Authority, Gender, and Midwifery in Early Modern Italy

Authority, Gender, and Midwifery in Early Modern Italy: Contested Deliveries explores attempts by church, state, and medical authorities to regulate and professionalize the practice of midwifery in Italy from the late sixteenth to the late eighteenth century.

Medical writers in this period devoted countless pages to investigating the secrets of women's sexuality and the processes of generation. By the eighteenth century, male practitioners in Britain and France were even successfully advancing careers as male midwives. Yet, female midwives continued to manage the vast majority of all early modern births. An examination of developments in Italy, where male practitioners never made successful inroads into everyday childbirth, brings into focus the complex social, religious, and political contexts that shaped the management of reproduction in early modern Europe. *Authority, Gender, and Midwifery in Early Modern Italy* argues that new institutional spaces to care for pregnant women and educate midwives in Italy during the eighteenth century were not strictly medical developments but rather socio-political responses both to long-standing concerns about honor, shame, and illegitimacy, and contemporary unease about population growth and productivity. In so doing, this book complicates our understanding of such sites, situating them within a longer genealogy of institutional spaces in Italy aimed at regulating sexual morality and protecting female honor.

It will be of interest to scholars of the history of medicine, religious history, social history, and Early Modern Italy.

Jennifer F. Kosmin is Assistant Professor of History at Bucknell University in Pennsylvania, USA. Her research focuses on the intersections of the history of medicine, gender history, the history of the body, and the popular display and study of anatomy in eighteenth-century Italy.

The History of Medicine in Context

Series Editors:

Andrew Cunningham (Department of History and Philosophy of Science, University of Cambridge) and Ole Peter Grell (Department of History, Open University)

Titles in the series include

Health and Welfare in St. Petersburg, 1900–1941
Protecting the Collective
Christopher Williams

The Afterlife of the Leiden Anatomical Collections
Hands On, Hands Off
Hieke Huistra

Civic Medicine
Physician, Polity, and Pen in Early Modern Europe
Edited by J. Andrew Mendelsohn, Annemarie Kinzelbach, and Ruth Schilling

Authority, Gender, and Midwifery in Early Modern Italy
Contested Deliveries
Jennifer F. Kosmin

For more information about this series, please visit: www.routledge.com/ The-History-of-Medicine-in-Context/book-series/HMC

Authority, Gender, and Midwifery in Early Modern Italy

Contested Deliveries

Jennifer F. Kosmin

Routledge
Taylor & Francis Group

LONDON AND NEW YORK

First published 2021
by Routledge
2 Park Square, Milton Park, Abingdon, Oxon OX14 4RN

and by Routledge
52 Vanderbilt Avenue, New York, NY 10017

Routledge is an imprint of the Taylor & Francis Group, an informa business

British Library Cataloguing-in-Publication Data
A catalogue record for this book is available from the British Library

Library of Congress Cataloging-in-Publication Data
A catalog record for this book has been requested

ISBN: 978-0-367-52022-9 (hbk)
ISBN: 978-1-003-05607-2 (ebk)

Typeset in Sabon
by Apex CoVantage, LLC

For my sister, Melissa

Contents

List of figures   ix
List of abbreviations   x
Acknowledgments   xi

Introduction   1

1   Midwives, medicine, and religion   15
The Church's interest 16
Baptism and the soul 17
Marriage, sexuality, and the courts 22
Childbirth, the sacred, and the Inquisition 24
Ordering the early modern medical marketplace 28
The impact and limits of legislation 31
Conclusion 35

2   Textual deliveries: reading early modern obstetrical treatises   43
The masculine origins of early modern midwifery manuals 44
An Italian midwifery manual? Scipione Mercurio's
    La Comare o Raccoglitrice *(1596) 48*
Eighteenth-century obstetrical texts and the emergence
    of a professional discourse 55
Theological embryology and the cesarean operation 68
Conclusion 73

3   The origins of public maternity care in Northern Italy   81
The maternity hospital as institution 82
"Those young women who imprudently lose their honor":
    Maternity care in Turin 85
Protecting honor, disciplining sexuality: Maternity wards
    in a longer frame 88
Daily life in an eighteenth-century maternity ward 94
Conclusion 98

4   Midwifery education and the politics of reproduction   106
    Populationism and pronatalism 107
    A school for midwives 110
    Recruitment 112
    Curriculum 116
    Expectations and realities 123
    Resistance and repercussions 126
    Conclusion 129

5   Surgical instruction and the clinicalization of the
    maternity ward   137
    Surgeons learn the trade 138
    Obstetrical machines and the instruction of touch 145
    Critiques of simulation 149
    The maternity ward becomes a clinic 152
    Conclusion 158

6   Contested deliveries   164
    Clients, communities, and conflict 165
    Midwives and surgeons 170
    Interprofessional rivalries 176
    Between church and state: the case of Marianna Boi 180
    Conclusion 185

    Conclusion   191

    Bibliography   196
    Index   217

Figures

2.1 Title page of the 1601 reprinting of Scipione Mercurio's
La Commare o Raccoglitrice   49
2.2 Position for difficult births that can be used profitably
for women experiencing prolonged labors   52
2.3 Birthing position recommended for large or
corpulent women   53
2.4 Dissected woman pointing to her extracted uterus from
Jacopo Berengario da Carpi's *Isagogae Breves* (1522)   54
4.1 Obstetrical models used by Giovanni Antonio Galli   119
4.2 Giovanni Antonio Galli's obstetrical machine,
mid-eighteenth century   120

Abbreviations

ACT	Archivio Comunale, Turin
AOSG	Archivio Ospedale S. Giovanni, Turin
ASDm	Archivio Storico Diocesano di Milano
ASDt	Archivio Storico Diocesano di Torino
ASMi	Archivio di Stato di Milano
ASP	Archivio di Stato di Padova
ASPa	Archivio di Stato di Pavia
AST, p.s.	Archivio di Stato di Torino, prima sezione
AST, s.r.	Archivio di Stato di Torino, sezioni reunite
ASTv	Archivio di Stato di Treviso
ASV	Archivio di Stato di Venezia
BA	Biblioteca Ambrosiana, Milan
BMV	Biblioteca Marciana, Venice
IPPAI	Archivio Storico dell'Istituto provinciale di protezione ed assistenza all'infanzia, Milan

Acknowledgments

This book would not have been possible without the generous support of a great number of people, and it is with much pleasure that I recognize their contributions. This project was born and fostered in the vibrant intellectual communities of Chapel Hill and Durham, North Carolina. I am incredibly fortunate to have been the recipient of the tireless support, enthusiasm, and encouragement of Melissa Bullard. I will be forever thankful for her guidance, careful reading of my work, and endless patience as this project developed into something quite different than initially envisioned. She will always be the model for the scholar I hope someday to become. I am also especially grateful to John Martin and Valeria Finucci, who, in addition to their valuable suggestions, have shared their love for and intricate understanding of Italian culture and history at all stages of this project. Seeing Venice through Valeria's eyes was a great pleasure. I also owe many thanks to Karen Hagemann and Konrad Jarausch for their valuable input on and stimulating discussion of many aspects of this research. Various others made my time in Chapel Hill one of constant growth, intellectual stimulation, and true community. Jamal Middlebrooks has been with me through the entire trip, and I deeply value his intelligence, wit, and friendship. Brittany Lehman, Alex Ruble, Julie Ault, Scott Krause, Josh Lynn, Rachel Levandoski, Shannon Eaves, Marry Mellon, and many others read parts of this work, and, most importantly, offered generous support and encouragement.

The faculty and staff in the history department at Bucknell University have been another source of continual support and encouragement. I am grateful to many of my colleagues who read chapters of this book and offered invaluable feedback.

I am deeply indebted to a great number of archivists, librarians, and other researchers for their assistance with the research on which this book is based. My research in archives across Northern Italy was facilitated and made most pleasurable by a number of talented researchers, archivists, and dedicated staffs. I would like to thank in particular the staffs of the Archivi di Stato of Turin, Milan, Venice, and Padua, as well as of the Archivo Storico Diocesano of Turin, the Archivio Storico Diocesano of Milan, the Archivo Comunale of Turin, and the Pinali Library for the History of Medicine at the

University of Padua. Gianpiero Viviano in Turin was both immensely help-ful in my archival searches as well as a pleasure to talk with about history in general. Daniela Caffaratto in Turin was incredibly helpful in my study of the Ospedale Maggiore di San Giovanni Battista and wonderfully generous in introducing me to her father's work on medicine in Piemonte. Maurizio Rippa Bonati generously welcomed me to and sponsored my research at the University of Padua. The incredibly kind Marina Cimino at the University of Padua was a source of unending knowledge about midwifery and obstet-rical texts published in Italy. In Milan, Flores Reggiani was most helpful and welcoming in letting me study materials in the archive of the Istituto provinciale di protezione e assistenza dell'infanzia di Milano.

I was fortunate to receive several fellowships that supported the archi-val research and writing of this book. The Social Science Research Council facilitated my first research trip to Turin in 2010 where the foundations of this project were laid. Since then I have benefitted immeasurably from the support of the Fulbright Foundation, the Gladys Krieble Delmas Founda-tion for research in the Veneto, the Medieval and Early Modern Studies program at UNC, UNC's Royster Society of Fellows, and generous research funding from Bucknell University.

Finally, I would like to thank my family, without whose love, encourage-ment, and laughter this journey would have been certainly less enjoyable, if not impossible. To Adam Domby and Lexi Domby Kosmin, I could not imagine doing this without you. Your unwavering support and encourage-ment are the most important things in my world. Thank you for always making me laugh. Finally, I could never thank my parents, Art and Kathy Kosmin, enough for their endless love and support – words simply fall short. To my sister, Melissa, I wish more than anything that you could read this.

Introduction

In March 1794, a midwife named Marianna Boi petitioned the Milanese medical authorities for reimbursement for the delivery of twins during the previous fall. Though tragically both newborns and their mother, Antonia Volpi, had died during the birth, Boi felt entitled to compensation for her time and efforts.[1] In and of itself, the recourse of a midwife to the Milanese health board for payment was not especially unusual; both medical practitioners and patients in the early modern care system were accustomed to litigation as a means of obtaining licenses, disputing cure agreements, and negotiating payments.[2] It soon became clear to investigators, however, that Boi's account of the birth – in which she delivered the twins and subsequently they and Volpi succumbed to illness – contradicted quite remarkably other witnesses' statements about what had happened.[3] According to a priest present at the birth and a surgeon who arrived soon after, Marianna Boi had performed a postmortem cesarean section in order to extract and baptize the two fetuses once she had determined that their mother had died.[4]

The medical authorities in both Milan and Pavia were deeply condemnatory of Boi's actions. Antonio Scarpa, a leading professor of anatomy at the University of Pavia, wrote in May 1794 that far from deserving payment for her services, Boi "should be reprimanded and severely admonished to abstain entirely from the use of surgical instruments in the practice of her profession."[5] Rather than a heroic act to save the lives of two infants, or at least allow for their baptism, Boi's actions were judged by the medical authorities in Milan as rash and negligent.

Despite Boi's censure, the act of performing a postmortem cesarean section to baptize a fetus was not in itself prohibited in late eighteenth-century Italy.[6] In fact, the Church launched a fervent campaign during this period to encourage the baptism of unborn children under almost any circumstance, including through the use of the cesarean operation when the mother died prematurely. A number of Italian theologians wrote lengthy treatises for audiences of priests, doctors, midwives, lawmakers, and officials on how best to ensure the salvation of the fetus's soul in every possible situation.[7] Fra Diodato da Cuneo argued, for instance, that a fetus should be baptized as soon as its delivery became difficult, even if a syringe had to be inserted into the mother's vagina to achieve this end.[8] As Claudia Pancino has observed, the Catholic Church's "preoccupation for the eternal life of the child" was only reinvigorated in the eighteenth century by intense debates over embryology and animation. The Church became more, not less, involved in medical practice in this period.[9] While this fact complicates traditional narratives of scientific progress and the secularization of medicine at the end of the eighteenth century, it is critical for understanding the place and practice of midwifery in early modern Italy.

Generally speaking, the early modern medical profession was respectful of the healing competencies traditionally reserved to the Church – baptism, exorcism, end of life care. In the case of Marianna Boi, however, the enactment of a surgical operation in the interest of ensuring eternal salvation for an unborn child illustrated the potential tensions that might exist between the Church and medical authorities in the context of early modern childbirth. Whereas Marianna Boi's parish priest defended and even praised her actions, the medical authorities condemned them. The medical profession was thus amenable to the Church's influence only to a point: when Boi was seen to overstep the professional bounds of midwifery and encroach upon the surgeon's territory, the medical authorities censured her, regardless of the fact that she had facilitated the baptism of two souls. Not only religion, then, but also gender and professional rivalries were factors that directly affected the practice of midwifery in early modern Italy. This book examines the varying and sometimes competing interests of the Catholic Church, state governments, and medical authorities in the practice of midwifery in Italy from the late sixteenth to the late eighteenth century.

Historians of early modern midwifery and childbirth have tended to focus in particular on the role and objectives of medical professionals. Indeed, in Europe between the sixteenth and eighteenth centuries, male medical practitioners increasingly invested themselves in women's health and reproduction, challenging women's special position as bearers of "women's secrets."[10] In addition to a proliferation of writing about reproduction by medical men across Europe, this period saw the emergence of new childbirth spaces, technologies, and techniques typically associated with the masculine appropriation of childbirth, such as forceps and pelvimetry. While female midwives continued to manage the vast majority of early modern births, the medical establishment sought to regulate and circumscribe the professional capacity of female practitioners. Scholars have often characterized the medicalization of childbirth in Europe and North America as a bitter struggle between men and women in which the knowledge and practice of traditional midwifery was rapidly eclipsed by masculine science.[11]

In Italy, however, this declension narrative is more complicated. Rather than maneuvering to usurp women's place in the birthing room as did male midwives in parts of England, France, and North America, medical practitioners in Italy aimed their efforts at professionalizing *female* midwives through new, formal courses of instruction. While this was true elsewhere, particularly in France, which had a highly sophisticated system of midwifery training, in Italy male practitioners were never able to fashion themselves as legitimate competitors for handling regular births.[12] The figure of the *accoucheur*, or man-midwife, was thus largely absent in Italy, though a number of elite surgeons did carve reputations for themselves as knowledgeable obstetrical practitioners who could intervene in difficult cases. By the mid-eighteenth century, a number of Italian cities had founded public midwifery schools, sometimes attached to small maternity wards, thereby merging paternalistic charity, Enlightenment-era reform efforts, and a new medical emphasis on clinical education. Childbirth in Italy thus remained largely in the hands of women throughout the early modern period, even as state officials and medical authorities targeted reproduction as central to their political and professional interests. Still, freed from focusing on the question of how men came to replace women as trusted and accepted birth attendants, this study highlights the considerable negotiation and accommodation between midwives and medical men in this period.

Of course, the professionalization of medicine was only partially responsible for changes to the practice of midwifery during the early modern period. State governments were intent on more rigorously enforcing licensing practices and creating new institutional spaces related to childbirth in this period for quite different reasons. Hospital maternity wards in Italy, for instance, developed primarily as institutional responses to long-standing concerns about shame, honor, and illegitimacy. Typically staffed by women, the first maternity wards in Italy did not originate with the interests of physicians or surgeons; rather, these sites signaled the state's assumption of the role of mediator of female honor in a society that disproportionately burdened women with the repercussions of illicit sexuality. Only in the late eighteenth and early nineteenth century did Italian maternity wards emerge as sites of true clinical training and research.

State officials' interest in faithfully examining and licensing midwives – which accorded with that of the medical authorities – was driven by concerns about infant and maternal mortality at a time when political theorists emphasized the twin goals of population growth and productivity as the basis for a nation's strength. Eighteenth-century Italian reformers such as Ludovico Antonio Muratori highlighted public health and maternal and child welfare as essential to what they referred to as the 'public happiness' and called on administrators to enact reforms in these areas.[13] Distinct from the concerns of the medical authorities, state efforts to license midwives and to establish maternity wards and midwifery schools during the eighteenth century reflected political preoccupation with high rates of infant mortality and fears about depopulation and military readiness.

Finally, as indicated in the case of Marianna Boi, the Catholic Church's interest in midwifery and childbirth expanded rather than retreated during the eighteenth century. The close relationship between parish priests and midwives, a legacy of Counter-Reformation initiatives to promote orthodoxy and enforce stricter sexual morality among the peasantry, received further impetus amidst debates about baptism, ensoulment, and embryology during the eighteenth century. Moreover, the Church should not be understood narrowly as a conservative force vis-à-vis the momentum of medical "progress" promoted by state and/or medical authorities. As with the case of the cesarean operation, the Church sometimes encouraged the development of aggressive interventions that we now associate with highly medicalized childbirth.

This book explores these competing interests by the Catholic Church, state governments, and the medical profession with regard to the practice of midwifery. Although the timeframe of the book extends back to the sixteenth century, my focus is on the development of new institutional spaces to care for pregnant women and formally train midwives during the eighteenth century. Whereas historians of medicine have traditionally viewed eighteenth-century hospital maternity wards and midwifery schools in light of later medical developments, this book situates these sites within a longer genealogy of institutional spaces in Italy aimed at regulating sexual morality and protecting female honor. Indeed, far from being strictly scientific spaces, hospital maternity wards shared much in common with convents and Counter-Reformation–era asylums for 'fallen' women. I argue, moreover, that not enough attention has been paid to the ample resistance leveled by a variety of actors to proposed changes to the management of childbirth. For instance, the impact of mandatory schooling and licensing programs on the actual practice of midwifery was often quite limited, as local resistance by midwives, clients, and even parish priests challenged such efforts well into the nineteenth century. The "professionalization" and "medicalization" of midwifery in eighteenth-century Italy were highly contested and multivalent processes that represented both breaks and continuities with the past.

* * *

Since the 1970s, historians of medicine and feminist critics of science have told and retold the story of how male medical practitioners came to displace traditional female midwives toward the end of the eighteenth century.[14] With a largely critical eye, these scholars documented the ways in which a professionalizing medical establishment invested itself in women's health and reproduction through the emergent fields of gynecology and obstetrics over the course of the long eighteenth century. According to this scholarship, male practitioners displaced women from one of the few areas where women's knowledge had traditionally dominated by medicalizing childbirth and removing it from the social realm. Men's better access to print and women's exclusion from the elite world of the university provided the grounds for a virulent smear campaign against "ignorant" female practitioners.

Although early twentieth-century histories of obstetrics had cited the forceps and use of surgical instruments as key to men's ascendancy in a traditionally female area, later generations of scholars argued that technological innovation in itself could not explain the rapid success of male midwives and obstetricians. Adrian Wilson, Lianne McTavish, Lisa Forman Cody, and others have all pointed out that there was in fact intense opposition from a variety of circles to male involvement in childbirth and that surgical intervention continued to be associated with poor outcomes during the eighteenth century.[15] Wilson argues that in fact it was largely women's own choice that created a space for men to establish authority over childbirth, as the use of a male midwife became a fashionable display of conspicuous consumption in some elite London circles.[16] McTavish argues that man-midwives engaged in careful and self-conscious acts of self-fashioning, particularly in their written texts, to facilitate their entrance into a traditionally female realm. Scholars have also become more discerning in their assessment of the extent to which early modern childbirth ever represented a moment of "female solidarity" or a "world turned upside down" where women's interests temporarily dominated.[17] Instead, much current scholarship highlights the tensions that sometimes existed among mothers, midwives, and other women, particularly when pre-marital sex or illegitimacy was involved.[18] Far from being a protected female realm, childbirth was understood and managed in ways that made the patriarchal structures of early modern European society manifest.

Through close studies of early modern obstetrical texts, anatomical illustrations, and three-dimensional models, scholars have also attended to the constitutive power of language and representation to shape social relations. Such studies have yielded a wealth of information about how male medical writers employed gendered discursive strategies in order to embed hierarchies of knowledge and authority into their discussions of anatomy and generation.[19] Researchers such as Ludmilla Jordanova and Lianne McTavish have studied the anatomical drawings found in such medical texts, arguing that the visual construction of bodies underpinned broader epistemological shifts that were essential to the production of a particularly masculine knowledge of reproduction and the female body between the sixteenth and eighteenth centuries.[20]

Although historians have increasingly challenged older historical commonplaces touting midwifery as a timeless and unchanging profession or early modern childbirth as a moment of unquestioned female solidarity, the scholarship on early modern midwifery still tends to focus on the basic question of how men came to replace women as trusted and expected birth attendants.[21] Whether the story is shaded more positively as one of medical professionalization and progress, or negatively as one of violence enacted by men on the bodies of poor and vulnerable women – what Lisa Forman Cody has colorfully described as "medical glory versus gory misogyny" – it tends nonetheless to begin at the end, with the triumph of male authority in an area once dominated by women.

This emphasis is in no small part because the bulk of English-language studies of early modern childbirth and midwifery have focused on England,

British North America, and France, where male intervention in childbirth was much more prevalent than elsewhere in Europe. Nadia Maria Filippini's masterful *Generare, partorire, nascere* (2018), which traces a *longue durée* history of reproduction in the West from antiquity to the twenty-first century is in fact one of the few texts in any language to center Italy in such a comprehensive history.[22] Because the practice of midwifery across much of the continent did not see, in any kind of sustained manner, the aggressive intervention by male practitioners that cities such as London and Paris did, our understanding of early modern childbirth has therefore been skewed toward an emphasis on gendered conflict and exclusion. By focusing on Italy, where the practice of midwifery underwent significant changes during the course of the long eighteenth century, but where female practitioners remained dominant, this study contributes an under-examined viewpoint on the medicalization of childbirth.[23] This book posits an alternative narrative in which the themes of negotiation, accommodation, and resistance better define the changing practices surrounding childbirth and midwifery in early modern Europe than do rejection and replacement.

Another dimension that a refocusing on Italy helps to illuminate is the role of the Catholic Church on the development of medicine in the eighteenth century. In recent years, historians of science and medicine have uncovered much about the complex and sometimes surprising interactions between the Catholic Church and scientific investigation in the early modern period. These studies have revealed that, far from being an antagonistic relationship, the Church often promoted innovative scientific practices during this period.[24] Nadia Maria Filippini's *La Nascita Straordinaria* (1995) richly charts the changing epistemological status of the fetus between the eighteenth and nineteenth centuries, particularly in Catholic countries.[25] According to Filippini, this period saw a dramatic deontological shift from preserving the mother's life during childbirth to that of the fetus, a shift that was in no small part driven by the Church's own changing views on embryology and animation. Filippini argues that while Protestant areas may have seen a decline in religious influence on childbirth by the eighteenth century, Catholic countries witnessed a renewed investment by clerics in certain areas of medical and scientific practice.[26]

The present study builds upon Filippini's intellectual history by attending carefully to the interactions between the Church and communities on a local level. I argue that parish priests were often important advocates of traditional midwives in their communities, even vis-à-vis newly trained midwives returning from formal instruction in the city. By rejecting male involvement in childbirth, the Catholic Church, at both a local and institutional level, played a fundamental role in shaping the management of childbirth in Italy. However, by promoting aggressive intervention during childbirth to save the soul of the fetus, including through cesarean section, the Church was not simply a conservative force in relation to the development of new childbirth practices and medical attitudes.

This book also draws on recent scholarship that has greatly expanded our understanding of the 'medical marketplace' in early modern Italy. David Gentilcore's investigation of medical pluralism and the *Protomedicato* in Naples has helped to develop a comprehensive picture of the early modern Italian medical marketplace.[27] Gentilcore's conception of early modern medicine as a complex interweaving of religious, learned, and popular spheres provides an especially useful context for considering the work of early modern midwives. According to Gentilcore, midwives were the only practitioners who embodied all three traditions at once, making them unique figures within the early modern medical landscape.[28] Additionally, Gianna Pomata's study of cure agreements and the agency of patients in Bologna has shown the ways in which practitioners and patients were on much more equal footing in a period when the medical arena overflowed with treatment options.[29] Sandra Cavallo, working in Piedmont, has argued that barbers and (most) surgeons occupied an artisanal social milieu rather than the elitist circles of university-trained medical professionals in which historians of medicine once placed them.[30]

Collectively, this scholarship has allowed historians to construct a picture of medicine in the early modern period that breaks down outmoded assumptions about professionalization and authority. Not only did licensed practitioners compete with empirics and itinerant charlatans in the early modern medical marketplace, but medicine was still very much a site in which science, religion, and popular knowledge intermingled. Building off these innovative studies, the present work contributes to our understanding of practitioner legitimation, patient involvement, and medical authority in the pre-modern medical marketplace. Midwives in particular embodied a type of medical practitioner whose authority still derived from community sanction long after other formal requirements were technically in place. The same can be said for the majority of early modern surgeons, another group that emerges as central to the negotiated authority surrounding childbirth in this period. This study attempts to fill in some of the significant gaps in our knowledge about how early modern surgeons outside of the university actually learned their trade. Before the introduction of university courses in obstetrics and specialized midwifery schools, where and how did surgeons learn to perform operations such as podalic version and embryotomy, or how to apply forceps and hooks? Did surgeons use these kinds of obstetrical tools commonly in practice? As one historian recently noted, "the study of surgery is still in its infancy."[31] This book will hopefully provide some pieces to this puzzle, by examining the ways surgeons learned about childbirth as apprentices to senior practitioners, through autopsy, on models and machines, and, eventually, at the bedside of women in maternity hospitals.

Finally, this book engages debates about the nature and existence of what is often termed "popular medicine."[32] As noted, scholars are aware that ahistorical assumptions about the authority of "regular" medical practitioners, including licensed and university-trained physicians and surgeons, must be recalibrated if we are to fully grasp the nature of early modern medicine, in which a wide variety of medical practitioners coexisted. Too often, the scientific and medical work performed by early modern women continues to be obscured because it defies modern assumptions about what these practices should look like and where they should take place.[33] The abiding use of descriptors such as 'domestic,' 'popular,' 'traditional,' 'untrained,' 'informal', and so forth to describe the work of female medical practitioners works to reinforce gendered hierarchies of knowing and to privilege the knowledge produced in particular settings, such as the university, over others, such as the home.[34] In this book, I have aimed to be as precise as possible when applying these kinds of qualifiers. Early modern midwives, while generally not formally educated, were also not untrained. Rather, they had typically undergone an extensive period of apprenticeship, gaining practical experience under the tutelage of a longer-practicing and community-authorized midwife. And although many of these women were unlicensed, they were not necessarily unregulated, if we understand regulation to imply a variety of systems that might be put in place locally to exert control over a particular kind of practice.

***

Contested Deliveries examines the practice of midwifery in three early modern northern Italian states – Savoy, Lombardy, and the Venetian Republic. In addition to tracing developments in the capital cities of Turin, Milan, and Venice, I devote particular attention to the interactions between the central governments located in these urban centers and the rural communities on whose compliance the success of reform programs depended. For instance, in Savoy, Lombardy, and Venice, initiatives to educate midwives by establishing schools in these capital cities were aimed above all at provincial women, who were expected to return to their home communities to spread the new, scientific knowledge of childbirth they had gained in the city. Resistance by local women to hiring such newly trained midwives, however, reveals just how contested the imposition of new practices by centralized states could be.

This study compares childbirth practices across Northern Italy to explore both regional variances and the ways in which "Italian" birth practices as a whole developed in contrast to those elsewhere in Europe. Because there was constant and sustained interaction and exchange between medical practitioners in these cities and the Continent, the specificities of Italian birth culture must derive from beyond the medical realm. Furthermore, these cities are noteworthy for developments in the context of Italian maternal and infant welfare. Turin saw the first public hospital maternity ward and midwifery school founded in Italy, at the city's San Giovanni hospital in 1728. Milan, under the direction of the famed German public health pioneer Johann Peter Frank, launched one of the first attempts in Italy to extend midwifery education throughout its vast provinces. Luigi Calza, professor of obstetrics in Padua, amassed one of the most complete eighteenth-century collections of wax and clay obstetrical models with which to teach his midwifery students. Midwifery in these three states therefore underwent significant changes during the early modern period; together, these states represent a varied cross-section of Italian approaches to controlling and regulating sexual and reproductive practices during the seventeenth and eighteenth centuries.

* * *

Chapter 1 introduces the wider social world in which early modern Italian midwives practiced. First, the chapter discusses the religious role of midwives and, in particular, the close relationship that the Catholic Church fostered between midwives and parish priests in the era of the Counter-Reformation. At once, midwives were indispensable bearers of religious values within their communities, entrusted with the rite of baptism, *and* figures who generated suspicion because of their association with the secrets of the female body and its attendant rituals. The Church saw midwives as a means of accessing information about and regulating sexual behavior, honor, and morality at a local level. This chapter concludes by considering the earliest efforts of medical authorities, particularly health boards and *protomedicati*, to regulate the practice of midwifery. Attempts to order the early modern medical marketplace were rarely more than partially successful, demonstrating both the distinct nature of the medical world of early modern Europe and the limits of state authority in this period.

Chapter 2 turns to the knowledge contained in obstetrical treatises published between the sixteenth and eighteenth centuries. I begin with a wide examination of European texts but then turn toward exclusively Italian material for the remainder of the chapter. Focusing primarily on vernacular midwifery manuals, I consider the visual and discursive strategies by which medical men attempted to exert their authority over childbirth. By the second half of the eighteenth century, a proliferation of specialized obstetrical treatises, as well as new written forms such as the case study and scientific journal, provided a textual space for Italian practitioners to promote their obstetrical expertise, anatomical knowledge, and manual skill, often at the expense of other male practitioners and female midwives.

Chapter 3 explores the origins of public maternity assistance in Italy. Scholars have, not incorrectly, critiqued early maternity wards as tools by which medical men gained practical experience with childbirth, typically on the backs of poor and marginalized women. In Italy, however, the first public maternity wards were largely resistant to male intervention. Rather than spaces in which medical men advanced their professional interests, Italy's first maternity wards were above all charitable sites aimed at protecting family honor and hiding the evidence of illicit sexuality. Staffed by women, these wards were less interested in promoting safer (or more "medicalized") childbirth than with providing a discrete and secure recovery for mothers of illegitimate offspring. This chapter argues that for much of the eighteenth-century, Italian maternity wards had more in common with Counter-Reformation–era asylums for women aimed at disciplining wayward sexuality. Only in the late eighteenth and early nineteenth centuries did maternity wards in Italy embrace 'scientific' clinical training and allow male practitioners regular access to the women that gave birth there.

In contrast, Italy's first midwifery schools, the focus of Chapter 4, did aim to introduce midwives to a more 'scientific' and theoretically informed understanding of childbirth. Directed by male professors of surgery or obstetrics, these courses more closely align with narratives of the medicalization and masculinization of midwifery and childbirth. At the same time, the catalyst for such programs was political concern about infant and maternal mortality in a period when political theorists were emphasizing population growth and production as essential to a strong state. As much as the ambitions of medical men, populationism and governmental pronatalism drove the professionalization of midwifery in eighteenth-century Italy. Moreover, as this chapter demonstrates, the existence of such programs in Italy was highly contested and only ever partially successful. Practicing midwives, mothers, and even parish priests all leveled intense opposition to outside intervention in the management of childbirth and the abrogation of local modes of legitimation.

Chapter 5 shifts away from midwives to consider how surgeons came to acquire the obstetrical skills that allowed them to intervene during the most complicated childbirth cases. Well before formal courses in obstetrics were offered to male practitioners, surgeons had assisted during difficult labors. While surgeons and physicians in such situations at times offered little more than non-specific remedies such as bleeding, purgatives, and fumigations, in other cases we know they also performed more specialized procedures such as podalic version, embryotomy and craniotomy, and postmortem cesarean section. How did early modern surgeons, who themselves often practiced without formal license, learn these kinds of manual skills? What kind of theoretical knowledge could surgeons claim with respect to childbirth? Later, in the context of formal courses in obstetrics and midwifery, what pedagogical methods were used to instruct surgeons? This chapter begins to fill in some of the lacunae that exist with respect to our knowledge of early modern surgeons' training. It concludes with an examination of how male practitioners did eventually come to have access to the vulnerable bodies of foundlings and public maternity patients in order to advance their professional interests and contribute to the production of obstetric and pediatric knowledge.

Chapter 6 explores moments of tension and conflict that arose between midwives and their communities. Rather than an event of unshakable female solidarity, childbirth could be a period of stress, discord, and even violence, especially in cases of illegitimate pregnancy. Moreover, there seems to have been little sense of professional solidarity that might have kept midwives themselves from fighting over clients and compensation. Such rivalries were compounded enormously during the second half of the eighteenth century when state efforts to enforce midwifery regulation became more comprehensive. Mothers typically preferred familiar, locally practicing midwives, eschewing those with formal educations and official license and thereby creating stark divides between licensed and unlicensed practitioners. Finally, midwives existed in competition, but also sometimes in solidarity, with local surgeons. This chapter argues that midwives' relationships with their clients and communities were neither static nor singularly harmonious. Loyalty toward clients could be tempered by economic considerations; surgeons might be the source of gendered professional rivalries, but also of respect and collaboration.

* * *

David Kertzer has written that "outside institutional forces – such as church and state – have long sought to influence reproductive behavior, not only through coercive measures (such as criminal laws), but [also] through social policy programs (such as poor relief for mothers and children)."[35] This book explores the latter type of control as it was manifested in eighteenth-century Italy in the guise of the maternity ward and midwifery school. It is interested in how and why Church, state, and the medical profession attempted to exert influence on women's bodies at the end of the early modern period. Above all, this book highlights the moments in which such efforts were resisted or negotiated by the women and men who came into contact with them.

Notes

1 Archivio di Stato di Milano (hereafter ASMi), *Sanità, parte antica*, c. 272, "Trucazzano." Marianna Boi's case is examined in greater detail in Chapter 6. The case is also discussed in Claudia Pancino, *Il bambino e l'acqua sporca: Storia dell'assistenza al parto dalle mammane alle ostetriche (secoli XVI–XIX)* (Milan: Franco Angeli, 1984), 150–159.
2 On cure agreements and patients' petitions before the medical tribunal in Bologna, see Gianna Pomata, *Contracting a Cure: Patients, Healers, and the Law in Early Modern Bologna* (Baltimore: The Johns Hopkins University Press, 1998).
3 Unfortunately, Boi's *supplica* itself is not to be found along with the other documents relating to the case; we can only piece together what was said through others' references to it.
4 On the history of the cesarean operation, see Renate Blumenfeld-Kosinski, *Not of Woman Born: Representations of Caesarean Birth in Medieval and Renaissance Culture* (Ithaca: Cornell University Press, 1990); Nadia Maria Filippini, *La Nascita Straordinaria: Tra Madre e Figlio la Rivoluzione del Taglio Cesareo* (Milano: Franco Angeli, 1995); Carmen Trimarchi, "Politica, cultura, religione e corpo delle donne: la pratica del parto cesareo (sec. XVII–XVIII)," in *Donne, politica e istituzioni: percorsi, esperienze e idee,* ed. M. Antonella Cocchiara (Rome: Arcane, 2009), 164–174. More broadly, scholars have explored the cultural, medical, and religious implications of the dissection of the female body in Renaissance and early modern culture. See, for instance: Katharine Park,

Secrets of Women: Gender, Generation, and the Origins of Human Dissection (New York: Zone Books, 2006); Jonathan Sawday, *The Body Emblazoned: Dissection and the Human Body in Renaissance Culture* (New York and London: Routledge, 1995).

5 ASMi, *Sanità, parte antica*, c. 272, "Trucazzano," Report of Antonio Scarpa, 6 May 1794.

6 In fact, the operation had been mandated in various synodal and conciliar legislation from at least the thirteenth century. See Kathryn Taglia, "Delivering a Christian Identity: Midwives in Northern French Synodal Legislation, c. 1200–1500," in *Religion and Medicine in the Middle Ages*, ed. Peter Biller and Joseph Ziegler (York: Boydell and Brewer, 2001), 86–87.

7 F. E. Cangiamila, *Embriologia Sacra, ovvero dell'Uffizio de' Sacerdoti, Medici, e Superiori, circa l'Eterna Salute de' Bambini racchiusi nell'Utero* (Palermo, 1745); P. Diodato, *Notizie Fisico-Storico-Morali Conducenti alla Salvezza de' Bambini Nonnati, Abortivi, e Projetti* (Venezia: Niccolò Pezzana, 1760); Girolamo Baruffaldi, *La Mammana Istruita per Validamente Amministrare il Santo Sacramento del Battesimo in caso di Necessità alle Creature Nascenti* (Venezia: Giambattista Recurti, 1746).

8 On debates surrounding the practice of cesarean section in the eighteenth century and the broader ideological and religious shifts which began to favor saving the soul of the infant over the life of the mother in this period, see Filippini, *La Nascita Straordinaria*; Elena Brambilla, "La medicina del Settecento: dal monopolio dogmatico alla professione scientifica," in *Storia d'Italia. Annali 7. Malattia e medicina*, ed. Franco Della Peruta (Torino: Einaudi, 1984), 5–147; José G. Rigau-Pérez, "Surgery at the Service of Theology: Postmortem Cesarean Sections in Puerto Rico and the Royal Cedula of 1804," *The Hispanic American Historical Review* 75, no. 3 (1995): 377–404; Adam Warren, "An Operation for Evangelization: Friar Francisco González Laguna, the Cesarean Section, and Fetal Baptism in Late Colonial Peru," *Bulletin of the History of Medicine* 83, no. 4 (2009): 647–675.

9 Claudia Pancino, "La Comare Levatrice: Crisi di un Mestiere nel XVIII Secolo," *Storia e Società* 15 (1981): 593–638, 620.

10 Park, *Secrets of Women*, 256.

11 See, for instance, Jean Donnison, *Midwives and Medical Men* (New York: Schocken Books, 1977), 21–41; Audrey Eccles, *Obstetrics and Gynaecology in Tudor and Stuart England* (Kent, OH: Kent State University Press, 1982), 124; Irvine Loudon, *Medical Care and the General Practitioner, 1750–1850* (Oxford: Oxford University Press, 1986), 90; Richard W. Wertz and Dorothy C. Wertz, *Lying-In: A History of Childbirth in America* (New Haven: Yale University Press, 1989), 47; Adrian Wilson, *The Making of Man-Midwifery: Childbirth in England, 1660–1770* (Cambridge, MA: Harvard University Press, 1995), 1–5; Lisa Forman Cody, *Birthing the Nation: Sex, Science, and the Conception of Eighteenth-Century Britons* (Oxford: Oxford University Press, 2005), 9.

12 On midwifery training in France and at the Hôtel-Dieu in Paris, see Margaret Carlyle, "Phantoms in the Classroom: Midwifery Training in Enlightenment Europe," *KNOW: A Journal on the Formation of Knowledge* 2 (2018): 111–136; Nina Rattner, *The King's Midwife: A History and Mystery of Madame Du Coudray* (Berkeley: University of California Press, 1999); Henriette Carrier, *Origines de la maternité de Paris. Les maîtresses sages-femmes et l'office des accouchées de l'ancien Hôtel-Dieu 1738–1796* (Paris: G. Steinheil, 1888).

13 Ludovico Antonio Muratori, *Della pubblica felicità: oggetto de' buoni principi* (Lucca, 1749), 142; Luigino Bruni and Stefano Zamagni, *Civil Economy: Efficiency, Equity, Public Happiness* (Bern: Peter Lang, 2007), 70–76.

14 See, for instance, Barbara Ehrenreich and Deirdre English, *Witches, Midwives and Nurses: A History of Women Healers* (Old Westbury, NY: The Feminist Press, 1973); Adrienne Rich, *Of Woman Born: Motherhood as Experience and Institution* (New York: W.W. Norton, 1976); Hilda Smith, "Gynecology and Ideology in Seventeenth-Century England," in *Liberating Women's History*, ed. Berenice A. Carroll (Urbana: University of Illinois Press, 1976), 97–114; Claudia Dreifus, ed., *Seizing Our Bodies: The Politics of Women's Health* (New York: Vintage Books, 1977); Jean Donnison, *Midwives and Medical Men: A History of Inter-professional Rivalries and Women's Rights* (London: Hinemann, 1977); Jane B. Donegan, *Women and Men Midwives: Medicine, Morality, and Misogyny in Early America* (Westport, CT: The Greenwood Press, 1978); Ann Oakley, *Women Confined: Towards a Sociology of Childbirth* (New York: Schocken Books, 1980); Barbara Katz Rothman, *In Labor: Women and Power in the Birthplace* (New York: W.W. Norton, 1982); Ann Oakley, *The Captured Womb: A History of the Medical Care of Pregnant Women* (New York: Basil Blackwell Publisher Ltd., 1984); Emily Martin, *The Woman in the Body: A Cultural Analysis of Reproduction* (Boston: Beacon Press, 1987); Mary Jacobus, Evelyn Fox Keller, and Sally Shuttleworth, eds., *Body Politics: Women and the Discourses of Science* (London and New York: Routledge, 1990).

15 Wilson, *The Making of Man-Midwifery*; Lianne McTavish, *Childbirth and the Display of Authority in Early Modern France* (Burlington, VT: Ashgate, 2005); Cody, *Birthing the Nation*.

16 Wilson, *The Making of Man-Midwifery*, 1–5.

17 This thesis was first posited by Natalie Zemon Davis in her essay "Women on Top," in *Society and Culture in Early Modern Europe: Eight Essays by Natalie Zemon Davis* (Stanford: Stanford University Press, 1975). Davis argued, referencing Mikhail Bakhtin, that childbirth was exemplary of how folk rituals in general were distinct from and represented a challenge to "official" ecclesiastical or feudal forms of power. Sarah Mendelson and Patricia Crawford, in *Women in Early Modern England, 1550–1720* (Oxford: Clarendon Press, 1998), and Adrian Wilson in his article "The Ceremony of Childbirth and Its Interpretation" argue that childbirth represented a moment of women's resistance to or insulation from a larger patriarchal culture. Wilson, "The Ceremony of Childbirth and its Interpretation," in *Women as Mothers in Preindustrial England*, ed. Valerie Fildes (London: Routledge, 1990), 94.

18 Laura Gowing, *Common Bodies: Women, Touch, and Power in Seventeenth-Century England* (New Haven: Yale University Press, 2003), 149–176.

19 Lynne Tatlock, "Speculum Feminarum: Gendered Perspectives on Obstetrics and Gynecology in Early Modern Germany," *Signs* 17, no. 4 (1992): 725–760; Caroline Bicks, "'Stones Like Women's Paps': Revising Gender in Jane Sharp's *Midwives Book*," *Journal of Early Modern Cultural Studies* 7, no. 2 (2007): 1–27.

20 Ludmilla Jordanova, *Sexual Visions: Images of Gender and Science Between the Eighteenth and Twentieth Centuries* (Madison: University of Wisconsin Press, 1989); McTavish, *Childbirth and the Display of Authority*.

21 On the development of the midwife as a figure with specialized knowledge within her community, see Monica Green, *Making Women's Medicine Masculine: The Rise of Male Authority in Pre-Modern Gynaecology* (Oxford: Oxford University Press, 2008), 127–128.

22 Nadia Maria Filippini, *Generare, partorire, nascere: Una storia dall'antichità alla provetta* (Rome: Viella, 2018).

23 A number of excellent studies have been carried out by Italian scholars, though they tend to be locally or regionally focused. M. T. Caffaratto, "L'assistenza ostetrica in Piemonte dalle origini ai nostril tempi," *Giornale di Batteriologia, Virologia ed Immunologia.* 6 (1970): 176–209; Gianna Pomata, "Barbieri

e comari" in *Cultura popolare nell'Emilia Romagna: Medicina, erbe e magia* (Milan: Silvana Editoriale, 1981), 161–183; Nadia Maria Filippini, "Levatrici e ostetricanti a Venezia tra sette e ottocento," *Quaderni Storici* 58 (1985): 149–180; Claudio Schiavoni, "L'attività delle levatrici o 'mammane' a Roma tra XVI e XVIII secolo: storia sociale di una professione," *Sociologia* 2 (2001): 41–61. One of the only book-length and comparative treatments of early modern Italian childbirth and midwifery remains Claudia Pancino's *Il Bambino e l'acqua sporca*; nonetheless Pancino focuses on the incommesaurability between the views of midwives and medical men.

24 See, for instance, several recent works on Prospero Lorenzo Lambertini, Pope Benedict XIV, and his patronage of science in the eighteenth century: Rebecca Messbarger, Christopher M. S. Johns, and Philip Gavitt, eds., *Benedict XIV and the Enlightenment: Art, Science, and Spirituality* (Toronto: University of Toronto Press, 2016); Lucia Dacome, "The Anatomy of the Pope," in *Conflicting Duties: Science, Medicine, and Religion in Rome, 1550–1750*, ed. Maria Pia Donato and Jill Kraye (London: Warburg Institute, 2009), 355–376.

25 Filippini, *La Nascita Straordinaria*.

26 Filippini, *La Nascita Straordinaria*, 15.

27 David Gentilcore, *Healers and Healing in Early Modern Italy* (Manchester: Manchester University Press, 1998); *Medical Charlatanism in Early Modern Italy* (Oxford: Oxford University Press, 2006); "'All That Pertains to Medicine': *Protomedici* and *Protomedicati* in Early Modern Italy," *Medical History* 38 (1994): 121–142.

28 Gentilcore, *Healers and Healing*, 3.

29 Pomata, *Contracting a Cure*.

30 Sandra Cavallo, *Artisans of the Body in Early Modern Italy: Identities, Families and Masculinities* (Manchester: Manchester University Press, 2007).

31 Paolo Savoia, "Skills, Knowledge and Status: The Career of an Early Modern Italian Surgeon," *Bulletin of the History of Medicine* 93, no. 1 (2019): 27–54.

32 For a good overview of current historical debates over the existence of a distinctive "popular" medicine in early modern Europe, see David Gentilcore, "Was There a 'Popular Medicine' in Early Modern Europe?" *Folklore* 115, no. 2 (2004): 151–166.

33 Susan Broomhall, *Women's Medical Work in Early Modern France* (Manchester: Manchester University Press, 2004), 6–9.

34 Meredith K. Ray, *Daughters of Alchemy: Women and Scientific Culture in Early Modern Italy* (Cambridge, MA: Harvard University Press, 2015), 5.

35 David Kertzer, "Gender Ideology and Infant Abandonment in Nineteenth-Century Italy," *Journal of Interdisciplinary History* 22 (1991): 2.

1 Midwives, medicine, and religion

Who were the midwives of early modern Northern Italy? Did their lives reflect similar social, cultural, and geographical patterns? Did they share a sense of professional identity? In what ways did they engage, negotiate, and form relationships with various members of their communities – priests, clients, neighbors, other medical practitioners? We know that early modern Italian midwives managed the vast majority of early modern births and did so with a mixture of medical knowledge, prayer, and a host of popular reproductive rituals. This combination of learned, popular, and religious expertise made midwives unique among early modern medical practitioners.[1] We know, moreover, that midwives' social identity extended beyond their role in the birthing room. Midwives might be involved in preparing women for marriage and guiding the religious activities of soon-to-be mothers during their pregnancies, especially given that childbirth in this period was always a potentially life-threatening endeavor.

In the case of emergency, it fell to the midwife to assume temporarily the religious authority of the priest and baptize the child to protect its soul. In addition, the midwife maintained a highly visible presence in the ritual life of Italian society. Traditionally, she carried the newborn whom she had delivered to the baptismal font for its spiritual birth and symbolic entrance into the community, often receiving the title of godmother (*"comare"*) in honor of her services. Midwives were also sometimes experts on a number of 'female' diseases, particularly those that affected menstruation and sexual functioning. As a result, those who lifted new life into the world might also deal in darker areas such as abortion, contraception, infertility, and infanticide. At the least, this was the concern of both religious and secular elites suspicious of the all-female activities surrounding childbirth. The still rudimentary understanding of the processes of reproduction across this period added an additional mysteriousness to midwives' work. Yet, even as such associations occasionally sprouted concerns about midwives' potentially illicit activities, this same knowledge proved instrumental to the workings of the early modern legal system. Midwives frequently gave testimony in cases in which a physical examination of the female body might be required, such as rape, marital discord, and infanticide. The importance of midwives' duties, both in the birthing room and the courtroom, made them respected and sanctioned figures in their communities, even though they often came from families of modest means.

This chapter introduces the figure of the midwife in early modern Northern Italy before the development of public maternity wards and formal programs of midwifery instruction in the eighteenth century. It aims to answer some of the questions posed earlier about midwives' social identity and intercommunity relationships, and, more specifically, to situate midwifery within the religio-political context of early modern Italy. Although their position at the intersections of multiple traditions found midwives targeted by new modes of ecclesiastical, state, and medical regulation between the sixteenth and eighteenth centuries, it was the Catholic Church that had the most sustained and intimate interest. Authorization by a parish priest was the only kind of formal sanction most early modern midwives received. Parish priests could attest to a midwife's character and respectability, and instruct her in the baptismal rite. These qualifications were central to a midwife's reputation, as were, of course, other women's own word of mouth appraisals of her skill and ability to handle difficult births. This close relationship between midwives and parish priests was fostered, in particular, because of the interests of the Counter-Reformation church. This chapter first discusses the Church's interest in midwifery; it then turns to the nascent efforts of state and medical authorities to impose outside regulation on the practice of midwifery, generally with very limited success. Above all, midwives' livelihoods and reputations were dependent on their relationships with clients and neighbors and their competition with one another.

The Church's interest

In early modern Europe, childbirth was an event at once mediated by and understood through religious practice. For pregnant women in a period when childbirth was fraught with danger and the looming potentiality of death, religious ceremony and ritual provided both comfort and the possibility of active intervention. In Catholic Europe, the Virgin Mary, who conceived without sin and delivered without pain, served as a powerful example to whom pregnant women could look for guidance. A host of saints represented additional intercessors, and many, such as St. Anne, became particularly linked to pregnancy and childbirth.[2] For those who could afford it, the birth itself was followed by an elaborately celebrated baptismal ceremony that marked the symbolic entrance of the newborn into the Christian community.[3] In early modern Italy, the midwife had the duty of supervising the religious regimen of birth, guiding the pregnant woman in a spiritual program before her delivery, and, most important, ensuring the salvation of the infant soul in an emergency.

Unsurprisingly, the Catholic Church was the first to assert its regulatory authority over the practices of midwifery. From as early as the twelfth and thirteenth centuries, Church decrees repeatedly mentioned the obligation of midwives to perform the sacrament of baptism in urgent situations. If the mother died during childbirth or even very late into her pregnancy, those present were directed to take extreme measures to ensure at least the salvation of the newborn's soul. The Councils of Canterbury (1236) and Trèves (1310) recommended that a midwife or surgeon perform a postmortem extraction of the fetus in order to baptize it.[4] Church decrees even counseled that the mother's mouth be propped open during the procedure to ensure that the baby did not suffocate.[5] Although documentation of such events is rare, artwork from this early period suggests that midwives may have at times undertaken this kind of surgical intervention.[6]

By the sixteenth century, Catholic reform brought renewed interest in the practice of midwifery. That interest was at least threefold. First, in the midst of the heated theological debates of the Protestant Reformation, baptism emerged as a fundamental point of disagreement. As Protestant theologians increasingly attacked infant baptism as practiced by the Roman Church, Catholic reformers placed even more emphasis on baptism's essentialness to Catholic ritual and Christian salvation. Second, in an effort to reinvigorate proper religious behavior, the contours of the Church began to stretch further into the daily lives of early modern Catholics. Marital and sexual practices came under increasing scrutiny by members of the secular clergy. Through her direct involvement in births, healing, and the intimate concerns of neighbors, the midwife represented a key point of access into local communities. By increasing their supervision over midwives' practice and instruction, the clergy envisioned a channel through which the tenets of Catholic reform and stricter moral standards might be relayed to their flock. Finally, the Counter-Reformation Church, intent on rooting out heterodoxy and ignorant superstition, looked with increasing suspicion upon the varied and often syncretistic forms of popular piety, healing, and sympathetic magic practiced by many early modern Italians. Reformers directed particular scrutiny toward the peasant population, with its strong traditions of popular healing and folk magic, both of which were associated with women and the female body. The host of folk traditions related to pregnancy and childbirth, coupled with the fact that birth itself was still a mysterious, female-controlled event, made this an area of particular concern for the Counter-Reformation Church.

Baptism and the soul

The Church's concern with baptism had brought midwives into the orbit of ecclesiastical regulation from an early date. As the fundamental rite of initiation into the Christian community and the essential condition for eventual entrance into the Kingdom of Heaven, baptism holds a singular place in Christian ritual and theology. In the sixteenth century, under attack from Protestant reformers who challenged how to correctly interpret and administer the rite, the Church in Rome responded by reaffirming baptism's centrality to the tenets of the Catholic Reform.[7] In this environment, baptism increasingly became the rite that distinguished Catholics not only from non-Christians, but also from other Christians. Midwives' role in delivering infants subsequently took on even greater significance in the eyes of the Church as guarantors of the souls of newborn children, who would otherwise be without a Christian identity and denied entrance to heaven.[8]

The official catechism for parish priests that emerged from the Council of Trent therefore paid direct attention to the role of midwives in baptism. In fact, "when accustomed to its [baptism's] administration, midwives are not to be found fault with if sometimes when a man is present who is unacquainted with the manner of its administration, they perform what may otherwise appear to belong more properly to men."[9] In this way, the Church entrusted midwives with a ritual performance that otherwise belonged solely to men.[10] Given the gravity of this responsibility, however, the Church dictated a close relationship between parish priests and local midwives. Pastors were "strictly bound to take care that . . . midwives, be well instructed in the manner of administering the sacrament."[11] Early seventeenth-century Church statutes stipulated that "no one should be permitted to perform the office of midwife, who does not hold the Catholic doctrine on the necessity of Baptism."[12] Church authorities continually warned that the sometimes chaotic atmosphere during birth might result in a midwife forgetting to baptize the infant or perhaps muddling the rite, and thus proper (and repeated) instruction was necessary.[13] To enforce this position, the 1614 *Rituale Romanum* issued by Pope Paul V required that Episcopal officials undertake regular visitations, during which they would inspect local practices with the aim of upholding faith and discipline and correcting any perceived abuses. During such visitations, officials regularly examined practicing midwives on their knowledge of the baptismal rite and recorded whether they were licensed in any way.[14]

Occasionally, such visitations generated more thorough investigations when midwives were seen to have perverted the baptismal rite in some way. For instance, the Friulian midwife Pasqua Guarini ultimately attracted the attention of the Inquisition for suspected abuse of the sacraments. Pasqua testified to the Holy Office that after delivering a local woman called Maria da Palazola, believing the newborn "was dying soon, I baptized her, with the name Maria," but "then the newborn revived, and I took her to the Church as her father and mother desired." When the priest asked Pasqua whether the child had yet been baptized, however, the midwife replied in the negative. She did not "believe that it was a great sin to baptize an infant twice" because she had "many times seen that priests, told that an infant was baptized at home . . . had poured water on the body another time in church."[15] Ultimately, Pasqua received little more than a verbal reprimand from the authorities. The Inquisition was not interested in prosecuting an uninformed midwife, only in ensuring that her ability to administer the sacrament of baptism was sound for future situations.[16] In fact, the final ruling emphasized a failure on the part of the local clergy and urged the parish to step up its instruction of midwives.[17]

On the other hand, some midwives were more rigorous administrators of religious rites than the parish priests from whom they were supposed to receive instruction on such matters. A case heard before the ecclesiastical courts in Turin called upon the testimony of a 60-year-old midwife named Maria Toretta.[18] Amidst claims that the local parish priest was neglectful of his duties, ignorant of religious rites, and often absent from his parish, Maria Toretta testified that on several occasions she had been compelled to baptize newborn infants herself because the priest was nowhere to be found. On one occasion when the priest, don Ronco, *was* present, Toretta had to step in when the ill-trained cleric stated, *"Ego te absolvo a peccatis tuis"* instead of the correct *"Ego te baptizo."* "When I realized [the error]," Toretta recalled, "I signaled with my head to make [the priest] understand that he had misspoken."[19] Although don Ronco eventually repeated the rite with the correct form, Toretta recalled that from then on, she always made herself especially alert at all baptisms, and in fact did have to intervene on other occasions. According to Oscar di Simplicio, it was precisely these moments of dissonance between the expected and actual behavior of the priest that might serve to sharpen the consciences of the faithful.[20]

As these examples demonstrate, baptism held real immediacy for early modern Italians that was not restricted to abstract theology. As Adriano Prosperi has written, the debates that emerged during the Reformation over how to understand baptism "were at the center not only of elaborate intellectual constructs and arduous theological definitions, but also of phenomena of great importance on which the political order of Europe and the forms of its expansion in the world was to depend."[21] On a local level, baptism stitched together the ritual fabric of early modern communities in a way that "transcended the crossroads between official religion and folklore tradition," and "transformed birth from a natural to a cultural fact."[22] In other words, baptism was of deep, material concern to the lives of everyday Europeans, particularly in a period when infant mortality was high. The wrenching emotional toil that parents might experience at the prospect of a child's soul banished to eternal damnation was something that European Catholics in even the remotest areas understood. The widespread phenomenon in the pre-Alpine regions of France, Italy, Switzerland, and Austria of the '*répit*' miracle, in which children who had died without baptism were briefly resuscitated, attests to the suffering parents felt in such cases.

Although not unknown before the Reformation, the practice of parents making pilgrimages to particular sites associated with the *répit* miracle became a regular and accepted practice in the years after, and continued well into the eighteenth century. According to Prosperi, there may have been some twenty of these sites in the Italian Alps, and as many as 230 in France.[23] What is especially notable about the *répit* sites, and indeed, about the ritual itself, is the involvement of women. At the Madonna of Terlago, near Trent, for instance, it was two women who were known to oversee the miracle in which dead infants would return briefly to life allowing for their baptism. With the women's attestation of the miracle, a certificate of baptism could be drawn up and, most importantly, the children finally laid to rest in consecrated ground.[24] In Carnia, near Udine, it was likewise to several women that "the bodies of infants who had died during childbirth were brought and these [women] would lay them out before the altar of the Madonna, celebrate the mass, say peculiar prayers, and suddenly shout that the Madonna had performed a miracle."[25] The babies would briefly move, cry, urinate, or make some other sign of life while the women would baptize them, after which they would return to death, prepared for reburial in Christian soil.

What also distinguished the *répit* miracle was the way it highlighted the differing interests of local communities and the Counter-Reformation Church. The foregoing description of the practice in Udine derives from the report of a representative of the Inquisition whose derision of the women's actions and of the rite in general is clear. Not only the feminization of the sacred embodied in the women's appropriation of the mass and baptism, but also the obvious prevalence of local superstitions drew the ire of the reform-minded Church hierarchy. Yet, individual parish priests were often sympathetic to the plight of grieving parents, and more or less accepting of such local practices that provided a reconciliatory function for the community as a whole.[26] Parish priests could be protective of the traditional childbirth culture that existed within their communities, and resistant to outside intervention in this area, whether by state or religious authorities.

Early modern Italians went to extreme lengths to ensure their infants were baptized because the alternative was unthinkable. To die without baptism meant to die without a soul, to be denied eternal salvation.[27] The soul was at the heart of the process of person making; it mediated between the material body and the individual, and between this world and the next.[28] The weight of the potential loss of this critical feature of identity therefore weighed deeply and heavily on the consciences of early modern parents, even those who abandoned their infants at foundling homes – these children were invariably left with notes that detailed whether they had yet received baptism.[29] Abortion and infanticide, by contrast, were an affront to God's justice, to the natural order, and to the social fabric of the community.

Midwives, given their medical knowledge and proximity to birth, were frequently discussed in relation to contemporary concerns about abortion and infanticide.[30] Midwives *were* likely familiar with recipes to bring about menstruation. That fact could lead to midwives being implicated in assisting women desperate to rid themselves of an unwanted pregnancy.[31] The Dominican friar and physician, Girolamo Scipione Mercurio, for instance, explicitly wrote in his midwifery treatise that midwives should be familiar with natural remedies to hasten delivery, such as drinks made from borax, hellebore, and castor – remedies that could easily be applied earlier in pregnancy to bring about abortion.[32] However, the legal and philosophical lines between healing and harming in such cases could be especially blurry. Ensoulment, which was traditionally correlated with quickening, when the pregnant woman could feel the child move, had long dictated at what point an abortion was considered sinful and criminal.[33] While religious writers debated the sinfulness of abortion before quickening, the Church saw the abortion of a quickened child as an unquestionable sin.[34] Moreover, beginning in the late sixteenth century, secular authorities increasingly concerned themselves with abortion, which they judged as a capital crime for all those involved.[35]

Midwives were not the only ones associated with abortion in early modern Italy. In fact, the community member perhaps most likely to be known to supply information or medicines to promote abortion was the procuress, for obvious reasons.[36] In an example discussed by David Gentilcore, it was common knowledge among members of the small Calabrian town of Pentidatillo that Anna de Amico, a foreigner, worked as a procuress and knew "the roots" used to induce an abortion. During a criminal investigation in 1710, Anna's reputation for arranging abortions in the community became central to the case's proceedings, and the courts turned to the expertise of the village midwife for assistance.[37] Maria Romeo, the 36-year-old midwife, testified that she had found Anna in the midst of a pool of blood in which "there were two small pieces of flesh, and attached to them two small bits of roots, so that, as a midwife and an expert [she] soon judged that the said Anna was pregnant, and had had an abortion because of the said roots."[38] In this case, there seems to have emerged in the court's mind a dichotomy between de Amico, a foreigner who traded in illicit sexual activity and unlawful healing, and Romeo, a trusted midwife whose actions were defined by honesty and uprightness. Whether these descriptions are accurate is impossible to tell; however, it is fair to say that successful midwives relied on the trust of their communities, something that might be tarnished by too great an association with illicit sexual or healing activity.

In addition to procuresses, physicians were also sometimes suspected of involvement in abortion given their traditional jurisdiction over internal remedies.[39] In the 1709 Bolognese infanticide case studied by Adriano Prosperi, Lucia Cremonini's mother had taken her illegitimately pregnant daughter to a physician to be bled.[40] As one of the most widely applied therapies at the time, bleeding was performed for a variety of medical conditions, including blocked menses. Historians have debated whether early modern men and women accustomed to thinking about health and illness in terms of balances and flows were consciously intending to induce abortions with the endless remedies designed to bring about the menstrual flow.[41] According to Cathy McClive, "methods used to regulate irregular menstruation and the meaning afforded to irregularity . . . depended heavily on the individual's marital status, socio-economic situation and the context in which regulation was sought."[42] In other words, one's physical condition was not conceived of independently of the social context in which she existed. Prosperi argues that in the case of Lucia, pregnant and unwed, she and her mother were indeed seeking to rid themselves of the fetus, which must also have been the conscious intentions of both physicians and midwives in some cases.[43]

Marriage, sexuality, and the courts

In addition to efforts to reform and better educate clergy and standard-ize Catholic ritual, the Counter-Reformation agenda extended to the dis-ciplining of everyday lives. In this environment, "concerns about the social order came to dominate spiritual agendas, and . . . the public and private spheres became intertwined as never before."[44] This broader project of moral supervision focused on a restructuring of marriage and the elimina-tion of concubinage, the reduction of illegitimacy, and the prohibition of pre-marital sex. Di Simplicio argues that the processes of confessionaliza-tion may even have shaped a uniquely Italian conscience based on the inter-nalization of the Church's strict attitudes toward morality and sexuality.[45]

Midwives were coopted into the Church's efforts in a variety of ways. Parish priests increasingly pressured midwives to report information about births in a timely fashion as the Church sought stricter record keeping in general.[46] In Venice, for instance, a midwife who did not report a birth within one day could be punished with public shaming in the Piazza San Marco or even exile.[47] In this way, the midwife was expected to oversee the moral vigor and proper functioning of the Christian community. Behind these requirements was the Church's increasingly strict enforcement of a sexual ethics that left no room for illegitimacy and that demonized mothers who aborted, abandoned, or killed unwanted children. At the same time, midwives who transported illegitimate children to foundling homes partici-pated in a system that disproportionately burdened women with the shame and guilt associated with illicit sexual relations.[48] If, as one historian has argued, "parish priests and confessors became the focal point of a com-plex power game in which the forces of local community life met with the reinforced structures of the church hierarchy," midwives came to represent a secondary intersection in this 'game' between community interests and those of the clergy.[49]

In some cases, midwives were not so ready to facilitate the Church's new-found interest in policing the sexual morality of the populace. The records of the Venetian health magistracy reveal several cases in which midwives pro-tected clients' secrecy in cases of illicit affairs and illegitimate pregnancies. In 1795, a man named Andrea Molin placed a young woman named Maria in the home of a local midwife and requested that she feed, clothe, and house the pregnant woman with great discretion – this despite prohibitions against exactly this kind of secretive behavior on the part of midwives. Only when the midwife did not receive compensation for all of these expenses did she take the case to the Venetian authorities.[50] Nevertheless, this case suggests that a midwife might choose to respect the wishes for the privacy of those who came to her for her services and aid, privileging community bonds – or perhaps simply her own financial interest – over the interests of the clergy.

As with illegitimate births, midwives' involvement with ecclesiastical courts clearly illustrates their role as intermediaries between community and clerical authority. Although early church regulations did not generally specify the medical knowledge a midwife should have, ecclesiastical authorities frequently deferred to midwives' anatomical expertise when it came to legal matters. The *Corpus juris cononici*, issued in 1580, stated that the testimony of midwives was admissible in ecclesiastical court.[51] Particularly in instances in which a physical examination might be necessary – for example, in cases of defloration, false promise of marriage, or the desired annulment of a marriage – the courts valued midwives' expertise and ability to make legible the female body. Midwives also testified in criminal cases related to sexual assault, abortion, and infanticide, though these were more likely to be tried in the secular courts. Ecclesiastical authorities did, however, demonstrate some concern about midwives being moved by loyalty to protect women in their community. Thus, in cases in which examination was required to corroborate a woman's virginity or pregnancy, the courts might summon "midwives from different parishes . . . to carry out inspections."[52]

In the wake of the Tridentine reform of marriage, which shifted the burden of managing heterosexual relations from the community to the Church, the flow of marital cases to ecclesiastical courts increased steadily. The Decree *Tametsi* reconfirmed marriage as a sacrament and formalized the proper manner in which a marriage could be formed and the (limited) reasons for which it could be annulled.[53] Sexual dysfunction that resulted in infertility or an unconsummated marriage were among the potential reasons for the dissolution of a union, each of which conditions midwives might help to verify with a physical exam. Furthermore, as marriage and sexual behavior became more strictly regulated, some women may actually have had better recourse to protest abuse or an unfavorable union. In Venice, for instance, Daniela Hacke has noted a significant rise in such marriage-related cases initiated by women following the reforms implemented at Trent.[54]

The case of a purported rape recorded in the ecclesiastical archive in Milan demonstrates both the reliance of early modern courts on the expert testimony of midwives and the significant cultural and legal repercussions wrought by the changes to marital practices after the Council of Trent. The case surrounded the apparent defloration in 1592 of a 14-year-old girl named Marta by one Giovanni Battista Ferrari in her home in the Porta Ticinese neighborhood of Milan. The sexual relationship allegedly occurred under the guise that Ferrari wanted to take Marta as his wife. The promise of marriage (*verba de futuro*) had traditionally been sufficient evidence of a couple's intentions to permit them to have sexual relations, though cases of broken marriage promises were common both before and after the Council of Trent. When Marta's father brought charges against

Ferrari for the deceit and defloration of his daughter, the latter began a smear campaign against the young woman. He contended that she was a loose woman who had already had sexual relations with men many times before he came along, accusations that Marta's father and sister vehemently denied. To determine whether Marta had been deflowered by the accused, a midwife named Ippolita de Santo Nazaro was called to examine the girl. Ippolita testified that:

> Having used the due diligence and procedures necessary in such things, and having diligently considered the [girl], I say it to be the truth that the girl by her husband was deflowered, but that she doesn't have the [physical] qualities to indicate that she has given birth, having found in her a narrowness such that makes me think and judge this way.[55]

In her testimony, the midwife alludes only vaguely to the examination she has performed, though there is clearly an implied standard of procedure in such cases. In the late sixteenth century, the midwife's authority remained tied to her practical knowledge of the female body rather than any formal educational or anatomical instruction. In this case, Ippolita made an unequivocal pronouncement based upon years of experience, and the court trusted the midwife's expertise. For the ecclesiastical authorities, the sexual encounter between Marta and Giovanni had been rendered illicit due to the new expectation that sexual relations would come only after a religious official consecrated the marital bond.[56]

Childbirth, the sacred, and the Inquisition

The Church's final point of interest in midwives' work centered on the host of peasant rituals associated with childbirth, which officials viewed as troublesome expressions of the rampant superstition and ignorance prevailing among the early modern populace. Childbirth, as the female-controlled ritual *par excellence*, was an obvious target, precisely because of the traditional lack of a male presence and its association with a range of popular prayers and rituals.

At the most basic level, folk practices surrounding pregnancy and childbirth were intended to assert some control over the apparent vagaries of life and death in an age of pre-modern medicine. The rituals associated with childbirth were numerous and widely employed. Taking stock of the various birth rituals encountered in his ministrations as a physician and Dominican friar, Girolamo Scipione Mercurio recounted the practice of girdling a woman with a belt of verbena gathered on a specific feast day. He also mentioned the lighting of a pilfered paschal candle at a mass said by a priest named Giovanni, and the common rural custom of the husband placing his hat over the women's pregnant belly.[57] Other contemporaries pointed to the use of various herbal remedies when labor proved difficult. Many women and midwives tried tying a magnet around one or both of the woman's thighs or placing seeds of coriander underneath the woman's skirts in order to hasten delivery.[58] An additional assortment of reproductive rituals and recipes worked to unblock fluids, increase fertility, and prevent miscarriage. Women used mandrake in remedies to facilitate conception, for instance, and, once pregnant, sometimes carried an eagle stone to protect the child in the womb.[59]

Often, women combined domestic superstitions and popular healing practices with orthodox religious rituals. Orthodox practices – such as prayer to the Virgin Mary, use of relics, and display of representations of biblical births or confinement scenes – were also important sources of mediation during childbirth.[60] Supplication to saints and relics linked to one's city or village gave these rituals a local character. What became a concern for the Church was the intermixing of the sacred and profane. Most troubling were cases in which midwives or other healers actually presumed to assert power over the sacred in a manner rivaling the authority of priests.

While most non-orthodox childbirth rituals did little more than exasperate reform-minded clergy, those practices that seemed to challenge the spiritual authority of priests garnered more intense efforts at re-Catholicization. From Venice to Southern Italy, wise women's healing abilities were closely tied to their perceived access to the divine through the practice of "signing."[61] In the late sixteenth century, a healer from the Veneto, Elena Crusichi, reported to the Inquisition how she would approach healing someone who had been bewitched: "I make the sign of the Cross three times and I say: I sign you . . . by the servant of the world . . . by the beard of Jesus, by the milk of the Virgin Mary, that every ill shall be undone from here and shall go away."[62] Clearly, Elena's healing infringed on the priests' monopoly to invoke the divine through exorcism and prayer. The previously-mentioned *répit* miracle, in which "babies who came out of their mother's wombs dead" were taken to certain women who attempted to resuscitate them, similarly incited the religious authorities for the popular (and feminine) appropriation of the priest's authority.[63]

The power of such rituals was often explicitly tied to strong peasant beliefs about the female body and a spiritual-religious understanding of sickness and malady.[64] In fact, as the Church attempted to evangelize the popular masses by consolidating its authority over the afterlife and by defending priests' monopoly to intervene in the sacred, it ran up against one of its strongest challenges in the power associated with the generative powers of the female body.[65] According to Luisa Accati, if the womb gives life, then it also has "the strength, by analogy, to confront and destroy that which was opposed to life and fertility" and thus "women were the most dangerous adversaries of the priests [as] they literally made problematic the priest's hegemony of the sacred."[66] Since men could not claim such bodily powers for themselves, they attempted to control its expression by women, as seen in inquisitorial records throughout the sixteenth and seventeenth centuries.[67]

Midwives not only had access to the womb, but also a certain power over it, an authority rooted in their knowledge of the secretive and mysterious processes of birth. The significance of this knowledge is evident in the ubiquitous presence of the womb in Italian folk beliefs. In the Friuli, for instance, witchcraft practiced by women in peasant communities was predicated on "the magical power of the female womb."[68] An intact caul or afterbirth was "a much sought after and highly treasured charm" which was believed "to bring special fortune and was preserved with great care."[69] In Venice, women used the caul in a variety of protective charms. Worn around one's neck, for instance, it prevented drowning. Midwives, with their obvious proximity and ease of access to the remnants of the amniotic sac, were often sought out for advice on caul beliefs and uses. More problematic was the practice of midwives secreting the caul with them when they took the baby to be baptized, as the Venetian midwife, Olivia, was accused of doing in 1591.[70] In fact, midwives were often believed to be paid to transport a variety of objects – not only cauls, but *brevi*, magnets, playing cards, etc. – with them when they took a baby to be baptized, thus imbuing these objects with religious power.[71]

Although caul beliefs in themselves might be considered relatively harmless, taking the caul (or other objects) secretively to be baptized was a much more serious infraction – the abuse of the sacraments.[72] In the case of Olivia, the repercussions were not particularly harsh: the midwife received only the warning "not to do such things, and [was] shown the great sin that it is, and the offence towards God, and the prejudice to her own soul and body that it could bring."[73] Still, the infringement on the priests' monopoly on the sacred clearly remained troublesome to early modern ecclesiastical authorities. A decree from the 1679 synod of the diocese of Otranto, on the southeast tip of Italy, speaks to very similar concerns about midwives' involvement with the sacred:

> We warn midwives, and command them under pain of excommunication, that whilst bringing infants to baptism or carrying them back home from baptism they abstain from all superstitious observances, nor place anything above [the infants] while they are being baptized, which could be used afterwards in sorcery, or (as they say) for remedies.[74]

This last phrase is telling; the religious authorities were articulating a disjunction between what midwives perceived themselves to be doing – healing – and how the Church wished to define such acts – as illicit magic.

Although midwives were certainly implicated in healing magic, they were not, at least in Italy, frequently associated with the kind of diabolical witchcraft that saw women burned at the stake in other parts of Europe.[75] Even when midwives *were* suspected of *maleficia*, or harmful magic, the elements of devil worship and Sabbath gathering that were present in inquisitorial cases elsewhere in Europe ware largely absent in Italy. Rarely did *maleficia* cases lead to capital punishment in Italy. Thus, when the Modenese wise woman and midwife, Diamante, was accused of harming her neighbor's children, the Inquisitors who investigated the case demonstrated skepticism and caution.

Diamante clearly had both supporters in her community, who had called upon her services for years, as well as detractors, who could target the woman's well-known use of incantations and healing magic. As many inquisitorial trials demonstrate, Italians were well aware of the notion that those who could heal could also do harm. Midwives, given their proximity to vulnerable infants and children, and their access to the powerful generative products of fertile bodies, were always potential suspects when the community's young became ill or died of uncertain causes.[76] Nevertheless, in Diamante's case, a reputation for magical healing did not prevent her from being well integrated into her community. In fact, one of the witnesses who came to her defense was her priest, who attested to her good reputation, even as he conceded she was known to perform magic and be able to heal children harmed by *maleficium* (or *guastare* as commonly referred to in Italy).[77]

Of course, even as authorities warned about midwives' potentially nefarious activities, they were also well aware that midwives might provide valuable information related both to local healing rituals and to the hidden activities of neighbors. As in the testimony of the Pentidatillo midwife Maria Romeo about her neighbor's involvement with local abortions, midwives sometimes provided just the kind of privileged information that Church officials sought.[78] In other words, "from their position as the priest's rivals, the midwives had to become allies and tools of the Church in the conquest of souls."[79] The events of one birth that became central to an inquisitorial investigation in Venice illustrate two points central to this idea: first, that female knowledge and tradition governed reproductive practice and, second, that midwives might act as important enforcers of religious orthodoxy during pregnancy and childbirth. In 1578, a midwife named Catherina was delivering the wife of the artisan Guglielmo Cromeri in the presence of Guglielmo's mother-in-law, Vienna Bertapaia. Some days after the happy birth of a baby girl, Vienna, at the forceful urging of her confessor, denounced her son-in-law to the Inquisition for heretical practices; specifically, the husband had mocked the invocation of the saints and displayed generally irreligious behavior in the home. Particularly troubling to Vienna was the fact that Guglielmo had infringed upon an entrenched tradition of calling on the Virgin Mary for protection and assistance during childbirth. According to Vienna, her son-in-law opposed such religious practices, doubting their efficacy, and saying that it was certainly enough "to pray to Christ" and "say the Lord's Prayer" rather than invoking the Virgin and saying the rosary.[80]

During the ensuing trial, Guglielmo's behavior at his wife's delivery was an important part of the proceedings. Catherina, the midwife, testified to the events of the birth: with Vienna kneeling before the parturient woman, "exhorting her to invoke the Virgin Mary," the women said prayers "as is always done" in order "for the baby to be alright" because "she [the new-born] was [in danger] for a bit." At the inquisitor's query about whether "one should invoke Christ and not the Madonna," at such times Catherina's reaction was vehement: "My Lord, no! O, Christ be blessed!"[81] Although Catherina ultimately testified that she was too intent on her work to take notice of the troublesome Guglielmo, she was nonetheless describing a scene in which women's knowledge and experience directed both spiritual and physical events. The moment of birth might therefore become a time when traditional patriarchy was destabilized and women's (religious) authority paramount.

Ordering the early modern medical marketplace

Straddling categories, midwifery was a specialty that in the early modern period was not fully conceived of as medical but yet boasted a specialized knowledge of the body that brought midwives into increasing contact with medical professionals. Because midwives' work involved the essential task of overseeing the reproduction of the population, the regulation of midwifery was also of increasing interest to both rulers and state-builders during this period. The following discussion briefly introduces the main bodies governing "official" medical practice in Northern Italy, particularly the health boards, medical colleges, and *Protomedicati*. The increasing medical oversight of midwifery beginning in the seventeenth century cannot easily be defined as either wholly positive or negative for the professional or social status of actual midwives. On the one hand, movements by state and medical authorities to license and regulate mid-wifery provided midwives with a stronger sense of professional identity and, at least theoretically, the potential for greater compensation. On the other hand, regulation tended to circumscribe midwives' right – at least officially – to manage difficult births and was often enjoined with a harsh and misogynistic invective against the "ignorance" of traditional midwives.

What is clear, however, is that attempts to regulate midwifery during this period tended to be just that – attempts. Licensing and examination requirements directed at midwives were rarely comprehensively applied or followed. The 1719 report of an irate official from the Venetian health board, the *Provveditori alla Sanità*, richly illustrates this fact. According to the report, despite repeated ordinances (issued in 1624, 1632, 1682, 1684, 1689, 1690, 1695, 1704) that required midwives to have formal licenses issued by the health board in order to practice legally, more than half of the 132 midwives active in the city were still operating without license.[82] Not only were these many unlicensed midwives purported to be "poorly or not at all learned," but they were also accused of being ignorant of the baptismal rite that they might be called upon to perform in an emergency, and therefore responsible for depriving "many innocent souls of the vision of God."[83]

In addition to oversight by health boards[84] like the one in Venice, medical practice in early modern Italy was regulated by medical colleges and corporations, or by official medical tribunals, called *protomedicati*.[85] The latter heard cases of malpractice and controlled the city's medical practitioners through examinations, licensing, and periodic inspections.[86] Across Italy during the course of the seventeenth century, these regulatory bodies attempted to bring the variety of medical practitioners in their territories under stricter oversight through regular licensing.[87] Such schemes, of course, had the added benefit of generating revenue. While not typically extravagant, licensing fees often proved to be deterrents for practitioners with modest means, including many midwives, surgeons, barbers, and empirics. Instead, these practitioners tended simply to eschew such requirements. In addition to revenue gathering, licensing was also aimed at enforcing the boundaries of a well-defined medical hierarchy with physicians at the top of the pyramid. The physician's overarching authority was implicit in licensing oaths that directed barbers "to swear not to let blood" and midwives not to prescribe oral medications "without the order of a physician." With similar aims, severe fines might be leveled "if a non-graduate physician or surgeon, mountebank, bone-setter, distiller, or other [practitioner] . . . impedes on the realm of physic."[88] Although surgeons, midwives, and a variety of other medical providers continued in this period to gain legitimacy and build their reputations upon the relationships they cultivated with clients, and not on the basis of a license, medical authorities tried effortlessly to bring the medical marketplace under stricter control.

For the most part, midwives were included in this new wave of regulation. In 1620, for instance, a decree from the *protomedicato* of the Papal States ordered that women healers could only receive licenses for the practice of midwifery. Women who attempted to heal in any other context were subject to fines of 25 *scudi*.[89] In 1627, the Roman *protomedico* added that, to practice, midwives "must first be examined and approved by the *protomedico* or one of his deputies."[90] Bologna and Siena followed this lead somewhat later; the *protomedicati* in these cities first began examining and licensing midwives in 1674 and 1686, respectively.[91] In Turin, by contrast, the *protomedicato* consistently omitted midwives from the list of medical practitioners it was responsible for examining and licensing.[92] The first formal efforts to regulate midwifery there came only with the establishment of a public midwifery school and maternity ward in the city in 1728.[93]

In Milan, confusion about what body was the proper authority to oversee midwifery meant that little effort was made to regulate midwives until the eighteenth century. In this case, jurisdictional conflicts between the *protomedicato* and the College of Barbers, both of which made some weak attempts to control midwifery licensing in the seventeenth century, demonstrated the imprecise position of midwifery within the official medical hierarchy and the often decentralized nature of medical oversight in this period generally. The result of this confusion was that most midwives eschewed any kind of licensing at all and continued to practice indifferently.[94] A report by the Milanese *protomedicato* in 1767 suggests, for instance, that most rural midwives continued to be chosen for their familiarity with and availability to their communities, and sanctioned by parish priests who would ensure they were conversant in the baptismal rite.[95] In the absence of any coherent licensing system by either the medical college, the college of barbers, or the *protomedicato*, midwives in Milanese territory retained traditional modes of ecclesiastical and community-based authorization well into the eighteenth century.

As mentioned, in Venice, the city's health magistrates, the *Provveditori alla Sanità*, began examining midwives in 1624 and posting the names of approved women on the city's official midwives' roll. The Venetian *Provveditori* justified their intervention into the regulation of midwifery because of "the confusion that follows a large number of women in time of birth and the loss of life and souls of infinite newborns because of the inexperience of many women who take on the office of midwife without having the required practice or experience."[96] To receive the license, Venetian midwives had to present a testimony from a midwife with whom they had apprenticed for a period of two years. Before the introduction of public schools for midwives, semi-formal local apprenticeships, often under the tutelage of female relatives, constituted the most common and important entryway into the practice of midwifery. Additionally, the Venetian statutes required that the midwife was to be examined by one doctor and "two women expert in the profession" who had already been approved by the *Provveditori*.[97] Lastly, aspiring midwives had to present written support from their parish priest certifying their ability to administer the sacrament of baptism in cases of necessity.

These early examples of midwifery regulation are largely similar in that they describe almost exclusively what midwives should *not* do rather than establishing a set of accepted practices for the delivery of babies. There was as yet neither the interest nor the practical experience on the part of the medical establishment to define and standardize the knowledge surrounding childbirth. Instead, the most important injunctions, repeated frequently, were against midwives letting blood, prescribing oral medications, or using surgical tools. Midwives were also directed to call in a surgeon as soon as a birth turned difficult. As with licensing in general, these prohibitions were aimed at defining and enforcing a medical hierarchy and protecting the authority of medical elites. As was the case with much medical practice in this period, however, the distinctions between types of healers and their respective professional prerogatives were constantly being blurred and crossed.

In a 1717 case heard before the Bolognese *protomedicato*, for instance, a midwife named Angela Nannini was investigated after the pregnant woman she was treating died. In danger of miscarrying early in her pregnancy, Virginia Calegari, at the behest of her mother, had called the midwife Angela who "took her [mother] to the apothecary, and there ordered some [drug] to eat . . . and . . . gave this to the patient."[98] Unfortunately, Virginia died several days later at Bologna's Hospital of Santa Maria Maddalena, at which time her husband, Lazzaro, brought charges against the midwife. Although Nannini was eventually reprimanded by the *Protomedicato*, the tribunal's condemnation lay not in the fact that her patient ultimately died, but that Angela had administered an oral prescription, something midwives were typically prohibited from doing since internal medicaments were the generally accepted preserve of physicians.

Nannini's case well illustrates both the extents and limits of medical oversight of midwifery in the early eighteenth century. On the one hand, Nannini, as a midwife, was clearly understood to be a medical practitioner whose work fell under the jurisdiction of the medical authorities and was subject to regulation and oversight. On the other hand, the authorities' response to Nannini belies an underlying assumption of female authority over women's reproductive matters. That is, for the *Protomedicato*, the issue at hand was one of professional boundaries, not of expertise. By administering an oral remedy Angela had violated the boundaries of her profession. Yet, as Gianna Pomata has pointed out, the authorities never questioned the nature of the concoction Angela prescribed nor its efficacy in treating a complicated pregnancy.[99]

The impact and limits of legislation

As medical legislation publically legitimized and granted a cohesive identity to midwives, it ultimately came to define the practice of midwifery in more limited terms. If the apprenticeship training advocated by the *Provveditori* in Venice protected traditional networks of knowledge transmission, the formal examination procedures implemented in Venice and by the *protomedicati* in cities such as Naples, Bologna, and Rome began a gradual process by which women's authority in the birthing room was eroded and replaced by the learned opinions of male physicians and surgeons. Other changes advocated by male medical professionals – such as the transition to the lithotomy (supine) position – transformed the cultural iconography and embodiment of birth as well.[100] The encroachment of male practitioners on midwives' traditional sphere of expertise was most obvious in calls for surgeons to handle an increasing variety of difficult cases. Scipione Mercurio wrote that "when . . . the Midwife finds herself in a very difficult situation," such as when there are sores or masses on the womb, or after normal remedies and purgations do not prove effective, she should "immediately make recourse to a doctor or surgeon."[101] There was thus the growing perception that midwives' duties encompassed only the birth itself and preferably only easy births at that.

Mercurio's midwifery text was significant not only for its presentation of "women's secrets" in the vernacular but also because it effectively became the standard handbook of midwifery in Italy until the eighteenth century. In 1689, when the medical authorities in Venice established new guidelines for examining and licensing midwives, they directly incorporated Mercurio's text. As was typical, the new requirements were first issued to the parish priests, and by them then made known to local midwives. The new procedures subsequently required that midwives:

> Be examined and approved as follows: they must know how to read, before every exam they are to be given for a text the "*Libro della Comare*," they must present a sworn certificate by an anatomist that that they have attended for two years demonstration of the matrice (womb) and the genital parts of woman, also [they must present] a testament certifying two years of practice with an approved midwife. Following, the examination of the *Magistrato*, is given by the *proto medico* in the presence of the priors of the College of Physicians and Surgeons and two midwives.[102]

As Daniela Pillon notes, the Venetian statutes represented a moment of transition, both theoretically and technically, with respect to the practice of midwifery.[103] For one, the elevation of midwifery to a science was predicated on the anatomical breakthroughs of the previous century. Along with the fact that the licensing of midwives was increasingly placed in the hands of (male) medical practitioners, this meant that the knowledge midwives were expected to have was based increasingly on an anatomical and theoretical understanding of childbirth. Personal experience of giving birth, the practical skills gained through apprenticeship and assisting neighbors, and a familiarity with the community and good relations with the parish priest – the traditional resume of most early modern midwives – were partially discredited as acceptable qualifications to practice midwifery. The story of midwifery legislation during the seventeenth and eighteenth centuries is therefore paradoxical: on the one hand, some midwives received public sanction and authorization through the acquisition of official licenses in a manner that elevated their art into a professional occupation; on the other hand, the midwife envisioned in new medical legislation was one whose duties had been sharply restricted. This reimagined midwife stood at a considerable distance from her traditional counterpart who had handled not only difficult births, but also all manner of pre- and postpartum complications. The space outside of "simple" deliveries was increasingly reserved, at least in theory, for male practitioners.

Such a conclusion would, of course, fail to acknowledge the ways in which midwives and community members may have openly or clandestinely resisted the novel forms of legislation introduced during the early modern period. In Venice, where from 1689 midwives had technically been required to attend dissections of the uterus and female genital parts in order to be licensed,[104] many midwives proved indisposed to such kinds of encroachment on traditional forms of instruction and authorization. Such resistance was rooted in a real skepticism of the value of such knowledge for their every-day practice. In 1719, for instance, Bortola Marchesini wrote a *supplica*, or petition, to the Venetian health board requesting a release from the requirement of attendance at a dissection. Marchesini noted that she had been instructed in how to perform an emergency baptism (also a requirement for midwives to be licensed) and was confident she could pass any exam without difficulty, but that she had not been able to attend a dissection of the uterus because she was "continually in company with my mother [an approved midwife] at births." Nor did Marchesini feel that this 'lapse' in training was significant since she she had "been present at many, many cases, both unusual and difficult ones . . . and . . . had occasion to learn all that the abovementioned dissection could show me."[105] A midwife named Lucietta Zaubina similarly wrote that she had not attended an anatomical demonstration because she had been repeatedly at the side of her mother and had attended many difficult cases at which she had learned extensively.[106] Both women, whose statements closely mirrored each other, indicated that they saw their presence at an anatomical dissection as a distraction from the most important source of their training – apprenticeship with an experienced mdiwife. Personal experience at numerous births counted more in their minds, and in those of prospective clients, than the theoretical discussion of anatomy that would have accompanied a dissection.

Traditional modes of authorizing a midwife, which hinged on local consensus, indeed represented another potent form of resistance to the efforts of medical authorities. Part of Lucietta's and Bortola's aversion to anatomical instruction, for instance, may have been their understanding that potential clients might see such training not only as unhelpful, but also even disquieting and offensive. This was the case of a midwife in Milan, whose clients found her anatomical training "disgusting."[107] The importance of choice was understood by medical officials even as they griped against it. When the Roman vice-*Protomedico*[108] in 1648 was angered that "the pregnant women and the people create midwives at their own whim, who then openly pass themselves off as such, without any recognition or experience at all,"[109] he was in fact articulating the confrontation between two competing methods of sanctioning medical practice in the early modern period, a traditional one resting on the wishes of the patients, and a professional one predicated on examination and licensing from above.

Gianna Pomata has compellingly discussed this patient-centered system as it existed in early modern Bologna. Pomata found that, in addition to passing an examination, Bolognese healers might successfully secure licenses by presenting testimonials from patients who had been treated successfully. Although testimonials were a strategy used most frequently by folk healers, they nonetheless reflected a medical system still characterized by "the coexistence of two sources of legitimization . . . the medical authorities, above, and the patients, below."[110] The fact that, at least initially, the medical authorities had to accommodate traditional forms of legitimation is evidenced by the virtual lack of fines or punishments meted out to unlicensed midwives in the records of the various *protomedicati*. In Rome, for instance, the first prosecution of a midwife for venturing beyond the limited scope prescribed by the medical authorities did not come until 1703, more than seventy-five years after the initial statutes were put in place.[111] Likewise, in Venice there is little evidence that midwives' lack of attendance at anatomical lectures prevented their acquisition of a license.[112] In city after city, statutes exhorting the necessity of midwives to be examined and licensed were repeated throughout the seventeenth and eighteenth centuries, suggesting that such attempts at regulation had only a limited impact.

Instead, communities retained a traditional system of validation that involved recognition from a parish priest based upon successful years of practice, good character, and local approval and recommendation. When discussing their qualifications, midwives referred to the apprenticeships they served with longer-practicing women and to an established record of assistance at neighbors' and relatives' births rather than to any kind of documentation. Many midwives learned their art from mothers or other female relatives; a specialized knowledge of birth – beyond the healing that most early modern women knew – was thus often passed down through generations. Although circumstances might vary significantly given the size or remoteness of a town or village, the path to becoming a midwife therefore followed an expected course. Clients also expected midwives to engage in an accepted course of actions and treatment, ranging from prayer to ritual to medicaments.

Given states' limited capacity to enforce licensing regulations, the extent to which medical authorities achieved any real oversight of midwives' activities in this period is therefore questionable. While statutes might theoretically circumscribe midwives' range of duties and prescribe the assistance of surgeons or physicians in difficult situations, a variety of factors often limited such intervention. For one, only an extremely limited number of male practitioners were trained in obstetrics until the second half of the eighteenth century when university and private courses began to be offered on the peninsula. A surgeon's capabilities before that were likely limited to traditional, non-obstetrical interventions, such as bloodletting. Some performed craniotomies to remove deceased fetuses, though many midwives likely undertook such procedures as well.[113] In fact, in remote areas, finding a surgeon to assist at a difficult delivery in a timely manner could be virtually impossible. In other words, despite prescriptive measures, state and medical authorities rarely had the ability to influence midwives' day-to-day actions.

In Milan, the archives of the public health board reveal only a handful of cases where midwives were censured for specific actions they undertook in the birthing room, and these only in the last several decades of the eighteenth century. In 1772, for instance, the midwife Matilde Bulgarelli was suspended from practice after a woman she had successfully delivered named Paola Maria died.[114] Following what seemed like the happy delivery of a baby girl, Bulgarelli assisted with the passing of the placenta as normal. When she had removed what she assumed to be the entire placenta, given its size and weight, she quickly disposed of the badly smelling mass, which was briefly seen by Paola's husband. Four days later, however, Paola was experiencing great pain, followed, according to her husband, by the emission of a partial membrane from the vagina. When doctors were subsequently called in, they were unable to remove the rest of the membrane, which still adhered to Paola's body; they instead treated the ailing woman with "appropriate" medicaments, both internal and external. In the evening, Paola experienced some relief and passed the remainder of what was later determined by the surgeon Bernardino Moscati to be the placenta from her earlier delivery.[115] Nonetheless, Paola ultimately succumbed to what was presumably infection from the fetid biological matter.

What emerged from the investigation into Paola's death reflected both the increasing oversight of midwives' actual birth room activities and an attendant circumscription of those duties. First, we might distinguish Matilde Bulgarelli's case from that of Angela Nannini, another midwife investigated by the authorities after a pregnancy-related death. While Nannini's censure in 1717 centered on her violating long-standing prohibitions on medical practitioners other than doctors prescribing internal treatments, Bulgarelli's 1772 reprimand cited a specific oversight in her actions related to managing a birth. Furthermore, given that Paola Maria went into labor with an already weak constitution, having a long history of health complications,[116] the medical authorities suggested that perhaps the case should not have been handled by a midwife at all.[117] In other words, by the second half of the eighteenth century, male practitioners were beginning to claim a wider and wider sphere of authority with respect to managing childbirth.

Conclusion

The ecclesiastical regulation of midwifery aimed both at controlling and utilizing midwives' authoritative position within the local community. The relationship between local midwives and parish priests was greatly strengthened as a result of Catholic reform, which tasked local curates with overseeing midwives and ensuring their knowledge of baptism, good morals, and demonstrated orthodoxy. The Church's stricter policies regarding record keeping and baptismal registration further facilitated the local surveillance of midwives and childbirth. This relationship typically provided midwives with a respected and valued position within the community. Sanctioned midwives had their names posted within their local churches, demonstrating the priest's approval and their place of significance within the local community. Furthermore, midwives' medical and healing expertise generally went unquestioned in this period.

This authority was gradually eroded, beginning in the seventeenth century, through state and medical efforts to more strictly regulate and license midwives. At the same time, the regulation of midwifery in early modern Italy was a process continually negotiated and contested by midwives, their local communities, religious officials, and medical and state authorities. Before the introduction of public midwifery schools in the eighteenth century, medical oversight of midwives tended to be minimal. Most midwives practiced unlicensed and continued to receive authorization from clients, neighbors, and local curates based on their intimacy and proven skill within their communities.

Notes

1 David Gentilcore, *Healers and Healing in Early Modern Italy* (Manchester: Manchester University Press, 1998), 82.
2 For a thorough discussion of the role of the Virgin Mary in early modern childbirth traditions, see Mary Fissell, *Vernacular Bodies: The Politics of Reproduction in Early Modern England* (Oxford: Oxford University Press, 2004), 14–24.
3 For evidence of lavishly celebrated lying-in and baptismal ceremonies, and the sumptuary legislation that regulated them in some areas, see Patricia Allerston, " 'Contrary to the Truth and also to the Semblance of Reality?' Entering a Venetian 'Lying-In' Chamber (1605)," *Renaissance Studies* 20, no. 5 (2006): 629–639.
4 Margaret Schaus, *Women and Gender in Medieval Europe: An Encyclopedia* (Boca Raton, FL: CRC Press, 2006), 104.
5 Renate Blumenfeld-Kosinski, *Not of Woman Born: Representations of Caesarean Birth in Medieval and Renaissance Culture* (Ithaca: Cornell University Press, 1990), 35.
6 Blumendfeld-Kosinski, *Not of Woman Born*, 61–63. For more on artwork related to early modern Italian childbirth, see Jacqueline Marie Musacchio, *The Art and Ritual of Childbirth in Early Modern Italy* (New Haven: Yale University Press, 1999).
7 Allyson M. Poska, *Regulating the People: The Catholic-Reformation in Seventeenth-Century Spain* (Leiden: Brill, 1998), 77–78.
8 Claudia Pancino, "La Comare Levatrice: Crisi di un Mestiere nel XVIII Secolo," *Storia e Società* 15 (1981): 614–615.
9 *The Catechism of the Council of Trent; Published by the Command of Pope Pius the Fifth* (New York: F. Lucas Jr., 1850), 121.
10 Records from foundling hospitals in Turin and Milan frequently refer to abandoned infants who had received "water from the midwife." See, for instance, AST, Istituto Provinciale per l'Infanzia, mazzo 3 (From March to December, 1781, at least seven infants were received at the foundling home having been baptized by a midwife.)
11 Archivio di Stato di Torino (hereafter AST), prima sezione, *Istituto Provinciale per l'Infanzia*, mazzo 3.
12 Lefebvre Desclee, "De Sacramento Baptismi," in *Rituale Romanum Pauli V, Pontificis Maximi, jussu editum et a Benedicto XIV* (Tornaci Nerviorum, 1896), 6.
13 Kathryn Taglia, "Delivering a Christian Identity: Midwives in Northern French Synodal Legislation, c. 1200–1500," in *Religion and Medicine in the Middle Ages*, ed. Peter Biller and Joseph Ziegler (Suffolk: York Medieval Press, 2001), 77–90.

14 Tommaso Astarita, *Village Justice: Community, Family, and Popular Culture in Early Modern Italy* (Baltimore: The Johns Hopkins University Press, 1999), 191–192.

15 "Processo per abuso di sacramenti contro Pasqua Guarini da Palazzolo (3 febbraio 1651)," in *I Processi dell'Inquisizione nella Bassa Friulana (1568–1781)*, ed. Benvenutio Castellarin (La Bassa: Associazione per lo Studio della Friulanita, 1997), 291–292.

16 On the lack of evidence that midwives were targeted in any systematic way by the inquisition in Italy, see, for instance, Jonathan Seitz, *Witchcraft and Inquisition in Early Modern Venice* (Cambridge: Cambridge University Press, 2011), 77; Ruth Martin, *Witchcraft and the Inquisition in Venice, 1550–1650* (Oxford: Blackwell, 1989), 33.

17 "Processo per abuso," 291–292.

18 Archivio Storico Diocesano di Torino (hereafter ASDt), 9.6.21 #11, Case Against the Curate of Santena, 1731.

19 ASDt, 9.6.21 #11, Case against the Curate of Santena, testimony of Maria Toretta, 1731.

20 Oscar di Simplicio, *Peccato, penitenza, perdono: Siena, 1575–1800; La formazione della coscienza nell'Italia moderna* (Milan: Franco Angeli, 1994).

21 Adriano Prosperi, *Dare l'anima. Storia di un infanticidio* (Turin: Einaudi, 2005), 186.

22 Prosperi, *Dare l'anima*, 197.

23 Ibid., 205.

24 Unbaptized infants were excluded from Christian burial. Prosperi, *Dare l'anima*, 208–210.

25 Quoted in Silvano Cavazza, "La Doppia Morte: Resurrezione e Battesimo in un Rito del Seicento," *Quaderni Storici* 17, no. 2 (1982): 551.

26 Cavazza, "La Doppia Morte," 555.

27 Prosperi, *Dare l'anima*, 175.

28 Ibid., 220.

29 Ibid., 192.

30 Statutes from the Venetian health board, for instance, specifically prohibited midwives from engaging in any activities that might produce an abortion, while suggesting that midwives were often persuaded by money to do so: "*L'esperienza ha spesso confermato che qualche d'una delle Levatrici scordata di Dio, e dell'Obligo suo, abbogliata dal denaro e speranza di gran lucro si è indotta ad adoperare rimedi per far disperdere la creatura, vengono pericò rigorosamente incaricate le medesime a scarso del loro impiego, onore, ed altre pene temporali prescritte dalle leggi criminali, anche dalla vita stessa secondo la grandezza del delitto, di non preparare, ne far preparare, meno di porgere a persona nessuna sia maritata o libera, delle medicine, bevande, polveri, ad altre cose per far sperdere la creatura sia vivo, o morta.*" Archivio di Stato di Venezia (hereafter ASV), *Sanità*, b. 591, "Istruzione per le Levatrici," n.d., likely 1794.

31 On midwives' role in regulating menstruation in various parts of Europe, see Merry E. Wiesner, *Women and Gender in Early Modern Europe* (Cambridge: Cambridge University Press, 2000), 54–56; Sara Read, *Menstruation and the Female Body in Early Modern England* (Basingstoke: Palgrave Macmillan, 2013), esp. Ch. 4.

32 Girolamo (Scipione) Mercurio, *La commare o raccoglitrice* (Venezia: Giovanni Battista Ciotti, 1596), bk. 2, 71.

33 Common opinion at this time held that the soul entered the fetus at the time of quickening, which was believed to be different for males and females. Thus, the Church stated that abortion was only illegal after forty days in the case of boys and eighty days in the case of girls. This ruling, of course, rests on the notion that

the sex of the fetus could be determined before birth, when in fact such determinations were as yet impossible.

34 There was much debate over the processes of fetal development in the seventeenth and eighteenth centuries. Some physicians and scientists held to an explanation based on preformationism, in which the form of the living thing exists before its development. Some preformationists suggested that all organisms were created by God at one time and thus were already in existence at the time of conception. Epigenesis, on the other hand, which was spurred on by the important seventeenth-century discoveries made by scientists such as Regnier de Graaf and William Harvey regarding the female ovum, held that living things come into existence through a number of stages of gradual development. For the relationship of these debates to concerns over ensoulment, the practice of cesarean section, and the crime of abortion, see Chapter 3 in this volume; Shirley A. Roe, *Matter, Life, and Generation: Eighteenth-Century Embryology and the Haller-Wolff Debate* (Cambridge: University of Cambridge Press, 1981); Angus McLaren, *Reproductive Rituals: The Perception of Fertility in England from the Sixteenth to the Nineteenth Centuries* (London: Methuen, 1984), 121; Nadia Maria Filippini, *La Nascita Straordinaria: Tra Madre e Figlio: La Rivoluzione del Taglio Cesareo (Sec. XVIII–XIX)* (Milano: Franco Angeli, 1995), 86–90; Marie-Hélène Huet, *Monstrous Imagination* (Cambridge, MA: Harvard University Press, 1993), 36–55; Eve Keller, *Generating Bodies and Gendered Selves: The Rhetoric of Reproduction in Early Modern England* (Seattle: University of Washington Press, 2011), 125–155.

35 Astarita, *Village Justice*, 156.

36 David Gentilcore, *From Bishop to Witch: The System of the Sacred in Early Modern Terra d'Otranto* (Manchester and New York: Manchester University Press, 1983), 148–149.

37 Astarita, *Village Justice*, 70–73.

38 Quoted in ibid., 73.

39 Prosperi, *Dare l'anima*, 250–252.

40 Ibid., 121.

41 It is important to remember that in early modern Europe early pregnancy was an incredibly ambiguous state, uncertain until quickening, and even then still open to interpretation. See Cathy McClive, *Menstruation and Procreation in Early Modern France* (Farnham and Burlington, VT: Ashgate, 2015), esp. Ch. 3.

42 McClive, *Menstruation and Procreation in Early Modern France*, 128.

43 Prosperi, *Dare l'anima*, 122.

44 Wietse De Boer, *The Conquest of the Soul: Confession, Discipline, and Public Order in Counter-Reformation Milan* (Leiden: Brill, 2001), 68. On the concept of 'social discipline' and its extents and limits in relation to the Counter-Reformation, see R. Po-chia Hsia, *Social Discipline in the Reformation* (London and New York: Routledge, 1989); Paolo Prodi and Carla Penuti, eds., *Disciplina dell'anima, disciplina del corpo, e disciplina della società tra medioevo e età moderna* (Bologna: Il Mulino, 1994); Giorgia Alessi, "Discipline: i nuovi orizzonti del disciplinamento sociale," *Storica* 2, no. 4 (1996): 7–37; Elena Brambilla, *Alle origini del Sant'Uffizzio: Penitenza, confessione e giustizia spirituale dal medioevo al XVI secolo* (Bologna: Il Mulino, 2000).

45 Di Simplicio, *Peccato, penitenza, perdono*.

46 On record keeping in relation to the Counter-Reformation Church's movement toward increased social control and community involvement, see Kasper von Greyerz, *Religion and Culture in Early Modern Europe* (Oxford: Oxford University Press, 2007), esp. 54–55.

47 Daniela Hacke, *Women, Sex, and Marriage in Early Modern Venice* (Burlington, VT: Ashgate, 2004), 157. Whether this form of punishment was ever actually applied is unknown, though there is good reason to be skeptical – expert midwives were always in need, particularly in Venice's densely populated confines.

48 Midwives commonly transported babies, often, but not always, illegitimate, to foundling homes. See, for instance, AST, *prima sezione, Istituto Provinciale per l'Infanzia, Esposti,* mazzo 3, "Registro degli Esposti e nati nell'Opera 'delle Partorienti,'" March 1781–June 1784.

49 De Boer, *The Conquest of the Soul,* 206.

50 ASV, *Sanità,* b. 181, Petition of Andrea Molin, 26 August 1795 and Petition of Antonia Basquesti, 21 August 1795.

51 Technically, canon law advised the consultation of seven midwives in such cases, though it is unlikely this standard was ever met in practice. *Corpus juris canonici, vol. 2, Titulus XIX, de Probationibus, Cap. IV* (Lipsiae: sumptibus Bernh. Tauchnitz Jun, 1839), 296.

52 Hacke, *Women, Sex, and Marriage,* 158.

53 The Decree *Tametsi* issued at Trent reconfirmed marriage as a sacrament, attempted to heavily suppress extra-marital sexual relationships such as concubinage (clerical and lay), and formalized the proper manner in which a legitimate marriage could be formed. Afterwards, proper marriage required a public ceremony performed before a priest and several witnesses preceded by marriage banns. In contrast to traditional practice, the consummation of the marriage could take place only *after* the marriage ceremony itself, rendering sexual relations entered into after just the promise to be sinful behavior in the eyes of the Church. See John Bossy, *Christianity in the West, 1400–1700* (Oxford: Oxford University Press, 1985), 25; Merry E. Wiesner, *Christianity and Sexuality in the Early Modern World: Regulating Desire, Reforming Practice* (London: Routledge, 2000), 106–108.

54 Hacke, *Women, Sex, and Marriage,* 40–52.

55 Archivio Storico Diocesano di Milano (hereafter ASDMi), Y6250, Trial of Tommaso Monasteri against Giovanni Battista Ferrari, 1593.

56 Giorgia Arrivo, *Seduzioni, promessi, matrimoni: Il processo per stupro nella Toscana del Settecento* (Roma: Edizioni di Storia e Letteratura, 2006), 12; Giorgia Alessi, "Il gioco degli scambi: Seduzione e risarcimento nella casistica cattolica del XVI e XVII Secolo," *Quaderni Storici* 75 (1990): 806; Simona Cerutti and Sandra Cavallo, "Onore femminile e controllo sociale della riproduzione in Piemonte tra Sei e Settecento," *Quaderni Storici* 44 (1980): 373.

57 Girolamo Scipione Mercurio, *Degli errori popolari d'Italia. Libri sette* (Venice: Giovanni Battista Ciotti, 1603), 382; Rudolph Bell, *How to Do It: Guides to Good Living for Renaissance Italians* (Chicago: University of Chicago Press, 1999), 108, 110.

58 Laurent Joubert, *The Second Part of the Popular Errors,* trans. Gregory David de Rocher (Tuscaloosa: University of Alabama Press, 1995), 189.

59 Musacchio, *The Art and Ritual of Childbirth in Renaissance Italy,* 140.

60 Ibid., 125–126.

61 Martin, *Witchcraft and the Inquisition in Venice,* 144–146.

62 Quoted in ibid., *Witchcraft and the Inquisition in Venice,* 145.

63 Quoted in Silvano Cavazza, "Double Death: Resurrection and Baptism in a Seventeenth-Century Rite," in *History from Crime,* ed. Edward Muir and Guido Ruggiero (Baltimore: The Johns Hopkins University Press, 1994), 1.

64 Barbara Duden, *The Woman Beneath the Skin: A Doctor's Patients in Eighteenth-Century Germany* (Cambridge, MA: Harvard University Press, 1998), 7–9; Piero Camporesi, *Il sugo della vita: Simbolismo e magia del sangue* (Milan: Edizioni

di Comunità, 1984), 16–18; Cristina Mazzoni, *Maternal Impressions: Pregnancy and Childbirth in Literature and Theory* (Ithaca: Cornell University Press, 2002), esp. Ch. 1.

65 The baptism of menstrual blood often served an important role in Italian love magic. See Gian Luca d'Errico, "I sortilegi," in *Sortilegi amorosi, materassi a nolo e pignattini. Processi inquisitoriali del XVII secolo fra Bologna e il Salento*, ed. Umberto Mazzone and Claudia Pancino (Roma: Carocci, 2008), 135–140.

66 Luisa Accati, "The Spirit of Fornication: Virtue of the Soul and Virtue of the Body in Friuli, 1600–1800," in *Sex and Gender in Historical Perspective: Selections from Quaderni Storici*, ed. Edward Muir and Guido Ruggiero (Baltimore: The Johns Hopkins University Press, 1990), 116.

67 Accati, "The Spirit of Fornication," 111, 118–119.

68 Ibid., 116.

69 Martin, *Witchcraft and the Inquisition in Venice*, 128.

70 Ibid., 128–129.

71 Ibid., 138.

72 Ibid., 175–176.

73 Quoted in ibid., 177. Original: ASV, *Sant' Uffizio*, b. 67, 16 May 1591.

74 Quoted in Gentilcore, *From Bishop to Witch*, 146.

75 The main academic source for the midwife-witch thesis was Thomas Forbes, *The Midwife and the Witch* (New Haven: Yale University Press, 1966), later essentially 'debunked' by David Harley's article "Historians as Demonologists: The Myth of the Midwife-Witch," *Society for the Social History of Medicine* 3 (1990). More recently, historians of the Roman Inquisition have come to understand that midwives were only infrequently denounced by the Holy Office. See Mary O'Neil, "Magical Healing, Love Magic, and the Inquisition in Late Sixteenth-Century Modena," in *New Perspectives on Witchcraft, Magic, and Demonology: Witchcraft, Healing, and Popular Diseases*, ed. Brian P. Levack (New York and London: Routledge, 2001), 172–199; David Gentilcore, "The Church, the Devil, and the Healing Activities of Living Saints in the Kingdom of Naples After the Council of Trent," in *New Perspectives on Witchcraft, Magic, and Demonology: Witchcraft, Healing, and Popular Diseases*, ed. Brian P. Levack (New York and London: Routledge, 2001), 200–221; Martin, *Witchcraft and the Inquisition in Venice*, 1989.

76 Prosperi, *Dare l'anima*, 29–44.

77 Mary O'Neil, "Discerning Superstition: Popular Errors and Orthodox Response in Late Sixteenth Century Italy," PhD dissertation, Stanford University, 1981, 90–94. See also, Mary O'Neil, "Magical Healing, Love-Making and the Inquisition in late Sixteenth- Century Modena," in *Inquisition and Society in Early Modern Europe*, ed. and trans. Stephen Haliczer (Totowa, NJ: Barnes and Noble, 1987), 88–114.

78 Wiesner, *Women and Gender in Early Modern Europe*, 54–56.

79 Prosperi, *Dare l'anima*, 38.

80 Many thanks to John Martin for alerting me to this case. John Martin, "Out of the Shadow: Heretical and Catholic Women in Renaissance Venice," *Journal of Family History* 10, no. 21 (1985): 27.

81 ASV, *Sant' Uffizio*, b. 43, Testimony of Guglielmo Cromeri, 30 May 1578. Also cited in John Martin, "Out of the Shadow," 27–28.

82 ASV, *Sanità*, b. 748, "Regolatione delle Comari Levatrici," 5 May 1719.

83 Ibid.

84 The permanent health boards that sprang up during the fifteenth and sixteenth centuries had their *raison d'être* in the prevention and amelioration

of the plague. However, the duties and jurisdiction of the health boards quickly expanded, coming to regulate not only the movement of people and goods during times of epidemic, but also the marketing of foods, sewage, beggars and prostitutes, burials, cemeteries, and the activity of hostelries, even during periods free of disease. Initially, the health boards were not strictly concerned with the regulation of medicine, though over time some did get involved in this area. For many years, however, most of the early modern health boards did not even have permanent physicians on their committees, though they might make recommendations for these in time of plague. Carlo Cipolla, *Public Health and the Medical Profession in the Renaissance* (Cambridge: Cambridge University Press, 1976), 20–23.

85 See Cipolla, *Public Health and the Medical Profession*; Michelle Anne Laughran, "The Body, Public Health and Social Control in Sixteenth-Century Venice," PhD dissertation, University of Connecticut, 1998; Pomata, *Contracting a Cure*.

86 David Gentilcore, "The Protomedicato Tribunals and Health in Italian Cities, 1600–1800: A Comparison," in *Living in the City*, ed. E. Sonnino (Rome: Casa Editrice Università La Sapienza, 2004), 407–430.

87 On the growth of professionalism in early modern medicine and historiographical debates over 'professionalization,' see Margaret Pelling, "Medical Practice in Early Modern England: Trade or Profession?" in *The Professions in Early Modern England*, ed. Wilfred Prest (London: Croom Helm, 1987), 90–128; Roy Porter, "William Hunter: A Surgeon and a Gentleman," in *William Hunter and the Eighteenth-Century Medical World*, ed. W.F. Bynum and Roy Porter (Cambridge: Cambridge University Press, 1988); Ramsey, *Professional and Popular Medicine in France, 1770–1830* (Cambridge: Cambridge University Press, 1988); Laurence Brockliss and Colin Jones, *The Medical World of Early Modern France* (Oxford: Oxford University Press, 1997); Thomas H. Broman's *The Transformation of German Academic Medicine* (Cambridge: Cambridge University Press, 1996) has a good overview of the historiographical debates over professionalism in its introduction, 1–13; Susan C. Lawrence, *Charitable Knowledge: Hospital Pupils and Practitioners in Eighteenth-Century London* (Cambridge: Cambridge University Press, 2002), esp. 16–19; Bridgette Sheridan, "Whither Childbearing: Gender, Status, and the Professionalization of Medicine in Early Modern France," in *Gender and Scientific Discourse in Early Modern Culture*, ed. Kathleen P. Long (Burlington, VT: Ashgate, 2010), 239–258.

88 Pelling, "Medical Practice in Early Modern England: Trade or Profession?"

89 Schiavoni, "L'attività delle levatrici o 'mammane' a Roma tra XVI e XVIII secolo," 45.

90 "Editto del Protomedico Generale alle Mammane – 1627 gennaio 28," in *Quattro secoli di vita del Protomedicato e del Collegio dei Medici di Roma; Regesto dei documenti dal 1471–1870*, ed. Garofolo Fausto (Rome: Pubblicazioni dell'Istituto di Storia della Medicina dell'Università di Roma, 1950), 35.

91 David Gentilcore, " 'All That Pertains to Medicine': *Protomedici* and *Protomedicati* in Early Modern Italy," *Medical History* 38 (1994): 131; Pomata, *Contracting a Cure*, 64.

92 A partial list of the practitioners that were mentioned includes: doctors, surgeons, apothecaries, barbers, druggists, sellers of live things, chemists, distillers, mountebanks, sellers of aquavita, and vagabonds. F. A. Duboin, *Raccolta per ordine di materia delle leggi. editti. manifesti, emanate dai sovrani della real Casa di Savoia sino all'8–12–1798*, 23 toms. (Turin, 1818–69), Lib. VII, Tit. XII, Cap. 3, p. 99.

93 F. A. Duboin, *Raccolta per ordine di materia delle leggi. editti. manifesti*, Bk. VII, Tit. XIX, Cap. 2, "Manifesto del Vicario di Torino, del quale notifica essersi stabilito nell'Ospedale di San Giovanni Battista un ricovero gratuito per le povere partorienti, ed una scuola practica per le ostetrici," 19 June 1728, 646.

94 ASMi, *Sanità, parte antica*, c. 186, Letter from the Protofisico 11 April 1679; Anna Parma, "Didattica e pratica ostetrica in Lombardia (1765–1791)," *Sanità, Scienza e Storia* 2 (1984): 102.

95 ASMi, *Sanità, parte antica*, c. 186, "Relazione della visita fin'ora eseguito nello Stato di Milano della Commissione della Facoltà medica," 2 May 1767.

96 Quoted in Daniela Pillon, "La comare istruita nel suo ufficio. Alcune notizie sulle levatrici fra il '600 e il '700," *Atti dell'Istituto Veneto di Scienze, Lettere ed Arti* 140 (1981): 67.

97 Nelli Elena Vanzan Marchini, ed., *Le leggi di sanità della Repubblica di Venezia*, vol. 1 (Veneto: Neri Pozza, 1995), 431, "Comari Allevatrici, 20 February 1624."

98 Quoted in Pomata, *Contracting a Cure*, 77.

99 Ibid., 77.

100 Mercurio, *La commare o raccoglitrice*, Bk. 2, 175–176; Jo Murphy-Lawless, *Reading Birth and Death: A History of Obstetric Thinking* (Bloomington: Indiana University Press, 1998), 37; Harold Speert, *Obstetrics and Gynecology: A History and Iconography* (New York: Parthenon Publishing, 2004), 266.

101 Mercurio, *La commare o raccoglitrice*, Bk. 2, 181.

102 Vanzan Marchini, *Le leggi di sanità*, 432, "Comari Allevatrici, 26 September 1689–Not. 19."

103 Pillon, "La comare levatrice," 69.

104 Vanzan Marchini, *Le leggi di sanità*, 432, "Comari Allevatrici, 26 September 1689–Not. 19."

105 ASV, *Sanità*, b. 589, Supplica of Bortola Marchesini, 15 December 1719.

106 ASV, *Sanità*, b. 589, Supplica of Lucietta Zaubina, December 1719.

107 ASMi, *Sanità, parte antica*, c. 269, Letter from the community of Abbiate Guazzone, 15 August 1768.

108 The vice-Protomedico was the Protomedico's representative in the countryside.

109 Quoted in Gentilcore, "'All That Pertains to Medicine'," 132.

110 Pomata, *Contracting a Cure*, 51.

111 "1703 – Processo contro alcune levatrici di Viterbro che medicavano in Chirurgia senza alcuna licenza," in Fausto, *Quattro Secoli*, 47.

112 Nadia Maria Filippini, "The Church, the State and Childbirth: The Midwife in Italy During the Eighteenth Century," in *The Art of Midwifery: Early Modern Midwives in Europe*, ed. Hilary Marland (New York: Routledge, 1993), 162.

113 Eve Keller, "The Subject of Touch: Medical Authority in Early Modern Midwifery," in *Sensible Flesh: On Touch in Early Modern Culture*, ed. Elizabeth D. Harvey (Philadelphia: University of Pennsylvania Press, 2003), 66.

114 ASMi, *Sanità, parte antica*, c. 271, Report of Francesco Raineri, Vice Prior of the medical school of Mantua, 31 October 1772.

115 Bernardino Moscati was the director of Milan's first midwifery school, opened just five years before Bulgarelli's case. For more on Moscati, see Chapters 4 and 5.

116 ASMi, *Sanità, parte antica*, c. 271, Report of Francesco Raineri, Vice Prior of the medical school of Mantua, 31 October 1772.

117 A petition on Bulgarelli's behalf also noted her impeccable sixteen years of service and her training under her mother, a midwife named Isabella. ASMi, *Sanità, parte antica*, c. 271, Supplica on behalf of Matilde Bulgarelli, 27 October 1772.

2 Textual deliveries

Reading early modern obstetrical treatises

In writing treatises on women's diseases and manuals for midwives, medical men began, in the sixteenth century, to expose the so-called secrets of generation, the knowledge of which had traditionally been linked to women's experiences of their own bodies. Medical men confronted this gendered barrier with their own brand of authority obtained through participation in the exclusive environment of the university and in the new anatomical sciences of the sixteenth century. Although some of these men had never been present at an actual birth, they had gained an alternative, invasive understanding of the female body through the practices of dissection. In urban centers such as Paris and London, midwifery manuals served in time as vehicles through which men established the rhetorical authority that would eventually lead to their actual presence in early modern birthing rooms. In response, by the end of the seventeenth century, prominent female midwives in France, England, and even Germany – Louise Bourgeois, Jane Sharp, and Justine Siegemund – had all published midwifery manuals which praised midwives for their practiced skill and argued that women's personal experience of birth provided them with knowledge men would never be able to obtain.[1]

By contrast, in Italy no woman wrote about pregnancy and childbirth until the last decades of the eighteenth century.[2] There was no desperate need to defend the midwife's role in childbirth because she was still the relatively unchallenged guardian of the knowledge and rituals surrounding pregnancy and parturition. Girolamo Scipione Mercurio's 1595 *La comare o raccoglitrice* was, in fact, the only Italian midwifery manual published until Sebastiano Melli's 1721 text, *La comare levatrice istruita nel suo ufizio*.[3] By the second half of the eighteenth century, however, the publication of Italian obstetrical manuals began to accelerate. Although there were often restrictions on male intervention in childbirth, increasing numbers of Italian surgeons and anatomists were introduced to a largely theoretical study of obstetrics.

In this chapter, I examine the evolution of the early modern midwifery manual into the more specialized and scientific eighteenth-century obstetrical treatise. The first half of the chapter discusses midwifery manuals published in the late sixteenth and seventeenth centuries: first, as they appeared on the

Continent and in England; second, the single manual published in Italy during that period. The remainder of the chapter turns to the eighteenth century and focuses on Italian obstetrical treatises directed at a more limited professional audience to consider how male writers employed the medium of print to develop their own professional discourse and identity as they sought to enter a traditionally female field for the first time.

Early modern midwifery manuals represented a textual space where issues of authority in childbirth were questioned and contested. While manuals published in the sixteenth and seventeenth centuries relied heavily on their authors' knowledge of anatomy and on the ancient wisdom of Galen, Aristotle, and Hippocrates, male authors by the eighteenth century had gained enough practical experience to assert their authority based on personal accounts of (at times exaggerated) heroic intervention. By the late eighteenth century, the case study had largely supplanted biblical anecdotes and classical references in obstetrical texts, though male authors continued to struggle to affirm their legitimacy as birth attendants in the face of both female midwives and competing male practitioners. In both their more popular and more specialized forms, midwifery texts revealed the contested nature of authority surrounding childbirth and its management. Earlier authors touted the revelatory power of anatomy but often had to concede the limitations of the bodily knowledge that might be gleaned from dissection. At times, manuals' images expressed messages that contradicted those in the accompanying text, belying the inconsistencies apparent when theory and practice were disconnected. In subsequent texts, male practitioners engaged in a project of theorizing childbirth, articulating a mechanical and predictable model of birth that nonetheless tended to highlight pathology and therefore the necessity of medical intervention.

The masculine origins of early modern midwifery manuals

Early modern midwifery manuals were, generally speaking, 'popular' texts. Not only did their subtly transgressive subject material attract readers with mainly lascivious interests, but midwifery manuals also presented a great deal of practical information about sex, conception, pregnancy, and common female diseases. These manuals shared much with the wider genre of "how to" books popular during and after the Renaissance. As Rudolph Bell notes, an eager sixteenth-century reader might easily have found advice manuals "telling farmers how to govern their wives, books telling priests how to use the confessional to guide their parishioners toward proper behavior, vernacular medical advice, herbals, books of secrets," and cookbooks.[4] Given the still mysterious nature of conception and generation, midwifery manuals' information on, for instance, how to conceive a boy, how to know if a woman is really pregnant, how to have a smooth delivery, and how to choose a good midwife or wetnurse represented a wealth of highly sought-after advice. The fact that these manuals often contained practical recipes and cures indicates that they could serve an important household function as well. Long digressions into biblical authority and examples from antiquity added story-like elements to these texts that would have been both familiar to early modern audiences and useful to maintain their attention. Finally, the important visual component of early modern midwifery manuals meant that they were theoretically accessible to even an illiterate audience. In any case, "readership" and "audience" were flexible terms in the early modern period, when the information available in a text might be passed on orally.[5]

As a genre, early modern midwifery manuals were highly formulaic; they shared a common structure, employed many of the same rhetorical devices, and were typically written in the vernacular.[6] They discussed comparable material, offered similar advice, incorporated the same biblical and classical anecdotes, and featured common visual conventions. In fact, because of the period's virtually nonexistent concept of intellectual ownership, the manuals sometimes borrowed outright from one another.[7] Typically divided into several parts or books, the manuals tended to discuss (in roughly the following order): female and male anatomy relevant to generation; sexual problems such as sterility; the processes of conception and generation; natural childbirth; complications that can arise as a result of the fetus's position or sickness of the mother; and often some treatment of the diseases of women and children more generally. As a result of the still wide dependence on traditional sources of authority in this period, little new information was actually produced in these manuals until the late seventeenth century, despite authors' frequent claims to originality and innovation.[8]

At the same time, midwifery manuals were emblematic of a new scientific tradition taking hold in the early modern period based on anatomical investigation.[9] Female anatomy and childbirth, topics traditionally couched in the language of "secrets,"[10] were popular topics in vernacular texts based on the new anatomy.[11] Early modern men writing about reproduction typically had limited experience with childbirth in practice. Though some were called in emergency cases that required surgical intervention, these often registered poor outcomes and instilled in male practitioners a distorted sense of the frequency of pathological births. Yet, these men shared a conviction in the superiority of their anatomical knowledge based on the practices of dissection. For the authors of early modern midwifery manuals, the direct observation of even one female body through dissection was privileged rhetorically over the practical knowledge a traditional midwife might gain through years of experience. Midwifery manuals provided a pivotal space for the establishment of male knowledge about reproduction and female anatomy, a textual justification for the real entrance of some men into the practice of midwifery and the basis for the creation of the new, 'scientific' field of obstetrics.[12]

In such texts, male authors attacked practicing midwives as ignorant, coarse, and dangerous precisely because they lacked a proper anatomical knowledge of the body. In one of the first published midwifery manuals, Jacob Rueff's *The Expert Midwife* (published originally in German in 1554), the author proclaimed that women, lacking anatomical knowledge of their own bodies, were like "a blind man, which is deprived of the benefit of the light."[13] Peter Chamberlen suggested similarly that a midwife ignorant of the practice of anatomy was "no more fitting for that Faculty, than a blind man to judge of Colours."[14] In 1651, Nicholas Culpeper called for midwives to recognize their own "ignorance" since they lacked "the exact knowledge of the Anatomy of" female reproduction.[15] According to Mary Fissell, the emphasis on anatomy expressed by men like Culpeper established "a new epistemology of female bodies, one in which women can learn only from men, not from each other."[16] The aforementioned authors' emphasis on sight reveals, further, the importance of visuality and exposure to male practitioners' claims to authority in this period.[17]

At the same time, sixteenth- and seventeenth-century midwifery texts were rife with examples of female bodies that challenged the anatomist's ability to accurately "read" their signs. The semiotics of virginity and pregnancy were as contentious as they were critical to ensuring the functioning of paternity, inheritance, and familial honor in the early modern social economy. Male medical writers who aimed to make legible the female body with a variety of tests and axioms frequently found themselves mired in contradictions. The well-known French surgeon Ambroise Paré, for instance, wrote that despite the hymen's purported existence in both ancient and contemporary sources, in all his experience with dissection, he "could never find it in any" of the many young women, "ages from three to twelve . . . that I had under my hands at the hospital of Paris."[18] Citing, however, a woman from Camburge who had had a surgical operation to, apparently, repair an imperforate hymen, Paré ultimately conceded the existence of the structure, but only as a monstrous or pathological condition.[19] For other writers, the hymen existed, but could not serve as a reliable marker of virginity because it could be destroyed in a variety of ways besides copulation – such as horseback riding, or even vigorous sneezing or speaking, the latter of which clearly reflected cultural associations between women's open mouths and open morals.[20] Nicholas Culpeper believed the hymen was sometimes broken by midwives, highlighting men's fears that women might render their own or other's women's bodies deliberately deceptive. In short, the hymen served as a marker of virginity in neither its presence nor its absence, despite the long efforts of anatomical writers to inscribe virginity on the female body.[21] Moreover, anatomical structures such as the hymen could typically only be discerned during dissection, creating "within its own terms the retroactive nature of the virginal body."[22] As in Paré's and other medical writers' accounts, the female body was subject to slippages among anatomy and pathology, health and disease, normality and aberration.

Pregnancy, like virginity, was a potentially ambiguous state, particularly in its early stages. Like the womb itself, the early modern pregnant body was both powerful and unruly; it could imprint its yearnings on a fetus or influence the child's gender. Without the aid of any kind of definitive pregnancy test, early modern midwives and physicians relied on a set of interrelated signs which could be read to determine whether a woman was with child. Popular medical texts referred to visible physical changes such as "eyes grow[n] hollow & wan . . . the lids loose, limber, and soft: the veins in the corners of her eyes more swollen. . . [and] breasts grow[n] big, and hard."[23] Other texts prescribed tests based on a humoral understanding of the body's flows and blockages. In some cases, writers' efforts to determine an accurate test for pregnancy aimed to diminish the importance of women's own embodied sensations. For instance, although physicians, jurists, and clergymen widely agreed upon the importance of a mother's sensation of the child quickening as the moment when a fetus was ensouled, most medical writers also continued to restate the Aristotelian assumption that this moment could be quantified mathematically at about forty days for boys and eighty for girls.[24] Some medical writers went further and directly questioned the reliability of women's self-knowledge. According to Culpeper, "Some Women are so Ignorant they do not when they are conceived of Child, and other so coy they will not confess when they do know it."[25] Contemporaries of course suspected that women hid pregnancies when they were undesirable or sought remedies to cure persistent "menstrual blockages."[26] Women's speech and reproductive knowledge were therefore always suspect, either because of ignorance or, worse, active deception.

Notwithstanding their concerted efforts to establish some kind of reliable guide, medical writers, jurists, and civic officials all acknowledged the indeterminacy and potential deception of the signs of conception. In his widely translated seventeenth-century midwifery treatise, Jacques Guillemeau emphasized both the difficulties of reading, and the potential consequences of 'mis-reading,' the female body for pregnancy. According to Guillemeau, the diligent surgeon had to be "very circumspect, in determining whether a woman be conceived, or no; because many have prejudiced their knowledge, and discretion, by judging rashly hereof."[27] In fact, in his own lifetime, Guillemeau witnessed the execution of a woman four months pregnant who had been deemed to be without child by experts.[28]

Despite their best efforts to claim otherwise, Guillemeau and other midwifery manual writers recognized the limitations of knowledge gained exclusively through dissection. The most certain way to determine pregnancy was, writers conceded, through the midwife's tactile knowledge and privileged access to the female body. The midwife, "by putting her finger into the wombe to touch the inner orifice thereof," will find it closed shut in a woman who is carrying a child, according to Guillemeau.[29] A midwife might also notice changes to the moistness or dryness of a woman's "natural parts." Midwives, in short, judged through touch, drawing conclusion based on their regular observation of the female body in both normal and non-normal situations. Their expertise was based on their practical and

tactile experience of their own and other women's bodies, not through anatomical training or presence at dissections.[30]

An Italian midwifery manual? Scipione Mercurio's *La Comare o Raccoglitrice* (1596)

It is a particular respect for midwives' vernacular knowledge that sets apart
the only Italian midwifery manual published during the seventeenth century.[31]
Like other male midwifery writers, Scipione Mercurio justified his foray
into writing about childbirth by referring to his anatomical knowledge –
as a student in Bologna he saw the dissection of "the natural site of the
human creature in the maternal womb."[32] He praised the anatomical breakthroughs initiated by Vesalius and included the now-infamous images of the
'vagina as penis' that were produced in the *Fabrica*. He could also be found
occasionally exasperated with and disparaging of excitable and superstitious midwives. Nonetheless, Mercurio tended to give midwives the benefit
of the doubt where other authors exaggerated their deficiencies. He readily
accepted that his own anatomical knowledge stopped short of providing
him unfettered access to live women's bodies. Mercurio's response to the
hymen controversy (he argued that all virgins *do* have one), for instance,
was based equally on his personal anatomical observations *and* on "reports
from numerous midwives experienced in these matters."[33] When considering the position of the fetus in the womb, Mercurio argued that the fetus
was upright facing the mother's front for much of the pregnancy only to
somersault before birth. Other medical writers had suggested that the fetus
was situated upward facing the mother's back, but Mercurio heartily denied
this, citing his own experience as well as the "multitude of very diligent
midwives in many Italian cities" who deemed it so.[34]

First published in Venice in 1595 and continuously reprinted in the seventeenth century, *La Commare o Raccoglitrice* became a kind of official catechism for Italian midwives. In Venice, midwives after 1689 were officially
required to have read the text in order to receive a license.[35] As noted, *La
Commare* was distinct for its appreciation of the orally and experientially
learned wisdom of local midwives. Unlike many of his contemporaries,
Mercurio seems to have made a concerted effort to develop relationships
with the midwives. Perhaps because of his experience as a *medico condotto*,
or salaried physician treating the poor in the Roman countryside, Mercurio
was aware that midwives handled not only all 'normal' deliveries, but also
the vast amount of difficult births they encountered. In a passage describing
the qualities a good midwife should have, Mercurio made the bold statement that "the wise and prudent midwife is as necessary to pregnant women
as the good physician, in fact more so, because, if he helps with advice, she
helps both with advice and her hands."[36] In this appraisal, a practiced touch
is the skill that most defines the midwife's practice and separates it from that
of men.

Figure 2.1 Title page of the 1601 reprinting of Scipione Mercurio's *La Commare o Raccoglitrice*.

Source: Wellcome Library, London. Wellcome Images.

In other midwifery texts, by contrast, it was midwives' tactile intervention at births that male writers most sharply condemned. Many authors criticized the midwife's touch as destructive and misguided, sometimes rashly pulling the child prematurely from the womb, other times deforming the infant's body with injurious hands.[37] In these representations, the midwife's touch lacked reason and restraint, qualities that were rhetorically reserved to men. A number of authors focused, for instance, on midwives' impatience and hastiness to manually break a laboring woman's water.[38] The *Compleat Midwife's Practice* warned that

> Some Midwiues either through ignorance, or impatience, or else by being hastned to go to some other womans labour, do teare the membranes with their nayles, and let foorth the water, to the great hurt and danger, both of the poore woman, and her child . . . which hath been the death of many women, and children.[39]

In an even more dreadful example, the deeply misogynistic English man-midwife Percival Willughby recounted that he had once been called to assist a woman who had been experiencing pain in her womb and heavy bleeding. Before he could arrive, however, a midwife assured the woman that she was pregnant and that

> Shee could ease and deliver her of the child. The poor woman in distresse, desirous to be freed of her tortures, hearkened and submitted to her skill. The midwife thrust up her hand into her body, and took hold of shee knew not what, and endeavoured violently to pull it away. But through her struglings and enforcements, great pains ensued, with a flux of bloud, and the woman being not able to endure such violence, the midwife was restrained from farther proceedings.[40]

Willughby's anecdote finished with the doctor's definitive pronouncement that the ailing woman had never been pregnant at all, but rather suffering from a "cancerous tumour in the womb."[41] Thus, not only was the midwife's touch violent and rash, but also in its inability to discern the difference between a fetus and a tumor, it embodied the ignorance that resulted from a lack of anatomical knowledge.

By contrast, Mercurio repeatedly highlighted the skillfulness of the midwife's touch. Noting the importance of midwives' "most tender" touch at birth, Mercurio referenced the Genoese midwives who were known "truthfully . . . to place the heads of the [newborn] babies almost in a mold (*stampa*) in order to give them the figure they judge optimal, without doing any harm."[42] Here, instead of a touch that resulted in aberration and injury, the midwife's hands manipulated in order to make the newborn more perfect. This message was reinforced through the incorporation of two rare woodcuts depicting the midwife's role in managing difficult births. In the first, with sleeves rolled up, the midwife's strong arms guide the child from its mother's womb.[43]

The laboring woman lies supine with hips positioned above her head using a stack of cushions, a position intended to open the pelvic brim and which later came to be known as Walcher's Position after the nineteenth-century German obstetrician.[44] Mercurio recommended the position for prolonged labors when the baby was head first but with neck angled such that the head was impeded from continuing down the pelvis, though he added that the position could be used profitably for a variety of contrary fetal positions. In the illustration, the physicality of the midwife's role is highlighted as her hands are depicted at the moment of delivery, disappeared into the laboring woman's uterus. At the same time, the scene is calm with only the two figures of midwife and mother present, rich decorations and bedding suggesting a positive and successful outcome. Although contemporary accounts of deliveries suggest that a birth with just the mother and midwife present would have been unusual, the woodcut's sparseness emphasizes the calm and order of the scene at a time when men often charged midwives with being reckless and flustered during difficult deliveries.

A second illustration depicts a midwife directing the scene of a delivery of an especially large woman, perhaps reflecting the more practical dilemmas Mercurio might have encountered working as a salaried physician in the countryside. In the woodcut, the midwife holds up one hand as if to call attention to the reader while pointing the other toward the laboring woman positioned in the background. The midwife here embodies both the knowledge and the manual skill to safely deliver what would otherwise be a difficult birth. Learned readers might have also noted the iconographic similarities between the midwife figured in this illustration and another famous anatomical woman, Berengario da Carpi's image of a dissected woman pointing to her own extracted uterus. If the earlier image indicated the authority of direct observation over the received wisdom of classical sources, Mercurio's illustration is an affirmation of the midwife's competency and skill, based on her own direct knowledge of childbirth.

Mercurio expects the Italian midwife to deal with any number of abnormal fetal presentations, to judge when it is necessary to break the laboring woman's water (something Guillemeau warned midwives never to do), and even to apply instruments herself when a surgeon or physician could not be found.[45] Mercurio also instructs the midwife on how to deal with a child who has died in the womb:

> First, cover the patient's face to keep her from seeing so frightening a procedure. Then, with the nail of her middle finger . . . dig into the dead baby's abdominal skin. . . [to] ease the passage of the rest. Next . . . try to get the creature into a headfirst position and use a hook . . . to pull it out. If the fetus is feet first . . . just hook as best you can, being very careful not to wound the mother.[46]

Figure 2.2 Position for difficult births that can be used profitably for women experiencing prolonged labors. Mercurio, *La Commare o Raccoglitrice*, Book II. Venice (1601).

Source: Wellcome Library, London. Wellcome Images.

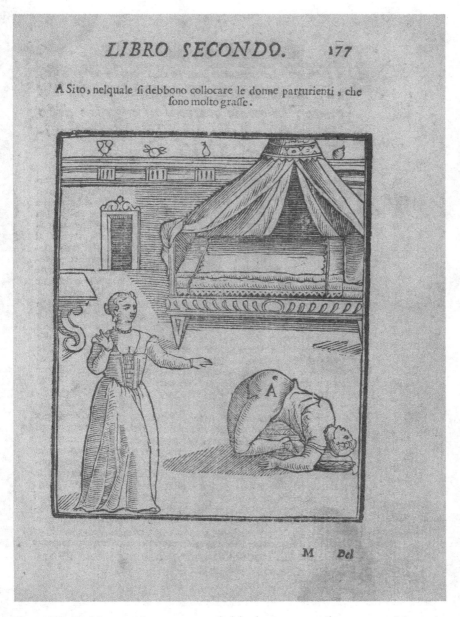

LIBRO SECONDO. 177

A Sito, nelquale si debbono collocare le donne parturienti, che sono molto grasse.

Figure 2.3 Birthing position recommended for large or corpulent women. Mercurio, *La Commare o Raccoglitrice*, Book II. Venice (1621).

Source: Wellcome Library, London. Wellcome Images.

DE ANATOMIA

❦Habes i vétre huius figuræ Matricem aper tam in qua vides punſ ſa aliq niſ gra indican tia capita venaæ quç dicuntur co tilidões: ha bes præteſ rea Matriſ cem inuerſ ſá extra véſ trem: & eſt illa figura ſupra q̄ viſ des Digitū indicē præſ ſentis figuſ ræ & in fun do Matricis eſt cerra de preſſio vt ui des/quç eſt illa quæ Diſ ſtinguit ſiſ nū Dextrū a ſiniſtro: nec in Maſ trice reperi tur alia Diſ uiſio:& illa punſta niſ gra ſunt co tilidones :& vides qualiter collum Matricis eſt ſine cotilidonibus :& viſ des qualiter collum aſſimilatur virgæ virili.

Figure 2.4 Dissected woman pointing to her extracted uterus from Jacopo Berengario da Carpi's *Isagogae Breves* (1522).

Source: Wellcome Library, London. Wellcome Images.

If the fetus is too large to be removed in one piece, the midwife should proceed to cut the body into pieces in order to evacuate it from the womb. Almost no other manual authors recommend the midwife attempt the removal of a dead fetus, arguing that such an operation was the prerogative of the surgeon.[47]

Eighteenth-century obstetrical texts and the emergence of a professional discourse

Mercurio's text remained the standard reference work on childbirth in Italian throughout the seventeenth century.[48] Though translations of continental works were available in Italy, no new Italian texts were produced until Sebastiano Melli's 1721 treatise, *La comare levatrice istruita nel suo ufizio* (The Midwife Instructed in her Duties).[49] Despite the lengthy interim, *La comare levatrice* presented little that was new in terms of either knowledge or praxis. Melli's text followed Mercurio's in form, beginning with a section on anatomy, followed by a discussion of normal and difficult births, and concluding with a consideration of the diseases to which parturient women and young infants might be prone. Like many of the midwifery manuals of the sixteenth and seventeenth centuries, Melli relied on the authority of traditional sources, particularly the Bible, Aristotle, Hippocrates, Soranus, and Galen. Melli aimed to legitimate his expertise by engaging in lively debates with the most prominent midwifery writers of the time, such as Gillemeau, Mauriceau, and Paré, underscoring the highly inter-textual and self-referential nature of these works. At the same time, Melli's text shared much of the philosophizing of earlier manuals, locating the origins of women's pain during childbirth in Eve's sin and pondering the wonders of human conception and generation, all the while discussing female reproductive anatomy in imaginative, though often borrowed, metaphor.[50]

Melli, like Mercurio and many continental authors, devotes particular attention to describing the ideal midwife. Melli agreed with Mercurio that the midwife has three main duties: first, to determine virginity and to discern, ahead of marriage, whether a woman and a man are both able to produce children; second, to know if a woman is pregnant or not; and third, to help women before, during, and after childbirth.[51] These first two responsibilities in particular demand a midwife who is discreet but also well-trained, given the severe consequences potentially involved. She must be punctual, attentive, knowledgeable, and experienced; agreeable and comforting in temperament; sober; charitable; and, especially, God-fearing. Melli then spends an entire page on the sin of abortion. The midwife, he continues, will also likely find herself in some occasion dealing with a young woman dishonored by an illegitimate pregnancy, a situation once again requiring the utmost discretion and prudence.[52] Melli's meandering presentation of the midwife's moral and spiritual obligations includes a digression on virginity and the inclusion of a passage from Ariosto discussing virtue in women. Only then does Melli write that the midwife should also know how to read and write, and to have a complete knowledge of female reproductive anatomy.[53]

Although ostensibly written for the improvement of midwives, Melli's text is curiously short on details related to normal births. Rather, the text overemphasizes malpresentations and other pathologies, reflecting medical men's exclusion before the eighteenth century from most uncomplicated births. *La comare levatrice* details chapter by chapter the various causes of difficult births, punctuating his discussion with a series of plates depicting the positions a fetus may take in the womb. These artistic renderings share much with their seventeenth-century French counterparts, which have been extensively studied by Lianne McTavish. According to McTavish, the illustrations in these texts participate in a self-conscious misrepresentation of the spatial reality of the womb. Full-term fetuses are shown floating, often completely extended, in wombs with ample space, quite unlike the actual cramped quarters that exist at the end of pregnancy. While the mother has been reduced to the womb, or perhaps a torso, in these depictions, the fetus, always male, is presented as the focus of an implied male expert. Though the text accompanying such images contrasted with the visual message they imparted – both the mother's labor and physicality, and the fetus's cramped positioning in the womb are highlighted in the written material – these images nonetheless served as "ideas in visual form that could guide the cerebral activity of practitioners asked to intervene in difficult deliveries."[54] By reducing an infinite number of possible malpresentations to a dozen or so "ideal" types, early modern representations of fetuses functioned as "diagrams meant to provide support for surgeon men-midwives' haptic acquisition of knowledge of the womb without offering a visual likeness of the womb."[55] Furthermore, the visual depictions of fetal presentations in Melli's text (figure 3) highlight the surgical intervention required to 'see' inside the womb. The flesh is cut and pulled back to offer a view of the fetus inside the womb, evoking men-midwives' frequent argument that their anatomical knowledge provided them a more thorough and scientific understanding of childbirth than midwives' traditional experience.

Melli's manual, published in 1721, presaged a marked shift in the nature of medical writings about childbirth. By the time the next spate of Italian midwifery texts were published, in the 1760s, courses in obstetrics for male surgeons were available in universities and academies.[56] The introduction of state-sponsored midwifery schools and public maternity wards meant that male practitioners were also increasingly exposed to clinical training in obstetrics, though they were still generally restricted from assisting at normal births. The impact of such changes on the obstetrical treatises produced after midcentury is notable; although structurally reminiscent to earlier midwifery manuals, the content in later texts has been much altered. In Italy, these texts were primarily authored by elite, university-trained surgeons (*medici-chirurghi*) who were often involved in the teaching of obstetrics, either at the universities, in local medical colleges, or even through private lectures in their own homes. Several of these writers also instructed female midwives at the first Italian midwifery schools: Giuseppe Vespa in Florence, Pietro Sografi in Padua, and Vincenzo Malacarne in Venice all wrote treatises on childbirth. A majority of these texts were directed at other surgeons, containing lengthy anatomical discussions and an emphasis on how to manage difficult births and other surgical complications, such as a uterine tumor.

Most distinctly, the later eighteenth-century texts were engaged in a self-conscious effort to define through print a new field of surgical practice in an area that had not traditionally even been considered medical. Unlike the sixteenth- and seventeenth-century midwifery manual writers, eighteenth-century authors were writing about a set of practices and beliefs for which they had begun to accumulate significant firsthand experience. Even in Italy, where male intervention in birth was more limited than on the continent or in England, surgeons generally expanded their capacity to assist at obstructed births and some male practitioners gained experience in hospital maternity wards during the second half of the eighteenth century. If earlier midwifery texts were "a combination of antiquarianism, irrelevance, salaciousness and the blindingly obvious," the obstetrical treatises of the later eighteenth century actually offered new knowledge, forged through the application of theory to practice.[57]

It is therefore not surprising that the Pavia obstetrics professor Giuseppe Nessi opens his treatise, *Arte Ostetricia Teorico Pratica* (1779), with claims to both textual mastery and practical experience: "The obstetrical treatise that I present to you . . . is the result of how much I have excavated from the writing of numerous Authors, and from many favorable and sinister observations made in various places, and at various times at the beds of Pregnant and Post-partum women."[58] Nessi thus holds the value of his treatise as much in his own direct experience as in the wisdom of either the ancients or other contemporary obstetrical writers. In fact, Nessi boasts that he has excised from his treatise much that bogs down other similar texts; he has abandoned "superfluous digressions, however erudite they might be, and useless reflections, however connected, touching instead on only those circumstances, which can instruct" and improve one's practice.[59] Decades before Nessi, the Florentine professor Giuseppe Vespa, who had been trained by the famed French obstetrician André Levret in Paris, made a similar pronouncement when he was named chair of obstetrics at the medical school of Santa Maria Nuova hospital. After disparaging the wandering, often senseless practice of studying only other authors, Vespa praises the practices of observation and experimentation in science and medicine. Was it not more fruitful, he questioned, "to interrogate [nature] with repeated experiments, penetrating into her secret recesses with the force of assiduous and well-thought-out observations?"[60] Likewise, Pietro Paolo Tanaron, professor of obstetrics and surgery at the University of Pisa, in his 1774 treatise, *Il Chirurgo-Raccoglitore Moderno*, wrote of obstetrics as a field that was constantly in the process of perfecting itself, rather than a discrete body of knowledge that could simply be transmitted from generation to generation. Even though many authors had written on the subject, Tanaron pointed out, observations and experiments made since "have illuminated many facts that were unknown in [those authors'] days."[61]

Although the obstetrical manuals published in Italy during the second half of the eighteenth century resembled their predecessors in structure, the content of these texts had undergone significant changes, reflecting new advancements in the field. Generally divided into three parts, the manuals move from a discussion of anatomy and the organs involved in generation, to labor, with a concentration on difficult and non-natural presentations, and are often concluded with a discussion of diseases related to childbirth, care for the newborn baby, false conceptions, abortion, and sterility. Unlike earlier texts, many of the eighteenth-century manuals also engage in theoretical discussions based on novel anatomical and physiological research about topics such as the development and nutrition of the fetus, the circulation of the blood in the fetus, and the forces that cause labor to begin.

These texts also stress the importance of pelvic anatomy to childbirth. Originating with the reflections of Hendrik van Deventer on the size, shape, and significance of the pelvis in labor, and the careful examination of normal births undertaken by William Smellie, obstetrical writers increasingly described birth as a mechanical process that followed unalterable principles. The practice of pelvimetry, or pelvic measurement, represented the promise of systematically determining if a woman would have difficulty giving birth ahead of time.[62] The result of new technologies such as the pelvimeter, which was developed specifically to measure pelvises, was the scientific classification of 'normal' and 'abnormal' pelvic types.[63] By carefully examining the relation between pelvic size and shape, the orientation of the uterus, and the position of the fetus in the womb, as well as the delivering woman's posture, Deventer believed that nearly all births could be completed without the introduction of instruments.[64] Coming to a different conclusion but nonetheless basing his obstetrical practice on pelvic geometry, the Frenchman Levret developed a new type of forceps mathematically designed to fit to the curve of the birth canal.

Thus, while Melli and his predecessors had barely mentioned the pelvis, writers after midcentury dedicated entire chapters to minutely detailing all the bones that composed the pelvic basin and how its size and the positioning of the womb within it determined how smoothly or difficultly a birth would proceed. Francesco Valle, in his 1767 treatise, *Trattato del Parto Naturale e dei Parti Divenuti Dificli per la Cattiva Situazione del Feto* (Treatise of Natural Birth and of Births become Difficult because of the Poor Situation of the Fetus), dedicates some twenty pages to his discussion of the pelvis. Likewise, the first lesson (titled "The Definition of Obstetrics and the Description of the Pelvis") in Pietro Sografi's manual, on which he based his instruction of both male and female students in Padua, considered a thorough knowledge of pelvic structure as the basis for obstetric practice.[65]

To determine the good or bad proportions of the pelvis, midwifery-manual authors also championed a new kind of internal examination to be performed on a pregnant woman before labor. Called *"il toccamento"* (the touching) or *"l'esplorazione"* (the exploration) in Italian manuals,[66] this exam would enable the midwife or surgeon to correctly determine virginity, sterility, pregnancy time to delivery, whether a woman was experiencing false or real labor pain, and, perhaps most importantly, whether delivery would be impeded in any way by a malformed pelvis.[67] Tanaron describes the procedure thusly:

> By 'Touching' is meant the introduction of one, or two Fingers into the *Vagina* of the Woman, after greasing them with oil, or butter (*butirro*), in order to touch the mouth of the Womb (*Matrice*), and to identify the figure of this, and to discover by this method that which certainly could not be identified otherwise.[68]

As they advocated for touching as an essential practice in obstetrics, however, male practitioners had to work hard "to counter the cultural norms that aligned touch with at best manual labor and at worst – given what they were touching – with out-right lechery."[69] The manual exploration of a woman's genitals had to be re-contextualized as an expression of scientific rationality and medical authority, all while maintaining decorum.

At the same time, touch was essential for extricating the management of childbirth from the whims of the pregnant woman herself. Instead of relying on the patient's word and interpretation of her own symptoms, the male practitioner could now make determinations based on his own systematic understanding and exploration of the female body. As Pietro Paolo Tanaron wrote, "all the ways women have thought to know if they are pregnant in the past are notoriously uncertain"; the only "true means [to know] is Touching."[70] Thus, while writers of sixteenth- and seventeenth-century midwifery manuals had emphasized their visual mastery of the female body, particularly through practices such as dissection and anatomy, eighteenth-century obstetrical authors worked to re-appropriate touch from midwives. Long considered the less-worthy counterpart to seeing, touching became, for male obstetrical writers in the eighteenth century, the most important expression of masculine and scientific rationality in the birthing room.[71]

* * * *

In addition to treatises written by surgeons, a smaller subset of eighteenth-century Italian midwifery texts were authored by physicians (*medici-fisici*). Traditionally, physicians might be called in by a pregnant woman to advise on matters of diet and regiment, or to prescribe a medication; surgical operations to deliver obstructed or deceased fetuses, on the other hand, had generally been considered the work of surgeons. During the eighteenth century, however, and perhaps more in Italy than elsewhere, university physicians also demonstrated considerable interest in obstetrics. A number of noted professors of obstetrics such as Giovanni Battista Galli in Bologna and Luigi Calza in Padua were physicians. Perhaps because of the generally high esteem in which surgery was held in Italy, there was considerable overlap among practitioners of physic and surgery, especially in the elite context of the university. There are occasionally some distinctions between physician-authored and surgeon-authored midwifery texts. Physicians might spend more time on theory and were more likely to engage in debates about physiology than about how to manage a difficult labor. In at least two cases in Italy, physicians also wrote treatises directed specifically at female midwives. Pared of the lengthy digressions and philosophical discussions of conception and generation found in earlier midwifery manuals, these physician-authored guides were often composed in dialogue form so as to be most easily understood by and useful to a female audience.

As male instructors such as Sebastiano Rizzo and Luigi Calza would do in their lectures to female midwifery students, physicians Natale Bernati and Giacomo Tranquillini employed the dialogue form in their texts so that 'coarse' female readers could conceive of the practice of midwifery as a series of more easily remembered questions and explanations.[72] Yet, unlike the surgical treatises discussed previously, neither of these physician-authored manuals purported to reveal new information; rather, their stated aim was to distill the best of the knowledge presently available into a more approachable form. Nonetheless, such manuals directed at midwives made implicit and explicit judgments about the intellectual abilities of women, the current state of midwifery, and the appropriate professional boundaries among various kinds of medical practitioners. For instance, the Trevisan physician Natale Bernati's use of the dialogic instills immediately a strict hierarchical relationship between doctor and midwife. The midwife's traditional mode of learning through long practice is quickly revealed as inadequate in the eyes of the physician:

Medico: But with what foundation do you practice your Trade?
Comare: I practice in the manner, that I have learned watching those other women older than me perform [the office of Midwife].[73]

This is all well and good, responds the doctor, when the birth is normal (which, he says, requires little study, and little effort), but what about when the fetus is poorly positioned and the woman finds herself in difficulty? The midwife responds that traditionally she has used cordials, powders, and waters to move along the birth, or else called in assistance from another midwife, a surgeon, or a physician. The doctor's response is patronizing: "My dear woman, if this is all you know, you are little expert in your Art, and it is necessary that you learn many things, if you want to exercise your Profession with honor and utility for your Clients."[74] Nevertheless, the midwife answers obsequiously that she will gladly be instructed by the doctor, whose knowledge vastly exceeds her own, as she often agrees elsewhere when the doctor notes her lack of understanding of various topics ("M: I see first of all, that you are little informed about the internal organs, and [anatomical] parts that everyday you are required to treat. Is that not true? C: Very true").[75] In these textually fabricated interactions, the physician can erase any suspicion about the nature of his authority with respect to childbirth. Much as obstetrical models would serve as passive stand-ins for real laboring women in the context of formal midwifery education, so too did textual midwives help imagine the hierarchical relationship that physicians and surgeons wished to assert in real life.

Tranquillini, a *medico-fisico* from Rovereto, wrote in the preface to his 1770 treatise that he was compelled to such an undertaking because of the great lack of initiative in Italy toward instructing its midwives, despite their unquestionably important service to the public good. At present, he wrote, doctors were loath to involve themselves in the training of women, and manuals on the subject were either too cumbersome and "poorly ordered, or too limited, and therefore obscure . . . or written in languages that our women do not possess," resulting in the fact that "this art is practiced by unlearned persons," causing many "pitiful disorders."[76] Tranquillini's manual is divided into 'dialogues' and is organized somewhat differently from the texts discussed earlier. In the first dialogue, Tranquillini engages his 'disciple' (*discepola*) in a conversation about the necessary qualities a midwife must have; the anatomical parts relative to generation; fecundity, conception, and sterility; and the growth of the fetus in the womb. The second dialogue covers the possible range of birth situations, including difficult births and false conceptions. The third dialogue diverges from other texts, however, by addressing a veritable compendium of 'diseases' and difficulties a pregnant or post-partum woman, or a newborn child might face, such as coughs, hemorrhages, swelling, venereal diseases, fevers, and so forth. Although beginning with the standard criticism of the great disorders caused by ignorant midwives, Tranquillini nevertheless takes a considerably less condescending tone toward his female readers than does Bernati, as demonstrated partly by his more complex treatise.

Hardly a brief treatise at some 270 pages, Tranquillini's manual indeed suggests a great deal of confidence in the abilities of a well-informed midwife. His lessons cover manually turning a mal-presenting fetus, how to perform a manual exam before labor to predict if there will be difficulties during the birth, how to check manually to see if the fetus is dead, how to extract a dead fetus, and the use of instruments in certain situations – all operations other authors suggested be in the hands only of male practitioners. As evidenced by Tranquillini's extensive information on the diseases of women and children, the physician implicitly acknowledged the reality many Italian midwives experienced on a day-to-day basis in the eighteenth century. While urban midwives might reasonably have timely access to a trained surgeon or physician, those in rural settings were largely on their own, regardless of whether a situation 'required' "the aid of art" (surgery or instruments). Thus, while surgeons with a personal interest in obstetrics emphasized in their writings the deference of female midwives to male practitioners and the necessity of calling in a surgeon immediately when labors became difficult, Tranquillini, as a physician less concerned with professional rivalry, may have felt freer to instruct midwives more comprehensively.

By contrast, when surgeons wrote to instruct midwives, their advice to female practitioners was quite different. The Bergamese surgeon, Orazio Valota, for instance, was much more conservative than Tranquillini in the instruction he gave to his female audience in his 1791 manual, *La Levatrice Moderna* (The Modern Midwife).[77] It may be useful here to compare several passages from the texts of Tranquillini, Bernati, and Valota to better understand the broader deontological differences among the works. For example, the following excerpts describe a midwife's responsibilities in a delivery made difficult by some abnormal presentation of the fetus (e.g. hands, neck, thighs, etc.). Bernati, explaining how a midwife should handle a fetus presenting with his hands above or close to the head, says that, if the woman had already delivered many children and has a "soft orifice," then the situation may not need much special handling at all, just that the midwife ensure that the head and hands are not set at angles from each other. If, instead, the midwife believes the positioning will render the birth difficult, she must:

I.   Transport the pregnant woman to bed, situated such that she is horizontal, or with her posterior slightly raised.
II. Push the fetus back lightly toward the back of the uterus, resting the end of your fingers above one of the shoulders.
III. Put the hands and the arms of the fetus back to their sides, and hold back the head close to the vaginal opening until a contraction occurs.
IV. Obtaining with this contraction, that the head penetrates the vaginal opening, meanwhile make sure that the hands and arm do not move.
V.   If it is difficult to direct the arms, and so if you fear a laborious birth, pull the fetus out by its feet.[78]

Tranquilli, after considering the reasons for such a presentation (hands first), instructs the midwife that:

> This position cannot be certified for sure, except after the waters have broken; before, therefore, that this part advances in the vagina, and that the waters have stopped flowing, position the mother in bed, with her buttocks raised, as I have told you other times; you will reintroduce into the uterus the hands which have come out, and immediately after, climbing with the hand up the body of the fetus, you will aim to find the

thighs of the same, which you will turn little by little toward the belly of the fetus, taking the legs, and next the heels, forcing them skillfully toward the mouth of the uterus; and if you can't grasp but only one thigh, force first this one, that in following you can easily find the other; in that manner, push the feet in the mouth of the uterus, and pull little by little, making sure that in the pulling, as in the turning of the fetus, if it comes with the face toward the front, you observe all the cautions, that I have taught you.[79]

Finally, in this situation,[80] the surgeon Valota instructs the midwife to do the following:

Since the fetus in the above-mentioned presentations always finds itself obliquely situated, thus the only remedy is the extraction of the fetus by its feet, an operation which belongs to the Surgeon; therefore the Midwife will have the diligence to know the part presented, and so will call the Surgeon.[81]

The difference between Vaolta's recommendations and those of Tranquillini and Bernati are striking. While the latter two authors clearly see the manual turning of the fetus in utero as well within the midwife's capabilities, for Valota the midwife's sphere of intervention has been circumscribed dramatically. Not only are those situations which might require a surgeon's tools out of the female practitioner's reach, but so, too, are a number of difficult natural situations traditionally handled by women.

In fact, Valota's text is clear evidence that even a midwifery manual written explicitly to *instruct* female midwives might not necessarily be destined to be *owned* or *read* by women independently. Valota's manual, for instance, includes a preface directed specifically to the "doctors and surgeons of Brescia," whom he implores to learn the art of obstetrics, particularly given the current situation in which "the midwives of my Province do not take care to train themselves in their art and continue in such a delicate moment to act with ignorance and presumption, *discunt periculis nostris, et experimenta per mortes agunt* (they acquire knowledge from our dangers and they experiment by way of our deaths)."[82]

Valota's invective against the ignorance of midwives was common in both texts directed at male practitioners and those intended to train midwives themselves, though of course there was overlap between these two categories. The Brescian surgeon writes that it was his compassion enlivened by the disastrous consequences of midwives' rash acts which most compelled him to write his treatise: "I have seen many miserable victims of their carelessness. How many mothers killed in the flower of their years because of inexpert Midwives! How many children torn apart, mutilated, killed because of the reckless attempts of the same!"[83] This oft-repeated, if dramatic, reproach against female practitioners functions to justify the

distinctly limited role Valota envisions for them while simultaneously rein-
forcing the need for the still controversial field of obstetrics, which was by
then conceivably taught and practiced by men.

Side by side with such polemic against female midwives in many midwifery manuals stood also the disparagement of other male practitioners.
In Lorenzo Nannoni's case studies, the obstetrician often finds himself summoned to situations that have been mishandled, not by midwives, but by
male surgeons or physicians before him who are little trained in obstetrics.[84] In the preface to his 1787 treatise, *Ostetricia Practica*, the Neapolitan
surgeon-obstetrician Pio Urbano Galeotti similarly devotes as much space to
deriding ignorant midwives who botch births as he does to inexperienced
surgeons who recklessly wield their instruments.[85] In one case related by the
Neapolitan surgeon, both mother and baby became "victims" of the unskilled
hands of an ignorant surgeon who did not know to rotate the infant during a
feet-first delivery, resulting in the head catching on the pubic bone and leading
to a severe infection.[86]

Galeotti argues that these kinds of disastrous results originate from a
lack of hands-on training. Galeotti's own knowledge, by contrast, gained
through personal experience as demonstrated by his case studies, is presented as clearly superior to that of manual writers whose information
is based predominantly on other texts. In discussing feet-first deliveries,
for instance, Galeotti finds it incredulous that many authors describe "as
natural" that kind of birth, though he admits he would not be so dubious
except that he has "seen in practice those problems the passage of the
head of the fetus is subject to" when delivered this way.[87] Even the use of
machines and models cannot recreate the same kinds of difficulties that
may arise during an actual birth and befuddle the male practitioner with
such limited experience. Giuseppe Nessi writes, in the same vein, that in
his text he has decided to omit entirely the inclusion of images of fetal
positions because there were, in fact, an endless number of ways the fetus
could position itself in the uterus. As such, Nessi believed dividing labors
into a discrete number of presentations could only ill-prepare practitioners for the variety of exigent circumstances they might encounter during
an actual delivery.[88]

* * * *

Given the many impediments that restricted early modern women's ability
to publish, print was a disproportionately masculine medium in the eighteenth century.[89] It was also one that became critical to the professionalization of medicine and the development of obstetrics in the late eighteenth
century. The establishment of new print forms, such as the scientific journal and the compendium of case studies, highlighted clinical findings and
fostered competition among male obstetrical practitioners. Their writings
became a fundamental component of the development of obstetrics as a distinct medical and professional field. As Jeanette Herrle-Fanning has argued

in her study of eighteenth-century British midwifery texts, obstetrics "was a profession which in many ways *wrote* itself into existence by evolving a system of publication and lecturing that disseminated a new kind of knowledge about reproduction."[90] By comparing his knowledge to other (male) practitioners' in print, a surgeon-obstetrician could help solidify for himself a position among the elite in a burgeoning field.

Whereas in the seventeenth century a manual writer could assert his authority through the mastery of classical authors, during the eighteenth century a reliance on acquired wisdom became insufficient. As a growing number of male practitioners gained practical experience, firsthand accounts of their interventions appeared more commonly in midwifery and obstetrical manuals. The case study, in which the male surgeon or practitioner could become the subject of the birthing event, became a critical tool with which an obstetrical writer might establish his own credentials. Moreover, case studies, which often highlighted and praised the manual skill of the male practitioner, tended to reflect the surgical nature of obstetrics and linked eighteenth-century midwifery manuals with earlier surgical treatises, which were sometimes printed together.[91] According to Lianne McTavish in her study of French treatises, despite their claims to originality, these case studies often followed closely to known narrative scripts:

> They typically begin by stating the date of the incident and providing information about the client, such as her husband's occupation. The tales then give an overview of the women's physical condition, stressing its dire nature while referring to the one or more previous practitioners who had only made it worse through mismanagement. The surgeon man-midwife's heroic entrance into the lying-in chamber is thereby positioned as a turning point; his intelligent interventions bring the woman, and sometimes even her child, back from the brink of death.[92]

Thus, while the authority of the case history rested upon its claims to unique personal experience, the genre as a whole tended to conform to expected conventions that reinforced popular perceptions of ignorant midwives or rash, instrument-wielding surgeons.

The case history also introduced a new kind of relationship between the male practitioner and female patient. As Eve Keller writes, the practitioners portrayed in case histories are "fully cognizant of the somatic experience of those they treat"; indeed, they "routinely and palpably engage their patients' bodies, touching, penetrating, manipulating them to ease delivery."[93] And yet, the result of this invasive engagement is the erasure of the delivering woman as a complete and present person, as she has been reduced to a series of discrete body parts the male practitioners must face and conquer.[94] Thus, in their case studies, male authors evoked female bodies that could be subjugated and mastered by rationality and "the modern transcendence of the masculine mind."[95]

Although Italian authors were less likely to include numerous case studies in their manuals than some of their Continental and British contemporaries, likely owing to their generally more limited intervention in actual births, there are a few examples which should be noted. For instance, the surgeons Lorenzo Nannoni and Pio Urbano Galeotti both included a series of case studies (*osservazioni*) in their midwifery treatises.[96] Nannoni's twenty-four case studies, studded throughout the text, do in fact generally conform closely to the model identified earlier by Lianne McTavish. In one *osservazione* concerning an obstructed birth, for instance, Nannoni writes that:

> A vigorous woman, wife of a farmer for the Monastery of San Ambrogio, had become pregnant for the first time around the age of forty. She reached the end of her pregnancy at the beginning of November 1784. The vaginal opening dilated sufficiently, the waters poured slowly, and the head presented, but the back of the head was turned facing upward, in the manner such that the head was presenting with its greatest width at the smallest part of the pelvic inlet (*stretto superiore*) and was immediately an obstacle to the good outcome of the birth. The pains kept up for some time, without any good result, when I was called in. I managed with some fingers to put the head in a better position, pushing back the frontal protuberances, and recalling the back of the head laterally, and I made an emission of blood to reduce the resistance of the external parts. The head was maintained in the same situation, and, so, having waited un-fruitfully for some hours, I resolved to operate, which I did with the pincers (*tenaglia*), which I put rather far internally, and grasping the head of the fetus, I noted, that still pulling in that manner, in which the head presented, it would give way, and so in that direction I pulled, and I extracted [the fetus] alive. . . . The woman has in succession become pregnant again, and gave birth successfully.[97]

Although there is no fumbling midwife or inexperienced surgeon to blame in this case history, Nannoni does present a situation that has become irresolvable except by his own skillful application of the surgeon's tools, which done, produces rather easily a happy outcome. Nannoni's case studies also highlight the wide extent of his knowledge, which includes not only obstetrics but also gynecology. Nannoni recalls, for instance, his treatment in 1782 of a young woman afflicted with a venereal disease which she had caught from her bookseller husband.[98]

Pio Urbano Galeotti's twenty-six case studies form the entire second part of the author's manual, following a very concise first part, which includes only brief discussions of generation, conception, the development of the fetus, and natural births. Clearly, Galeotti's text represents a shift away from the lengthy theoretical treatise to obstetrical manuals structured entirely around cases and a practitioner's personal experiences and observations. Galeotti's cases also conform closely to McTavish's script, frequently featuring erring midwives; at least three times, the author is called in to assist when a mid-wife has misidentified the part of the fetus presenting, mistaking a shoulder or thigh for the fetus' head. Yet, Galeotti's case studies at times differ from those described by Eve Keller in treatises by mid-eighteenth century British practitioners such as Edmund Chapman and Percival Willughby. Keller writes that the case studies in British texts reflect the broader "shifts in the self-presentation of the practitioners and in their constructed connection to others in the birthing process."[99] In particular, these accounts reveal a "childbearing woman" who is "decreasingly present as a subject in these texts. Her verbal participation becomes either irrelevant or obviated alto-gether," as are the voices of others present at the scene.[100]

While it is true that Galeotti, like Nannoni, presents himself as the central figure of the birthing events he describes, he is at times also intensely aware of the pregnant woman under his care. In a case which the surgeon describes as one of his most difficult, when a baby presented with its shoulder for-ward and the pregnant woman's water had broken three days before he was called in, Galeotti recalls that he was almost unsuccessful in completing the necessary maneuvers because "the screams of the pregnant woman and the difficulty that I encountered in turning the fetus filled me with confu-sion."[101] Galeotti also emphasizes with some sympathy the youth of the woman, who, illegitimately pregnant, was attempting to keep her condi-tion secret from her parents and had been attended during her labor only by a young servant. Galeotti relates that the friend, a maid, had been so troubled by seeing the girl in such great torment and "brought so low, and fearing death, she put aside every regard, and confided to the mother her [daughter's] wretched situation."[102] In another case, Galeotti is not so much overwhelmed but aided by the woman under his care: "I found this woman lying on her back in bed, all afflicted . . . and when she saw me she began to recommend herself to me, giving me signs of courage, and [she was] very disposed to doing all that I instructed her to do."[103]

Thus, while in some instances Galeotti could perform the kind of mater-nal erasure described by Keller – he describes one case in which he extracted a dead fetus from a mother without relating any aspect of the woman's reac-tion or mental state[104] – he also at times showed himself intimately aware of the living woman he was treating and allowed the collaborative work of practitioner and patient to be expressed in his writings. The case study as employed in Italian obstetrical manuals was therefore a rhetorical device with several overlapping, and even potentially conflicting, meanings. On the one hand, the case study was employed ostensibly to instruct. On the other hand, the case study was clearly a tool employed by male practition-ers to re-center themselves as subjects in the birthing event; to emphasize the individual writer's skills and practical experience (often at the expense of both midwives and other less-accomplished surgeons); and textually to refashion childbirth as an event which could be rationally ordered, under-stood, and managed. The fact that some writers included those cases with tragic outcomes, where mother and/or baby died, or mentioned the screams and miserable circumstances of their patients meant that even highly trained male practitioners were not always successful at conforming to the infallible and stoic image they wished to present of themselves.

Theological embryology and the cesarean operation

A final aspect common to all the eighteenth-century Italian midwifery texts, which bears considering, is their emphasis on baptism.[105] While most manual authors dedicated a chapter to the necessity of instructing midwives and other practitioners in the baptismal rite, so that they could perform it in the case of emergency, some religious writers devoted entire texts to the subject. The Ferrarese priest Girolamo Baruffaldi's 1746 treatise, *La Mammana Istruita per Validamente Amministrare il Santo Sacramento del Battesimo* (The Midwife Instructed in how to Validly Administer the Holy Sacrament of Baptism) ran nearly seventy pages and included twenty chapters detailing the situations in which a midwife might be called on to perform a baptism, the correct procedure, what to do if the child then survived, and whether or not a Christian midwife could deliver a Jewish mother.[106] As Claudia Pancino notes, a particular focus on the midwife's religiosity and good Christian character made clear sense in the sixteenth and seventeenth centuries amidst religious controversy and in a period when midwifery was overseen and regulated almost exclusively by the Church. Yet, the Church's involvement in debates over reproduction and childbirth only grew in the era of the Enlightenment. Whereas studies of eighteenth-century midwifery are often framed by a background of growing secularization, Italian midwifery texts produced in this period suggest just the opposite. In this period, the Catholic Church's preoccupation with the salvation of newborn souls dramatically influenced not only intellectual debates but also actual praxis.[107]

Part of the impetus for this preoccupation with baptism in the eighteenth century derived from new scientific discoveries relating to embryology and the heated debates about ensoulment and animation which resulted. While some argued that the advanced organization of the animal embryo attained during development existed complete in some form from the time of conception (preformationists), others held that the embryo developed gradually from unorganized matter (epigeneticists).[108] The notion behind preformationism that essentially an entire human being was present at conception, only waiting to be revealed over time during development, appealed to theologians who seized on the opportunity to harness science to support a religious worldview. To such thinkers, the preformation thesis allowed for the argument that human ensoulment began at conception, something that aligned well with the idea of Mary's Immaculate Conception. Nevertheless, this view represented a quite drastic revision of traditional Aristotelian and Thomistic doctrine on ensoulment which held that animation began at between thirty and forty days for males, and seventy to eighty for females.

These figures had long provided the basis for both Church and legal codes. That is to say, abortion was typically considered a crime only if carried out after these supposed points of animation. They also shaped women's own perceptions and understandings of pregnancy, as, in the early stages after conception, there was not generally seen to exist a child, but rather an unformed mass that could still be false pregnancy (*mole*), retained menses signaling some kind of ill health, or even something more malicious or monstrous.[109]

One of the works inspired by the Catholic rigorism of this era was the extraordinarily influential treatise of Francesco Emmanuele Cangiamila, *Embriologia sacra: Ovvero dell'uffizio de' sacerdoti, medici e superiori circa l'eterna salute de' bambini racchiusi nell'utero* ("Sacred embryology: That is, on the duty of parish priests, physicians, and officials with respect to the eternal well-being of infants still in the womb").[110] A priest and jurist when he wrote his treatise, Cangiamila eventually rose to bishop of the dioceses of Palermo and head inquisitor of Sicily. Deeply influenced by the thought of preformationists who argued that the soul entered the embryo at or directly after conception, Cangiamila was also acutely aware of existing theological debates over the fate of babies who died without baptism.[111] While adherents of Probabilism, especially Jesuits, tended toward a less rigid interpretation, Rigorists held that unbaptized infants were denied salvation. As Probabilism fell out of favor at the end of the seventeenth century, some clergy became strident proponents of extreme measures to ensure fetal baptism.

Although non-surgical interventions, such as inserting a syringe filled with holy water into the uterus during a distressed delivery, had long been discussed by theologians and clergy, the validity of such measures was increasingly called into question by the eighteenth century.[112] Instead, it was the postmortem cesarean operation that emerged as the resounding consensus on how to avoid what Cangiamila and his followers viewed as a massacre of innocent souls.[113] Cangiamila, whose own pastoral work in Sicily brought him face to face with the tragedy of infant and maternal death, was deeply concerned about questions of salvation, particularly amidst what he perceived as rising rates of abortions. In many cases, Cangiamila wrote, no efforts had been made to baptize these countless unborn fetuses.[114] His treatise was thus both a call to arms and a means of instruction aimed at familiarizing a wide audience with the cesarean operation.

As a work meant for a varied audience of clergy, laymen, jurists, and medical practitioners, the *Embriologia Sacra* was as much a practical handbook as it was a learned theological discussion. The text therefore included chapters on the causes of voluntary and involuntary abortion (miscarriage), how priests might help to prevent them, whether animation begins at conception, and the procedures for baptism in a variety of cases. A bestseller with wide support from the Church, the *Embriologia Sacra* was translated into numerous languages and remained a relevant and much-cited work well into the nineteenth century.[115] In fact, the *Embriologia Sacra* even had a direct influence on legislation in Cangiamila's native Sicily. The work received both Papal support and the endorsement of the Spanish King of Sicily, Charles III (later to assume the Spanish crown), who went so far as to issue a decree in 1749 making the cesarean operation mandatory for women who died while pregnant (even if there was only the suspicion of pregnancy).[116] Endorsement of the postmortem cesarean was not limited to the south; similar edicts followed in Venice and Milan in the 1760s.[117] In fact, the language in the latter statutes suggested that relatives who impeded such an operation might legally be viewed as assisting in murder.

Overall, Cangiamila's position on baptism and the cesarean operation was an extreme one, if not entirely new. Owing to his belief that ensoulment followed closely if not immediately after conception, the priest argued that baptisms should be performed on all abortions, even those occurring in the early days of a pregnancy.[118] The *Embriologia Sacra* explained in detail how the fetus can survive for short periods in the womb even after the mother's death, cause according to Cangiamila to intervene with a postmortem cesarean at such times. Most unusually, he advocated that the cesarean operation be performed not only on all dead women who were suspected or known to be pregnant, but also in certain cases on live women as well, even though surgical conditions at the time effectively ensured the mother would die in the latter situation. As Adriano Prosperi notes, "in the cesarean section . . . the priest and the physician exchanged roles, and the life of the soul was the prize gained with the physical death of the mother and fetus."[119] Indeed, it was parish priests, according to Cangiamila, who would have to be ready and willing to perform the procedure themselves, as the reluctance of relatives to the dissection of the pregnant woman or the non-payment of a surgeon might prevent others from acting.[120]

By contrast, the official decrees on the subject emanating from governments in Venice and Milan were more cautionary. Officials were skeptical of priests or midwives undertaking a serious surgical operation and advocated that such procedures only be performed by capable surgeons or physicians. In Venice, for instance, a list of capable practitioners was to be posted at all apothecaries so that community members would know whom to call in such a situation.[121] Johann Peter Frank, director of public health in Lombardy, was deeply concerned that an extreme position such as Cangiamila's might result in an overzealous priest or other untrained person operating on a woman who was in fact still alive. He not only outlined several tests to ensure that the mother was truly dead, but also concluded that the occasional loss of a fetus was not worth a massacre of child-bearing women.[122] Moreover, Frank thought undertaking the operation in the very early stages of pregnancy was not only useless but barbaric since the fetus had no possibility of being viable.[123]

Despite the differences in tone between Cangiamila and officials such as Johann Peter Frank, the underlying assumptions in such discussions marked a profound shift in thinking about the relationship between mother and fetus. With the introduction of theories which potentially moved animation all the way back to conception, religious writers such as Cangiamila began to think of the fetus, if not as an individual, then at least as a creature independent of the mother that was deserving of the tutelage of the state. According to Cangiamila, the fetus "becomes animated" in the first few days and therefore, "however small . . . it nonetheless is living . . . and is therefore never licit to murder it."[124] Frank, too, wrote with a new consciousness about the nature of the being contained in the womb, and his words would have a deep impact on public health legislation not only in Lombardy, but also in Europe as a whole.[125] In his *Sistema completo di polizia medica*, Frank asked, "Are not the citizens still enclosed in their mother's wombs nonetheless members of the state?"[126] Influenced as much by the political arithmetic of populationism and new conceptions of the state as he was by the spiritual concerns of Cangiamila, Frank nonetheless concluded that the unborn fetus was deserving of the protection of the state through laws that, among other things, would compel qualified practitioners to perform a postmortem cesarean operation.[127] In both cases, the cesarean operation signaled something much more consequential than the development of a new medical intervention. As Nadia Maria Filippini has argued, the new sensibilities gestured to a "profound rupture of tradition, one that disrupted the hierarchy of moral, professional, and social ethics."[128] For the first time, the life/soul of the fetus was considered equally, if not paramount, to that of the mother.

It was not only priests and lawmakers who discussed the cesarean section in print. Many medical writers considered the procedure as well. If medicine was still largely conceived of in underlying theological terms in the eighteenth century, the cesarean operation symbolized "a bond . . . between theology and medical science, under the aegis of the state."[129] Subtle shifts in the physician's understanding of the relationship between mother and fetus had therefore also been under way for some time.[130] As early as the late sixteenth century, Mercurio had described the cesarean operation in glowing terms, having seen it performed on a woman in France during his training. A Dominican friar as well as a physician, Mercurio even claimed that the cesarean could be safely executed on a living woman, though he recommended that only surgeons and physicians attempt the operation.[131] By the second half of the eighteenth century, few Italian midwifery manuals failed to engage the topic. Several entire texts were devoted to the operation, such as the Venetian Girolamo Persone's *Dissertazione sopra l'Operazione Cesarea* published in 1778.[132] An advocate of the operation, Persone, who was a member of the Venetian college of physician-surgeons, attempted in his dissertation extensively to detail the reasons why the cesarean operation was non-lethal and could be performed on a living subject. Making comparisons to other surgical procedures commonly practiced at the time, such as the removal of kidney stones, Persone argued for the safety of the cesarean section and claimed to have performed it himself several times on women in Venice.[133]

Even among champions of the operation, there were disagreements about when, how, and by whom it should be undertaken.[134] Tanaron was a promoter of surgeons performing the procedure postmortem, and even potentially when the mother was still alive. If the child's passage was undeniably blocked yet the infant suspected still to be alive, were there men, he queried, "so barbarous, and so deprived of humanity, that they could plunge a knife into the breast of a poor, little infant (*creatura*) and cut it to pieces . . . so that it could be pulled out?"[135] The cesarean section was therefore presented as the more humane option when compared with the horrors of an embryotomy. In fact, Tanaron went so far as to argue that the learned practitioner who failed to perform the cesarean operation in a situation where it could be of aid should be judged in line with any other murderer:

> Princes, and Magistrates judge to be the offenders those prostitutes, and other women, known to have caused the deaths of their children, either through a procured Abortion, or an Infanticide; so why not punish similarly those, who because of fault, or negligence, cause to perish within the womb those unfortunate infants . . . even though they could have saved them with the application of their profession? Since this question concerns [the loss of] the physical life, no less than the spiritual one, and as there should be equal consideration for the one as for the other crime, then any Practitioner (*Professore*) who out of negligence, or, even more if out of politics, or maliciousness omits [to perform] the Cesarean Operation he should receive a severe penalty, as grave as that for the perpetrator of Homicide.[136]

Although Tanaron, a practicing surgeon, never advocated for a midwife, priest, or other layperson to undertake the cesarean operation, there were some medical authors who did. Considering the situation practically, some writers conceded that there might be situations, particularly in the countryside, where a midwife was the only qualified person present to undertake the operation. Orazio Valota, another proponent of the cesarean operation, accepted the possibility that either a midwife or a parish priest could be called upon to perform the procedure in postmortem cases and was confident in their abilities if well instructed.[137] In the case of living women, Valota did not rule out the cesarean but cautioned that only a physician or surgeon should perform the operation.

Although there were obviously differences in how eighteenth-century religious figures, medical practitioners, and laymen thought the cesarean operation might best be applied, there was overall a wide general consensus on its utility, especially in postmortem cases. Surgery and theology had combined in this instance to reimagine the nature of the relationship between mother and fetus. According to Prosperi, the prospect of the cesarean operation had dramatically "changed the social condition" of the *creature* that existed in their mothers' wombs; they had "become the object of great investment by powers and disciplines of all kinds, just as a special system of surveillance had been put into place over unmarried mothers."[138] By investing the fetus with a greater humanity than ever before, the changed theological and medical landscape of the eighteenth century brought women, particularly those who might be suspected of abortion or infanticide, under greater scrutiny and legal supervision. As is the case today, the development of reproductive technologies was never independent of religious and cultural sensibilities.

Conclusion

Early modern midwifery manuals written in the vernacular introduced medical ideas about women's health, childbirth, and the still-mysterious processes of conception and generation to a wide audience. Men's involvement in childbirth in this earlier period was nonetheless largely confined to the literary realm. Men might hope to restore patriarchal equilibrium and confront their generative anxieties in print, but few male practitioners at this time had much practical experience with childbirth, instead basing their claims on a combination of ancient wisdom and anatomical observation.

Only in the eighteenth century did male involvement in normal births allow surgeon-obstetricians such as William Smellie and Hendrik van Deventer to conceptualize a theoretical understanding of childbirth based on "the relationship between pelvic anatomy, the position of the uterus, and . . . the fetus."[139] With a firmer foundation on which to intervene in births, both normal and difficult, male practitioners' print projects became increasingly about establishing a good professional reputation. Eighteenth-century midwifery texts played a critical role in the establishment and general recognition of 'obstetrics' as a distinct branch of surgery and field of inquiry in its own right. Through print, obstetrics practitioners could tout the vital importance of their field for saving the lives of mothers and children, define their own distinguished position in a centuries-old lineage of childbirth writers, and demonstrate their esteemed practical experience through, generally felicitous, case studies. By imagining themselves as heroic subjects of the birthing room, male obstetrical writers of the second half of the eighteenth century literally helped create – through print – the profession which they hoped ultimately to control.

Notes

1 Louise Bourgeois, *Observations diverses sur la sterilité perte de fruict foecondité accouchements et maladies des femmes et enfants nouveaux naiz* (Paris, 1609); Jane Sharp, *The Midwives Book, or, the Whole Art of Midwifry Discovered* (London: S. Miller, 1671); Justine Siegemund, *Die Chur-Brandenburgische Hoff-Wehe-Mutter* (Cologne: A. D. Spree, 1690).

2 The French midwife Teresa Ployant, working in Naples during the eighteenth
   century, produced the first female-authored midwifery manual in Italian in
   1787, *Breve compendio dell'arte ostetricia* (Naples, 1787).
3 Sebastiano Melli, *La comare levatrice; istruita nel suo ufizio; secondo le regole
   più certe, e gli ammaestramenti più moderni* (Venice: Gio. Battista Recurti,
   1721).
4 Rudolph M. Bell, *How to Do It: Guides to Good Living for Renaissance Italians*
   (Chicago: University of Chicago Press, 2000), 5.
5 On literacy and reading habits in early modern Italy, see Bell, *How to Do It*,
   12–16.
6 Lianne McTavish, *Childbirth and the Display of Authority in Early Modern
   France* (Burlington, VT: Ashgate, 2005), 25–27. McTavish points out the generic
   nature of and common conventions employed in French obstetrical texts of the
   period.
7 Bell, *How to Do It*, 8.
8 McTavish, *Childbirth and the Display of Authority*, 25; Eve Keller, "The Subject
   of Touch: Authority in Early Modern Midwifery," in *Sensible Flesh: On Touch
   in Early Modern Culture*, ed. Elizabeth D. Harvey (Philadelphia: University of
   Pennsylvania Press, 2003), 62–80, 158.
9 On the rebirth of anatomy in the sixteenth century, see Andrew Cunningham,
   *The Anatomical Renaissance: The Resurrection of the Anatomical Projects of
   the Ancients* (Abingdon and New York: Ashgate, 1997); Andrew Wear, Roger K.
   French, and I. M. Lonie, eds., *The Medical Renaissance of the Sixteenth Century*
   (Cambridge: Cambridge University Press, 1985).
10 On the "books of secrets" and "secrets of women" genres, see William Eamon,
   *Science and the Secrets of Nature: Books of Secrets in Medieval and Early Mod-
   ern Culture* (Princeton: Princeton University Press, 1994); Monica Green, *Making Women's Medicine Masculine: The Rise of Male Authority in Pre-Modern
   Gynaecology* (Oxford: Oxford University Press, 2008), esp. Ch. 5; Katherine
   Park, *Secrets of Women: Gender, Generation, and the Origins of Human Dissection* (Brooklyn, NY: Zone Books, 2006), Ch. 2.
11 Jonathan Sawday, *The Body Emblazoned: Dissection and the Human Body
   in Renaissance Culture* (London and New York: Routledge, 1995), esp. Ch. 1,
   "The Autopic Vision"; Cynthia Klestinec, *Students, Teachers and Traditions
   of Dissection in Renaissance Venice* (Baltimore: The Johns Hopkins Univer-
   sity Press, 2011); Andrea Carlino, *Books of the Body: Anatomical Ritual and
   Renaissance Learning*, trans. John Tedeschi and Anne C. Tedeschi (Chicago:
   University of Chicago Press, 1999); Park, *Secrets of Women*; Gianna Pomata,
   "Observation Rising: Birth of an Epistemic Genre, 1500–1650," in *Histories of
   Scientific Observation*, ed. Lorraine Daston and Elizabeth Lunbeck (Chicago:
   University of Chicago Press, 2011), 45–80.
12 For further discussion of early modern midwifery manuals and their significance
   for male claims to professional authority, see Pomata, "Observation Rising,"
   45–80; McTavish, *Childbirth and the Display of Authority*; Keller, "The Subject
   of Touch", 62–80; Lynne Tatlock, "Speculum Feminarum: Gendered Perspectives
   on Obstetrics and Gynecology in Early Modern Germany," *Signs* 17, no. 4 (1992):
   725–760; Caroline Bicks, " 'Stones Like Women's Paps': Revising Gender in Jane
   Sharp's *Midwives Book*," *Journal of Early Modern Cultural Studies* 7, no. 2
   (2007): 1–27; Ludmilla Jordanova, *Sexual Visions: Images of Gender and Science
   Between the Eighteenth and Twentieth Centuries* (Madison: University of Wisconsin Press, 1989). On Italian treatises, see Giulia Calvi, "Manuali delle Levatrici
   XVII–XVIII Secolo," *Memoria* 3 (1983): 108–113; Anna Parma, "Didattica e

Pratica Ostetrica in Lombardia (1765–1791)," *Sanità, Scienza e Storia* 2 (1984): 101–155; Claudia Pancino, "La Comare Levatrice: Crisi di un Mestiere nel XVIII Secolo," *Storia e Società* 15 (1981): 593–638; Bell, *How to Do It.*

13 Jacob Rueff, *The Expert Midwife, or an Excellent and Most Necessary Treatise on the Generation of the Birth of Man* (London, 1637), 44.

14 Peter Chamberlen, *Dr. Chamberlain's Midwifes Practice: Or, a Guide for Women in That High Concern of Conception, Breeding, and Nursing Children* (London: Thomas Rooks, 1665), author's preface to the reader.

15 Nicholas Culpeper, *A Directory for Midwives: Or, A Guide for Women in their Conception, Bearing, and Suckling Their Children* (London: Peter Cole, 1651), 5v.

16 Mary Fissell, *Vernacular Bodies: The Politics of Reproduction in Early Modern England* (Oxford: Oxford University Press, 2004), 149.

17 This would change in time as male practitioners gained increasing practical experience with childbirth; then, it was touch that was stressed as the most important skill of the surgeon-obstetrician, who often had to perform internal operations without seeing. See Chapter 5 in this volume for a discussion of how midwifery instructors aimed to cultivate a reasoned touch in students with the use of obstetrical machines.

18 Ambroise Paré, *The Workes of That Famous Chirurgion Ambrose Parey Translated Out of Latine and Compared with the French*, trans. Th. Johnson (London, 1649), 630.

19 Ibid., 631.

20 Diane Cady, "Linguistic Disease: Foreign Language as Sexual Disease in Early Modern England," in *Sins of the Flesh: Responding to Sexual Disease in Early Modern Europe*, ed. Kevin Siena (Toronto: Centre for Reformation and Renaissance Studies, 2005), 168.

21 The late medieval period saw a significant shift toward the medicalization of virginity. While patristic writers in the early medieval period had presented virginity as most importantly a spiritual state, marked by the virtues of purity, silence, obedience, and piety, early modern commentators increasingly conflated virginity with physical markers – in particular the hymen. Yet despite early modern practitioners' readiness to write virginity onto the female body, definitive markers of chastity remained contested and elusive. Early modern anatomy texts reflected visually the confrontation between ideology and empirical reality which was inherent in what Marie Loughlin has called "the ultimate inaccessibility and ephemeral nature of the hymen." Marie H. Loughlin, *Hymeneutics: Interpreting Virginity on the Early Modern Stage* (Cranbury, NJ: Associated University Presses, 1997), 27–28. See also Valeria Finucci, *The Prince's Body: Vincenzo Gonzaga and Renaissance Medicine* (Cambridge: Harvard University Press, 2015), esp. Ch. 1, "The Virgin Cure," 28–61.

22 Loughlin, *Hymeneutics*, 45.

23 Jacques Guillemeau, *Child-Birth or, the Happy Deliverie of Women* (London, 1612), 4.

24 On contemporary debates over quickening as a sign of pregnancy, see Cathy McClive, "The Hidden Truths of the Belly: The Uncertainties of Pregnancy in Early Modern Europe," *Social History of Medicine* 15, no. 2 (2002): 215–218.

25 Culpeper, *A Directory for Midwives*, 125.

26 Cathy McClive, *Menstruation and Procreation in Early Modern France* (Abingdon and New York: Routledge, 2016), 186.

27 Guillemeau, *Child-Birth*, 4.

28 Cathy McClive, "Blood and Expertise: The Trials of the Female Medical Expert in the Ancien-Regime Courtroom," *Bulletin of the History of Medicine* 82, no. 1 (2008): 86–108.

29 Guillemeau, *Child-Birth*, 7.

30 Laura Gowing, *Common Bodies: Women, Touch, and Power in Seventeenth-Century England* (New Haven: Yale University Press, 2003), 45.

31 Another Italian midwifery text was not produced until Sebastiano Melli published *La Comare Istruita nel suo Ufizio Secondo le Regole più Certe e le Ammaestraenti più Moderni* in 1721.

32 Girolamo (Scipione) Mercurio, *La commare o raccoglitrice* (Venezia: Giovanni Battista Ciotti, 1621), 16.

33 Ibid., 9.

34 Ibid., 17.

35 Daniela Pillon, "La comare istruita nel suo ufficio: Alcune notizie sulle levatrici tra il '600 e il '700," *Atti dell'Istituto Veneto di Scienze, Lettere, ed Arti* 140 (1981–1982): 65–98, 69.

36 Mercurio, *La commare o raccoglitrice*, 80.

37 For an example of this negative portrayal in European manuals, see Parè, *The Workes of That Famous Chirurgion* (1634), 934, 594, 289; Chamberlen, *Dr. Chamberlain's Midwifes Practice*, esp. author's preface to the reader.

38 It should be noted that female midwives often accused man-midwives and surgeons of exactly the same thing. Both Louise Bourgeois and Elizabeth Nihell, for instance, accused man-midwives of being rash and all-too hasty to use instruments. For Bourgeois, see Wendy Perkins, *Midwifery and Medicine in Early Modern France: Louise Bourgeois* (Exeter: University of Exeter Press, 1996), 109–112; for Nihell, see Doreen Evenden, *The Midwives of Seventeenth-Century London* (Cambridge: Cambridge University Press, 2006), 181.

39 Hugh Chamberlen, *The Compleat Midwife's Practice Enlarged* (London, 1680), 94.

40 Percival Willughby, *Observations in Midwifery: As also the Countrey Midwifes Opusculum or Vade Mecum*, ed. Henry Blenkinsop (Warwick: H.T. Cooke and Sons, 1863), 9.

41 Willughby, *Observations in Midwifery*, 9.

42 Mercurio, *La commare o raccoglitrice*, 122–123.

43 Woodcuts in midwifery manuals depicting birth scenes were rare and may have become even more so over time. The only two other woodcuts I am familiar with that show a midwife actively aiding a delivery include those in Eucharius Rösslin, *Der schwangeren Frauen und Hebammen Rosegarten* (Strasbourg, 1513) and Jacob Rueff, *De conceptu et generatione hominis et iis quae circa haec potissimum consyderantur* (Zurich: Christopher Froschoverus, 1554).

44 Lawrence D. Longo and Lawrence P. Reynolds, *Wombs with a View: Illustrations of the Gravid Uterus from the Renaissance Through the Nineteenth Century* (Basel: Springer, 2016), 40.

45 Mercurio, *La commare o raccoglitrice*, Bk. 2, Chap. 16, 136. See also Adriana E. Bakos, "'A Knowledge Speculative and Practical': The Dilemma of Midwives' Education in Early Modern Europe," in *Women's Education in Early Modern Europe: A History, 1500–1800*, ed. Barbara J. Whitehead (New York: Routledge, 1999), 272.

46 Mercurio, *La commare o raccoglitrice*, Bk. 2, Chap. 27, 161–164.

47 See John Pechey, *The Compleat Midwife's Practice Enlarg'd* (London, 1698), 140; Paré, *The Workes of That Famous Chirurgion Ambrose Parey*, 4; Chamberlen, *Dr. Chamberlain's Midwifes Practice*, 138.

48 Pancino, "La comare levatrice," 594.

49 Melli, *La comare levatrice istruita nel suo ufizio secondo le regole piu certe.*

50 Ibid., Bk. 1, Ch. 7, 90–94.
51 Ibid., Bk. 2, Ch. 2, 145.
52 Ibid., Bk. 2, Ch. 2, 149.
53 Ibid., Bk. 2, Ch. 2, 152.
54 McTavish, *Childbirth and the Display of Authority*, 188.
55 Ibid., 190.
56 Courses of instruction in obstetrics were offered to surgeons and physicians in Turin (1732), Ferrara (1750), Bologna (1757), Florence (1758), Siena (1762), Pavia (1764), Milan (1768), Padua (1769), Venice (1773), Rome (1786), and Genoa (1799). Pancino, "La Comare Levatrice," 630.
57 Helen King, "As If None Understood the Art That Cannot Understand Greek: The Education of Midwives in Seventeenth Century England," in *The History of Medical Education in Britain*, ed. Vivian Nutton and Roy Porter (Amsterdam: Rodopi, 1995), 184–198, 189.
58 Giuseppe Nessi, *Arte Ostetricia Teorico Pratica* (Venezia, 1797), iii.
59 Ibid., iii.
60 Giuseppe Vespa, *Dell'Arte Ostetricia Trattato di Giuseppe Vespa Professore di Chirurgia, diviso in tre parti procedute da vari ragioanmenti* (Firenze: Appresso Andrea Bonducci, 1761), 2.
61 Pietro Paolo Tanaron, *Il Chirurgo-Raccoglitore Moderno* (Bassano, 1774), xiv.
62 Adrian Wilson, *The Making of Man-Midwifery: Childbirth in England, 1660–1770* (Cambridge, MA: Harvard University Press, 1995), 179–182.
63 Alfonso Corradi, *Dell'Ostetricia in Italia dalla metà dello scorso secolo fino al presente. Parte II* (Bologna: Gamberini e Parmeggiani, 1877), 861–866.
64 Wilson, *The Making of Man-Midwifery*, 181–182.
65 Pietro Sografi, *Corso Elementare dell'Arte di Raccogliere i Parti, Diviso in Lezioni* (Padova: 1788), 27.
66 Vincenzo Malacarne, *L'Esplorazione Proposta come Fondamento dell'Arte Ostetricia* (Milano: Giacomo Barelle, 1791); Tanaron, *Il Chirurgo-Raccoglitore Moderno*, 145–158; Nessi, *Arte Ostetricia Teorico Pratica*, 43–46.
67 Several manual authors note that bone malformations may be caused by childhood or adult cases of rickets. See, for instance, Tanaron, *Il Chirurgo-Raccoglitore Moderno*, 18; Vespa, *Dell'Arte Ostetricia*, 61; Nannoni, *Trattato di Ostetricia*, 37.
68 Tanaron, *Il Chirurgo-Raccoglitore Moderno*, 145–146.
69 Keller, "The Subject of Touch," 169.
70 Tanaron, *Il Chirurgo-Raccoglitore Moderno*, 148.
71 Mark M. Smith, *Sensing the Past: Seeing, Hearing, Smelling, Tasting, and Touching in History* (Berkeley: University of California Press, 2007), 100–101. Smith notes that obstetrical writers also gendered touch, making their touch represent rationality and restraint, while the midwife's touch was depicted as irrational, reckless, and harmful.
72 Giacomo Tranquillini, *Dottrina della Comare, o sia Breve Compendio d'Arte Ostetricia* (Verona, 1770); Natale Bernati, *Breve Istruzioni dell'Arte Ostetricia ad uso delle Comare Levatrici* (Treviso: Giannantonio Pianta, 1778).
73 Bernati, *Breve Istruzioni dell'Arte Ostetricia ad uso delle Comare Levatrici*, 9.
74 Ibid., 10.
75 Ibid., 11.
76 Tranquillini, *Dottrina della Comare*, v–vi.
77 Orazio Valota, *La Levatrice Moderna, Opera Necessaria alle Comari, ed Utile ai Principanti d'Ostetricia, ed ai Reverandi Parrochi* (Bergamo: Locatelli, 1791).
78 Bernati, *Breve Istruzioni dell'Arte Ostetricia ad uso delle Comare Levatrici*, 34–35.

79 Tranquillini, *Dottrina della Comare*, 104.
80 In fact, when the fetus's neck, shoulder, back, chest, abdomen, arm, hand, or hip presents, Valota's instructions are all the same.
81 Valota, *La Levatrice Moderna*, 124.
82 Ibid., viii. The Latin quote comes from Pliny, *Naturalis Historia*, 29.18, describing greedy Greek doctors out only to make money for themselves.
83 Ibid., viii.
84 Nannoni, *Trattato di Ostetricia*, eg. 102 (*osservazione* xvii), 106 (*osservazione* xix), 203 (*osservazione* xxii).
85 Pio Urbano Galeotti, *Ostetricia Practica, Ove si Dimostra il Metodo più Semplice, e più Facile per Assistere i Parti Divenuti Difficli per la Cattiva Situazione del Feto, con un Breve Discorso sopra la Generazione, ed Avanzamenti della Gravidanza, e Parto Naturale* (Napoli: Donato Campo, 1787), xi.
86 Ibid., 75–76.
87 Ibid., 71–72.
88 Nessi, *Arte Ostetricia Teorico Pratica*, iv–v.
89 Merry E. Wiesner, *Women and Gender in Early Modern Europe* (Cambridge: Cambridge University Press, 2000), 190–192.
90 Jeanette Herrle-Fanning, "Of Forceps and Folios: Eighteenth-Century British Midwifery Publications and the Construction of Professional Identity," unpublished PhD dissertation, City University of New York, 2004, iv.
91 Nancy G. Siraisi, *Medieval and Early Renaissance Medicine: An Introduction to Knowledge and Practice* (Chicago: University of Chicago Press, 1990), 170–172; McTavish, *Childbirth and the Display of Authority*, 40; Joseph P. Byrne, *Health and Wellness in the Renaissance and Enlightenment* (Santa Barbara: ABC-CLIO, 2013), 130.
92 McTavish, *Childbirth and the Display of Authority*, 40.
93 Eve Keller, *Generating Bodies and Gendered Selves: The Rhetoric of Reproduction in Early Modern England* (Seattle and London: University of Washington Press, 2007), 159.
94 Ibid., 180.
95 Ibid., 159.
96 Lorenzo Nannoni, *Trattato di Ostetricia e di lei Respettive Operatzioni* (Siena: Luigi e Benedetto Bindi, 1788). Francesco Valle also occasionally makes references to his personal experiences treating women in his manual.
97 Ibid., 214–215.
98 Ibid., 98–99.
99 Keller, "The Subject of Touch," 70.
100 Ibid., 70.
101 Galeotti, *Osservazione Ottava*, 92.
102 Ibid., 90.
103 Galeotti, *Osservazione Decimaterza*, 112.
104 Galeotti, *Osservazione Duodecima*, 109–111.
105 Pancino, "La Comare Levatrice," 614–621.
106 I refer to the 1774 reprint. Girolamo Baruffaldi, *La Mammana Istruita per Validamente Amministrare il Santo Sacramento del Battesimo in caso di Necessità alle Creature Nascenti* (Venezia: Pietro Savioni, 1774). The treatise was first published in 1746.
107 Pancino, "La Comare Levatrice," 615.
108 On the debate over preformationism in Italy, see Ivano dal Prete, "Cultures and Politics of Preformationism in Eighteenth-Century Italy," in *The Secrets of Generation: Reproduction in the Long Eighteenth Century*, ed. Raymond

Stephanson and Darren N. Wagner (Toronto: University of Toronto Press, 2015), 59–78.

109 Barbara Duden, *Disembodying Women: Perspectives on Pregnancy and the Unborn* (Cambridge, MA: Harvard University Press, 1993), especially 56–61, 79–82 and *The Woman Beneath the Skin: A Doctor's Patients in Eighteenth-Century Germany* (Cambridge, MA: Harvard University Press, 1998), 159–160.

110 F. E. Cangiamila, *Embriologia Sacra, ovvero dell'Uffizio de' Sacerdoti, Medici, e Superiori, circa l'Eterna Salute de' Bambini racchiusi nell'Utero* (Milano: Giuseppe Cairoli, 1751); all quotes have been taken from the 1751 Milanese edition, though Cangiamila's text was first published in Palermo in 1745.

111 Nadia Maria Filippini, *La Nascita Straordinaria: Tra madre e figlio la rivoluzione del taglio cesareo (sec. XVIII–XIX)* (Milan: Franco Angeli, 1995), 59–63, 81–84.

112 Adriano Prosperi, *Dare l'anima: storia di un infanticidio* (Turin: Einaudi, 2005), 215.

113 Filippini, *La Nascita Straordinaria*, 75.

114 Ibid., 60. Cangiamila spoke in terms of both voluntary and involuntary (what today would be called miscarriages) abortions.

115 Ibid., 61.

116 Adam Warren, "An Operation for Evangelization: Friar Francisco González Laguna, the Cesarean Section, and Fetal Baptism in Late Colonial Peru," *Bulletin of the History of Medicine* 83, no. 4 (2009): 652. In fact, there may have been as many as 225 postmortem cesarean sections performed in Sicily in just the two-year period between 1760 and 1762. Warren's data here come from J. Paul Pundel, *Histoire de l'operation cesarienne: Etude historique de la césarienne dans la médecine, l'art et la littérature, les religions et la législation* (Brussels: Presses Academiques Europeennes, 1969), 91.

117 Pancino, *Il bambino e l'acqua sporca*, 146.

118 On ideas about ensoulment in this period, see Adriano Prosperi, *Dare l'anima*, esp. 218–99.

119 Ibid., 216.

120 Cangiamila, *Embriologia Sacra*, Bk. II, Ch. VIII, 138–142.

121 Pancino, *Il bambino e l'acqua sporca*, 146.

122 Ibid., 147–148.

123 Filippini, *La nascita straordinaria*, 129.

124 Cangiamila, *Embriologia Sacra*, 16.

125 Prosperi, *Dare l'anima*, 217.

126 Frank, *Sistema completo di polizia medica*, vol. II, 166.

127 Filippini, *La nascita straordinaria*, 117–121; Prosperi, *Dare l'anima*, 216–217.

128 Filippini, *La nascita straordinaria*, 13.

129 Prosperi, *Dare l'anima*, 216.

130 Ibid., 252–265.

131 For an interesting discussion of the sensibilities of Mercurio's instructor in Bologna, Giulio Cesare Aranzio, see Prosperi, *Dare l'anima*, 253.

132 Girolamo Persone, *Dissertazione sopra l'Operazione Cesarea* (Venezia: Antonio Zatta, 1778).

133 Ibid., 22–24.

134 The Dutch obstetrician Hendrik van Deventer, who opposed surgical intervention during childbirth in general, was probably the most well-known and respected critic of the cesarean operation. William Osborn and many other English practitioners also opposed the operation. Cesareans on live women,

though written about in many medical texts, were in practice extremely rare in eighteenth-century Europe.

135 Tanaron, *Il Chirurgo-Raccoglitore Moderno*, Bk. III, 26. At the time, apart from the cesarean section, the only sure method for delivering an obstructed fetus was to perform a craniotomy or embryotomy and pull the baby out in pieces, a procedure typically performed by a surgeon. This was seen as the safest procedure for the mother.

136 Tanaron, *Il Chirurgo-Raccoglitore Moderno*, Bk. III, Ch. III, 95.

137 Valota, *La Levatrice Moderna*, *La Levatrice Moderna*, 156–159.

138 Prosperi, *Dare l'anima*, 217.

139 Herrle-Fanning, "Of Forceps and Folios," 32.

3   The origins of public maternity care in Northern Italy

In 1728, the village of Lombriasco, outside of Turin, was the site of a "great scandal."[1] For months, the priest and local schoolmaster, Giovanni Caomino, had been frequenting the house of a surgeon named Giovanni Mioli, avowedly to carry out an intimate relationship with Mioli's daughter, Appolonia. In what was clearly a well-known secret in the town, Caomino and Appolonia had been engaged in a sexual affair since around Carnival time two years prior.[2] The scandal came to a head when Appolonia became pregnant. As soon as her condition became visible, she fled from the town, presumably with Caomino's financial support, to give birth in secret on the outskirts of Turin.[3] Appolonia successfully abandoned the infant, though witnesses noted that when she returned home less than a month later her health had not yet recovered from the ordeal.[4]

Although Appolonia and Caomino's relationship was widely known, and clearly provided the village with an enticing scandal about which to gossip, the affair between a priest and a young, unmarried woman was apparently not offensive enough to spur drastic action against either party. The tangible evidence of an illegitimate child, for whom the burden of care would fall upon the broader community, was, on the other hand, unsupportable.[5] Only when Appolonia became pregnant and the evidence of her shame tangible was the young woman compelled to leave home. While an illegitimate offspring might have been absorbed by the community in an earlier period, attitudes toward illegitimacy had become more rigid by the eighteenth century. Significant changes to the social, legal, and economic landscape of early modern Italy had weakened the communal bonds that might have once overlooked or helped to remedy the transgressions of certain members of the community. Appolonia, faced with an unwelcome pregnancy at the hands of a priest, was thus pressured to absent herself when her physical state threatened to upset the community's equilibrium. She exploited the anonymity of the nearby capital to give birth far from scrutiny, perhaps at the home of a distant relative or an urban midwife contracted by Caomino himself. Although foundling homes, where women might deposit burdensome or illegitimate children, were familiar components of Italian charity since the late medieval period, no formal institution yet existed in Turin where women like Appolonia could give birth safely and secretly and leave with their honor intact.

In the same year that Appolonia journeyed to Turin to give birth, however, Duke Victor Amadeus II of Savoy announced plans for a novel project in the sphere of public welfare and maternal assistance. Victor Amadeus's proposal to establish a maternity ward in the capital with public funding was the first of its kind in Italy. Directed at precisely those women who, like Appolonia, were otherwise of good background, but whose honor had been compromised with an illegitimate pregnancy, the maternity ward would offer a secure and secret place to give birth and deposit the child. Through this expression of paternalistic charity, the Savoyard state asserted its right to act as custodian of female honor, a role traditionally played by community and religious networks. This chapter explores the development of specialized institutions for maternity care in Italy. Instead of focusing on these sites as evidence of the 'medicalization' of childbirth, I argue that such institutions originated out of much more traditional concerns about honor, sexuality, and shame. Eighteenth-century Italian maternity hospitals shared much in common with Counter-Reformation–era conservatories for fallen and at-risk women. Moreover, the provision of assistance for illegitimately pregnant women was not entirely new. In Italy from at least the sixteenth century, small, semi-formal arrangements were sometimes provided for women in need to give birth at both hospitals and convents. This chapter considers the relationship between these earlier sites and the more specialized, state-sponsored institutions that emerged in the eighteenth century, revealing both continuities and breaks with the past. As Sherrill Cohen notes, "Institutions emerge as solutions to perceived social problems."[6] It was only during the eighteenth century that state-sponsored institutional remedies emerged specifically for the problem of unwed mothers. The reasons for the changing societal perceptions of this particular group of women are the focus of this chapter. We will also return to the maternity hospital in Chapter 5, to consider its transformation around the turn of the nineteenth century. It was in that period that the maternity hospital *did* become a central locus of midwifery and obstetrical instruction, clinical study, and research. In fact, maternity hospitals were sometimes founded in this later period with the explicit intention of serving as sites of training for midwives and surgeons, rather than to protect and assist illegitimately pregnant women.

The maternity hospital as institution

During much of the early modern period, hospitals functioned as institutions of charity and welfare provision. Traditionally, Italian hospitals' main function was to succor and provide for the impoverished, aged, disabled, and incurable sick of the population. Early modern Italian hospitals also often doubled as depositories for orphans and foundlings, a role that might extend to acting as long-term custodians for these children, particularly girls who needed both tutelage and, eventually, a dowry. In fact, the greatest percentage of expenditures at Italy's largest hospitals typically went to the care and upkeep of foundlings, rather than to medicines, the salaries of medical professionals, or other "medical" costs.[7] At the same time, however, many hospitals in Italy had taken decisive steps toward the provisioning of highly specialized medical care and the cultivation of a true clinical medicine. From the seventeenth century on, hospitals such as Turin's San Giovanni and Milan's *Ospedale Maggiore* were staffed by networks of highly competent physicians, surgeons, and trainees. For surgeons in particular, service in large general and military hospitals became a path toward career success and recognition. By the eighteenth century, medical education for both physicians and surgeons tended to include an emphasis on practical training in a hospital. In Turin, for instance, the Savoy dukes, as part of major university reforms in the 1720s, fostered the establishment of a department within the city's main hospital for the purposes of clinical study. This *studio* was run by professors nominated by the University of Turin and became a focal point of exchange between the university and the hospital, drawing the two sources of medical education ever closer together.

These developments foreshadow the so-called birth of the clinic in the late eighteenth and nineteenth centuries. According to this narrative, the early nineteenth century saw a transformation of the epistemology of Western medicine, evident in new emphases on statistical enumeration, pathological anatomy (autopsy), and, according to Foucault, the emergence of the modern medical patient, separated by the 'medical gaze' from his 'person' and reduced to his 'disease.'[8] Together, these changes can be classified under the rise of clinical medicine, which transformed the role of the hospital in medical thought and praxis. The ability to amass statistical information and the availability of bodies for postmortem dissection rendered the hospital a central locus of medical advancement and professional development from the late eighteenth century on, and began to strip the hospital of its traditional charitable and religious identities. At the same time, historians of the hospital such as Guenter Risse remind us to give proper attention to the complex interplay between "society and the production of medical knowledge."[9] Thus, even amidst efforts to medicalize and secularize the hospital, older traditions and interests continued to shape hospital policies and practices in Italy and elsewhere.

The maternity hospital well encapsulates these tensions and contradictions. Initially, hospital care for pregnant patients was not primarily concerned with improving birth outcomes or tending to complications. In fact, early maternity hospitals typically did not cater to sick or at-risk women. Regulations for the first Italian wards often explicitly denied entrance to such categories of patient.[10] Moreover, in many cases hospital maternity wards actually contributed to maternal and infant mortality, especially through the abetment of puerperal fever. As Nadia Maria Filippini reminds us, a specialized medical institution for pregnancy is also, in a sense, paradoxical as pregnancy in and of itself is not a pathological event (though it can be pathological in its development).[11] Thus, even as early modern male medical writers emphasized the dangers of childbirth in their treatises to justify increased male involvement in the field, the first maternity institutions were not primarily concerned with difficult births that required specialized medical care. Instead, the primary rationale behind early proposals for public maternity wards in Italy was concern for female honor. By the end of the century, however, maternity hospitals *were* emerging as centers for clinical instruction, research, and a variety of novel medical experiments, such as vaccination and artificial feeding.[12] Indeed, obstetrics was a medical specialty that grew up in the clinic, with even university training centered in or combined with bedside training in maternity wards. Poor women and children in this environment risked becoming the reductive medical patients described by Foucault. This 'clinicalization' of the maternity ward is discussed more fully in Chapter 5, while we focus here on the Italian maternity hospital's origin story.

Despite the multiple impulses driving the development of new childbirth spaces in eighteenth-century Italy, early maternity hospitals have most typically been considered by historians of medicine within a narrative framework of medical progress.[13] Since the nineteenth century, historians have associated the creation of European maternity hospitals with the professionalization of medicine, the emergence of obstetrics as a viable medical practice for male practitioners, and the desire of those practitioners to gain a foothold in childbirth when propriety and custom largely kept them from attending women at home. According to Margaret Connor Versluysen, the maternity hospital was a defining element in both the medicalization and masculinization of childbirth: "lying-in hospitals brought immediate professional rewards to doctors," provided men-midwives with "invaluable . . . clinical experience," and served to position the "midwife as subordinate to the doctor."[14] Whether viewed positively, as medical advancement, or negatively, as male appropriation of a formerly female sphere of knowledge and influence, the development of specialized maternity hospitals has generally been understood as the critical first step in the male domination of obstetrics and the near-universal hospitalization of birth that exists in the West today. This medical view masks the fact that institutional maternity care was also intimately tied up in paternalistic efforts to manage wayward female sexuality.

A strict focus on such institutions' medical character has also resulted in the maternity hospital being the recipient of much condemnation. In addition to critiques of the hospitals as exploiting the bodies of poor and vulnerable women so that inexperienced male practitioners could gain the practical experience they required to launch careers as male-midwives and obstetricians, they have been almost universally condemned for their poor health outcomes. Citing poor hygiene, high mortality rates, and frequent outbreaks of infection, especially puerperal fever, historians of medicine such as Thomas McKeown have argued that "when first introduced, and for many years after . . . institutional confinement [of pregnancy] had an adverse effect on mortality."[15] Another historian has bluntly called the hospitals "a disaster," suggesting that "it would have been better if they had never been established before the introduction of antisepsis in the 1880s."[16] While there is much truth to these claims, they obscure the central purpose and ideology of these kinds of institutions when they first emerged in Italy – which was to preserve female honor and protect communities from evidence of sexual shame, not necessarily to improve birth outcomes. Furthermore, during the eighteenth century maternity wards in Italy tended to be staffed by female midwives and nurses with limited male involvement, meaning that gendered conflict cannot be the only lens through which to consider the nature of power and exploitation in such spaces.

"Those young women who imprudently lose their honor": Maternity care in Turin

In 1728, Duke Victor Amadeus II presented plans for a maternity ward to be installed at San Giovanni hospital, the central hospital in the Savoyard capital of Turin. Part of Victor Amadeus's broad program of economic and institutional reforms, the maternity ward project was a much-touted example of the Duke's desire to see "private, spontaneous Christian charity . . . institutionalized under state control."[17] A maternity ward in the capital city's central hospital symbolized a concerted effort to bring the tutelage of female sexuality and honor within the ambit of state control. The primary objective of the maternity ward was to offer unmarried pregnant women and poor married women in need of a secure and private location to give birth and, if necessary, abandon the child. The project proposals promised secrecy and compassion "for those young women who imprudently lose their honor," as well as "Christian uplift" to poor married women with nowhere else to give birth.[18] The intended recipients of the ward's services thus included not only the illegitimately pregnant, but also women who, either "devoid of permanent residence, [or] because of their poverty, have neither space nor assistance sufficient to give birth in their homes."[19] Nevertheless, it was unmarried women compelled to conceal illegitimate pregnancies in order to protect their honor that were agreed to be the main beneficiaries of the new public institution.

A secondary objective was to provide for the formal training of midwives, something that many contemporaries thought was urgently needed. Victor Amadeus II's proposal mentioned the Savoyard state's lack either of a sufficient number of qualified midwives to serve the general population or of the kind of institution capable of training them. Officials proposed a program of midwifery education on the lines of that at Paris's *Hôtel Dieu*, where young women would receive both practical and theoretical instruction in a hospital setting. In fact, Victor Amadeus lost no time in enlisting the esteemed Parisian surgeon Pietro Simone Rouhault as a primary consultant for the project.[20] According to the plans that emerged from this collaboration, the pregnant women who applied to the maternity ward would be cared for by an expert midwife, initially someone herself trained at the *Hôtel Dieu*. This head midwife (*maestro levatrice*) would then also have the responsibility of "instructing others not least for the service of the hospital [San Giovanni] as for the public."[21] In sum, the Turin maternity ward would serve the public good by protecting women's honor and the lives of children put at risk of abortion, abandonment, or infanticide, as well as by providing formal training for Savoy's midwives.

Despite these promised benefits, the maternity ward proposal was met with immediate opposition by San Giovanni's board of governors, a body composed of lay and ecclesiastical city elites. Such resistance reflected in part the newness of the venture. As noted, Italian hospitals, while important centers of public charity, did not typically extend services to pregnant women. Additionally, the governors raised financial and logistical concerns. Any space given to a maternity ward would come at the expense of several new rooms intended for the hospital's already overflowing population of foundlings, who, according to the board, suffered severe ill health as a result of overcrowding and poor conditions.[22] The hospital governors were also irked by the fact that the royal instructions had placed the financial burden of the new ward, including salaries for the director and head midwife, solely upon the hospital itself. The maternity ward project was in fact a major infringement on the hospital's traditional prerogatives and authority, part of a larger appropriation of the hospital for the Savoyard's state interests begun with the university reforms of the 1720s.[23]

At the same time, at least rhetorically, the opposition leveled by the hospital board concerned neither finances nor even power, but rather propriety. Administrators worried that the proximity of the proposed ward to the great number of young female foundlings would have the effect of inciting the girls to "great scandal."[24] The board, well aware of the steep financial and social challenges facing female orphans, feared that this already vulnerable group would fall into similar patterns of promiscuity as they believed had any woman who required a public maternity ward's services. Much the same reasoning drove women pregnant with illegitimate children from their homes, as moralists argued such evidence of shame would incite others in the community to sin and scandal.[25]

Concerns about the physical proximity of foundlings and parturient women in the cramped quarters of the hospital may also have been influenced by the medical logic of the day. Theories of 'moral contagion' current at the time held that the *corpuscules* emitted by individual bodies "were imprinted with the mark of that person's temperament and physical condition" and that persons in close proximity could very literally transmit "psychological states through the skin."[26] With similar reasoning, medical officials in Turin and elsewhere warned that wetnurses had to be carefully selected both for their physical health *and* upright character, as breast milk was believed to pass on moral qualities, such as temperance and charity or, less favorably, licentiousness and depravity.[27] Such concerns mixed with the knowledge that wetnurses, who often came from lower social strata than the babies they succored and who were often popularly associated with lewdness, might also transmit more tangible diseases, especially syphilis.[28] Indeed, wetnurses employed in foundling homes were increasingly subject to invasive physical exams during this period. In this way, the morally suspect women who came to the ward to give birth were considered a real threat to the precarious moral situation that already existed for the hospital's young female foundlings.

In fact, maternity wards and foundling homes would prove to be two sides of the same ideological coin. As the majority of babies born in early maternity hospitals were illegitimate, a nearby location to deposit the children advanced both institutions' *raison d'être* of protecting women from shame and preventing abandonment and infanticide. Furthermore, foundling hospitals, perpetually overcrowded, came to rely on the maternity wards' stream of new mothers to serve as wetnurses for periods of up to a year or more as repayment for the services they had received during labor. This symbiotic relationship continued well into the nineteenth century. For instance, after the 35-year-old widow Elena Bossa gave birth in Milan's maternity hospital in August 1775, she is noted as having been 'made wetnurse' in September.[29] Annuziata Ascorti, a 28-year-old widow who gave birth in March 1775 was made wetnurse in April, though she was suspected of having a venereal disease and so was ultimately dismissed from the hospital.[30]

In Turin, when official regulations governing the maternity ward were drawn up, they concentrated most pointedly on the protection of female honor and the maintenance of propriety. First and foremost, the ward's statutes emphasized the importance of keeping secret the identities of the women, known as *gravide occulte* or "secretly pregnant women," giving birth there. Repeated verbal gestures toward the preservation of "secrecy and honor," "precise secrecy," and "good order" suggest that both Royal reformers and the hospital governors were sensitive to potential concerns about the presence of pregnant women within the wider context of the hospital. The strict separation of the maternity ward's clientele from the rest of the hospital population aimed to limit the contact between these groups as much as possible.

It is evident from surviving records that the Turin maternity ward served an acute and growing need. From an initial outlaying of eight beds, arrangements for an additional twelve beds were under way already by 1729, and grew steadily from there. By 1782, the ward's total capacity had increased to 125. For the ten-year span of 1736–1745, we know that 936 women delivered children in the ward. For the next period for which we have accurate accounts, the seven-year period from 1760–1766, 847 women gave birth, an annual increase of 27 births. By the end of the century, those numbers had risen even more dramatically. From 1788–1800, more than 3600 women gave birth at San Giovanni, 282 per annum on average.[31] The majority of the babies born at the hospital were, moreover, illegitimate children born to single mothers. Across the period from 1736–1800, approximately 73% of the women who gave birth in the hospital were single women.[32] Married women cited extreme poverty as cause for appealing to the maternity ward's services, or sometimes the death of or abandonment by a spouse. As early as 1739, officials were praising the maternity ward's success in preventing infanticides and touting it as a prime example of the Enlightened beneficence of the Savoyard state. Indeed, other Italian states often looked to Turin as a model when they envisioned similar proposals for maternal assistance and midwifery education.[33]

Protecting honor, disciplining sexuality: Maternity wards in a longer frame

The maternity ward in Turin was followed by similar institutions founded in Italy during the second half of the eighteenth century. In some cases, maternity wards were located in general hospitals in larger cities and attached to preexisting foundling homes; often, they were associated with newly established midwifery schools. In other places, assistance for unwed mothers continued to be provided by smaller hospitals and hospices.[34] Whatever form a maternity ward assumed, the institutional care of pregnancy was almost always intimately connected to foundling assistance. Both maternity wards and foundling homes shared the same guiding principles of protecting women from shame and dishonor, of preventing infanticide and abandonment, and of ensuring that all babies were baptized. Furthermore, as mentioned previously, foundling homes became increasingly reliant on the maternity wards' new mothers to help remedy their own chronic lack of milk.

In addition to these structural links with foundling homes, eighteenth-century Italian maternity wards also shared much in common with Counter-Reformation–era sites of female reform and moral recuperation, such as conservatories for abused wives, repentant prostitutes, or at-risk girls. Together, these spaces were designed to protect female honor, discipline wayward female sexuality, and reform immoral behavior of all kinds. These earlier institutions had resulted from the socio-religious tensions of the Counter-Reformation.[35] According to Monica Chojnacka, "it was a combination . . . of spiritual conviction mixed with social anxiety" that resulted in certain groups of women becoming the targets of new institutional attempts to curtail wayward female sexuality in the late sixteenth century.[36] Both religious and lay authorities agreed upon the need for new institutional solutions to manage certain popultions of socially disruptive women, especially reformed prostitutes (*convertite*), poorly married women (*malmaritate*), and at-risk girls (*zitelle*).

As these women typically could or would not take vows, they required institutions that would combine the disciplinary, reformative, and spiritual components of the convent, but which would aim at eventual reintegration into society. Across Italy between the late sixteenth and eighteenth centuries, a constellation of such custodial institutions dotted the landscape. As Sherrill Cohen notes, these sites tended to blend voluntary and compulsory elements as part of their governing policies, in much the same way that eighteenth-century maternity wards would.[37] For instance, just as women who gave birth in maternity homes were faced with strict restrictions on their personal autonomy and the obligation to serve the hospital after their deliveries, daughters of prostitutes were sometimes taken against their will to homes for *zitelle*, and their mothers risked being sent to *case delle convertite* if they were seen to become disruptive to civic order.[38] By the late eighteenth century, many of these custodial institutions had in fact transformed into or become nearly indistinguishable from more explicitly correctional sites, increasingly overseen by civil police rather than religious authorities.

In all of these kinds of custodial institutions, personal autonomy was limited, and inmates were compelled to follow strict schedules and to cut themselves off from the outside world. Both maternity wards and reform houses were also, at least in theory, sites of rehabilitation, both in a physical and spiritual sense. Female sexuality had to be disciplined (or in the case of *zitelle*, protected) through confinement, work, and religious tutelage.[39] The aim was to restore honor where it had been lost and prepare women for reintegration back into society so that they could be properly married or otherwise overseen by a male authority. In some cases, the link between the two types of institutions was explicit. In Catania (Sicily), mothers who gave birth at the *Casa del Santo Bambino*, a maternity institution founded by a nobleman in 1783, had the choice after eight days of returning to the world or of entering the local refuge for repentant sinners.[40]

In addition to the new types of female custodial institutions founded in the era of the Counter-Reformation, there were also a small number of spaces already devoted to the care of unwed mothers in sixteenth- and seventeenth-century Italy. Though these earlier forms of assistance have usually been treated as distinct from the supposedly more medically oriented materntiy institutions founded in the eighteenth century, there is often little that distinguishes this earlier care aside from the scale on which it was provided. Typically, such assistance was an extension of local, private, and religious charity. In cities such as Milan, Florence, and Arezzo, some form of institutionalized maternity care had been offered to women at risk since as early as the sixteenth century. Most commonly, these institutions were associated with convents or conservatories. The Orbatello in Florence, for instance, which was founded to aid widows and older women, also came to accept unmarried pregnant women. In some cases, foundling homes or small hospitals, such as San Cristoforo in Arezzo, also accepted indigent and unmarried pregnant women.[41]

In Milan, from as early as 1528, pregnant women in need had been accepted at the small San Celso hospital, which had long housed foundlings and wetnurses. Given San Celso's primary identity as a foundling hospital, the women who gave birth there generally went on to serve for some period as wetnurses or as attendants in exchange for the medical care and lodging they had received. In fact, San Celso proved to be a kind of self-sustaining institution. Not only did women who gave birth there typically stay to wet-nurse as many as two to three additional children for periods of up to several years, but also in some cases, such women can later be found serving as nurses or midwives themselves. The case of Francesca Danielli richly demonstrates the way a woman might move through the hospital in different roles. Danielli first appeared in San Celso's records in 1594 as a wetnurse, though it is unclear whether or not this came after her own delivery in the hospital. From 1594–1597 she served as wetnurse but then Danielli is listed in 1597 as an attendant for weaned children; in 1599, at age 35, as a caretaker for older children; and finally from 1600–1603, as a midwife.[42]

In a trajectory that was even more common, girls born as foundlings at San Celso often went on to become midwives at the hospital. Proximity to births and experience gained through the assistance some of these girls likely offered during labors must have provided them with sufficient training to take over birthing duties themselves as they aged.[43] While the seventeenth-century statutes governing San Celso directed that midwives who worked there had to have good reputations, be of mature age, and be knowledgeable in their trade, there were no specific references made to the training or skillset these women should have.[44] The dearth of information that accompanied the hospital's record of a midwife being fired in 1712 for lacking the necessary expertise suggests that, well into the eighteenth century, it remained the prerogative of existing midwives to select, train, and judge the skill of their counterparts.[45]

Although sixteenth- and seventeenth-century maternity hospices functioned similarly to the state-sponsored wards of the eighteenth century, there were some changes over time. One point of distinction is that the earlier instititons may have been more inclined to seek out the fathers of illegitimate children, much as foundling homes had tended to do in an earlier period.[46] At San Celso, for instance, at least until the mid-seventeenth cetury, midwives were directed to question the women under their care about the baby's father, the name of which they would then discretely record for the hospital to use to seek out financial support.[47] Additionally, women seem to have stayed for relatively short periods during the sixteenth and seventeenth centuries, often entering only upon labor rather than in their seventh or eighth month as became common for illegitimatly pregnant women in the eigheenth century.[48] Additionally, in many early maternity hospices, which were often of an explicitly disciplinary nature, only illegitimately pregnant women were accepted. What seems consistent among these early sites of maternal assistance is that demand was growing. At San

Cristoforo in Arezzo, where pregnant women were admitted beginning in 1579, the recourse of *gravide occulte* to the hospital was initially small and represented only a fraction of the hospital's total number of patients. By 1660, however, the thirty-five pregnant patients admitted that year constituted more than half of the hospital's sixty patients, and this number had increased to an even greater percentage by the end of the century.[49]

In Milan, by 1671, demand for greater supervision and an expansion of services resulted in the transfer of the foundlings, wetnurses, and pregnant women of San Celso to the much larger *Ospedale Maggiore* where they were housed in a section of the hospital known as the *Quarto delle Balie*. According to Flores Reggiani, the relocation of the Milanese maternity ward to the *Ospedale Maggiore* saw not only a general rise in hospital births, but also a dramatic increase in the number of married women who gave birth there, as well as the number of native Milaense women who did.[50] As we saw in Turin, the demand for public maternity services was growing during the eighteenth century. So were the numbers of abandoned children. To fully understand the phenomenon of infant abandonment in early modern Italy, however, it is necessary to consider the changes to the management of sexuality, honor, and reproduction that resulted from the disciplining impulses of the Counter-Reformation.

* * *

In the wake of the Council of Trent in the late sixteenth century, the Catholic Church had significantly altered the customary relationship between sexual activity and marriage. The Decree *Tametsi* issued at Trent reconfirmed marriage as a sacrament, attempted to suppress extra-marital sexual relationships and concubinage, and formalized the proper manner in which a legitimate marriage could be consecrated. Afterward, marriage required a public ceremony performed before a priest and several witnesses preceded by marriage banns. More importantly, whereas custom had legitimated pre-marital sexual relations contracted under the promise of marriage, the post-Tridentine Church redefined such sexual activity as sinful behavior.[51]

The Church's adherence to strict sexual guidelines in the era of the Counter-Reformation mirrored the state's and the community's interest in protecting familial status and inheritance. As central to the proper functioning of the early modern social economy, the female reproductive body had to be regulated and controlled. A woman who engaged in illicit sexual relations jeopardized patriarchal structures and threatened social discord, shaming the woman's family as much as herself. A woman whose honor was tarnished faced diminished marital prospects and therefore a potential financial burden for her family. At the same time, pre-marital sexual relations or an illegitimate pregnancy that could be funneled into marriage between the partners (or at the least compensated with the equivalency of a dowry) had traditionally been satisfactory to restore a woman's compromised honor.

Even after Trent, communities might therefore tolerate a fair amount of pre-marital sexual activity. For a time, community structures were such that illegitimacy could be absorbed into everyday life without seriously threatening the gender or social order.

By the late seventeenth century, however, economic and demographic shifts affecting both rural and urban life contributed to hardened attitudes toward illegitimacy.[52] Whereas an illegitimate pregnancy might have been absorbed by the community in the sixteenth century, by the eighteenth century social and legal conventions tended to exculpate men and victimize women for sexual transgression, leaving unwed mothers with the burden of supporting unwanted children.[53] Whereas the community's management of marriage had once protected female honor by pressuring men who broke marriage promises to marry or dower the woman,[54] over time increased social mobility and urban migration disrupted these kinds of local safeguards. Even in cases that could not be so easily remedied, institutions such as foundling homes had once tended to seek out fathers of abandoned children to pay for their upkeep. Yet, by the eighteenth century, both communal and institutional pressures on fathers had diminished. Promises of marriage were less commonly used to hold men responsible for pre-marital sexual relations, and foundling homes became less assertive in tracking down fathers to make them financially accountable for their illegitimate children.[55]

In this environment, the public response to illegitimacy was increasingly punitive and suspicious. Midwives were often targeted as potential facilitators of sexual immorality. Across Italy, midwives were pressured to immediately report any woman they suspected of carrying an illegitimate child. In Milan in the 1770s, midwives were absolutely forbidden to take women into their own homes to give birth unless they first informed the authorities.[56] Both illegitimately pregnant women and any persons who concealed them were threatened with exceedingly harsh punishments, including, in some cases, even death.[57] This hostility toward illegitimately pregnant women also rapidly altered the nature of foundling assistance in Italy. According to Jeffrey Watt, after the sixteenth century, "preserving the mother's honor by keeping the birth secret eventually displaced saving the life of the baby" as the *reason d'être* of most foundling homes.[58] Adriano Prosperi likewise affirms that, especially by the eighteenth century, the objectives of "foundling hospitals had profoundly changed with respect to the period of their origins."[59] The result of this transformation was the adaptation of a previously existing institutional solution to fit new needs, in particular the protection of female honor.

Women who found themselves with an illegitimate pregnancy were increasingly pressured to conceal the evidence of sexual sin by leaving their communities temporarily. Maternity wards typically allowed such women to be admitted as early as their seventh month to avoid scandal. For their part, foundling homes, reoriented toward the preservation of female honor, became less likely to actively seek out information about the fathers of abandoned children, even though such indifference signaled a loss of financial support for these already overburdened institutions. Simona Cerutti and Sandra Cavallo argue, further, that not only had pre-marital "sexual intercourse lost its character as a prelude to the state of marriage" but also "for the first time, sexual practice came to be associated explicitly with a moral concept of guilt."[60] The basic result of this gradual transformation in the community's sense of morality and shame was that a "responsibility which once had been widely" shared, that is, the responsibility for supporting illegitimate offspring, was now "concentrated on the woman" alone.[61]

Indicative of the changes in societal attitudes toward illegitimacy were particularly harsh legal responses to abandonment and infanticide. A revised Savoyard criminal code issued in 1729, for instance, prescribed capital punishment for women convicted of infanticide and abortion, as well as for any accomplices to such crimes. Mothers who abandoned their children outside of foundling homes were to be publically flogged or exiled.[62] If the state was going to assume the responsibility of protecting female honor through public maternity wards, then it would apparently give no leeway to women who were seen to take matters into their own hands.[63] At the same time, elsewhere in Europe, there were calls for the decriminalization of infanticide as the figure of the desperate mother compelled by circumstances to grievous action received greater sympathy among moralists and novelists.[64] Italian reformers such as Cesare Beccaria also rallied for the decriminalization of infanticide and abortion, though legal codes in Italy continued to prescribe harsh punishments for these crimes throughout the century.[65]

Compounding preexisting and deep-seated attitudes toward shame and illegitimacy in the eighteenth century was also the widespread belief that the strength of a nation lay in the vitality and size of its labor force. The pronatalism of eighteenth-century economic policies and populationist thinking added a new valorization to motherhood and heightened disapproval of those who would renounce this duty.[66] Contemporaries influenced by populationism viewed infanticide as more than just a moral or religious crime; a murdered newborn meant not only the loss of life and a soul unbaptized, but also the loss of a "future citizen."[67] Johann Peter Frank, the famous eighteenth-century public health architect, wrote in support of public assistance for illegitimately pregnant women, arguing that "the conditions of pregnancy in unwed mothers is as estimable as in married women; both carry a citizen and a creature of God's making under their hearts."[68] For Frank and others, the spiritual transgression implied in the act of infanticide was compounded by its civic repercussions. Even if the punishments meted out to women accused of these crimes were often less severe in practice than prescribed in criminal codes, the attention to the crime and the severity of the language with which it was addressed indicate the chord which infanticide struck in the public discourse.[69] For instance, in a particularly gruesome case of infanticide heard before the highest criminal court in Turin, in which a young mother buried her newborn son when, according to an expert, he might still have been alive, the judge sentenced the mother to death and declared her "an enemy of the state."[70] Infanticide was no less than an attack on the integrity and well-bring of the society as a whole.

The continued criminalization of infanticide and abortion, and the decreased accountability of fathers of illegitimate children seem to be clear markers of more oppressive attitudes toward women during the eighteenth century. At the time, however, many contemporaries praised Italian maternity wards as examples of Enlightened beneficence and even a softening of attitudes toward illegitimately pregnant women.[71] Popular pamphlets and literature from this time also began to address illegitimate mothers with at least some degree of sympathy, presenting them as victims of predatory masculinity rather than irredeemable vixens or sinners. Contemporary reformers praised public institutions such as the Turin maternity ward and the *Quarto delle Balie* in Milan for offering illegitimate mothers a "voluntary, free, and secret refuge, beyond any jurisdictional and penal ambit."[72] Although reformers thought it was clear that such women had committed shameful acts and were in need of moral and spiritual recuperation, no criminal action would be taken against them. As the statutes of one later maternity hospital stated, no longer should "a lack of asylum and fear of shame . . . serve as an excuse for mothers to kill their child[ren]."[73]

Daily life in an eighteenth-century maternity ward

Daily practice in Italy's eighteenth-century maternity wards was shaped foremost by the concern to ensure secrecy and privacy for the mothers housed there. Because contemporaries assumed that poverty, immorality, and illegitimacy were interrelated conditions, even married women who gave birth at a public institution were tinged with shame and suspicion by association.[74] Maternity wards therefore aimed both to protect otherwise upright women whose honor had been compromised by an illegitimate pregnancy, and impoverished women, married or not, for whom an additional birth might lead to sinful acts such as abortion and infanticide, or prostitution and theft. Anonymity protected both the mothers who gave birth at public maternity wards and their home communities from association with sexual sin and immoral behavior.

The bylaws that governed these institutions therefore placed heavy restrictions on who could enter and exit, and under what circumstances. In Turin, the small maternity ward in San Giovanni hospital was initially composed of three rooms[75] which could be entered only by those with a written license from the ward's director and head midwife.[76] In addition, two "robust" female assistants guarded the doors to the ward, allowing entrance and exit only to those with the proper approvals.[77] Even sanctioned visitors were to be accompanied by one of the assistants to the bed of the woman being visited and not allowed to wander elsewhere so as not to disturb any women who did not want to be seen or known.[78] In Milan's *Quarto delle Balie*, midwives and other attendants were "absolutely prohibited" from inquiring into the personal information a pregnant woman did not wish to disclose, including the identity of the baby's father. Provisions in more than one maternity hospital even considered the possibility that a woman might come to the hospital masked in order to conceal her identity, in which case the staff were expected to do their utmost to keep the woman's presence secret.[79] Additionally, the directors of the *Ospedale Maggiore* in Milan made it expressly known that a woman's having given birth in the public maternity ward would never serve as evidence "for judgments hostile to the parturient woman, nor ever will the *Casa* give testimony or a certificate" stating that the woman gave birth at the hospital. In other words, pregnant women could give birth in full assurance that their stay would never be revealed against their wishes, especially to police or other authorities. Admitted women were requested only to record their full name and bed number on an envelope, which would then be sealed and transported with the patient throughout her stay, to be opened exclusively in the event of her death in order that her husband or relatives be notified.[80]

Although the maternity wards in Turin and Milan extended their assistance to both married and unmarried women, they did not receive patients indiscriminately. For instance, unmarried women could be admitted as early as the seventh month of pregnancy, to avoid scandal in their home communities.[81] By contrast, married women were only to be admitted in their ninth month, and then only with a certificate from their parish priest attesting to their poverty and the permission of their husbands. Such differences in policy toward married and unmarried women reflected the broader concerns that married women might further burden already over-crowded foundling hospitals by abandoning legitimate children, a practice that hospital administrators desperately wished to curtail. In fact, authorities in Turin outright prohibited the abandonment of legitimate children, threatening offenders with legal and financial penalties, though such deterrents seem to have had little impact.[82]

Although contemporaries often assumed illegitimacy and poverty went hand in hand, the bylaws of Milan's *Quarto delle Balie* suggest that it was not just poor women who took refuge in the hospital. Maternity patients were in fact divided into four categories depending on how much they were able to contribute to their own care. At one extreme, the wealthiest patients paid three *lire* per day and received the comfort of a private room and were governed by the most stringent restrictions on who could enter.[83] These patients were also protected from being cared for by training midwives or surgeons. Women in the second tier paid one *lira* and ten *soldi* per day and, though joined together in one room, were nonetheless kept distinct from the lowest two classes, had individual beds, and were to be served only by trained midwives and the head physician-obstetrician. These two highest-paying classes of patient were also treated to a comfortable lying-in which approximated that of a typical mother of the middling classes, with all the expected domestic accoutrements, including "an individual servant, the finest linens, and better furniture."[84]

By contrast, the poorest women admitted to the hospital paid nothing and were required to present a certificate from their parish priest attesting to their poverty.[85] Further, they were subject to the least hospitable conditions, being housed together with patients of the third class (who paid a relatively modest ten *soldi* a day), and, depending on the availability of space and linens, might be required to bed together. Significantly, the women of the third and fourth classes, who comprised the majority of patients, were made available for visitation by training midwives and even male surgeons, a provision that was still unusual in Italian maternity wards at this time.[86]

Apart from the limited provisions for training surgeons to visit maternity patients in Milan, eighteenth-century Italian maternity wards were largely female-controlled spaces. While always nominally under the authority of male physicians or directors, it was the head midwives who took responsibility for day-to-day activity within the wards. They maintained the wards' provisions, including firewood and patients' daily allotment of food; directed the small number of servant women and midwives under them; received new patients and registered them; and managed the vast majority of actual births when patients went into labor.[87] In many cases, it was the head midwife who made administrative decisions about which women would be admitted. In Milan, she was the one who performed an examination to determine how far along in their pregnancies were desiring entrants.[88] The only time a surgeon or physician might be involved in a woman's admittance was if there was suspicion that she was infected with a venereal disease, especially syphilis, in which case she might be sent elsewhere for specialized treatment.[89]

In general, medical oversight by male physicians or surgeons at maternity wards was minimal, though it varied across the Italian peninsula. While in Milan a professor of surgery from the *Ospedale Maggiore* was officially required to visit the maternity ward each morning to attend to all persons, even returning after lunch if needed, the maternity ward in Turin only required a surgeon to make two annual inspections. Moreover, in Turin young male surgeons were strictly prohibited from using the ward for any kind of clinical instruction throughout the eighteenth century, regardless of a patient's economic status. A male surgeon might be called to the ward to draw blood, but he was directed to leave immediately after completing his operation and not to go to any other bed except that of the woman being attended. If needed to draw the blood of a woman in labor, the surgeon, having performed the operation, was to remove himself promptly and not to remain during the delivery.[90] When faced with a difficult birth, the midwife was directed to call for the assistance of a male surgeon only when it became clear that the delivery required instruments. In such cases, however, male trainees were prohibited from accompanying their instructors into the ward.[91] In all other cases, male surgeons and physicians were strictly forbidden from entering the ward, *especially* during deliveries.[92]

Midwives were generally trusted to perform a wide range of therapeutic procedures. Although she was prohibited from prescribing internal medicines (the preserve of physicians), the head midwife in Turin *was* sanctioned to draw blood and perform enemas when warranted, with the authorization of a physician.[93] Hospital midwives also likely continued to employ the countless recipes, fortifying cordials, and topical medicaments that had long been at their disposal, as well as practiced skills such as massage, manual dilation of the cervix, and turning of the fetus in the womb. In addition to handling births, midwives working in wards attached to foundling hospitals might also assume some care of the children. In Milan, Maria Teresa Robbles, who first came to the maternity ward to give birth, became noted in the hospital community in the 1720s for her unguent to treat ringworm and for developing a binding that was so effective in controlling hernias that at least twenty-nine children were prevented from having to go under the surgeon-*norcino*'s knife.[94]

Eighteenth-century maternity hospitals also continued to merge physical care with spiritual recuperation. Religious education was stressed from the outset for the pregnant inmates, who were presumed to have engaged in shameful behavior. In Turin, a chaplain visited the women twice a week, and in times of emergency, "urging them to make their devotions, and always encouraging in them sentiments of piety."[95] Contemporaries were convinced that such moral 'recovery' was best "pursued through a rigid separation from the outside."[96] As had been the case in earlier women's refuges and conservatories, eighteenth-century maternity wards thus restricted contact with the outside world. Moreover, before delivery, the women were expected to engage in useful labor, such as spinning, shoe-making, or agricultural labor.[97] Care and discipline thus merged in the setting of the maternity ward, though not always seamlessly.

Despite careful measures to maintain order and propriety, maternity wards were constant sources of complaints and misbehavior that officials never seemed able to curtail. In Milan, such disorder was one of the reasons cited for transerring San Celso's inhabitants to the *Ospedale Maggiore*. Reports described rowdy behavior by pregnant women and wetnurses socializing against regulations in the parlor and a rogue wetnurse whose milk supply had dried up continuing to lodge at the hospital with dire consequences for the infants under her care. Other women met with relatives and friends in defiance of restrictions on visitors or simply left the hospital at their will. Even after the transfer, various offences continued to be recorded. Around 1716, a three-year old boy was found dead with bruises on his face, leading to the discovery of an attendant who beat the children and even "ripped at their skins with her nails."[98] In another case, a woman named Annunziata who was training with the head midwife had to be restrained because she was found to take little care with the children.[99] And in defiance of the expectation that they perform morally recuperative labor, some pregnant women paid the wetnurses or other women in the ward to perform their chores, such as sweeping or washing clothes.[100]

In Turin, the maternity ward fared no better. The ward's first head midwife, Chevassus, was censured for a littany of abuses, including accepting women before their seventh month of pregnancy, failing to prevent unwanted visitors from entering the ward, being indiscriminate about the women allowed to serve as birth attendants, and even for consuming more than her fair share of the food and resources allocated for the entire ward.[101] In addition, she was cited for overstepping her professional bounds by administering excessive doses of medicine, causing sicknesses and even two deaths in the ward.[102] On one point, the head midwife may not have been wholly to blame: a number of pregnant women *had* apparently attempted to be admitted early by feigning labor pains.[103] There were problems with the training of midwives as well. Although anatomical demonstrations were supposed to be performed twice a year, these seem to have happened only rarely. Likewise, the incorporation of written lessons for the student midwives had apparently ceased altogether.[104]

These abuses were matched by repeated reports calling attention to the high infant mortality in San Giovanni's maternity ward and foundling home. This was the case in Milan as well. In one regretful incident, an infant was suffocated when the wetnurse with whom he was sleeping (because of a lack of crib space) rolled over on him.[105] Moreover, despite attempts to identify and reject pregnant women and wetnurses infected with contagious diseases, especially syphilis, infections continued to spread at alarming rates.[106] In Milan, where the mortality rate for the *Ospedale Maggiore*'s foundling population was upward of 43%, critics blamed poor ventilation, overcrowding, and an insufficient availability of wetnurses to supply adequate milk.[107]

Conclusion

The steady rise in entrants to Italian maternity wards during the eighteenth century makes clear that such institutions were serving a palpable social need. In large part they were attending to transformations that had begun in the era of the Counter-Reformation but had accelerated during the eighteenth century. During this period, according to Silvana Baldi, local communities were subject to disruptive forces from multiple sources, all of which had the cumulative effect of weakening traditional bonds of cohesion and self-regulation. The " 'promise' that fiancés exchanged prior to marriage," for instance, "progressively lost its protective function with respect to female honor and of control and legitimization of pre-marital sexual practices."[108] Additionally, the rural population became increasingly mobile, migrating toward the city for greater job opportunities, and at the same time "rendering . . . more difficult a paternity search."[109] Together, these disruptions of traditional controls rendered it more difficult to remedy an illegitimate birth with a subsequent marriage, and almost impossible to compel a father to recognize an illegitimate child by the mother's "simple declaration."[110]

As these shifts began to introduce a new sexual ethics into society, maternity wards represented an institutional solution based on the principles of confinement and moral rehabilitation that could both conceal and absorb the effects of sexual deviance. While local solutions to such problems were not unknown in the past – convents and hospices had received limited numbers of pregnant women in some cities – the maternity wards that emerged in Italy in the eighteenth century were the first such institutions to be promoted and supported by state governments and intended to serve populations on a large scale. While discussions of eighteenth-century maternity institutions have typically focused on their role in increasing male involvement in childbirth, this narrative fails to capture the contours of maternity care in Italy. In Italy, institutionalized maternity care was driven by traditional concerns about honor, shame, and sexuality. Although these institutions strived to provide certain women a safe place to give birth, they were, at least initially, quite resistant to the interests of male medical practitioners.

Notes

1 Archivio Storico Diocesano di Torino (hereafter ASDt), *Tribunale Archivescovile*, 9.6.20, Fasc. 21, Trial of Giovanni Caomino, 1728.
2 Ibid., Testimony of Lorenzo Michele Leona.
3 Ibid., Testimony of Lorenzo Michele Leona.
4 Ibid., Testimony of Antonio Sbodio.
5 Eleonora Canepari, "Svelare o Occultare? L'eco delle Nascite Illegittime (Roma, XVIII Secolo)," *Quaderni Storici* 41, no. 1 (2006): 101–132, 102.
6 Sherrill Cohen, *The Evolution of Women's Asylums Since 1500: From Refuges for Ex-Prostitutes to Shelters for Battered Women* (Oxford: Oxford University Press, 1992), 4.
7 Brian Pullan, *Rich and Poor in Renaissance Venice: The Social Institutions of a Catholic State, to 1620* (Cambridge, MA: Harvard University Press, 1971), 135.
8 Michel Foucault, *The Birth of the Clinic: An Archaeology of Medical Perception*, trans. A. M. Sheridan (London: Tavistock, 1973), 10–15. Foucault drew his conclusions primarily from his study of the hospital in post-Revolutionary France.
9 Guenter B. Risse, "Before the Clinic was 'Born': Methodological Perspectives in Hospital History," in *Institutions of Confinement: Hospitals, Asylums, and Prisons in Western Europe and North America, 1500–1950*, ed. Norbert Finzsch and Robert Jutte (Cambridge: Cambridge University Press, 1996), 75–96.
10 Franca Pizzini and Lia Lombardi, *Corpo medico e corpo femminile: parto, riproduzione artificiale, menopausa* (Milan: Franco Angeli, 1999), 34.
11 On this point, see Nadia Maria Filippini, "Ospizi per partorienti e cliniche ostetriche tra Sette e Ottocento" in *Gli ospedali in area Padana fra Settecento e Novecento*, ed. Maria Luisa Betri and Edoardo Bressan (Milano: Franco Angeli, 1992), 395; Peter McCaffery, "The Politics of Midwifery: Introduction," in *Midwifery and the Medicalization of Childbirth: Comparative Perspectives*, eds. Edwin Van Teijlingen, George Lowis, Peter McCaffery, and Maureen Porter (New York: Nova, 2004), 293.

12 This is discussed in Chapter 5.

13 Alfonso Coarrdi, *Dell'ostetricia in Italia dalla metà dello scorso secolo fino al presente* (Bologna: Gamberini e Parmeggiani, 1872), 6; T. M. Caffaratto, *L'Ospedale Maggiore di San Giovanni Battista e della Città di Torino: Sette secoli di assistenza socio-sanitaria* (Turin: U.S.L., 1984), 61–72; Elena Spina, *Ostetriche e Midwives: Spazi di autonomia e identità corporativa* (Milan: Franco Angeli, 1998), 41–46.

14 Margaret Connor Versluysen, "Midwives, Medical Men, and 'Poor Women Labouring of Child': Lying-In Hospitals in Eighteenth-Century London," in *Women, Health, and Reproduction*, ed. Helen Roberts (London: Routledge, 1981), 42.

15 This negative view remains persistent, though it has been challenged recently by Lisa Forman Cody who makes a thorough comparison between mortality rates and conditions within London maternity wards and those which existed at large, arguing that they were comparable. See Lisa Forman Cody, "Living and Dying in Georgian London's Lying-In Hospitals," *Bulletin of the History of Medicine* 78, no. 2 (2004): 309–348.

16 Irvine Loudon, *The Tragedy of Childbed Fever* (Oxford: Oxford University Press, 2000), 59.

17 Geoffrey Symcox, *Victor Amadeus II: Absolutism in the Savoyard State, 1675–1730* (Berkeley and Los Angeles: University of California Press, 1983), 199. For a contemporary and highly celebratory account, see A. Guevarre, *La mendicita sbandita col sovvenimento dei poveri* (Turin, 1717).

18 Archivio Ospedale di San Giovanni Battista (hereafter AOSG), Cat. 1, Cl. 3, fasc. 1, 1732.

19 AOSG, Cat. 10, Cl. 1, Fasc. 3, "Memoriale per lo stabilimento di una sala per le donne gravide," 6 May 1728.

20 Rouhualt was also the main author of the maternity ward's first official "*Regolamento*" published in 1732.

21 F. A. Duboin, *Raccolta per ordine di materia delle leggi, editti, manifesti, emanate dai sovrani della real Casa di Savoia sino all'8–12–1798*, 23 Bks. (Turin, 1818–69), Bk. XII, Tit. XIX, Chap. II, 644.

22 AOSG, Cat. 2, Cl. 5, fasc. 1.3, 20 January 1728.

23 According to Sandra Cavallo, the hospital board's reservations about the maternity ward and the Royal government's unwillingness to compromise were expressions of a broader struggle for control over the institution in a period when Victor Amadeus was attempting to limit precisely the kind of local autonomy represented by the hospital and its governors. The installation, dating from this period, of a *Regio Prottetore*, essentially a Royal representative, onto the hospital board was an instance – met with considerable indignation by the traditional hospital elites – of tangible Royal interference in the daily governance of the hospital. In this view, the hospital board should not be seen narrowly as a conservative force putting up "strenuous resistance to the medical reform of hospitals, advocated for by the more progressive medical profession and more enlightened representatives of the state" but rather as an entity struggling with encroachment by a new class of state functionaries on its traditional prerogatives. As Cavallo's point makes clear, viewing the installation of a maternity ward in Turin through a purely medical filter leads to a distortion of the actual motivations and pressures on the actors involved. Sandra Cavallo, *Charity and Power in Early Modern Italy: Benefactors and Their Motives in Turin, 1541–1789* (Cambridge: Cambridge University Press, 1995), 185, 191.

24 AOSG, Cat. 2, Cl. 5, fasc. 1.3, 20 January 1728.

25 David I. Kertzer, *Sacrificed for Honor: Italian Infant Abandonment and the Politics of Reproductive Control* (Boston: Beacon Press, 1993), 52–53.

26 Christopher E. Forth, "Moral Contagion and the Will: The Crisis of Masculinity in fin-de-siècle France," in *Contagion: Historical and Cultural Studies*, ed. Alison Bashford and Claire Hooker (London: Routledge, 2001), 63.

27 Antonia Pasi, "Mortalità infantile e cultura medica in Italia nel XIX secolo," in *Malaltia I Cultura*, ed. Josep L. Barona (Valencia: Seminari d'Estudis Sobre la Ciencia, 1995), 131; Gioseffo Jacopo Plenk, *Elementi dell'arte Ostetricia* (Venezia: Francesco di Nicolò Pezzana, 1798), 86–90; Simon Richter, *Missing the Breast: Gender, Fantasy, and the Body in the German Enlightenment* (Seattle: University of Washington Press, 2006), 97; Daniela Franchetti, *La scuola ostetrica pavese tra Otto e Novecento* (Milan: Cisalpino, 2012), 36.

28 In Europe, physicians were aware that syphilis could be passed down through breastfeeding from at least the early sixteenth century. See David I. Kertzer, "Syphilis, Foundlings and Wetnurses in Nineteenth-Century Italy," *Journal of Social History* 32, no. 3 (1999): 589–602. For a long-term historical perspective on the associations between syphilis and wetnursing, see Beatriz M. Reyes-Foster and Shannon K. Carter, "Suspect Bodies, Suspect Milk: Milk Sharing, Wetnursing, and the Specter of Syphilis in the Twenty-First Century," in *Syphilis and Subjectivity: From the Victorian to the Present*, ed. Kari Nixon and Lorenzo Servitje (London: Palgrave Macmillan, 2018), 91–112.

29 Archivio Storico EX IPPAI Milano (hereafter ASI.Mi.), *Ospedale Maggiore*, 1 D, Gravide et balie, n. 1, 1775–1776.

30 Ibid.

31 Silvana Baldi, "L'assistenza alla maternita' a Torino nel XVIII secolo," *Sanità, Scienza, e Storia* 1, no. 2 (1992): 129.

32 Ibid., 136. According to Baldi, 28.5% of the babies born in the hospital in that period died.

33 This was the case in Milan during the planning stages of the midwifery school there. ASMi, *Sanità, Parte Antica*, c. 268.

34 Brian Pullan, *Tolerance, Regulation and Rescue: Dishonoured Women and Abandoned Children in Italy, 1300–1800* (Manchester: Manchester University Press, 2016), 150.

35 These institutions have been well documented, though usually treated within individual contexts. See, for instance: Daniela Maldini, "Donne sole, 'figlie raminghe,' 'convertite' e 'forzate.' Aspetti assistenziali nella Torino di fine Settecento," *Il Risorgimento* 33 (1980): 115–138; Lucia Ferrante, "L'onore ritrovato. Donne nella Casa del Soccorso di S. Paolo a Bologna (sec. xvi–xvii)," *Quaderni Storici* 18, no. 53 (2) (1983): 499–527; Daniella Lombardi, "L'Ospedale dei Mendicanti nella Firenze del seicento. 'Da inutile serraglio dei mendici a conservatorio e casa di forza per le donne'," *Società e Storia* 24 (1984): 289–311; Alessandra Camerano, "Assistenza richiesta ed assistenza imposta: Il conservatorio di S. Caterina della Rosa di Roma," *Quaderni Storici* 28, no. 82 (1993): 227–260; Silvia Dominici, "Il conservatorio di Santo Spirito in Sassia di Roma: Condizioni, risorse e tutela delle donne nel Settecento," *Studi Storici* 44, no. 1 (2003): 191–250.

36 Monica Chojnacka, "Charity and Community in Early Modern Venice: The Casa delle Zitelle," *Renaissance Quarterly* 51 (1998): 68–91, 73.

37 Cohen, *The Evolution of Women's Asylums*, 116–118.

38 Camerano, "Assistenza richiesta ed assistenza imposta," 82.

39 Carlo Decio, *Notizie storiche sulla ospitalità e didattica ostetrica Milanese* (Pavia: Successori Fusi, 1906), 78.

40 Silvana Raffaele, "Il problema degli esposti in Sicilia (secc. XVIII–XIX). Normativa e risposta istituzionale: il caso di Catania," in *Enfance abandonnie et sociiti en Europe XIVe–XXe siecle* (Rome: Ecole francaise de Rome, 1991), 920–922.

41 On the hospital of San Cristoforo in Arezzo, see Deanna Sardi, "In nome di Maria: Madri illegittime e partorienti povere nella Toscana moderna. Il caso di Arezzo fra Sei e Settecento," *Ricerche Storiche* 32 (2002): 81–99. On the Orbatello in Florence, see Lucia Sandri, "Matrimoni mancati. 'Pericolate' e 'gravide occulte' dell'ospizio di Orbatello di Firenze nel XVIII e XIX secolo," in *Nubili e celibi tra scelta e costrizione (secoli XVI–XX)*, ed. M. Lanzinger e R. Sarti (Udine: Forum, 2006), 71–92.

42 Decio, *Notizie storiche sulla ospitalità e didattica ostetrica Milanese*, 95–96.

43 Ibid., 96.

44 Ibid., 96.

45 Ibid., 113.

46 Pullan, *Tolerance, Regulation and Rescue*, 149.

47 Decio, *Notizie storiche sulla ospitalità e didattica ostetrica Milanese*, 92. Many women gave false names or claimed to be ignorant of the father's identity.

48 Sardi, "In nome di Maria," 94.

49 Ibid., 89.

50 Flores Reggiani, "Responsabilità paterna fra povertà e beneficenza: 'I figli dell'Ospedale di Milano fra Seicento e Settecento," *Ricerche Storiche* 27, no. 2 (1997): 287–314, 293.

51 Giorgia Alessi, "Il gioco degli scambi: Seduzione e risarcimento nella casistica catolica del XVI e XVII Secolo," *Quaderni Storici* 75 (1990): 807–808; John Bossy, *Christianity in the West, 1400–1700* (Oxford: Oxford University Press, 1985), 25.

52 Giovanna Cappelletto, "Infanzia abbandonata e ruoli di mediazione sociale nella Verona del Settecento," *Quaderni Storici* 53 (1983): 421–443, 423–424.

53 Joanne M. Ferraro, *Nefarious Crimes, Contested Justice: Illicit Sex and Infanticide in the Republic of Venice, 1557–1789* (Baltimore: The Johns Hopkins University Press, 2008), 4, 158–159; Cappelletto, "Infanzia abbandonata e ruoli di mediazione sociale nella Verona del Settecento," 423–424.

54 Alessi, "Il gioco degli scambi," 806.

55 Cappelletto, "Infanzia abbandonata e ruoli di mediazione sociale nella Verona del Settecento," 433; Reggiani, "Responsabilità paterna fra povertà e beneficenza," 287–314, 297.

56 ASMi, *Sanità, Parte Antica*, c. 186, "Regolamento del Regio Direttorio della Facoltà Medica nella Lombardia Proposto da Giuseppe Cicognini, Consigliere della Regia Deputazione," n.d.

57 Adriano Prosperi, *Dare l'anima: Storia di un infanticidio* (Torino: Einaudi, 2005), 68–70.

58 Jeffrey R. Watt, "The Impact of the Reformation and Counter-Reformation," in *Family Life in Early Modern Times, 1500–1789*, ed. David I. Kertzer and Marzio Barbagli (New Haven: Yale University Press, 2001), 125–156, 150.

59 Prosperi, *Dare l'anima*, 68.

60 Simona Cerutti and Sandra Cavallo, "Onore femminile e controllo sociale delle riproduzione in Piemonte tra Sei e Settecento," *Quaderni Storici* 44 (1980): 373.

61 Ibid., 373.

62 The law assumed only women committed infanticide; see Prosperi, *Dare l'anima*, 67–71. On the revised criminal code, see Symcox, *Victor Amadeus II*, 193–194; Mario Viora, *Le Costituzioni Piemontesi, 1723, 1729, 1772. Storia Esterna della Compilazione* (Turin Fratelli Bocca, 1928), Chapter 20; Duboin, *Raccolta per ordine di materia delle leggi*, Bk. VI, Ch. VIII, 82.

63 Kertzer, *Sacrificed for Honor*, 32.

64 Prosperi, *Dare l'anima*, 70–80.

65 Margaret Brannan Lewis, *Infanticide and Abortion in Early Modern Germany* (New York: Routledge, 2016), 172. Silvana Baldi has noted that in Turin the severity of the punishments for these crimes did diminish markedly in practice

during the last quarter of the century. See Baldi, "L'assistenza alla maternita," 136–140.

66 Baldi, "L'assistenza alla maternita," 141–142.

67 Lewis, *Infanticide and Abortion in Early Modern Germany*, 172. For an extended treatment of populationism, see Leslie Tuttle's excellent study on France, *Conceiving the Old Regime: Pronatalism and the Politics of Reproduction in Early Modern France* (Oxford and New York: Oxford University Press, 2010), and Chapter 5 in this book.

68 Johann Peter Frank, *System einer vollständigen medicinischen Polizey*, vol. 2.4 (Mannheim: C. F. Schwann, 1779–1780), 7–8, 419, quoted in Mary Lindemann, "Maternal Politics: The Principles and Practice of Maternity Care in Eighteenth-Century Hamburg," *Journal of Family History* 9, no. 1 (1984): 45. For an English translation of Frank's monumental work, see Johann Peter Frank, *A System of Complete Medical Police*, trans. E. Wilim (Baltimore: The Johns Hopkins University Press, 1976).

69 AST, *Sezione Reunite, Senato di Piemonte, Sentenze Criminali, 1724–1802*. Although contemporaries often spoke of infanticide as a growing problem, an examination of the sentences meted out by the criminal court in Turin between 1724–1801 reveals a rather steady and marginal three to four related cases per year. On contemporaries' understanding of the relationship between infanticide, illegitimacy, and poverty, see Baldi, "L'assistenza alla maternita," 136–140; Maria Pia Casarini, "Maternità e infanticidio a Bologna: Fonti e linee di ricerca," *Quaderni Storici* 17, no. 1 (1982): 275–284; Prosperi, *Dare l'anima*, 71. Gregory Hanlon argues that, at least in rural Tuscany between the sixteenth and eighteenth centuries, infanticide was practiced even by married couples on a "not insignificant scale," Gregory Hanlon, "L'infanticidio di coppie sposate in Toscana nella prima età moderna," *Quaderni Storici* 38, no. 2 (2002): 467.

70 AST, *Sezione Reunite, Senato di Piemonte, Sentenze Criminali 1724–1802*, March 1772, also cited in Baldi, "L'assistenza alla maternita," 134.

71 Filippini, "Gli ozpizi," 400.

72 Ibid.

73 Léon Le Fort, *Des maternités: Étude sur les maternités et les institutions charitables d'accouchement à domicile, dans lesprincipaux états de l'Europe* (Paris, 1866), 141, quoted in Filippini, "Gli ozpizi," 400.

74 On contemporaries' understanding of the relationship among infanticide, illegitimacy, and poverty, see Baldi, "L'assistenza alla maternita," 121–178, 136–140.

75 These included: a modest main room with eight "curtained beds"; a small delivery chamber with a fireplace, in front of which were a handful of beds for laboring women; and a third room nearby to house the personal living quarters of the head midwife "so that both day and night she can promptly care for the women in labor." AOSG, "Memoriale per lo stabilimento di una sala per le donne gravide," 6 May 1728.

76 AOSG, Cat. 1, Cl. 3, fasc. 1, 1732.

77 AOSG, "Memoriale per lo stabilimento di una sala per le donne gravide," 6 May 1728.

78 Ibid.

79 Ibid.

80 ASMi, *Pii Luoghi, Parte Antica*, c. 389, "Istruzione delle Pia Casa degli Esposti, e Partorienti," 1781.

81 AOSG, "Memoriale per lo stabilimento di una sala per le donne gravide," 6 May 1728; while the 1728 document states that at seven months unmarried women should be permitted to enter the hospital, the regulations issued in 1732 amended this to eight months. Both allow for earlier admittance in the case of emergency.

82 Pullan, *Rich and Poor*, 155.

83 ASMi, *Luoghi Pii, Parte Antica*, c. 389, "Avviso prescritto intorno al metodo da Sua Maestà pel ricevimento delle Donne gravide nello Spedale di Santa Caterina alla Ruota," 20 September 1784.

84 Felice De Billi, *Sulla I.R. Scuola di Ostetricia ed Annesso Ospizio delle Partorienti* (Milano: Società degli Editori degli Annali Universali delle Scienze e dell'Industria, 1844), 14.

85 Eventually, these women were also required to have approval from the "Regulators of Poverty," a new committee instituted in each parish. ASMi, *Luoghi Pii, Parte Antica*, c. 389, "Istruzioni alla Giunta per gli Esposti, Gravide, e Partorienti," 1784.

86 ASMi, *Luoghi Pii, Parte Antica*, c. 389, "Avviso prescritto intorno al metodo." The only marked difference between women of the bottom two classes was that women of class three paid only half the normal fee in the event that they wished to abandon their child at the foundling home; further, they did not have the obligation to remain at Santa Caterina as a wetnurse. Women of class four paid no fee to leave a child but were required to serve as wetnurses.

87 AOSG, Cat. 1, Cl. 3, fasc. 1, 1732.

88 ASMi, *Luoghi Pii, Parte Antica*, c. 389, "Istruzione della Pia Casa degli Esposti, e Partorienti," 1781.

89 Decio, *Notizie storiche sulla ospitalità e didattica ostetrica Milanese*, 67.

90 AOSG, "Memoriale per lo stabilimento di una sala per le donne gravide," 6 May 1728.

91 AOSG, Cat. 1, Cl. 3, fasc. 1, 1732.

92 AOSG, "Memoriale per lo stabilimento di una sala per le donne gravide," 6 May 1728.

93 AOSG, "Memoriale per lo stabilimento di una sala per le donne gravide," 6 May 1728. This was amended in the official regulations released four years later, in 1732, when midwives were prohibited from drawing blood, especially without a surgeon or physician present. See AOSG, Cat. 1, Cl. 3, fasc. 1, 1732.

94 Decio, *Notizie storiche sulla ospitalità e didattica ostetrica Milanese*, 112.

95 AOSG, Cat. 1, Cl. 3, fasc. 1, 1732.

96 Chojnacka notes the important distinction that, while the women's refuges sought as did convents to create "a secluded environment of prayer, discipline, and contemplation," they differed from the latter in that the refuges' ultimate aim was to prepare the female inmates to reenter society. Chojnacka, "Charity and Community," 85.

97 ASMi, *Pii Luoghi, Parte Antica*, c. 389, "Istruzioni per la Giunta per gli Esposti, Gravide, e Partorienti," 1784.

98 Decio, *Notizie storiche sulla ospitalità e didattica ostetrica Milanese*, 111.

99 Ibid., 111.

100 Ibid., 112.

101 AST, *prima sezione, Materie Ecclesiastiche, Luoghi Pii di qua da Monti*, Mazzo 17, Fasc. 7.

102 Ibid.

103 Ibid., Fasc. 8.

104 Ibid.

105 Decio, *Notizie storiche sulla ospitalità e didattica ostetrica Milanese*, 111.

106 The infectious disease most associated with early maternity hospitals, puerperal fever, does not, however, seem to have been a problem in Italy during the eighteenth century. Decio notes that while the disease theoretically could have been present, the sheer lack of reference to any episodes of extreme morbidity and mortality among post-partum women makes this very unlikely. This absence may well be linked to the limited involvement of surgeons in these wards' day-to-day activity. Decio, *Notizie storiche sulla ospitalità e didattica ostetrica Milanese*, 106–107.

107 The mortality rate among foundlings in eighteenth-, and especially nineteenth-century Milan (when abandonment rates peaked) was higher than in most other large European foundling hospitals at the same time, an anomaly noted by contemporaries. See Volker Hunecke, *I Trovatelli di Milano: Bambini esposti e famiglie espositrici dal XVII al XIX secolo* (Bologna: Il Mulino, 1989).

108 Baldi, "L'assistenza alla maternita," 127.

109 Ibid.

110 Ibid.

4 Midwifery education and the politics of reproduction

Francesca Mazzuchelli, a peasant woman from Gallarate, a rural community about 40 kilometers northwest of Milan, was among the first class of midwives to be trained at the city's new midwifery school. Opened in 1767 in Milan's large central hospital, the *Ospedale Maggiore*, the midwifery school was the first of its kind in Austrian Lombardy. The reformers who had proposed the school were particularly intent on recruiting provincial women like Mazzuchelli, who they hoped would act as ambassadors, bringing to remote communities the new knowledge of childbirth gained in the city. Yet, despite her success at school (we are told that Francesca "gracefully completed her final exam"), Mazzuchelli's return home was met with disillusion and financial desperation. Instead of the expected benefits of formal education and official license, such as increased pay and a wider client base, Mazzuchelli found herself in a losing competition with two other midwives, Camilla Ceriana and Orsola Brambilla, both of whom had continued to practice without proper approvals in her absence. In fact, Mazzuchelli discovered upon her return that she was rarely called on as a midwife. Her economic prospects became so dire, according to a petition she wrote to the authorities in Milan, that she was unable to feed her large family.[1] Far from an isolated episode, Mazzuchelli's experience was one that was shared by many of the midwifery school's newly licensed graduates when they returned to their home communities. Rather than embrace this new corps of 'professional' midwives, many women shunned something they viewed with suspicion and doubt. Neither theoretical training nor an official license made much of an impact on women who judged the skill of their birth attendants by trusted recommendation earned through years of practice and intimate knowledge of the community. In fact, the continued operation of midwifery schools during the eighteenth century was often in question.

Although historians have been quick to highlight the gendered contests that resulted from efforts to medicalize childbirth, Francesca Mazzuchelli's story suggests that the conflicts that emerged between women over who could claim legitimacy and authority in this area were just as important. Particularly in Italy, where male midwives were virtually non-existent, tensions ran not only along gender, but also along class and geographical lines.

Moving away from a strict focus on gendered conflict reveals the complex relationships that existed among midwives, mothers, wetnurses, and other community members. Not only did professional and traditional midwives challenge one another for the right to manage local births, but mothers made decisions about who to care for them that were not always in line with larger state efforts to regulate and professionalize the practice of midwifery. Moreover, parish priests, often seen by state and medical authorities as critical liasions with local communities, might choose to support long-practicing but informally trained midwives, despite efforts to replace this group with formally educated midwives.

This chapter considers the emergence of formal midwifery schools in the second half of the eighteenth century and the multiple sources of resistance that challenged the existence of such institutions. In the preceding chapter, I explored the societal conditions that provided the imperative for public maternity assistance in Italy during the eighteenth century. This chapter keeps these concerns in mind while examining in detail the quite differently motivated efforts by both state officals and medical men to professionalize midwifery and base its practice on scientific principles. Whereas maternity wards in eighteenth-century Italy represented new institutional solutions to long-standing pressures surrounding shame, honor, and illegitimacy, the programs of formal midwifery instruction instituted in the second half of the century were inspired by different concerns. Midwifery schools reflected the belief that it was the state's responsibility to involve itself in public health. They also advanced the interests of administrators who sought to utilize the biopower of subject populations to buttress their states in international competition. Although maternity wards in Italy had initially been insulated from efforts by medical men to bring childbirth within the orbit of professional medicine, midwifery schools aimed to do just that. Even though in Italy it was generally assumed that female midwives would remain the primary birth attendants, officials and medical practitioners argued increasingly that childbirth should be understood as a medical process that could be approached through theoretical knowledge and formalized standards of practice. Networks of midwifery schools directed by male professors trained in anatomy, surgery, and obstetrics could provide female midwives with the proper clinical and theoretical training it was believed they lacked.

Populationism and pronatalism

The governmental push to professionalize midwives in eighteenth-century Italy was articulated in the language of the public good and the spirited pronatalism of that era's political and economic theory. Before Malthus, European states generally viewed procreation as "an unqualified political benefit," a political arithmetic supported by the belief that the strength of a nation rested on the vitality and growth of its population.[2] This emphasis on procreativity as the path to productivity had far-reaching consequences through policies aimed at regulationg the reproductive and marital lives of everyday Europeans. European states' pronatalist efforts in the eighteenth century "drew private sexual behavior into the public arena, judging its worth not on the hallowed teachings of the Church but on the modern criterion of productivity."[3] In addition to various incentives and penalties applied to divorce, illegitimacy, abortion, infanticide, and procreativity, European states also became increasingly interested in ways to make childbirth itself safer. Thus, at the same time that medical men were advancing the newborn field of obstetrics at the expense of traditional midwifery, midwives came under particular scrutiny by state governments as the perceived weak links in the preservation of invaluable maternal and infant lives.

With widespread concerns about the state of childbirth assistance, administrators in cities such as Turin, Milan, Florence, Bologna, and Venice raised the prospect of formal educational programs to train midwives.[4] As early as 1749, Ludovico Antonio Muratori had recommended in his *Della Pubblica Felicità* that because midwives had a responsibility that was "of such public import for the well-being of communities," it was the rightful duty of the city or its ruler to designate a physician or other person sufficiently trained in anatomy and obstetrics to direct a school for their instruction.[5] Only then could states circumvent the severe consequences caused by the "ignorance of unlearned midwives, and the savage audacity of many inexpert surgeons."[6] Reformers argued, further, that educational efforts should be directed at provincial women, "since the most urgent need arises in the countryside," where, it was believed, midwives were especially inept.[7] An extended discussion of the proposal for a midwifery school in Milan in the 1760s clearly illustrates these concerns about governmental responsibility and populaton growth:

> There is no doubt that in countries especially fertile, and abounding in the things necessary for survival, the happiness of the state grows together with the number of people inhabiting it. . . . Legislators in all times have always efficaciously sought to increase the population of their respective countries, at times through punishing bachelordom with public disapproval, at others [through] moderating the excessive luxury of marital dowries, and at still others by awarding those who bring to the world a great number of children. Now, a powerful means apart from those mentioned for obtaining the same end is to assure, to the extent possible, to make childbirth a happy event, so that fewer future subjects are lost, and as many fertile mothers as possible are conserved for the State; therefore it can be seen in our time many Princes who, for the happiness of their subjects, and for the interest of the public good, have adopted all of the most valuable means with which to efficiently promote the advancement of the Art of Obstetrics.[8]

State interventions to promote maternal welfare thus symbolized both the *illuministi*'s novel conception of the public good and the harnessing of what Foucault has termed 'biopower' through the extension of state power over the physical bodies of subject persons.[9]

Such initiatives were reinforced by reports, particularly from rural areas, that painted a likely exaggerated canvas of abuses and ineptitude among practicing midwives. Muratori, for instance, wrote of the "ignorance and inexpertness of midwives" that led to high infant and maternal mortality.[10] Similarly, in 1766, a Milanese official tasked with surveying practices in local villages described with alarm the presence of midwives who were "completely ignorant and impudently bold . . . undertaking operations," with the use of prohibited surgical instruments and hooks.[11] Critics also alleged that midwives hesitated far too long in emergency situations to call in a surgeon or physician for assistance and that they were susceptible, as women, to over-excitement and rash behavior during the chaotic time of labor.[12] Apart from these critiques of midwives' practical skills, both state and ecclesiastical officials bemoaned the unruly persistence of many folk traditions, superstitious beliefs, and heterodox childbirth rituals perpetuated by both mothers and midwives. Finally, many administrators distrusted midwives' close ties with their communities, fearing that they would choose loyalty to their clients over their obligation to report illegitimate pregnancies or, even worse, that they would assist in the abortion, abandonment, or murder of an unwanted child.[13]

Although a patchwork of medical licensing requirements for midwives was in place by the eighteenth century, a report by the Milanese medical faculty in 1767 was probably not inaccurate in its claims that "for the most part, the priest of the village selects the oldest woman, or the least hampered by a husband and children [to become midwife], he instructs [her] in the formula of baptism, and then publishes her name at the altar," so that she will be known publicly as midwife.[14] Indeed, midwives in the mid-eighteenth century learned their trade much as they had for years, through apprenticeship and firsthand experience with relatives, friends, and neighbors.[15] Legitimacy derived foremost from a midwife's long and intimate experience within her community and accepted, if informal, standards of practice. In cities, midwives might be subjected to slightly stricter oversight than in the countryside, but the situation there was by no means uniform either. In Milan, some midwives touted licenses from the Milanese *protomedico*, others from the College of Barbers, and still others displayed outdated certificates that had been issued to their own mothers or even more distant relatives. This multiplicity of potential authorizing bodies, both secular and religious, had created a situation characterized by indeterminancy over what exactly constituted the proper certification for a practicing midwife. Even where midwives were subject to licensing by medical faculties or public health offices, approval generally rested on the passage of an examination rather than on formal or standardized instruction. Moreover, licensing was notoriously hard to enforce, especially outside of major cities. State-run midwifery schools, through which aspirant midwives would have to pass in order to be licensed, provided eighteenth-century governments an appealing solution both to concerns about infant and maternal mortality and endemic problems related to the regulation of medical practitioners in their territories.

A school for midwives

In Milan, while authorities were largely in agreement by mid-century that some kind of formal midwifery instruction was needed, there was little agreement on what shape this kind of training should take. By this time, the field of obstetrics had been widely accepted as a discrete branch of surgery. University courses where training surgeons and physicians could gain a predominantly theoretical knowledge of reproduction were established in many Italian medical schools during the second half of the century. Yet, the relationship between university obstetrics and the everyday practice of midwifery was far from straightforward. For one, should midwives be trained in theory as well as pratice? And who exactly should be in charge of midwifery instruction?[16] The question therefore remained of who should be responsible for educating midwives and where should such instruction take place.

It was not only the fact that obstetrics was a relatively newly recognized part of the medical curriculum that raised questions about how to train female midwives. Because the students of any midwifery school would necessarily be women, both state officials and members of the medical faculties agreed that, by virtue of their gender, they couldn't be instructed or examined in the same manner as male students. The director of the medical faculty in Milan, Giuseppe Cicognini, mused that "dealing with women, it doesn't seem appropriate (*decente*) to subject them to the examination [administered by] the College . . . as is done with surgeons."[17] Other reformers worried whether women would be able to handle the rigors of classroom education and theoretical study at all. Responding to an early outline for the midwifery school in Milan, Bernardino Moscati, the head surgeon at the *Ospedale Maggiore* and soon-to-be first director of the midwifery program, noted his skepticism that "coarse," uneducated women from provincial communities would ever succeed in mastering both the theory and practical skills he believed a trained midwife required.[18]

The fact that many reformers saw formal midwifery instruction as a remedy primarily for abuses occurring in rural areas added another dimension to the question of what shape such instruction might take.[19] Midwifery schools would most practically be located in major cities in proximity to large hopsitals or universities but would have to house provincial women for the duration of their studies.[20] As state chancellor Wenzel Anton von Kaunitz reminded his colleagues in Milan, the aspirant midwives they would be dealing with would be "for the most part peasants . . . needed for labor in the fields, and for the raising and education of children."[21] Women in such communities could not be expected simply to up and leave their families or farms for long periods.[22] Not to mention that such women would be traveling far from home without male supervision, meaning that concerted efforts would have to be made to ensure that the housing of a number of young, rural women at the behest of the state would not result in embarrassment or scandal.

The decision that many governments took to house midwifery schools in hospitals alongside foundlings and maternity patients reflected the symbiotic nature of these populations. In Turin, for instance, where midwifery instruction was initially in the hands of the head midwife of the maternity ward, the vast majority of training consisted of caring for the ward's pregnant patients.[23] Although twice yearly anatomical demonstrations by the hospital's head surgeon were officially prescribed in the midwifery school's bylaws, these seem to have fallen off quickly, as did the written and theoretical instruction the ward's first head midwife was supposed to impart to trainees based on her own training at the *Hôtel Dieu* in Paris.[24] Significantly, when the generally disliked French midwife was replaced, her successor was a former foundling who had grown up in the confines of the hospital and who had continued on as a birth attendant in the maternity ward when she came of age.[25] Moreover, in the same way that foundling homes came to rely on newly delivered women from maternity wards to supply milk, midwifery schools benefited from close proximity to public maternity wards and their steady supply of patients.

The extent to which such bedside training represented a true clinicalization of the maternity ward is questionable for this period. In Turin, where the public maternity ward was managed by an entirely female staff with only very minimal oversight by a male surgeon and physician, the hallmarks of clinical training – anatomical pathology, statistical analysis, increased use of diagnostic techniques – do not seem to have been emphasized, at least during the eighteenth century. Only in the nineteenth century, under the French administration, does evidence exist that midwives were trained to take systematic case histories, to follow patients from pregnancy through their post-partum recovery, and to keep detailed records of each case. Even at this date, training was entirely restricted to female midwives, though with much greater oversight by a head surgeon who provided the theoretical lessons at the school and supervised clinical activities. In other words, midwifery schools might sustain in an institutional setting relatively traditional modes of instruction.

In Milan, by contrast, Bernardino Moscati suggested housing a midwifery school alongside the *Quarto delle Balie* in the *Ospedale Maggiore* precisely because of the accessibility to pregnant patients in the maternity ward and the availability of human material for anatomical study.[26] According to Moscati, "nowhere else [wa]s there available the amount of cadavers of pregnant women, and fetuses, or the frequency of occasions to observe the many situations . . . related to the theory, and practice of childbirth."[27] Midwifery instruction in Milan was thus based from the beginning on the principles of clinical education and pathological anatomy that would become hallmarks of modern medical practice.[28]

This fact also illustrates the point that while midwifery schools might benefit from the availability of maternity patients, they did not necessarily share the maternity wards' concerns regarding issues of shame and honor. In fact, when Lombard officials were discussing proposals for a second midwifery school, this time near the university in Pavia, the Lombard medical director Johann Peter Frank asserted that "the object of the Pavia house is not to give place to pregnant women in search of seclusion, but to accept pregnant women for the instruction of [student] midwives."[29] In this way, midwifery schools can be seen as important drivers, particularly by the turn of the ninteenth century, of a changing kind of maternity care in Italy, one that was less concerned with protecting female honor than it was with the advancement of clinical medicine.

Recruitment

From the outset, officials intended not only to educate midwives but to reshape the social profile of the profession. In Milan, circulars sent to local parishes detailed the desired qualities of potential students: "other than good, and regular health, and stature," students should exhibit "a certain natural intelligence, and the capacity . . . to learn," not to mention "a natural docility and acute discretion."[30] Ideal candidates for the school were notably young, between 22 and 32, in sharp contrast to the advanced age of many practicing midwives. Initially, it was hoped these women would be married (with their husband's written consent), or widows without young children, but by the 1790s even unmarried women were welcomed.[31] The women were expected to dress modestly and "have shoes and a sufficient store of linens."[32] Officials explicitly forbade women deemed to be of a "scandalous life, or those who [were] wives or widows of husbands who exercise[d] infamous trades."[33] In Venice, prospective midwives were warned to refrain from all "superstitious words, gestures, or means," indicating that lingering concerns about religious orthodoxy and women's infringement on the sacred continued to plague Italian towns well into the eighteenth century.[34] In some cases, parish priests were even requested to speak to new students before they departed and provide them with "some benevolent advice adapted to the task ahead of [them], especially with respect to prompt obedience, pleasant modesty, and Christian piety."[35]

The optimal midwife therefore had to possess a combination of physicial, intellectual, and moral qualities suggestive of the sometimes delicate situations a childbirth attendant might confront in an early modern society which hinged around sexual and familial honor and which policed illegitimacy with severity. She also had to be upstanding and suitably tractable so as not to cause scandal while boarding far from home. Despite the fact that many practicing midwives were mature women, familiar with their communities and with a long record of assistance at births, officials seem to have targeted young women precisely because they would be less steeped in the lay traditions and beliefs surrounding childbirth.

The expectation that the candidates be able to read and write proved to be a perpetual stumbling block in recruiting students. Bernardino Moscati thought these skills were essential. He was doubtful that an entirely verbal instruction "could . . . amount to great advantage, either because of the frequent repetition of the same things [which would be] necessary, or for the easy forgetting of these."[36] With similar reasoning, midwifery trainees in Turin were expected to know "at least how to read, so that they could profit from those lessons that will be given in writing and explained."[37] Even though the women who entered midwifery schools ultimately exhibited a range of skills, literacy, and experience, the aforementioned concerns voiced by professors help to underscore the novelty that these institutions represented at the time. Although a handful of notable women, such as Laura Bassi (1711–1787), Cristina Roccati (1734–1814), and Maria Pellegrina Amoretti (1756–1787), earned university degrees in early modern Italy, higher education was something that was, except in rare cases, closed to women.[38] A license from a midwifery school was not a universty degree, but it was a peculiarity at the time: evidence of a rigorous educational program that required both theoretical and practical training and distinct from almost any other occupational certification open to women.

When midwifery schools opened in cities such as Milan, Venice, Padua, Bologna, and Florence in the second half of the eighteenth century, administrators found that identiyfing young, literate women of good backgrounds to train as midwives was more difficult then they would have hoped. In fact, most schools struggled to find more than a handful of women willing to enroll, particularly during these schools' first years of operation. The fact that many of the midwifery schools were most interested in recruiting women from the countryside seems to have only exacerbated the issue, as such women were hesitant to make long journeys and leave families, dependent children, and farms for long periods. A curate from the village of Binasco, near Milan, wrote in response to the state's request for a woman to attend the city's new midwifery school that

> Having made every due diligence in all of the communities of my delegation, up until now in none of these has there been found a woman who wants to come to the Venerable *Ospital Maggiore* of Milan to learn such a calling (*virtù*) . . . already in all of the communities there is a woman who practices this art, but all these persons are unlearned (*grossolane*), such that not one knows how to read . . . but nevertheless in that pious practice the midwives know what they do, and surely all the women who are served by them are content with them.[39]

In the parish of San Donato, about 10 kilometers southeast of Milan, the local civic authorities encountered a similar lack of interest. No woman could be found who wished to enroll in the course in Milan. The woman currently serving as midwife, a 45-year-old widow named Anna Maria Maiocca, was perfectly "ready to submit to any exam, but not to take residence at the hospital, having herself children who need constant care."[40] In Vaprio, on the Adda River, the response again echoed the earlier sentiments: although the city council had already nominated one woman for the midwifery school, and sent her name back to Milan, the community was forced to send an apologetic note soon after. Apparently, the elected woman, though regretful, "absolutely did not want to move [to Milan] . . . regardless of persuasions made by the deputies [of the *Estimo*]."[41] In other cases, communities reported back that they simply could not find any women fitting the description in the circular.[42] The potential candidates were too old in some cases, unable to read or write in others, or had never practiced midwifery before.[43] At the same time, the words of the Biansco curate suggest that there was not major concern over the lack of qualified or interested candidates. These provinical midwives apparently demonstrated an acceptable combination of moral uprightness and practical skill to serve their communities without much concern on the part of local authorities.

The tepid response to Milan's recruitment efforts was not unique. When a school was opened in Como in 1791, then director Giuseppe Nessi reported back to Johann Peter Frank that, despite a circular issued to the nearby communities advertising the school, "not one woman, either from the city or from the countryside" presented herself for the lessons.[44] In the Veneto as well, the various challenges posed by extended travel away from home and family, overlaid by suspicions about the moral correctness and necessity of such training, more than tempered any enthusiasm the midwifery courses might have been expected to generate. In one case, the parish priest of Castelbaldo, a community about 55 kilometers southwest of Padua, wrote to the Venetian health magistracy that he had tirelessly tried to persuade the midwife Domenica Ferrari to attend the new midwifery course in Padua, only to be repeatedly rebuffed. Domenica cited her "poor health, her numerous family, her miserable [economic] condition, and her inexperience in reading and writing" as reasons for her disinterest.[45] A more "lively" woman, also named Domenica, was the priest's next choice. While Domenica Feltivato was healthier and could read, she refused the nomination as well, arguing that her family was sustained more by her husband's labor than by the meager earnings she received from her practice as a midwife.[46]

Although many women cited financial hurdles, a husband could also present a potential impediment, even if a woman did wish to attend a midwifery school. For instance, the Venetian woman Teresa Rizzi said she was honored to be selected to attend the midwifery course in Padua yet could not because of her husband's steadfast objections. Although it is unclear on exactly what grounds Rizzi's husband's refusal was based, it is likely that he found the long absence of his wife undesirable. It is possible that he was also opposed to the anatomical instruction that would have been a part of Rizzi's training at the new midwifery school. Years later, Rizzi wrote to the Venetian Health Board upon her husband's death, requesting a dispensation from attending school in order to be licensed as a midwife. At that point, she was advanced in age and did not want to undertake an entire course; however, she had clearly continued to practice as a midwife without license. She wrote that she was confident in her abilities and ready to undertake any kind of exam as soon as possible, given her urgent need for a source of income to support herself.[47]

In other cases, parishes reported no candidates for midwifery schools, though for rather different reasons. The local priest from Carceri, located about 30 kilometers southwest of Padua, wrote that with 250 families in his parish, some 7,000 in the immediate surrounding territories, and only one midwife able to travel (two elderly women also practiced but because of age had very limited mobility), he felt he simply could not put his community at risk by removing the one childbirth expert available.[48] Even when a woman could be convinced to enroll in a midwifery school, her eventual attendance was still questionable, at least according to a priest from Villanuova. After much effort, he wrote:

> I was able to persuade Angela Molesina, midwife in my care, to trans-port herself to Padua to be instructed in the art of Obstetrics . . . putting in front of her eyes the obligation of her conscience since, not having the required knowledge in her profession, she is in danger of making great errors in prejudice of innocent infants. For the moment she is persuaded to embrace this encounter, as long as she remains stable in her opinion, of which I cannot assure you, since I know the female sex to be very changeable.[49]

In addition to appealing to her sense of morality, the priest had also made the argument to Angela that her increased knowledge would enhance her reputation and thus her economic circumstances. At least one of these motivators was apparently sufficient to convince the woman, who did ultimately enroll in the Padua midwifery school in 1774 without chang-ing her mind.

At the other extreme were communities that lacked midwives entirely or had only an insufficient number and desperately wanted women trained in the new midwifery school. For instance, the parish priest of Cologna, about 46 kilometers west of Padua, wrote to that city's health board in 1780 lamenting the "disorders born even recently due to the inexperience, and lack of able midwives to serve the numerous population" of the town and its surrounding territories.[50] Cologna had already sent one woman to the midwifery school, but a single trained midwife proved unable to han-dle the demands of the entire community. Thus, the parish priest entreated the health board to accept a second candidate, Lucia Regazzi, to the school as well.[51]

Although resistance to the new midwifery schools was widespread, it is clear that some women – or at least their communities – were open to the opportunities such schools presented. Whether these women were persuaded by spirited priests, or enticed by the prospect of living in the city, or by the expected professional and economic benefits of an official license, it is often impossible to know. Yet, for women like Catterina Bramano, a 29-year-old widow from the parish of Incino, in Lombardy, who had never practiced midwifery before and whose two children were already old enough to be self-sufficient, the anticipation of travel and the eventual financial security of a paid occupation were evidently appealing. In fact, given the age requirements, many enrollees to the new midwifery schools were similar to Catterina Bramano in that they had never practiced midwifery before. Others arrived with limited experience. For several related reasons a community's most senior midwife was rarely selected. Not only was she likely to be older, and often unable or unwilling to travel because of her advanced age, but also as the only midwife around, she was an irreplaceable resource in her community. The absence of such a woman for many months or even several years was unthinkable. Furthermore, it was apparently perplexing to many such women, who had been practicing as midwives for years, if not decades, that they should be expected to travel long distances and live in a foreign city in order "to learn" a trade they had clearly already been authorized to practice by long-established consensus from their neighbors and parish priest. The schools seem to have had better luck over time attracting women with little experience in midwifery, and therefore with less sense that they were being forced to relearn skills that they had already mastered.

Curriculum

Based upon the principles of obstetrics, the curricula developed for the new midwifery schools emphasized both practical skills and the study of theory and anatomy. Above all, such courses aimed to elevate the "practices" of midwifery into a discrete science. Courses typically began with instruction in theory and then advanced to practical skills, rehearsed first on machines and cadavers, and eventually performed on live patients. Often, these courses employed one of the obstetrical texts written in this period, and thus often followed a similar structure to the texts described in Chapter 2. During the theoretical component of the course, midwives might learn about the processes of generation, the causes of sterility and abortion, the signs of pregnancy and of false pregnancy, multiple births, the causes of a variety of birth complications, and, finally, problems that might arise after birth in both the post-partum woman and the newborn child. Students were also exposed to a systematic instruction in anatomy based on drawings, models, and cadavers. During the practical part of the course, students were trained in manual skills on obstetrical machines and at the bedside of patients.

Influenced by popular understandings of the human body as governed by mechanical processes, eighteenth-century obstetrics argued that childbirth could be reduced to a set of universal axioms and predictable outcomes based on certain criteria, such as pelvic size. The new midwifery courses followed this logic and encouraged students to think about childbirth in a systematic way. For instance, the midwifery curriculum Bernardino Moscati devised in Milan carefully differentiated birth situations that were normal from those that were difficult or preternatural, divided labor into stages, and taught midwives to predict potential problems by comparing a patient's pelvic shape and size to that of the fetus. Based on the mechanical understanding of childbirth he had learned while working with the French obstetrician André Levret in Paris, Moscati was adamant that the successful management of birth began with a mastery of anatomy. A well-trained midwife must know "the exact anatomy of the parts that serve in conception, [the] bones, muscles, [and] veins." Then, she must "master the mechanism of birth: the directions, pushes, forces . . . passages, stages," and the "changes that the [anatomical] parts of a woman undergo during birth."[52]

To this end, midwifery schools made particular use of the most up-to-date obstetrical atlases compiled by some of the era's most famous obstetricians, such as William Smellie and William Hunter. Moscati recommended displaying on the walls of the midwifery school drawings of "the gravid uterus, and positions of the fetus" as depicted in the works of "[Johann Georg] Roederer, Hunter, [and] Smellie." Beneath each illustration would be a written description with "an explanation suitably adapted to the need of the midwives."[53] Moscati hoped his student midwives in Milan, particularly those with minimal literacy, would take advantage of these instructional aides, observing the images at their leisure and according to their own ability. At the same time, such images underscored the school's emphasis on observation and visual learning, a hallmark of the new clinical medicine emerging in the late eighteenth century. In contrast to traditional midwifery's hands-on training, the use of anatomical illustrations reflected the "belief that visibility itself can reveal the 'facts'" and reinforced obstetrical knowledge as, above all, "a 'seen' knowledge."[54]

Midwifery schools also emphasized more direct anatomical training, both through attendance at dissections and through the study of prepared anatomical specimens. Anatomical demonstrations and prepared wet and dry specimens furthered the aforementioned project of making visible the internal structures of the female body and the fetus in utero. Collections of specimens also advanced the reputations of their owners and facilitated research that gained international attention for professors such as Vincenzo Malacarne and Ambrogio Bertrandi when they published their findings in journals or presented them to professional societies. In such collections, students might view preserved fetuses at various developmental stages, as well as those with pathologies, such as spina bifida. These kinds of collections also highlighted various examples of "monstrous" births – such as fetuses lacking eyes, a nose, or other body parts – alongside other more traditional obstetrical specimens. One catalogue for the obstetrical collection in Milan lists, for example, "a fetus of seven months arranged to show the origins of the vessels of the umbilical cord, the urethra, the urinary bladder, etc."[55]

At the *Ospedale Maggiore*, Moscati enthusiastically wrote about the opportunities students had to

> Observe in practice the most interesting cases which the large size of our hospital and the great number of patients produce yearly, so that the women were able comfortably to see in life the *mole* (false conception), mutations, the site of the gravid uterus; the substance, the joints, the shape, the natural size of the placenta, [and] the dissection of many cadavers.[56]

Students thus gained a thorough anatomical knowledge of the pregnant body, but in a way that often emphasized pathology. For obvious reasons, available cadavers and anatomical specimens typically resulted from labors that had ended disastrously. Moreover, as Pietro Sografi, midwifery instructor in Padua, noted, the dissection of a woman not pregnant could serve only to demonstrate normal anatomy and not the changes the body underwent during pregnancy.[57] In Venice, Sebastiano Rizzo unapologetically hoped that each class of midwives would be able to attend an anatomy of at least one pregnant or post-partum woman who had died of complications. During these occasions, the students would examine both the external and internal anatomy related to generation, as well as practice certain skills, such as inserting a syringe into the bladder to extract urine in the case of retention, and supporting the uterus with a pessary to correct a prolapse.[58] Thus, even in the context of teaching relatively standard skills, there were lingering reminders that childbirth could easily turn pathological.

Although midwifery instruction did value the visualization of internal structures, touch and the cultivation of manual skills were also central to learning in Italy's midwifery schools. Instructors employed a variety of obstetrical models and machines to help students coordinate their visualization of internal structures with their tactile sense of the placement and movement of the fetus in utero. Constructed from a range of materials, including leather, cloth, glass, clay, and wax, obstetrical reproductions had been employed since at least the seventeenth century in Europe to aid the instruction of midwives and surgeons. They varied significantly in size, construction, and complexity, though many incorporated detachable body parts and deliverable fetuses, and some were mechanized, with dilating uteri and shifting fluids. On models and machines, midwives could practice manual skills, such as podalic version, and become familiar with a more scientific and standardized vocabulary related to touch. As Sografi explained, series of models, like those in the extensive collection at the midwifery school in Padua, allowed students to see the changes the pregnant body – down to the changes of the umbilical vein and artery before and after birth – underwent over time and to compare side by side different types of potential complications. Students could both see and feel the ways in which various kinds of abnormalities – a pelvis distorted by rickets, a fetus with an enlarged head – could block the normal progression of a labor.[59] As Lucia Dacome points out, obstetrical models "provide[d] a comprehensive overview of the world of generation . . . a visual and material archive of pregnancy and childbirth where the models' orderly arrangement promised to turn the complex and mysterious domain of childbirth into a distinctly accessible site of learning."[60]

The most extensive collection of obstetrical models in mid–eighteenth-century Italy belonged to the Bolognese obstetrician, Giovanni Antonio Galli.[61] By the early 1750s, Galli could boast that he owned some 170 anatomical models, which he used to instruct midwives and surgeons privately out of his home.[62] Later in the century, Luigi Calza's collection of models in the obstetrical cabinet at Padua, many of which were made by modelers

Figure 4.1 Obstetrical models used by Giovanni Antonio Galli. Palazzo Poggi, Bologna.

Source: Elena Manente.

trained in Bologna, would rival the extent of Galli's.[63] The Bolognese models, at least twenty of which were produced by the renowned wax modeling husband-wife team of Giovanni Manzolini and Anna Morandi Manzolini, were derived directly from drawings made during the dissection of female reproductive structures.[64] In addition to wax and clay models, Galli also incorporated at least one obstetrical machine in his teaching.[65] Distinct from the clay and wax models, which tended to be limited to disembodied wombs, Galli's machine comprised a torso with legs cut abruptly at the upper thigh. The machine's pelvis was composed of wood, while its uterus, sized to a full-term pregnancy, featured a glass womb. This most distinctive feature of Galli's machine allowed for students to view a stuffed leather fetal doll in various positions in the womb, and observe as Galli performed the proper procedures to manage various situations. In time, the students themselves would practice these maneuvers as Galli observed and corrected.

As Lucia Dacome has eloquently described, the most spectacular aspect of Galli's obstetrical instruction was his practice of testing midwives on the machine blindfolded. These moments, Dacome writes, "combined training and surveillance with a striking performance. By blindfolding the midwives, Galli could downplay their visual skills and, at the same time, subordinate their tactual expertise to his own visual control."[66] In this way, the use of the obstetrical machine validated touch as essential to obstetrical practice

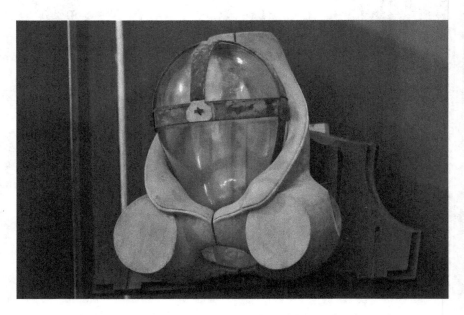

Figure 4.2 Giovanni Antonio Galli's obstetrical machine, mid-eighteenth century.

Source: Courtesy of Museo di Palazzo Poggi – Systema Museale di Ateneo – Alma Mater Studiorum University of Bologna, Bologna, Italy.

yet maintained a (gendered) hierarchy that placed sight at the pinnacle of the senses. Galli was also recreating the drama of birth with new protagonists. While the mother herself had been subordinated and silenced – reduced to nothing more than a torso – the midwife became the figure under scrutiny, acting strictly by touch and memory, the professor the protagonist guiding events to their successful conclusion.

An even more remarkable obstetrical machine was commissioned by Vincenzo Malacarne in 1791 in anticipation of the opening of a midwifery school in Pavia.[67] Quite distinct from Galli's, the Pavia obstetrical machine featured a wholly embodied woman.[68] The life-like model, which had an abdomen and external genital parts that were partially elastic and could distend to a point, was accompanied by two fetal dolls. The Florentine obstetrician Giuseppe Galletti, who designed the machine, emphasized the importance of its interior devices, which caused the uterus to contract, such that a student attempting to reposition the fetal doll would feel resistance. Most striking was the incorporation of eyes that moved when excessive pressure was applied to the genital area, producing an effect that, according to Galletti, seemed to bring the "automaton to life."[69] This unique inclusion, while at first glance an eccentric or farcical addition, seems to have been made in earnest.[70] Although this feature clearly rendered the machine a potentially sexual and sexualized object – one that Malacarne felt compelled to cover in the name of modesty – it also reconnected the ostensibly mechanical processes of birth to the rational, embodied subject of the mother.

Feminist historians of science have been particularly critical of obstetrical machines, arguing that by distancing instruction from actual labor, they helped to facilitate the entrance of male practitioners into the management of childbirth when they were limited by convention or law from attending normal deliveries. Obstetrical machines have also been accused of sanitizing delivery and engaging in a project of maternal erasure. It is true that obstetrical machines (Malacarne's machine excluded) tended to "concentrate on the parts of generation and the womb at the expense of the whole body," mirroring the erasure of the pregnant woman's holistic role in her own labor perpetuated by mechanistic theories of childbirth that emphasized the womb's almost independent activity.[71]

While there is certainly some truth in these criticisms, reducing obstetrical models to a tool in a gendered game of control over childbirth is too simplistic. For one, in Italy, obstetrical models were used as much for the instruction of female midwives as they were for male practitioners. Moreover, obstetrical models presented a number of legitimate advantages for instruction in midwifery. Professors such as Galli, Moscati, and Malacarne praised models for their capacity to demonstrate comparative anatomy and to depict temporal change in a single space. Midwives familiar with judging changes in breast size, vaginal wetness, or the dilation of a cervix could easily grasp the usefulness of seeing such changes side by side and being able to compare the body's transformations at different stages of pregnancy.

For both male and female students, it was believed that training in a calm atmosphere where procedures could be repeated under the careful instruction of a professor was the most humane way to teach the manual skills required of midwives and surgeons.[72] To protect women who took recourse to public maternity hospitals from the prying eyes of trainees and the torture of repeated procedures, the public health expert Johann Peter Frank argued that obstetrical models were a necessity in the training of midwives and surgeons.

At least one Italian woman capitalized on the great interest in obstetrical machines in this period. Lucia Landi, a midwife from Siena, petitioned Grand Duke Pietro Leopoldo in 1774 for permission to sell two obstetrical machines of her own invention that aimed to instruct students in how to perform operations "to extract the foetus from the womb."[73] Although Landi's petition languished for years before finally being approved in 1786, her designs were apparently so well received in Siena that even male surgical students pushed for the machines to be made available as soon as possible. According to Francesca Vannozzi, Landi's machine may have indeed had a great impact on obstetrical training in the city, if it is the same to appear in the 1862 inventory of the school's *Gabinetto di Chirurgia Operatoria* (Cabinet of Operative Surgery). The inventory describes a machine consisting of "a woman without legs or chest, but with a pelvis lined with hide [*pezze al naturale*], and with a foldable foetus also of skin [*pelle*]."[74] In any case, Landi's example shows that women, too, might embrace the possibilities presented by obstetrical machines to advance their careers.

At the conclusion of their course, students generally faced some kind of comprehensive exam before receiving an official midwifery license. In Venice, to be eligible to sit for the final exam, the candidate had to submit a signed certificate from the director of the midwifery school attesting to her capacity and regular attendance, a certificate from the anatomical instructor,[75] and a certificate from an approved midwife attesting to two years of apprenticeship.[76] The exam itself was to be overseen by a health commissioner (*provveditore alla sanità*), the *protomedico*, priors of the two colleges of physicians and surgeons, and two licensed midwives. In Pavia, the final exam consisted of two parts, one verbal, the other practical. The first, delivered in equal parts by the dean of faculty at the University of Pavia, the professor of obsetrics, and two professors of surgery knowledgeable in obsterics, covered a wide range of topics, including female anatomy, the marks of virginity and defloration, the signs of pregnancy and of false pregnancy, the signs and progress of labor, normal fetal presentation, and various kinds of malpresentation and what to do in each circumstance, what to do after the birth, and how to perform a baptism. For the practical exam, the student midwife would select three tickets from a large container; each ticket indicated a fetal presentation. The professor would then prepare an obstetrical machine according to each ticket and the student would have to perform the necessary operation to correctly manage the delivery. Examples might include a breach presentation, the delivery of twins, or how to perform fetal version. Students were expected to verbalize their actions and decision making as well as to answer questions posed by the instructor.[77]

Expectations and realities

As already mentioned, the proponents of midwifery schools in eighteenth-century Italy had a distinct vision of the kind of women they believed should become trained midwives. Young and literate, exposed to the most scientific and up-to-date instructional methods, the professional midwife would be an expression of the Enlightened state's active involvement in public health. The goal of focusing training on women from the countryside was ultimately to extend that involvement into even the remotest areas of the state. In practice, however, midwifery education was tempered by the realities of low recruitment and unmatched expectations. Out of sixty-one women selected to attend the first session of the Milanese midwifery school, only forty-five were actually present at the school's official opening on 26 November 1767. These women's average age was 34, much older than hoped. Fifteen were widows and the remainder married women. They displayed a range of practical experience, and, in contrast to the school's emphatic insistence on literacy, many could not read or write well or at all.[78] Five of the women left before the end of December, and at the end of the year only twenty-four out of the starting forty-five were approved to practice and presented with a license.[79] Those women who had practiced midwifery to some extent prior to school proved, unsurprisingly, to be the most successful, although they tended to be older than the reformers had hoped.[80]

Lengthy programs of study also proved difficult for many women to complete. At the most basic level, attendance at school might represent an untenable financial and familial burden for rural women or those with small children. In Venice, Sebastiano Rizzo complained, for instance, that some women enrolled over and over again in the midwifery course (at the state's expense) for as long as ten years or more because demands at home prevented them from faithfully attending the lessons.[81] In other cases, even adverse weather during rainy or cold seasons might prevent students from attending lessons.[82] A report from Venice issued in 1786 was not unusual in noting a chronic lack of attendance at the school, where rarely were six students in attendance, and more commonly only two or three.[83]

Midwifery professors also discovered they had constantly to adapt planned curricula to accommodate a number of unexpected challenges. In his reflections on the first year of school in Milan, director Bernardino Moscati noted the obstacles represented by his students' widely varying backgrounds and degrees of preparation. Some were "completely inexpert in this profession," while "others had already a certain degree of instruction, which the practice of some years, and the training under some older midwife had given them."[84] As a result, "even in the same school and under uniform direction," the relative benefit of training to individual women was uneven.[85] Similarly, Sebastiano Rizzo reported variable results among his Venetian students who ranged in age, experience, and degrees of literacy. Some students succeeded "marvelously," he recounted, while others seemed to be "born mute: deaf in the questions, and mute in the responses."[86]

Faced with students who represented a range of experiences and capabilities, instructors such as Bernardino Moscati, Giuseppe Nessi, Sebastiano Rizzo, and Luigi Calza employed a variety of instructional methods to accommodate diverse needs. Rizzo favored a dialogic method.[87] Describing these lessons as a kind of catechism in which the students would study and memorize a series of concise questions and answers, Rizzo reported variable results.[88] On the one hand, his young students were generally quite successful in comprehending and retaining the daily lessons, "having the organs of memory ready as much to receive the notion as to commit it firmly and strongly . . . to memory."[89] On the other hand, older students tended to struggle. Rizzo noted regretfully that he needed to spend twice as much effort on the older students, repeating lessons over and over such that with time these women would at least be able to achieve "a servile practice, most useful to . . . the aim of simple, manual practice."[90] In Padua, Luigi Calza also used a catechistic formula based on easily memorizable questions and answers. To reduce the onerous repetition that Rizzo complained of, Calza encouraged the women best able to read to repeat these questions to their fellow students in their off hours.[91]

Even repetition outside of the classroom proved inadequate for some students, however. In a report from February 1777, Calza had to admit that only with much difficulty could "words alone commit completely new and unfamiliar ideas in the minds of unlearned and aged women." Instead, Calza found he could achieve better results if he "resort[ed] to the help of the senses, endeavor[ing] to put before their eyes, and make them touch with their hands" the principles he was attempting to teach.[92] Fortunately, Calza could rely on his extensive collection of wax obstetrical models to instruct students struggling with written and verbal lessons. The professor even took it upon himself to adopt the Venetian dialect and local colloquialisms to describe various concepts.[93]

Midwifery schools also highlighted urban/rural divides in the attitudes of students toward formal instruction. In Padua, acknowledging both the differing work demands and diverse educational backgrounds among rural and urban students, the health board determined that it would be most beneficial to keep the two groups separate. As such, rural midwives would attend school during a condensed four-month program, from December to March; urban midwives would have lessons during the remaining months of the year, but only two or three days a week, over a two-year period. Progress reports from Luigi Calza to the health board in Padua indicate that even though his rural students were on the whole less literate, and less likely to have significant midwifery experience, they achieved much success (particularly with some of the adaptive instructional techniques described earlier), demonstrated excellent natural ability, and were consistently able to complete the course successfully. Moreover, Calza wrote that his rural students were well behaved and "participate with every assiduity and attention at my lessons."[94] By contrast, Calza's experience in training urban midwives, who had often been practicing in the city without license, proved much different. Instead of the deference and malleability of his rural students, many of the urban women at first "demonstrated great resistance . . . and were determined not to obey."[95] Urban midwives, whose compensation was generally much higher than their rural counterparts, may have seen less incentive to attend a lengthy course of instruction that might interfere with attention to their own clients in the meantime.

****

An additional set of challenges arose as a result of the living conditions established to house rural midwives during their studies. Administrators needed a safe and secure environment for women who would be traveling far from home without male supervision, and one that would also facilitate the women's educational program. In Milan, officials argued that boarding the training women in a wing of the hospital[96] where they would also be instructed represented the most efficient way of controlling both their learning and behavior.[97] The rooms at the *Ospedale Maggiore* designated for the female students were believed to be ideal because they were "secluded from every sight, and communication with males, especially those young trainees in the hospital."[98] Moreover, the rooms were separate from but within easy communication of the *Quarto delle Balie* which contained the hospital's foundlings, wetnurses, and maternity ward.

Much like the maternity wards discussed in the previous chapter, the midwifery students were subject to strict regulations and restrictions on personal autonomy. For instance, entrance to and exit from the student dormitory in Milan was regulated through a single doorway, which was to be kept locked at all times and guarded by a door keeper.[99] The students themselves were governed by a highly structured daily schedule in order to minimize idle time. Rising at five or six in the morning depending on the month, the women would have an hour for prayer and housework, a half hour each for mass and breakfast, three or four hours of instruction and study, and finally two hours for lunch and recreation. Lessons would resume in the afternoon, followed by several hours of dedicated study time, an hour and a half for dinner and recreation, and lastly prayers before bed. On Sundays, the late-morning hours typically devoted to lessons were reserved for religious education, while after lunch the students were permitted to take a walk, provided they "went in company [of another student] and with [a female] attendant" escorting them. Once a month, after completing their duties for the day, the students would be allowed to leave school grounds in the company of a relative or other approved individual.[100] Additional regulations dictated how the women could dress: the pupils, "as much inside the school as out must dress decently according to [their] own means."[101] Prohibited were "low-collared dresses" or other garments that could be considered indecorous or incongruous with the women's social status. In fact, the rules were so stringent that one Milanese official warned that such an "[excessively] rigid . . . discipline would not do but to dishearten [the students] and could seem to them more a prison, than a school."[102]

In Padua, where students were housed in the former convent of San Leonino, the women faced similar, though perhaps slightly less rigid, arrangements. Visitors were limited to family members but seem to have been allowed fairly regularly. Students also had more freedom to leave the premises, subject only to a midnight curfew, after which time the guardian of the house would close and lock the doors. Oversight outside of lessons was provided by an on-site female guardian, while a deputy *Provveditore* from the health magistracy was responsible for monitoring the "conduct and behavior of these women, who would live in a Christian manner, and in peace with one another under the governance of the custodian, and in the case of scandal, or turbulence, the most disruptive would be dismissed" and replaced with another woman.[103]

Despite the strict governance of student midwives, administrators were dismayed to hear of scandals arising at the schools. Intermittent reports of disorders at San Leonino were noted almost immediately after the Padua midwifery school's opening in 1774. By the late 1780s, however, the lax oversight at the house and blatant disregard for its regulations resulted in an alarmed memo to the health board. Much of the responsibility for the lack of discipline was ascribed to the governess, whose "depraved connivance" had apparently encouraged "licentious behavior" among the student midwives.[104] According to the report, the students often failed to come home by their curfew in the evening, and they received visitors who were not relatives at all hours of the night. To make matters worse, the church of San Leonino, adjacent to the residence, was currently lacking a priest, so the female students were not receiving regular moral and religious guidance as per the health board's regulations.

Resistance and repercussions

Despite the occasional reports of misbehaving midwives outside of the classroom, and the constant struggles with recruitment, most midwifery school professors were generally content with the progress demonstrated by the women who did attend their courses. At the same time, midwifery programs had a relatively limited impact on licensing practices as a whole, much to the disappointment of the state officials who had assumed the programs would serve as a major corrective. Officials had optimistically hoped that all prospective midwives would eventually be required to matriculate through a midwifery school in order to practice their trade. However, conceding that all currently practicing midwives could not simply be rendered illegal overnight, many states initially accommodated practicing midwives by allowing them to undergo an exam instead of requring them to attend school in order to be licensed.[105]

Yet, even given such compromises, both urban and rural communities continued to report widespread licensing abuses throughout the century. Four years after the midwifery school opened in Milan, the city's Medical Faculy described the "unyielding resistance of many women" to the new requirements for licensing: "these women being even now without the approval to practice . . . the art of midwifery, cause public scandal and . . . great danger to the lives of babies, no less than their mothers."[106] Giuseppe Cicognini was especially angered that despite his efforts to make the burden of travel and expenses for the midwifery school manageable for rural women, "a large part" of the state's midwives continued "audaciously to exercise the art of midwifery" without license, leading to "frequent scandals resulting from badly assisted births."[107]

In Padua, similarly, almost a decade after the midwifery school was opened, Pietro Sografi bemoaned the "very grave disorders, which frequently occur in the practice of Obstetrics because of abuses, and the inexperience of the practitioners of that art."[108] According to Sografi, under present conditions, any woman could "at her pleasure undertake the vocation of midwife, and can practice it without an exam . . . and . . . without any obligation in doubtful or difficult cases to call the Public Professor of Obstetrics[109] or another able surgeon to undertake any necessary operations."[110] Additional reports cited midwives who continued independently to administer internal medicines, use instruments, and perform simple operations.[111]

In some cases, the resistance of midwives to official regulations and licensing practices was also supported by local curates. In a letter from Maria Teresa to officals in Milan, the empress noted with disdain that "some parish priests refuse to publish at the altar the names of the midwives . . . qualified to practice that art with patent from the Medical Faculty. . . [and] that these [priests] presume with undeserved impertinence to be entitled even now to the right to sanction this practice."[112] The priests' obstinacy was all the more irking to Maria Teresa because she recognized the necessity of their interaction with midwives. It was the priest's responsibility to instruct the midwife in the correct manner of delivering the baptismal sacrament in cases of necessity. Yet, it was also sometimes the parish priest who represented the biggest challenge to state governments in recruiting women from the countryside to urban midwifery schools and in enforcing more stringent licesning practices.[113]

Parish priests frequently advocated on behalf of long-practicing midwives in their communities, regardless of whether such women were formally approved and licensed by the medical faculty. In the parish of Incino, for instance, the local priest petitioned on behalf of the community's traditional midwife, Cristina Appiana. Appiana, who had trained as a midwife under her well-respected mother-in-law, was already past the desired age for entrance into the midwifery school when the first announcements reached the small town in 1767. Nor did Appiana, by now advanced in age, necessarily want to undertake the hardship of travel and relocation to Milan even if the school's director was willing to make an exception for her. Arguing that the parish's one midwife who did have an official license was not sufficient to care for the entire population, the parish priest pleaded with the medical faculty in Milan to permit Cristina Appiana to continue practicing. She would undergo an exam if necessary but did not desire to attend formal lessons far from home in Milan.[114]

Similarly, in the Venetian neighborhood of S. Niccolo it was the governers of the local fraternity devoted to the poor who wrote on behalf of the traditional midwife, Tommasa Nani. Although Nani herself was not officially licensed, her mother, whom Nani had followed for thirty years, had been. Following her mother's death, Nani continued to practice, demonstrating a great capacity for Christian charity in the impoverished parish. Even though many women there could offer Nani no payment for her services, the midwife nonetheless continued to serve her neighbors indiscriminately, and even provided alms herself when possible, according to the members of the *Fraterna de' Poveri*. More than that, Nani was apparently quite capable: two surgeons from nearby towns and a member of the confraternity were ready to submit sworn testimony as to Nani's ability to handle with skill not only simple deliveries, but also emergencies. Yet, as the brothers' petition continued, Nani's inability to read had dissuaded her from ever applying for an official liecense or attending anatomical demonstrations or other lessons, something that had made Nani a target of the health board's reinvigorated efforts to stamp out abusive midwives. For the fraternity members, it was not Nani's anatomical or theoretical knowedge of childbirth that rendered her qualified as a midwife, but rather her demonstrated Christian charity, goodwill, and proven competence.[115]

In other cases, the opposition of potential clients presented an impediment to the new midwifery schools. In the village of Abbiate Guazzone, Angela Maria Caima had been selected for and attended the first course of midwifery instruction in Milan in 1767. Much like Francesca Mazzuchelli, whose story opened this chapter, Caima had returned to her home community with official license in hand, only to face determined resistance from the women there, who continued to prefer the services of a longer-practicing but unlicensed midwife. In a letter pleading for assistance, the council members in Abbiate Guazzone stated that while it was customary practice in the village to pay the midwife ten *soldi* for each birth, in addition to provisions during the labor and immediate pre- and post-partum periods, the townswomen refused to pay Angela Caima more than five *soldi* per birth and would not provide her with food or lodging because they found

her "disgusting . . . for having been in the Hospital and having seen anatomical demonstrations during the time of the [midwifery] course."[116] Nor
was Angela Maria Caima's experience an isolated event. In the village of
Binasco, the newly trained midwife Maria Maddalena Oliva found herself
in similar competition with the community's familiar and long-exercising,
but unapproved, midwife, Catterina Mazzoletti.[117] As in Abbiate Guazzi-
one, the women in Binasco preferred to seek assistance from midwives
whose practice and skills had been sanctioned locally and who had not been
exposed to practices at the midwifery school that they deemed both repul-
sive and unnecessary.

Conclusion

During the eighteenth century, Italian states increasingly sensitive to their
moral responsibility for the public health of their subjects and the potential
biopower of the same, and a jealous medical profession intent on delimiting
the sphere of influence of potential competitors, sought to reform the practice of midwifery. Midwifery schools aimed to elevate traditional midwifery
into a scientific discipline based on anatomical study, mathematical principles, and a clear division of labor between midwives and surgeons. However, midwifery schools and the new forms of instruction and regulation
they promoted were often viewed as an affront to the traditional authority
of the community and local church. Midwives, whose practice had long
been authorized primarily by their neighbors and parish priest, now found
these customary sources of legitimation and approval to be undermined by
outside entities. Authorization from below nonetheless continued to super-
cede official licensing as the most important source of legitimation for most
practicing midwives throughout the eighteenth century. In this way, midwives, mothers, and parish priests had a signifiant amount of leverage with
which to resist the efforts of state and medical authorities to formalize the
training of midwives.

   In fact, midwifery schools' permanence was often in question during this
period. In Milan, for instance, the midwifery program was initially meant as
a kind of pilot project with resources allocated for only a few years. In 1769,
just two years after its opening, the school was officially suspended, though
Bernardino Moscati continued to provide lessons on a more informal basis
to midwives and surgeons who desired such training.[118] Only in 1791, after
the entire *Quarto delle Balie* had been transferred out of the *Ospedale Maggiore* to a nearby site at the ex-convent of Santa Caterina alla Ruota, was
midwifery instruction officially reorganized under Pietro Moscati. Similarly, in Venice, the midwifery school, which had first opened in 1770, was
closed temporarily in 1795 because of financial concerns. The school was
reopended shortly thereafter, though the responsbility for its administration
and financial expenses was transferred from the Venetian health magistracy
to the medical-surgical college.[119]

In Turin, midwifery education, though introduced with much fanfare in 1728, does not seem to have remained a priority during the eighteenth century. Immediate reports that almost no written lessons were being offered and that anatomical demonstrations were rare suggest that the state was unable or unwilling to more thoroughly overhaul midwifery education. Instead, the materity ward at San Giovanni continued to operate under the authority of a head midwife who trained other women in the trade through apprenticeship without major shifts in educational practices. Professor of surgery Ambrogio Bertrandi may have introduced more formal training for midwives (though not surgeons) in 1761. There are indications that midwives at this time received some theoretical training, pratice on obstetrical machines, and anatomical training, though archival documentation about midwifery education in Turin is scarce until the French domination in the nineteenth century.[120]

These examples demonstrate that while midwifery schools were opened in Italy with ambitious goals, there were often considerable challenges to their success and overall impact. Not only midwives' intransigence, but also financial and logistical concerns often complicated efforts to provide public education for women with diverse social backgrounds. As is discussed in the following chapter, attempts to systematically train surgeons in obstetrics were likewise fraught during the eighteenth century, both for the reasons cited in this chapter and because there remained in Italy during this period significant resistance to men involving themselves in childbirth.

Notes

1 ASMi, *Sanità, Parte Antica*, 269, Ricorso di F. Ponti Mazzuchelli, 11 ottobre 1768.
2 Leslie Tuttle, *Conceiving the Old Regime: Pronatalism and the Politics of Reproduction in Early Modern France* (Oxford and New York: Oxford University Press, 2010), 6.
3 Carol Blum, *Strength in Numbers: Population, Reproduction, and Power in Eighteenth-Century France* (Baltimore: John Hopkins University Press, 2002), x.
4 Claudia Pancino, "La comare levatrice: Crisi di un mestiere nel XVIII secolo," *Storia e Società* 13 (1981): 629–631.
5 Ludovico Antonio Muratori, *Della pubblica felicità: oggetto de' buoni principi* (Lucca, 1749), 142.
6 ASMi, *Sanità, Parte Antica*, c. 186, "Relazione della visita fin'ora eseguita nello Stato di Milano dalla Commissione della Facoltà Medica," 2 May 1767; ASMi, *Sanità, Parte Antica*, c. 268.
7 ASMi, *Sanità, Parte Antica*, c. 268, Report of Teodoro della Somaglia, 22 October 1767.
8 ASMi, *Sanità, Parte Antica*, c. 268.
9 Michel Foucault, *The History of Sexuality, Volume 1: An Introduction*, trans. Robert Hurley (New York: Vintage Books, 1990), esp. part five; Silvana Baldi, "L'assistenza alla maternità a Torino nel XVIII secolo," *Sanità, Scienza, e Storia* 1–2 (1992): 127–128; Claudia Pancino, ed., *Politica e salute: dalla polizia medica all'igiene* (Bologna: CLUEB, 2003).

10 Muratori, *Della pubblica felicità: oggetto de' buoni principi*, 142.

11 ASMi, *Sanità, Parte Antica*, c. 186, "Relazione della visita fin'ora eseguita nello Stato di Milano dalla Commissione della Facolta'Medica," 2 May 1767. Although midwives were prohibited from the use of obstetrical and surgical tools, it was nonetheless probable that midwives, particularly in remote areas, would have some kind of 'instrument.' This would most likely be some kind of a crotchet, which could be used to extract a dead child piece by piece. There is little evidence that midwives were overly quick to use any such tools, or that a male surgeon's or physician's use of them would have resulted in better outcomes because in most cases instruments were applied only in the event of the fetus's death in the womb. See, for instance Margaret Connor Versluysen, "Midwives, Medical Men, and 'Poor Women Laboring of Child': Lying-in Hospitals in Eighteenth-Century London," in *Women, Health and Reproduction*, ed. Helen Roberts (London: Routledge, 1981), 31; Jo Murphy-Lawless, *Reading Birth and Death: A History of Obstetric Thinking* (Bloomington: Indiana University Press, 1998), 55; Pancino, "La comare levatrice," 600–603; Lisa Forman Cody, *Birthing the Nation: Sex, Science and the Conceptions of Eighteenth-Century Britons* (Oxford: Oxford University Press, 2005), 181–183.

12 ASMi, *Sanità, Parte Antica*, c. 268, Letter from Firmian to Kaunitz, 31 October 1767.

13 Ibid.

14 ASMi, *Sanità, Parte Antica*, c. 186, "Relazione della visita fin'ora eseguita nello Stato di Milano dalla Commissione della Facoltà Medica," 2 May 1767.

15 At times, the bishop might intervene in this process to confirm the midwife's capacity in regard to the administration of the baptismal sacrament; episcopal visitations were known to include an inspection of all practicing midwives for just this reason.

16 ASMi, *Sanità, Parte Antica*, c. 186, "Avvertenze per le Ostetrici," n.d.

17 Ibid.

18 Moscati also noted that between "the *Protofisico*, and the Colleges of Physicians and of Barbers" there were long-standing and "unresolved judicial grudges surrounding [these bodies'] respective competences, and ability to approve experts in the practice of Obstetrics," which might complicate matters further. ASMi, *Sanità, Parte Antica*, c. 268, "Riflessioni di Bernardino Moscati intorno allo stabilimento della nuova Scuola pe' Parti," 1767.

19 For instance, ASMi, *Sanità, Parte Antica*, c. 268, Printed Circular, 28 October 1767.

20 ASMi, *Sanità, Parte Antica*, 268.

21 ASMi, *Sanità, Parte Antica*, c. 268, Letter from Kaunitz, 30 November 1767.

22 Ibid. Kaunitz recommended lessons in both the morning and afternoon hours, the latter spent in practical training with a practicing physician and expert midwife. In this way, according to Kaunitz, the women should be able to be trained in only three months. In this area, Kaunitz's recommendations went unheeded – the course of instruction remained scheduled for November through April.

23 F. A. Duboin, *Raccolta per ordine di materia delle leggi, editti, manifesti, emanate dai sovrani della real Casa di Savoia sino all'8–12–1798*, 23 Toms (Turin, 1818–69), Bk. XII, Tit. XIX, Ch. II, 644.

24 AST, *Sezione Corte, Materie Ecclesiastiche, Luoghi Pii di qua da Monti*, Mazzo 17, Fasc. 8.

25 Ibid., Fasc. 7.

26 ASMi, *Sanità, Parte Antica*, 268, "Riflessioni di Bernardino Moscati intorno allo stabilimento della nuova Scuola pe' Parti," 1767.

27 Ibid.

28 In particular, the training of surgeons. On the emergence of clinical training, see Othmar Keel, "The Politics of Health and the Institutionalization of Clinical Practices in Europe in the Second Half of the Eighteenth Century," in *William Hunter and the Eighteenth-Century Medical World*, ed. F. W. Bynum and Roy Porter (Cambridge: Cambridge University Press, 1985), 207–258; for the clinical practices at the *Ospedale Maggiore di Milano* specifically, see Pio Pecchiai, *L'Ospedale Maggiore di Milano nella Storia e nell'Arte* (Milan: Pizzi e Pizio, 1927), esp. Ch. 8.

29 ASMi, *Sanità, Parte Antica*, c. 273, "Istituzione della Scuola Pratica d'Ostetricia nella Regia Università di Pavia al Leano," 3 October 1792.

30 ASMi, *Sanità, Parte Antica*, 268, "Istruzione," 28 October 1767.

31 Ibid.

32 Ibid.

33 ASMi, *Sanità, Parte Antica*, c. 186, "Regolamento del Regio Direttorio della Facoltà Medica nella Lombardia," 1767.

34 Ibid.

35 ASMi, *Sanità, Parte Antica*, c. 268, "Istruzione," 28 October 1767.

36 ASMi, *Sanità, Parte Antica*, 268, "Riflessioni di Bernardino Moscati intorno allo stabilimento della nuova Scuola pe' Parti," 1767.

37 AOSG, Cat. 1, Cl. 3, fasc. 1, 1732.

38 Rebecca Messbarger, *The Century of Women: Representations of Women in Eighteenth-Century Italian Public Discourse* (Toronto: University of Toronto Press, 2002), 8.

39 ASMi, *Sanità, Parte Antica*, c. 268, Letter from the Regio Cancelliere Delegato nel Vicariato di Binasco, 10 November 1767.

40 ASMi, *Sanità, Parte Antica*, c. 268, Letter from S. Donato, n.d.

41 ASMi, *Sanità, Parte Antica*, c. 268, Letter from Vaprio, n.d.

42 The representative from Porlezza wrote back, for instance, that Giuseppa Tencalla had been elected "with the consent of her husband," that she was a woman "of spirit, that knows how to read, but I confess of the age of forty-three, and thus outside [of the age] prefixed in the instructions." ASMi, *Sanità, Parte Antica*, c. 268, Letter from Porlezza, 28 November 1767.

43 ASMi, *Sanità, Parte Antica*, c. 268, eg. Letter from Rosate, 26 November 1767.

44 ASMi, *Sanità, Parte Antica*, c. 273, "Stabilimento della Scuola d'Ostetricia nelle Diverse Città dello Stato, e Destinazioni de' Locali."

45 Archivio di Stato di Padova (hereafter ASP), *Sanità*, b. 153, Letter from Castelbaldo, 13 November 1774.

46 ASP, *Sanità*, b. 153, Letter from Castelbaldo, 13 November 1774.

47 ASV, *Sanità*, b. 175, 26 August 1784.

48 ASP, *Sanità*, b. 153, Letter from Carceri, 28 November 1774.

49 ASP, *Sanità*, b. 153, Letter from Villanuova, 30 November 1774.

50 ASP, *Sanità*, b. 154, Letter from Cologna, 6 November 1780.

51 Ibid.

52 ASMi, *Sanità, Parte Antica*, c. 268.

53 ASMi, *Sanità, Parte Antica*, c. 268, Letter from Bernardino Moscati, 1767.

54 Murphy-Lawless, *Reading Birth and Death*, 34.

55 Felice De Billi, *Sulla I.R. Scuola di Ostetricia ed Annesso Ospizio delle Partorienti* (Milano: Società degli Editori degli Annali Universali delle Scienze e dell'Industria, 1844), 66–67.

56 ASMi, *Sanità, Parte Antica*, c. 268, Letter of Bernardino Moscati, 10 April 1768.

57 Pietro Sografi, *Corso elementare dell'arte di raccogliere i parti* (Padova: nell stamperia del Seminario, 1788), 1–2.

58 ASV, *Sanità*, b. 591, Report of Sebastiano Rizzo, 16 March 1796.

59 Sografi, *Corso elementare dell'arte di raccogliere i parti*, 1–25.
60 Lucia Dacome, *Malleable Anatomies: Models, Makers, and Material Culture in Eighteenth-Century Italy* (Oxford: Oxford University Press, 2017), 164.
61 For Galli's collection of obstetrical models in Bologna, see Marco Bortolotti, "Insegnamento, ricerca e professione nel Museo Ostetrico di Giovanni Antonio Galli," in *I materiali dell'Istituto delle Scienze* (Bologna: CLUEB, 1979), 239–247; Olimpia Sanlorenzo, *L'insegnamento di ostetricia nell'Università di Bologna* (Bologna: Alma Mater Studiorum Saecularia Nona, 1988), 27–37; Olimpia Sanlorenzo, *Ars obstetricia bononiensis: catalogo ed inventario del Museo Ostetrico Giovan Antonio Galli* (Bologna: Editrice CLUEB, 1988); Viviana Lanzarini, "La Scuola Ostetrica di Giovanni Antonio Galli," in *Nascere a Siena. Il parto e l'assistenza alla nascita dal Medioevo all'età Moderna*, ed. Francesca Vannozzi (Siena: Nuova Immagine Editrice, 2005), 25–34; Dacome, *Malleable Anatomies*, Ch. 5; Lyle Massey, "On Waxes and Wombs: Eighteenth Century Representations of the Gravid Uterus," in *Ephemeral Bodies: Wax Sculpture and the Human Figure*, ed. Roberta Panzanelli (Los Angeles: Getty Research Institution, 2008), 83–105.
62 Giambattista Fabbri, "Antico Museo Ostetrico di Giovanni Antonio Galli, restauro fatto alle sue preparazioni in plastica e nuova conferma della suprema importanza dell'ostetricia sperimentale," in *Memorie dell'Accademia delle Scienze dell'Istituto di Bologna, serie III, tomo II* (Bologna: Gamberini e Parmeggiani, 1872), 129–166, 130.
63 Marian Cimino and Andrea Cozza, "Modelli Ostetrici nella Collezione della Clinica Ostetrica di Padova," in *Le Collezioni di Ostetricia. Scuola Italiana di Storia della Medicina. Giornate di Museologia Medica. Atti.*, ed. Viviana Lanzarini (Chieti: Edicola, 2013), 15–20.
64 Messbarger, *The Century of Women*, 80.
65 Fabbri mentions two machines, though it is possible that one was designed but never actually realized. See Dacome, *Malleable Anatomies*, 174.
66 Dacome, *Malleable Anatomies*, 174.
67 Despite a great deal of planning, the Pavia school was not actually opened until the second decade of the nineteenth century. See Daniela Franchetti, *La scuola ostetrica pavese tra Otto e Novecento* (Milan: Cisalpino, 2012).
68 The closest examples to the Pavia machine may be a series of eight obstetrical models produced by the Roman anatomist and wax sculptor, Giovanni Battista Manfredini, who was active in Bologna in the 1770s. The models, produced in coloured terracotta for instructional use at the midwifery school in Modena, feature full-size women from the head to mid-thigh, such that seated on a table they appear standing. The models move from an intact full-term pregnant belly to greater and greater penetration into the womb, often with the woman holding open her own skin (as was a familiar convention in Renaissance anatomical drawing). These models are not, however, machines. They have no internal mechanisms and were not intended to be practiced upon. On Manfredini, see Owen, *Simulation in Healthcare Education*, 125; Thomas Schnalke, *Diseases in Wax: History of the Medical Moulage*, trans. Kathy Spatschek (Carol Stream, IL: Quintessence Publishing, 1995), 38–39.
69 Galletti, *Elementi di Ostetricia*, xiv.
70 ASMi, *Sanità, Parte Antica*, c. 273. Letter from Vincenzo Malacarne, 9 November 1792.
71 Dacome, *Malleable Anatomies*, 166.
72 G. B. Monteggia, trans., "Osservazioni Preliminari," in *Arte Ostetricia di G.G. Stein*, vol. 1 (Venice, 1800), 5–6.

73 Francesca Vannozzi, "Fantocci, marchingegni e modelli nella didattica ostetrica senese," in *Nascere a Siena. Il parto e l'assistenza alla nascita dal Medioevo all'età moderna*, ed. Francesca Vannozzi (Siena: Nuova Immagine, 2005), 40.

74 Vannozzi, "Fantocci, marchingegni e modelli nella didattica ostetrica senese."

75 Apparently the practice of stealing and selling such certificates was not unknown; it was enough of a problem, in fact, that the Venetian authorities issued a special notice stating that the anatomical instructor should always pass these certificates individually and in person to the appropriate student so as to avoid any abuses. ASV, *Compilazione Legge*, b. 277, Terminazione 24 March 1774.

76 ASV, *Sanità*, b. 109, Terminazione 14 May 1770.

77 ASMi, *Sanità, Parte Antica*, c. 273, "Istituzione della Scuola Pratica d'Ostetricia nella Regia Università di Pavia al Leano," 3 October 1792.

78 ASMi, *Sanità, Parte Antica*, c. 268, "Tabella delle Donne Forensi accettate nel Venerando Ospitale Maggiore di Milano." In addition, six women from Milan (who did not lodge at the Ospedale Maggiore since they lived in the city) joined those selected from the countryside at the school.

79 ASMi, *Sanità, Parte Antica*, c. 268, "Catalogo delle Donne Forensi admesse nel Venerando Ospitale Maggiore di Milano per la Scuola dell'Arte Ostetricia . . . Esaminate, ed approvate dal Dottore Bernardino Moscati Lettore Delegato dal Governo."

80 In fact, all the women eventually approved and licensed after the first year of school had worked as midwives for at least a year before attending the midwifery course. ASMi, *Sanità, Parte Antica*, c. 268, "Catalogo delle Donne Forensi."

81 ASV, *Sanità*, b. 591, Report of Sebastiano Rizzo, 25 January 1796.

82 ASV, *Sanità*, b. 591, Report of Sebastiano Rizzo, 21 January 1795.

83 ASV, *Sanità*, b. 176, Report of Anzolo Giustinian, 1 September 1786.

84 ASMi, *Sanità, Parte Antica*, c. 268, Letter of Bernardino Moscati, 10 April 1768.

85 Ibid.

86 ASV, *Sanità*, b. 591, Report of Sebastiano Rizzo, 21 January 1795.

87 As author of a midwifery manual himself, Rizzo was familiar with the use of the dialogue form as a popular structure for such texts, particularly those directed at female midwives. For more on these texts and the power and gender dynamics inherent in the dialogue form, see Chapter 2.

88 ASV, *Sanità*, b. 591, Report of Sebastiano Rizzo, 21 January 1795.

89 ASV, *Sanità*, b. 591, Report of Sebastiano Rizzo, n.d.

90 Ibid.

91 Ibid.

92 Ibid.

93 ASP, *Sanità*, b. 152, "Quelli interessanti oggetti di salute, e di preservazione de'suddetti, che indussero l'Eccellente Senato ad instituire col Decreto 2 Maggio 1770 la Scuola Ostetricia in questa dominante, lo hanno pure determinate ad estendere eguali provvidenze anche nella terraferma, onde impedire la continuazione de' gravi disordini derivanti dalla imperizia delle Levatrici," 11 December 1775.

94 ASP, *Sanità*, b. 152, Report of Luigi Calza, 13 February 1777.

95 ASP, *Sanità*, b. 152, Report of Luigi Calza, 5 June 1777.

96 Florence, by contrast, initially favored a kind of apprenticeship structure wherein trainees from the provinces would live with and be supervised by those already approved midwives active within the city.

97 ASMi, *Sanità, Parte Antica*, c. 268, "Piano della scuola della ostetricia da erigersi nel Venerando Ospitale Maggiore di Milano," 10 October 1767; ASMi, *Sanità, Parte Antica*, c. 268, Letter from Firmian to Kaunitz, 31 October 1767.

98 ASMi, *Sanità, Parte Antica*, c. 268. Letter from the delegates of the Ospedale Maggiore, 10 October 1767

99 Ibid.

100 De Billi, *Sulla I.R. Scuola di Ostetricia ed Annesso Ospizio delle Partorienti,* Tavola A: Orario e Disciplina, 77.

101 De Billi, *Sulla I.R. Scuola di Ostetricia ed Annesso Ospizio delle Partorienti*; ASMi, *Sanità, Parte Antica,* c. 268, Letter from Kaunitz to Firmian, 1767.

102 ASMi, *Sanità, Parte Antica,* c. 268. Letter from Kaunitz to Firmian, 1767.

103 ASP, *Sanità,* b. 152, 11 December 1775.

104 ASP, *Sanità,* b. 152, 5 May 1787.

105 Kaunitz in particular had cautioned that it would be unwise and reckless to prohibit women with long experience as midwives from practicing, even though their age or personal situation might impede them from attending school. Particularly in the first years of the schools' existence, allowances were made for such women who, nonetheless, had to demonstrate their abilities by taking an exam. Of course, many women simply continued to practice without undergoing an exam or attending any courses at the midwifery school. F. A. Duboin, *Raccolta per ordine di materia delle leggi, editti, manifesti,* Bk. VII, Tit. XIX, Ch. II, "Manifesto del Vicario di Torino, del quale notifica essersi stabilito nell'Ospedale di San Giovanni Battista un ricovero gratuito per le povere partorienti, ed una scuola practica per le ostetrici," 19 June 1728, 646.

106 ASMi, *Sanità, Parte Antica,* c. 269, 12 August 1771.

107 ASMi, *Sanità, Parte Antica,* c. 269, Letter from Cicognini, 1 August 1771. The medical faculty had petitioned numerous confraternities and other "*luoghi pii,*" both from the rural communities themselves and from Milan, to contribute to the expenses incurred for the midwives' upkeep in Milan so that many of the women could be trained at no cost to themselves or their families. Cicognini also made it possible for some already-practicing midwives to be approved by local authorized physicians or surgeons, rather than having to travel to Milan to sit for the exam there. Seventy-eight out of the 200 midwives approved from 1767–1771, for instance, were exempted from paying the normal seven *lire* fee for the examination/license.

108 ASP, *Sanità,* b. 152, "Parere del Sig. Pietro Sografi sopra La Scuola di Mammane," 6 October 1784.

109 Because Padua and its surrounding territories lacked hospitals which accepted pregnant women, it became the duty of the Professor of Obstetrics himself to attend personally any difficult births in the city for which a midwife called assistance. ASP, *Sanità,* b. 152, "Parere del Sig. Pietro Sografi sopra La Scuola di Mammane," 6 October 1784.

110 Ibid.

111 Ibid.

112 ASMi, *Sanità, Parte Antica,* c. 269, Letter from Maria Teresa, 13 December 1770.

113 A circular was issued on 15 April 1771 from the Bishopric in Cremona to all parishes reiterating the government's position on midwives.

114 ASMi, *Sanità, Parte Antica,* c. 270, Letter from Bosisio, n.d. This request was denied and called out as a spurious attempt to circumvent the newly approved midwife, Isabella Castelnuova, in favor of the long-practicing Appiana. ASMi, *Sanità, Parte Antica,* c. 270, Letter from the *Reale Giunta Economale,* 19 July 1768.

115 ASV, *Sanità,* b. 589, 4 March 1771.

116 ASMi, *Sanità, Parte Antica,* c. 269, Letter from the community of Abbiate Guazzone, 15 August 1768.

117 ASMi, *Sanità, Parte Antica,* c. 269, Letter from the community of Binasco, 14 September 1768.

118 Renzo Dionigi, *Bernardino Moscati: Maestro di Chirurgia e Riformatore della Sanità Milanese nel Settecento* (Milan: EDRA, 2017), 85.
119 Corradi, *Dell'Ostetricia in Italia*, 754.
120 T. M. Caffaratto, *Storia dell'Ospedale S. Anna di Torino (Opera di Maternità)*, in supplemento *Annali dell'Ospedale Maria Vittoria di Torino*, vol. lxiii, 7–8 (1970), 13.

5   Surgical instruction and the clinicalization of the maternity ward

In March 1714, the Turin surgeon Paolo Bernardo Calvo was called in to assist at the delivery of 24-year-old Angela Francesca Morano.[1] Morano, who had already been troubled with pain and the discharge of a fetid fluid earlier in her pregnancy, was now vomiting, feverish, and experiencing severe abdominal pain. After more than a day where the woman's labor had not progressed, the midwife called in the noted Turin physician and anatomist Giovanni Battista Bianchi along with Calvo. Taking into account Morano's worsening symptoms, the discovery of a mass on the woman's uterus, and his suspicion that the fetus was already dead, Calvo persuaded Morano's family to allow him to manually explore the woman's genitals to assess the situation, something they initially opposed but eventually consented to. Calvo noted that his efforts were largely in vain, feeling as though he had "entered into a dark labyrinth, not having for assistance the light of even a little candle," and thus unable to determine if the cavity he was touching was actually the uterus or not. Nonetheless, the woman's fever and pain were severe, and a rigidity near her navel suggested fluid leaking into her abdominal cavity.

Given the severity of the symptoms, Calvo recommended recourse to the surgical extraction of the fetus and the removal of any other putrid tissue that might be contributing to Morano's high fever. This, too, was at first strongly opposed by the woman's family, though, in time, Bianchi and Calvo succeeded in convincing Morano's husband, who also happened to be a surgeon, to consent to the operation. Cutting into Morano's abdomen, Calvo extracted a fetus in horrendous condition, with a head that looked pulverized, and a fetid, decaying umbilical cord torn from the placenta. Calvo and Bianchi determined that the reason why Morano's labor had never progressed was that the fetus had in fact developed outside of the uterus. After extricating the fetus, Calvo attempted as best he could to remove the remaining decaying material in Morano's abdominal cavity, inserted a dressing (*piumaciuolo*), and applied an unction and bandage to the abdomen. Despite these efforts, Morano died eleven days later.

Where did Paolo Bernardo Calvo, who one historian has called "a thoroughly unremarkable surgeon,"[2] learn to perform a manual exploration of a pregnant woman's genitals? To know the signs of a fetus that had died in its mother's body? To be aware of the importance of removing all pieces of the placenta after a delivery (or in this case, an operation)? To perform a cesarean operation? While there was no formal obstetrical instruction for Turin surgeons in 1714, an ambitious, urban surgeon like Calvo could clearly acquire a certain amount of knowledge and practical experience related to childbirth and fetal development. Calvo, faced with an extremely difficult case, did not hesitate to intervene, even though the outcome was certainly less than desirable. This chapter fills in some gaps in our knowledge about how surgeons learned about childbirth, both before and after the emergence of formal midwifery schools in Italy. As such it contributes to our broader understanding of how early modern surgeons were instructed and how they honed practical skills. Well into the eighteenth century, the surgeons called to handle emergency childbirth cases were trained primarily through apprenticeship and firsthand experience. Graduate surgeons with university degrees may have had some theoretical instruction in obstetrics, but they, too, would have lacked any systematic clinical training.

How, then, did surgeons learn to perform procedures such as craniotomy, podalic version, or cesarean section? After the introduction of schools for midwifery training, how did the instruction of surgeons differ from that of midwives? In what ways did the maternity ward become an important site of medical research and experimentation, in which surgeons could promote their own reputations and boost their careers? This chapter considers these questions in turn, arguing that there were a number of similarities between the professionalization of surgeons and midwives. Like midwives, many surgeons practiced unlicensed into the eighteenth century. They often learned their trade through apprenticeship, and their reputations relied on their good relationships with clients and neighbors more than they did on official endorsements. When formal instruction in midwifery began to be offered to surgeons, one of the most critical instructional tools was the obstetrical machine, on which male students might practice techniques repeatedly in a controlled environment. Such machines became part of discussions during the eighteenth and nineteenth centuries that centered the importance of touch in medical practice, engaged with debates over mechanism and vitalism, and questioned the epistemological status of the fetus. The chapter concludes by considering the clinicalization of the maternity ward and its transformation into a site of medical research at the turn of the nineteenth century.

Surgeons learn the trade

Formal obstetrical training for male surgical students during the eighteenth century was initially limited to theoretical instruction. While many Italian universities had chairs in obstetrics by mid-century, clinical obstetrical training emerged much more unevenly across the peninsula and was dependent on several factors, in particular the presence or absence of a public maternity hospital. By the end of the eighteenth century, however, clinical obstetrical training in hospitals and specialized maternity wards was increasingly seen as necessary, a shift reflective of broader changes in medical epistemology that made clinical instruction and pathological anatomy central to medical learning. Maternity wards also became sites of innovative medical research related to fetal deformity, vaccination, and artificial nutrition. Beneficiaries of the changes that made the hospital indispensable to medical education and practice, surgeons experienced a significant shift in their social status and professional identity between the seventeenth and eighteenth centuries. Just as obstetrical writers aimed to establish a scientific midwifery through a precise anatomical and physiological understanding of the body, so too had surgical reformers undertaken major steps in this period to elevate surgery from its traditional associations with empiricism and manual training into a theory-based, professional specialty.

Indeed, the most influential Italian surgeon-obstetricians of the eighteenth century embodied the heightened status of surgery in this period. Cultured and university trained, elite surgeons specializing in obstetrics, such as Ambrogio Bertrandi, Vincenzo Malacarne, Lorenzo Nannoni, Bernardino Moscati, and Pietro Paolo Tanaron, were very much the peers of the physicians alongside whom they worked, corresponded, and collaborated. Such men were cosmopolitan, engaging in lively correspondence with renowned practitioners across Europe and belonging to national and international academic societies.[3] Malacarne was the Enlightenment surgeon *par excellence*. He was deeply interested in history, literature, and philosophy in addition to medicine; he cultivated fruitful relationships with a variety of European intellectuals, including the Swiss naturalist, Charles Bonnet, with whom he discussed ideas about the nature of intelligence and the location of the soul in the cerebellum.[4] While Italy had known a tradition of elite, university-trained surgeons even before the eighteenth century, reforms in this period aimed to eliminate the reliance of surgery on empiricism and apprenticeship in favor of a systematic, anatomically based instruction. Increasingly, all surgeons wishing to receive a license were expected to be literate, to have undergone significant anatomical training, and to have been exposed to surgical theory in addition to practical experience. In short, surgery distanced itself from the world of barbers and empirics, and moved increasingly closer to that of medicine.[5]

Of course, this transformation reflected the reality for only a portion of practicing surgeons and barbers. Just as midwives resisted increasing efforts to control and license their practice, so too did surgeons defy the regulatory aims of official medicine. In the Savoyard state in the late seventeenth century, for instance, a significant portion of surgeons and barbers operated without license; at least 40% in the provinces and 20% in the cities practiced abusively. As was the case with midwifery, surgery was a trade that was regulated internally and from below as much as it was from above.

That is, as Sandra Cavallo has described for Turin surgeons, local reputations, professional contacts, and past experience provided greater validation and credibility in the eyes of prospective clients than did a formal license.[6] Well into the eighteenth century, the majority of surgeons did not attend formal courses but gained practical experience through apprenticeship, in the shops of master surgeons, and walking the wards of hospitals. And when reformers attempted to enforce stricter educational requirements, such as attendance at anatomical demonstrations, many surgeons resisted these impositions on the grounds that they were not necessary for a thorough surgical preparation. As with midwifery, surgical expertise was commonly transmitted through kinship networks. For surgeons, these relationships were not restricted to fathers passing on knowledge and equipment to sons but might include apprenticeships or resource sharing between siblings, uncles and nephews, and in-laws.[7] Well into the eighteenth century, familial dynasties with particular specialties, such as treating hernias, can be identified in Italy's major hospitals.[8]

That is not to say that surgeons lacked any theoretical understanding of the body. Surgeons like Paolo Bernardo Calvo seem to have possessed a sophisticated sense of the relationship between external symptoms and internal physiology. Calvo, whose father had been a surgeon, had learned his trade apprenticing in barber surgeons' shops, eventually coming to operate his own shop and serving his entire career in the same neighborhood in Turin. Nevertheless, he was quite familiar with a variety of surgical texts, both ancient and modern. In his writings, Calvo frequently cites classical sources such as Hippocrates, Galen, Aristotle, Avicenna, and Celsus, though he was certainly also familiar with more modern writers, including Ambroise Paré, Gabriele Falloppio, and Fabricius. Moreover, scholars have increasingly cautioned against assuming a strictly oppositional nature between categories such as empirical and theoretical, learned and unlearned.[9] This may have been especially true in Italy, where historians have revealed the rich and generally unhostile exchanges that took place between non-graduate surgeons, graduate surgeons, and physicians.[10] Italian physicians were, on the whole, not disdainful of surgical practice – a number of physicians practiced or taught surgery (including obstetrics) at the university level – and it was also hardly unheard of for a surgeon to climb the ranks and himself become a professor of medicine.[11] In Italy, both physicians and surgeons wrote about, taught, and specialized in obstetrics.

What is clear is that, like midwives, most Italian surgeons who undertook obstetrical operations before the mid-eighteenth century did not receive formalized instruction or enroll in specialized schools to learn such procedures. In some cases, surgeons or physicians called in to assist a pregnant patient offered no specific obstetrical remedies at all, prescribing instead general therapies such as bloodletting or purgation. In other cases, surgeons may have been exposed to some specialized writing about obstetrics if they had access to published books. Calvo, for instance, referred to looking for the signs of a dead fetus that other authors had cited.[12] Because no new Italian obstetrical manuals were published during the seventeenth century, the most likely sources of information would have been translations of the works of well-known Continental practitioners, such as the French obstetricians Jacques Guillemeau and Francois Mauriceau, or the Dutchman, Hendrik von Deventer, all of whose obstetrical treatises were popular in Italy. As discussed in Chapter 2, these texts would have provided an overview of reproductive anatomy, some theoretical discussion of conception, infertility, abortion, and false pregnancies, and more or less detailed information about how to manage difficult births, the removal of a dead fetus, and serious complications such as uterine hemorrhage or rupture.

Surgeons could also find practical information about childbirth in general surgical treatises, such as the Paduan Filippo Masiero's *Opere Chirurgiche*, first published in 1707. In addition to instructing his readers about how to explore a pregnant woman's genitals to determine the stage of her pregnancy and how to manually turn a malpresenting fetus, Masiero listed the signs that might indicate a woman had aborted and described how to facilitate the delivery of a dead fetus with a variety of methods, including several different kinds of fumigations, pessaries, and suppositories.[13] Of course, the surgeon might also need to use hooks (*uncini*), which Masiero advised should always be kept out of sight of the mother, and suggested that when removing a fetus by embryotomy it was prudent to shield the mother's eyes with some kind of veil.[14]

Some surgeons may also have encountered instruction in obstetrics in the private lessons offered occasionally in the homes of respected surgeons and physicians.[15] Giovanni Battista Bianchi, for instance, ran what was essentially a private school out of his home in Turin where he taught a variety of courses, but above all, anatomy. From his writings, we can assume that Bianchi would have introduced his students to theoretical discussions of human generation, as well as to the causes of preternatural births, monstrous births, extrauterine pregnancy, and other defects of the uterus.[16] In fact, Bianchi wrote extensively about the cesarean operation, dividing it into three types, depending on the location of the fetus. An 'internal cesarean section' referred to the extraction of the fetus from the uterus; however, the extraction of the fetus from either the fallopian tube or ovary ('medium cesarean'), or from the abdominal cavity ('external cesarean'), were distinct operations, according to Bianchi.[17] The operation Calvo performed on Angela Francesco Morano would therefore have been classified as an 'external cesarean operation' that did not actually entail cutting into the mother's uterus.[18] By contrast, Bianchi believed that a 'true' internal cesarean should never be performed on a living woman, given the near certain death of the mother that would result from such an operation.

Apart from some theoretical instruction, any practical experience surgeons might have with difficult childbirths came in the field. If lucky, a surgeon might observe such a case first as an apprentice or assistant to a more experienced practitioner. A surgeon might also have seen the aftermath of a complicated birth during the dissection of a fetus or of a woman whose labor had gone bad. In Angela Francesco Morano's case, Calvo immediately took the fetus home with him to autopsy and later, in the presence of "the most celebrated professors of medicine and surgery," also dissected Morano to better understand the mechanisms by which a fetus might develop outside the uterus. Additionally, a surgeon might have gained some firsthand experience with normal female reproductive anatomy during the dissection of a woman who had died naturally or of non–childbirth-related causes. For instance, Calvo refers in his written account of Morano's case to his dissection of an 80-year-old woman and his operation on a younger woman with a cancerous mass in order to make relevant comparisons.[19]

While surgeons like Calvo could thus gain a certain amount of theoretical knowledge from books and varied practical experience in the field, many practitioners agreed that the atmosphere in Italy was particularly hostile to male intervention in childbirth. At a speech delivered to the Venetian health magistrates in 1776, for instance, Sebastiano Rizzo lamented that, particularly in Italy, obstetrics had for so long been kept out of the hands of "serious men" because of women's "irrational modesty" (in France, he pointed out, at least the Royal family set the example of having surgeons and doctors attend births):

> This modesty in pregnant women is of grave damage, when dealing with a difficult labor. The midwives . . . for as much skill as they have in their Art, never surpass the knowledge of Obstetrics. They will never be in a position to discern accurately the various indications, which present themselves according to the circumstances.[20]

For those who shared Rizzo's sense that the advancement of obstetrics had been impeded in Italy, training abroad might present an appealing means of gaining practical experience in a more open environment. In fact, many of the first generation of elite Italian obstetrical practitioners were instructed abroad.[21] Italian practitioners who wanted to see obstetrical operations first hand and obtain systematic training often spent time in France. This was the case with Ambrogio Bertrandi, Bernardino Moscati, the Tuscans Pietro Paolo Tanaron, Giuseppe Vespa, and Lorenzo Nannoni, Domenico Ferrari in Naples, and Francesco Asdrubaldi in Rome.

Moscati and Ferrari were in fact sent for instruction abroad with state funds in anticipation of their assuming posts as directors of midwifery schools. At the behest of Empress Maria Teresa, who was a vocal proponent of midwifery education, Moscati spent time in Paris training with the famed obstetrician, André Levret. From Levret, Moscati gained practical experience and extensive training in forceps delivery. When he returned to Milan, he introduced Levret's forceps design, defined by the long length of the arms and a mathematically derived curve intended to perfectly match the contours of an idealized birth canal.[22] In addition to the technological know-how he gained in France, Moscati was deeply influenced by Levret's mechanical understanding of birth, upon which the latter's understanding of forceps design and application were based.[23] For the Frenchman, childbirth was a "natural and truly mechanical operation susceptible to geometric demonstration. . . . The knowledge of the Mechanical Laws of childbirth is essentially necessary to all who are destined for the Art of *accouchement*."[24] For Levret, and, subsequently, for Moscati, such a mathematically precise tool as the curved forceps would help distance obstetrics from earlier associations that equated surgical assistance at childbirth with pain, desperation, and death.

In Turin, the proposals for a maternity ward and midwifery school were based on and inspired by the example of the Hôtel-Dieu, in which midwives received both theoretical and clinical training in a hospital setting. The original architect of the project, Pierre Simone Rouhualt, was himself a French transplant. A highly respected surgeon and member of the French Royal Academy of Sciences, Rouhault had been recruited by Victor Amadeus to professionalize surgical practice in Turin during the 1710s.[25] Ambrogio Bertrandi, who taught obstetrics in Turin in the 1760s, not only learned under Rouhault, but also, with financial support from Charles Emanuel III, spent three years in Paris and London.[26] During his time abroad, Bertrandi gained practical experience in obstetrics and forged long-term professional contacts with leading surgeons, such as the reformer of surgical education, Antoine Louis. Bertrandi was deeply influenced by Louis's vision for a surgical practice based upon extensive theoretical, anatomical, and physiological knowledge, which students should master before entering into clinical practice and training in manual operations.[27]

In major cities, then, even before clinical training was available in a maternity ward, surgeons could gain practical experience alongside more senior practitioners with obstetrical expertise acquired, at least in part, abroad. This was the case for the Venetian surgeon Benedetto Maja who claimed in a letter to Luigi Calza in 1766 to be the first in the *Serenissima* to have employed the forceps successfully without harm to either mother or child.[28] Maja had first been exposed to the Levret forceps when the surgeon Francesco Pagiola brought them back from France. Pagiola, another student of Levret, tutored Maja on forceps when he returned to Venice. In one case, Pagiola applied the forceps with great skill yet was still unable to execute a safe delivery, causing Maja to wonder about the risk to maternal and infant lives from surgeons who used instruments *without* such careful training. Concluding that any limitations in that case had been due, not to Pagiola, but to the design of the forceps itself, Maja undertook in the following years to revise the Levret forceps design so as to produce an instrument that "delicately embraces the head of the fetus in the same way that the hands of an expert Professor do."[29] When Maja petitioned the Venetian health board some years later to approve and endorse his forceps design, he encouraged the authorities to consult Pagiola, who could best comment on the innovation and usefulness of the new model.[30]

Even after obstetrical courses for male surgeons began to be offered, students still often gained practical experience by accompanying more senior practitioners to cases. Another surgeon-obstetrician who spent time training at the Hôtel-Dieu, Lorenzo Nannoni, frequently notes the presence of students when he is called in to assist at difficult births. In one case of a 37-year-old woman who began experiencing pains and shortness of breath when six months pregnant, Nannoni noted that he had with him a number of students who "deign to follow me in my visits, and treatments." In fact, when he was called away to deal with the more immediate demands of a birth in progress in which the woman's pelvis was poorly shaped and the fetus's head large, he sent his students to check in on the first woman in his absence.[31] When the original case ultimately turned fatal – severe pericardial effusion had apparently caused the woman's breathing difficulties and resulted in miscarriage – Nannoni conducted an autopsy in the presence of several colleagues and two advanced students. Another time, Nannoni assisted a woman whose labor had failed to progress for hours because the fetus's head had become lodged perniciously against the mother's pelvis. After attempting extraction with forceps, trying to manually reposition the fetus, and, finally, resorting to craniotomy, Nannoni was so physically exhausted that he called on his student, Giuseppe Giudetti, to complete the removal of the dead body.[32]

Although the recourse to a surgeon during childbirth in this period was still often interpreted as a sign of imminent death, practitioners who wrote about such difficult cases stressed the importance of postmortem autopsy to better understand the structural or physiological reasons that had caused the pathological outcome. Thus, for Nannoni in the cases described earlier, neither the pedagogical instruction he describes nor his own self-fashioning as an obstetrical specialist are entirely dependent on a successful delivery. In the same way, Paolo Bernardo Calvo's published account of his experience with an extra-uterine pregnancy concentrated less on the tragic outcome of the case than on the opportunities his dissection of the fetus and mother represented for the production of obstetrical knowledge. Certainly, Italian obstetrics writers had heroic stories to tell, too, ones in which they remedied the poor decisions of a reckless midwife or overeager male practitioner and provided critical surgical aid to save the life of a mother and/or child. However, Nannoni's and Calvo's writings, which stressed their postmortem investigations, suggest that eighteenth-century surgeons could exploit even grim cases to advance their careers and reputations.

Surgeons might even take extreme measures to ensure this kind of investigation. In a case in which Malacarne was called into a labor with an arm presentation that was failing to progress, he arrived with his student to see that the mother's symptoms, which included convulsions and fainting, were worsening.[33] Upon their arrival, Malacarne and his student noted that the woman's cervix was swollen and inflamed, and that the baby's right arm was not only already partially delivered, but dark and cold, indicating the baby was likely dead. Assiduous attempts were made by Malacarne, the midwife, and Malacarne's student, Girolamo Sburlato, to manually reposition the baby so that it could be delivered. Malacarne recorded that he had considerable trust in Sburlato, who, under his direction, "had already extracted a number of placentas, and poorly positioned fetuses, with success."[34] Nonetheless, these efforts proved fruitless and the woman's condition only worsened, resulting in her death only a few hours later.

Given the difficulty and unusualness of the case, including a surprising lack of blood during the entire ordeal, Malacarne was desperate to perform an autopsy. He was, however, "with threats, absolutely denied" by the woman's family. In an act that Malacarne painted as part of the medical practitioner's noble pursuit of knowledge, the surgeon, with the help of Sburlato and a gravedigger (and some money, "opportunely dispensed"), retrieved the body from the cemetery so that he could dissect it.[35] These efforts revealed that the woman had suffered a severe uterine rupture, and that the baby's foot had pushed the amniotic sac through the tear. After this preliminary investigation in the field, Malacarne proceeded to separate the woman's pelvic region from the rest of the corpse so that he could more calmly and thoroughly dissect the uterus at his home. Although Malacarne had been sensitive to the woman's agony during the labor, once dead, her body became an equally valuable laboratory for anatomical investigation and the production of obstetrical knowledge.

Obstetrical machines and the instruction of touch

If early modern surgeons learned how to perform obstetrical operations primarily through observation and apprenticeship, the establishment of public midwifery schools across the Italian peninsula during the second half of the eighteenth century introduced new possibilities for acquiring such skills. In particular, the widespread use of obstetrical machines and models aimed at cultivating in students, both male and female, a reasoned, theoretically based tactility through which they could assess and manage a variety of childbirth situations. As Susan Lawrence has pointed out, however, "teaching about sensations is fraught with ambiguities. Words serve uneasily to reify experience."[36] In addition to the difficulties of verbalizing the sense of touch, instructors had to work against at least two opposing tendencies. First, critiques of both midwives and man-midwives in this period often presented such practitioners' touch as dangerous and harmful.[37] Women's touch was uneducated and impatient. Man-midwives' and surgeons' was aggressive and clumsy, made especially perilous by the incorporation of unwieldy surgical instruments. In both cases, touch was destructive; hands delivered babies that were misshapen, broken, or scarred. Second, the early modern period increasingly saw touch, long associated with eroticism and carnality, "subordinated to the senses that support a greater distance between bodies"; that is, to sight and hearing.'[38] In *The Birth of the Clinic*, for instance, Michel Foucault suggests that eighteenth-century visual representations of pathological anatomy functioned to redirect the sensory knowledge derived from touch and smell into a multisensory gaze in which sight is the predominant mode of knowing.[39] Obstetrical machines resisted these impulses and provided a controlled space for both male and female practitioners to cultivate touching as a legitimate, embodied, and scientifically rational mode of knowing the body that was as (if not more) important as seeing.

Midwifery instructors such as Bernardino Moscati, Luigi Calza, and Vincenzo Malacarne stressed the importance of obstetrical models and machines to overcome precisely the kinds of limitations that a solely apprenticeship-based type of learning posed. For one, given the extremely limited obstetrical training most provincial Italian surgeons could claim in this period, Moscati cautioned that it would be inhumane to practice techniques on live patients without repeated and regular exercise of skills on machines first.[40] Additionally, the charged atmosphere during a difficult birth could make systematic learning impractical. Moscati's colleague, the surgeon Giovanni Battista Monteggia, argued that because in practice surgeons typically saw only pathological labors and their operations often took place in haste, it was almost impossible "to reason scientifically on individual cases and operate composedly behind the true principles of the art, without rushing to deliver the woman as quickly as possible with a blind touch, dictated as often as not by instinct, rather than by a wise and rational theory."[41]

It was thus on machines or cadavers, rather than at the bedside of living patients, that the professor could unhurriedly "exercise the hand[s] of the students to know" the shape and contours of the gravid uterus and the placement of the fetus within. Under careful scrutiny, the professor could instruct students on how to turn and extract the fetus according to a particular situation. The flexibility and repeatability of the obstetrical machine allowed for students to gain a sense of "the natural situation of the fetus [in the womb], in order to then understand to what extent difficult births had moved away from the norm, and with what easiest means could the problem be resolved."[42] Most importantly, students could reflect on their progress calmly, "far from the commotion caused by the screaming of the pregnant patient and the consternation of onlookers."[43]

For Malacarne, obstetrical models could also help male students learn how to touch the most intimate parts of female bodies in a way that wouldn't jeopardize either party's reputation. This was of particular concern for Malacarne, who wrote a lengthy treatise championing the importance of the 'esplorazione,' a thorough internal examination of a woman's genitals that could help male practitioners judge the state of a woman's pregnancy and predict potential difficulties that might arise during birth.[44] In addition to practice on machines, Malacarne advised students to perfect this technique by exploring "the state of the genital parts of various cadavers, of different ages, and body types."[45] Only after considerable practice might students seek out opportunities to examine, "with the greatest integrity and decency possible," live women. Critically, students needed to gain familiarity with the feel of these parts in their 'natural' condition in order to make necessary distinctions and assessments later on. Students therefore needed to know

> The normal volume, weight, and mobility of the Uterus; the expanse, depth, and normal roughness (*rugosità*) of the Vagina; the toughness, the lubricity of the inner and outer labia of the Vulva; the shape, the direction, and position of the neck and opening of the Uterus.[46]

In this way, Malacarne was providing his students with a vocabulary to understand touch in a comparative, systematic, and scientific manner.

Distancing touch from its associations with both manual labor and sexual knowledge was critical to overcoming traditional cultural barriers that prevented men from assisting women at childbirth. Embedding touch within a scientific discourse aimed at distilling knowledge from sensation protected men from charges of lechery and licentiousness. Touch conceived of scientifically entailed subdividing tactile sensations into conceptual categories such as shape, texture, resistance, and moistness, from which expectations and norms could be defined. Monteggia argued that touch of this kind provided a knowledge that could not simply be conveyed through lectures or textbooks. Recalling a case in which he explored a decesased woman who had had complications during labor involving a uterine laceration, Monteggia was surprised that the practitioner who had delivered her was not aware of the injury. That was because, he conlcuded, the laceration occurred near the top of the vagina rather than on the uterus proper (as was typically taught in textbooks). For Monteggia, practitioners too often based their diagnoses on the "uncertain meanings of the . . . signs deduced from symptoms," rather than the direct understanding of the situation that touch provided.[47]

It may have been Malacarne's concern over just these kinds of issues that compelled him to commission an obstetrical machine rather unlike any of those in use in Italy at the time. As described in Chapter 4, the Pavia machine was distinct from those employed by other obstetrics instructors in that it was a wholly embodied woman.[48] The lifelike model was equipped with mechanical internal devices that would help to recreate as naturalistic an experience as possible for students practicing on the machine. For instance, mechanisms caused the uterus to contract, such that a student attempting to reposition the fetal doll would feel resistance.[49] As Giuseppe Galletti, the machine's designer, argued, teaching students about the various positions a fetus might assume in utero could not accustom them to feeling, and learning how to negotiate, the strong resistance the uterus might exert at its opening or around the fetus, or the innumerable ways it might furrow.[50] What also made Malacarne's device unique among existing obstetrical machines was the model's extreme lifelikeness and beauty. In fact, Malacarne admitted that because the machine was "so elegant and seductively naturalistic," he felt compelled by decency to cover it with a sheet when used for instruction.[51] The machine's most distinctive features were eyes that moved when excessive pressure was applied to the genital area, producing an effect that, according to Galletti, seemed to bring the "automaton to life."[52]

Whereas the Bolognese midwifery professor Giovanni Antonio Galli's famed glass-wombed machine had intentionally eschewed realism in favor of instructional capacity, the Pavia machine was apparently modeled with the explicit intent of erasing, or at least reducing, the conceptual boundaries between model and body. Indeed, for Galletti, the machine mimicked the movements of the human body so "splendidly . . . that it was almost as if it were produced by the secret workings of nature."[53] Even the accompanying fetal dolls were constructed so as to mimic nature as closely as artificial means would allow. They were elastic, bendable at the joints, and contained internal structures that provided an accurate feel and sense of the resistance of bone. According to Galletti, the fetal head "presents its membranous spaces, the interstices of the skull, and is suceptible to enlongation and compression."[54] Thus, the obsterical machine in Pavia did not encourage haste or excessive force as some scholars have charged against such devices.[55] Instead, it cultivated a touch that was sensitive to the natural feel of the fetus and attuned to the delicacy of newborn skin and bone.

While the machine was distinct among its immediate counterparts in important ways, it was in others a perfect exemplar of its age. Like other obstetrical machines, the Pavia model reflected the belief of many eighteenth-century obstetricians that childbirth was an event driven by mechanical principles. Exact pelvic measurements could predict whether a birth would be difficult; the uterus could be understood as a pump that functioned in a larger hydraulic system. Moreover, Galletti's reference to the Pavia machine as an 'automaton' was no accident. Although automata of various sorts had existed as technical marvels since antiquity, eighteenth-century automata were, according to Jessica Riskin, "philosophical experiments, attempts to discern which aspects of living creatures could be reproduced in machinery . . . and what such reproductions might reveal about their natural subjects."[56] In other words, the project of making a lifelike obstetrical model was intended not simply as a kind of referential simulation but as a true recreation of the mechanisms that guided and animated physiological processes.

At the same time, the incorporation of responsive eyes and aesthetic touches remind us that contemporaries were also deeply interested in questions about sensibility and sensitivity, particularly with respect to sexuality and sexual pleasure and their relation to generation. Darren Wagner writes, for instance, that in this period even mechanist medical writers often accepted the idea of 'nervous fluids' or 'animal spirits' that coursed through the body and were essential to "mental and physical sensitivity, awareness, impressions, and responses."[57] Sexuality was therefore "understood and represented through the movement and influence of animal spirts between the body and mind – or, more specifically, between the salacious, sensitive genitalia and the rational, thinking brain."[58] The Pavia machine therefore embodied the late eighteenth-century's fascination both with the mechanical recreation of life and with the physiological processes that produced sensation, desire, passion, and pleasure.[59]

Even the inclusion in the Pavia machine of eyes that responded to pressure applied to the genital area seems to have been a deliberate decision made in earnest.[60] Although this feature clearly rendered the machine an object of potential sexual appeal – such that Malacarne felt compelled to cover it in the name of modesty – it also reconnected the ostensibly mechanical processes of birth to the feeling, embodied subject of the mother. At least in theory, the machine's responsive eyes reminded practitioners of the vital fluid that connected purely physical sensations to an individual's rational brain. Was the womb just its own kind of automaton, independent of the larger automaton in which it resided, and responding in a predicatble way to external stimuli?[61] What caused labor to be set in motion?[62] What were the pathways by which sensation, emotion, and imagination coursed from the mother to the fetus?[63] Obstetrics writers in this period devoted countless pages to these questions. The Pavia machine, produced amidst these debates, thus combined mechanism with attention to sensitivity and sensibility, though in a body that nonetheless responded mechanically and could be managed with the proper knowledge and skills.

As men like Malacarne endeavored to appropriate touch as a legitimate modality and mechanism of expertise, they may have sought novel means of cultivating compassion and sensitivity in their students, particularly young, male surgeons. Encouraging students to be aware of how their touch was received by the women they were delivering suggests the opposite of the dehumanizing effect some scholars have associated with the obstetrical machines of the British man-midwife, William Smellie.[64] Moreover, unlike the anatomical Venuses[65] or similar wax models that had become popular in public museums and in traveling shows, the obstetrical machine in Pavia was explicitly *not* intended as an object of entertainment or prurient curiosity.[66] Although Malacarne was clearly aware of the model's aesthetic appeal, he was adamant that under no circumstances was it to become a "spectacle for the curious," even if they offered to pay for a visit to the mechanical woman.[67] For Malacarne, obstetrical machines were the reserve of those with specific qualifications and expertise.[68]

Critiques of simulation

It is clear that the use of obstetrical machines was widespread in Italy by the end of the eighteenth century. As observers like the German public health expert, Johann Peter Frank, noted, in Italy a combination of entrenched custom and female modesty meant that male professors were still limited in their opportunities to instruct students at the bedside of patients. Even at the largest public maternity homes, like that at Santa Caterina in Milan, where poverty and desperation eroded such resistance, the number of live births was not always sufficient to train a large number of surgeons. Models and machines could fill in the gaps and, in areas without public maternity hospitals, might comprise the majority of practical instruction.[69] Yet, while most contemporaries deemed models necessary, there were some, like Frank, who also warned of their limitations

Frank, who, as health inspector general of Austrian Lombardy, was heavily involved in midwifery education in the state, favored training on live patients and cadavers where possible.[70] Though Frank conceded the need for obstetrical models to assist training, he also argued that it was difficult for students to gain an accurate sense of the feel of the fetus in utero with bulky dolls. Nor was it possible for surgical students to practice procedures like embryotomy on cloth or leather puppets. He advocated instead for the use of recently deceased fetal cadavers in conjunction with pelvic simulators, ideally made with a pelvis from a woman who had died during or soon after childbirth.[71] In 1770, the Macerata obstetrics professor, Antonio Santimorsi, developed an obstetrical machine with just this kind of instruction in mind. Santimorsi's machine featured a stuffed leather uterine cavity lined with waxed silk to make it waterproof. In this way, students could practice on fetal cadavers, including performing embryotomies, without damaging or staining the machine itself.[72] When the cadaver began to flake and disintegrate, it would be replaced with another.[73]

Frank's position on simulated training came from his firm belief in the primacy of touch for the practice of midwifery and obstetrics. "What does the eye have to do with obstetrics?" he asked rhetorically, referring to the tendency of some professors to demonstrate techniques and point out reproductive structures to rooms filled with young surgeons. How could one expect students to comprehend what a professor was doing with his hands while they were moving *inside* the uterus? Or understand how to maneuver forceps from watching at a distance? It was learning by touch, Frank argued, "that should be the only pursuit that has a place in obstetrics."[74] Recalling his own experiences learning obstetrics, Frank cautioned that performing fetal maneuvers only on immobile models poorly prepared him for the actual sensation of turning the fetus in the face of uterine contractions.[75] Galli's glass simulator was thus arguably of less value, despite its potential for visual theatrics, than Malacarne's obstetrical machine, the mechanisms of which allowed for simulated contractions and resistance to the practitioner's touch. Neither, however, could perfectly recreate the sensations of the fetus in utero and the impressive force a contraction might yield.

In fact, the Milanese surgeon Monteggia contended that 'playing around' with padded dolls and pelvises was largely a waste of time. In 1800, Monteggia outlined his own method for preparing cadavers for practical training. First, the intestines and bladder should be removed from a recently deceased female cadaver, then the vagina and rectum above the flexor muscles of the anus should be cut out from the inside.[76] At this point, a deceased fetus could then be introduced into the woman's empty abdominal cavity and positioned as desired for whichever skills or procedures were being taught. Monteggia noted that initially the progress of the fetus might be blocked by the prolapse of any remaining parts of the peritoneum, vagina, or intestine, which would act as a strong bridle on the fetus's head, though this would resolve with additional 'deliveries' as the tissues stretched. Implicit in Monteggia's critique of artificial models is the understanding that the human body cannot be recreated with materials that themselves have not once been alive and that lack intrinsically human qualities.

Looking back on the development of theoretical and practical obstetrics from the nineteenth century, the Ferrarese physician, Augusto Ferro, articulated just this kind of distaste for mechanical aids. At a speech delivered at the *Accademia Medico-Chirurgica* in Ferrara in 1852, Ferro spoke passionately on the subject. Obstetrics, he argued, is learned

> in the dark, [and] he who is a practitioner must have eyes on his fingers, and fingers exercised on parts that resist, and that move with their own force; and not from some mechanical impulse they receive from shapeless dolls, placentas made of rags, stuffed pelvises, and uteruses of wire!!!!! Oh, tragic blinding of the mind! Oh, most disastrous hardening of the heart!![77]

This impassioned plea may reflect changing understandings after 1800 of what animated living beings. Although mechanistic understandings of the body had been challenged already during the eighteenth century, vitalist conceptions of nature strengthened by the end of the century and became prevalent in the next. Vitalism, "the theory that life is generated and sustained through some form of non-mechanical force or power specific to and located in living bodies," opposed the notion that living beings could be defined entirely by mechanical laws.[78]

Enlightenment discussions about vitalism had particular relevance for the field of embryology, as a range of interested parties, from medical practitioners to theologians to jurists, debated whether fetuses developed in discrete stages (epigenesis) or grew from preformed parts (preformationism).[79] Ferro's objection to the possibility that mechanical devices could ever recreate the intrinsic force that animated pregnant bodies and fetuses suggests a rejection of mechanical thinking about the body. In this view, obstetrical machines could never sufficiently simulate childbirth precisely because they lacked the unique vital forces that constitute living things and that are absent in inert ones. Although obstetrical machines continued to be used in the nineteenth century, it is clear that some practitioners had begun to question whether wax and wood bodies, even those as ingeniously constructed as Galletti's obstetrical machine, could truly instill students with the human compassion and manual sensitivity required to attend real women.

The maternity ward becomes a clinic

Practitioners such as Malacarne, Frank, and Ferro all agreed that first-hand experience with living patients was the optimal method of obstetrical instruction, better even than the most naturalistic obstetrical machine could provide. For bedside training to become a primary mode of obstetrical instruction, however, a transformation of the identity of the public maternity ward needed to be effected. As we have seen, the relationship between foundling homes, maternity wards, and midwifery schools varied across Italy. In Turin, while these spaces were intimately tied together from an early date, they remained resistant to male intervention throughout the eighteenth century. In Milan, by contrast, the establishment of a midwifery school in 1767 also provided the justification for the expansion of male surgical training at the adjacent maternity ward. In Venice, with its preference for decentralization, foundling and maternal assistance was never unified in a central hospital, and midwifery instruction took place initially in the private home of the instructor. In Padua, which became known for its extensive collection of obstetrical models and fetal specimens, practical training never relied on a public maternity ward, as one did not exist in the region until the nineteenth century.

This variety reflects in part the fact that such spaces were initially governed by divergent aims. Foundling homes and maternity wards had their origins in traditional concerns for the protection of female honor and the provision of Christian charity. Over time, however, they came to intersect more directly with the interests and aspirations of a professionalizing medical establishment and an expanding public health apparatus. If maternal and infant care, on the one hand, and obstetrical instruction, on the other, were largely separate ventures during much of the eighteenth century, the same could not be said for the nineteenth. As these two areas merged, the vulnerable bodies that populated sites such as foundling homes and maternity wards were identified as valuable experimental material for both specialized obstetrical training and public health research.

In Milan, where these shifts are well documented, the transformation of the *Quarto delle Balie* from a primarily charitable space to a more scientific one occurred in steps during the last decades of the eighteenth century. The first moment of transition took place in 1781 when the entire population of foundlings, wetnurses, midwives, and pregnant women was transferred to its own site at the ex-convent of Santa Caterina alla Ruota, located on the *Naviglio* (canal) close to the *Ospedale Maggiore*. At Santa Caterina, the foundling hospital-maternity ward complex was separated from the *Ospedale Maggiore* in an ideological as well as a physical sense. As medical care was becoming increasingly specialized and the hospital increasingly medicalized, the support of pregnant women, whose condition was neither fully pathological nor 'normal,' and foundlings, who were traditionally a focus of charity, and yet among whom disease was common, troubled categories in a care system that was still working to define itself.

At Santa Caterina, the foundling home was detached from the maternity ward.[80] The two spaces shared a kitchen, wardrobe, and several administrative offices but were otherwise distinct sites. The separation reflected the hospital reformers' belief that it was the proximity of diverse groups of women, many of whom were morally suspect, that had fostered the abuses which so plagued the *Quarto delle Balie*. At the same time, the emphasis on physical separation, which both Bernardino and Pietro Moscat endorsed, may have been an attempt to partition the more domestic space of the foundling home from the increasingly specialized and medicalized spaces of the maternity ward and school. The latter now contained an amphitheater for lectures, a room for anatomical demonstrations, and an anatomical cabinet. On the upper floor were six private rooms reserved for paying pregnant women, and large dormitory-style rooms with up to sixty-six beds for the remaining pregnant women and the student midwives. There were also two rooms with four beds each for sick pregnant women and three rooms for sick postpartum patients. In contrast to earlier maternity wards, then, Santa Caterina was equipped to handle normal and difficult births *and* women who were or became sick during or after their pregnancies.

An even more significant shift in the identity of the maternity ward in Milan took place in 1791 when the midwifery school, which had officially been closed since 1769, was reopened under the direction of Pietro Moscati. From this point forward, the medical supervision of the maternity ward was stressed in a variety of ways. First, Moscati, in his position as Royal Professor of Surgery at the *Ospedale Maggiore*, would reside at Santa Caterina to handle any emergencies that might arise during the night.[81] In addition, Santa Caterina would serve the dual function of providing training to both surgeons and midwives. Surgical students began with a semester-long theoretical course, which included anatomical demonstrations, followed by two months of practical training in the maternity ward. Both Moscatis incorporated models and machines to assist their training and to perfect students' manual skills before their advancement to handling patients in the maternity ward. Under Pietro, students also practiced on cadavers to increase their familiarity with the feel and resistance of human tissue. The possibility of turning the maternity ward into a real clinic, however, was most aided by a rapidly expanding client base. Male surgeons, who were restricted to assisting the poorest patients and managing difficult cases, were increasingly able to amass sustained clinical experience as the population of pregnant patients at Santa Caterina grew. While in 1775–1776, the *Quarto delle Balie* had assisted only 100 women, in 1801, 200 women gave birth at Santa Caterina, and by midcentury, that figure had grown to more than 500 births per year.[82]

The nature of the bedside training for both midwives and surgeons had also changed dramatically since the first iteration of the midwifery school in 1767, becoming increasingly systematic and comprehensive. When a patient entered the ward, her case was assigned to a student midwife who was responsible for her care and the minute recording of her case throughout her stay. Upon a patient's arrival, the midwife assigned to her began by taking a detailed patient history and performing a thorough physical examination that included not only a manual exploration of the woman's reproductive organs but also, in time, auscultation. The student midwife would then be expected to verbalize her findings with regard to the conformation of the pelvis and whether there were any indicators of a difficult delivery. Though the two most senior midwives might direct female students during the actual labor, the preliminary evaluations were always undertaken under the supervision of the obstetrics professor.

In the event of a difficult labor, the professor would explain in the presence of both midwifery and surgical students the physiological causes of the problem and also demonstrate on an obstetrical machine how to manage the delivery. During a patient's post-partum stay, as well, student midwives were expected to follow their assigned patients' progress attentively, including whether the new mothers were successfully breastfeeding. Each morning, the head professor would question each midwife about her patient and whether any changes had occurred since his last visit.[83]

By the early nineteenth century, Santa Caterina's identity had clearly shifted from being a site of charitable assistance for pregnant women seeking a safe refuge to a medical space where women experiencing difficult labors might go to receive specialized surgical care. Giovanni Battista Monteggia recounted a case in 1800 in which a woman experiencing a protracted labor because of the baby's arm presentation was eventually taken to Santa Caterina for surgical assistance. In this case, Monteggia's report was intended as a rapprochement of rural midwives who waited too long to seek medical assistance and overestimated their own abilities – the midwife in this case had tried repeatedly to reposition the fetus herself, resulting only in the extreme inflammation of the uterus and, ultimately, gangrene. What is most significant about this story, though, is the fact that when the precariousness of the situation became undeniable, the pregnant woman was sent to Santa Caterina rather than being assisted in her home.

Over time, Santa Caterina became associated with a tendency toward interventionist obstetrics, following the so-called French school. During the nineteenth century, surgeons at Santa Caterina performed a proportionally high number of risky surgical procedures such as symphysiotomy and cesarean section.[84] Paolo Assalini, one of Moscati's successors at Santa Caterina, argued that this kind of intervention was necessary because of the prevalence of women who came to the maternity ward with malformed bone structures caused by complications arising from malnutrition. Diseases such as rickets and osteomalacia, which caused pelvic deformities, were indeed common among the women, often desperately poor, who turned to public maternity wards. In fact, Assalini spent many years experimenting with different forceps designs to lessen the impact of the device on the fetus.[85]

If the most obvious aspect of the clinicalization of Santa Caterina was the close relationship between the maternity ward and midwifery instruction, the foundling population was also a target of novel medical research in this period. For example, many of the first experiments with inoculation in Italy exploited foundlings as a ready source of human material. Because inoculation was commonly feared and resisted by local populations, foundlings, without parents to object to the procedure, were ideal early test subjects. In 1788, Pietro Moscati performed the first public inoculation of smallpox in Milan on 24 foundlings from Santa Caterina. Moscati followed the method of variolation, or the use of live virus taken from patients with mild cases of the disease, developed by the Dutch physician, Jan Ingenhousz.[86] On the first day, Moscati administered to the children a powdered mixture with the anti-viral component, after which almost all the children vomited. The regiment then called for the children to be given a mercury-based purgative on the third day, and on the sixth day a second, smaller dose of the original smallpox compound, concluding with a second dose of the mercury mixture on the eighteenth day. By the fifth or sixth day, most of the children had developed pustules, and by the seventh, a fever which gradually diminished. The exhibition was largely a success, with the vast majority of the children responding as predicted with mild cases of the infection (two did not develop smallpox at all, and one developed a severe case), an achievement made all the more meaningful as smallpox was then raging in the city.[87]

The availability of foundlings became even more important after the development of the cowpox vaccine by Edward Jenner in 1796 and more widespread public health campaigns to vaccinate populations on a large scale. Apart from local resistance, one of the main difficulties in administering the cowpox vaccine extensively was that it required a steady supply of fresh virus, which was almost impossible to preserve outside the body. It was quickly understood that the cowpox vaccine could be transferred arm-to-arm from those with an active infection, the virus reproducing itself in each subject; however, this always demanded the presence of a previously vaccinated subject with open pustules to continue the chain of vaccination. In the environment of the overflowing foundling homes of the nineteenth century, this supply could be nearly endless. Luigi Sacco, a colleague and friend of Pietro Moscati, and one of the most vocal proponents of cowpox vaccination in Italy, related how in Milan the city's orphanages had been "put to my disposal to perform public experiments."[88] At Santa Caterina, he had organized a medical-surgical commission to introduce the vaccine there. Sacco noted that when he left Milan to continue these efforts in Emilia, he took with him three foundlings from Santa Caterina who were "a few days earlier vaccinated by me [and] from whom I was sure to have sufficient

material to introduce the vaccination" elsewhere, having in the past vaccinated 130 subjects with "a single pustule."[89]

In addition to performing demonstrations of smallpox inoculation and,
later, cowpox vaccination, Pietro Moscati almost certainly instructed the
midwives and surgeons at Santa Caterina in the theory of inoculation. In
fact, he commissioned two instructional wax models demonstrating the
principles of cowpox vaccination that were based on real cases. The first
model consisted of two arms, one of which was the arm of a "girl with
the 'real' vaccine grafted in winter . . . which came to be marked by 11
graduated pustules," and the second, the arm of a girl showing the quality
of the "spurious, benign vaccine," that is, a vaccine made from pustules
that did not actually carry or derive from the cowpox virus. The second
model showed the appearance of both "true" (carrying the cowpox virus)
and "false" pustules on the udder of a cow infected with cowpox.[90] In this
way, Moscati could provide students with a clear presentation of not only
how to administer the vaccine, but also how to distinguish the real from the
false virus and so avoid the dangerous circumstance of introducing material
that had no protective properties.

Instruction in inoculation was also emphasized at the midwifery schools
in Venice and Padua by at least the 1790s. Pietro Sografi, director of the
midwifery school in Padua after Luigi Calza, recorded that he would incorporate in his lessons a discussion about "the utility of the smallpox graft
(*innesto*) [meaning inoculation], the distinction between its good and bad
quality, the proper time to administer the inoculation . . . its preparation,
the mechanism of inoculation, and given its development, the method of
managing it." These lessons would be adapted so as to be intelligible not
only to surgeons, but also to the student midwives, with the ultimate aim
of "persuasively disseminating the practice of inoculation, for the salvation
of subjects, and in turn the public economy."[91] In fact, the requirement that
the midwifery professor incorporate instruction about vaccination into the
curriculum had been formalized in an official *terminazione* (decree) issued
by the Venetian state in 1794.[92]

Educating midwives about vaccination made particular sense. Authorities across Italy interested in mass vaccination programs quickly realized
the important role midwives might play as ambassadors, bringing the scientific interests of the state to local populations, which were often hesitant or downright resistant to vaccination efforts. Not only were midwives
sometimes tasked with administering the vaccine themselves, but also, more
importantly, state authorities hoped to capitalize on the trust and intimacy
midwives shared with their communities to ameliorate fears and "convince
mothers that vaccination was safe and beneficial to their infants."[93]

In addition to vaccination, foundlings were also the constant subjects
of experiments with artificial lactation. Both because of a perpetual lack
of sufficient wetnurses and because of concerns that infants born infected
with syphilis might infect healthy wetnurses, early modern medical

practitioners had long sought alternative sources of milk. At San Celso in the late sixteenth century, for instance, there were attempts to use goat milk, though with few positive results. Often, infected children were simply paired with wetnurses who themselves were determined to be carrying the disease. According to Flores Reggiani, hospital staff in the early eighteenth century experimented with the use of fresh goat and cow milk delivered with a sponge.[94] Only toward the end of the century, however, did efforts to develop a safe and effective artificial nutrition receive systematic treatment. Bernardino and Pietro Moscati experimented with having infants suckle directly from goats, although this proved difficult logistically in the often crowded space of the foundling home.[95] Furthermore, Pietro worked for years on a method to cure infantile syphilis by delivering a mercury treatment directly to the goats from which the infants would then nurse. This method never registered much success since the mercury sickened the animals.[96]

On the one hand, artificial feeding experiments represented the embryotic stage of the development of pediatrics as a medical subspecialty. As an obvious extension of obstetrics, infant care was often addressed in both published obstetrical treatises and midwifery courses. Surgeons and obstetrics professors also recognized that the continued interdependence of maternity wards and foundling homes could facilitate medical research that began with childbirth and continued through childhood. The relative absence of legal protections for foundlings mean that medical practitioners were largely free to experiment with this population. At the same time, the dreadfully high mortality rates at foundling homes provided an almost endless supply of bodies for anatomical investigation. In this way, foundling homes, too, during the nineteenth century became a kind of clinical space in which medical knowledge might be produced.

On the other hand, efforts to develop a safe and efficient means of artificial nutrition were part and parcel of an increasingly mistrustful attitude toward the lower-class wetnurses traditionally responsible for the care of infant foundlings. Authorities of course recognized the necessity of these women, and even toyed with a variety of means, including increased pay, to attract healthy women to serve as wetnurses either in or (preferably) out of foundling homes. Yet, in the context of greater attention to health and hygiene generally, there was a steady stream of criticisms directed against the kinds of women associated with public institutions. It was assumed that these women's bodies were in some way afflicted and therefore dangerous – the women either carried syphilis, had "debilitated constitutions" resulting from chronic diseases such as rickets and scrofula, or were living in unhygienic conditions.[97] Although artificial feeding experiments were never more than marginally successful during this period, the potential development of an effective method of artificial feeding represented the capacity for science to reduce the state's reliance on allegedly unreliable and morally compromised female bodies.

Conclusion

Like midwives, many early modern surgeons practiced their trade unlicensed and without having ever taken a formal course. Before the mid-eighteenth century, surgeons who assisted at difficult deliveries might have gained some knowledge of obstetrics from printed books, by assisting senior surgeons, or by serving in some capacity in a hospital. Surgeons with significant resources might have traveled abroad to London or Paris to gain practical experience and train with established men-midwives like William Smellie and André Levret. As obstetrics began to be taught at the universities, surgeons were more systematically introduced to a thorough, but predominantly theoretical obstetrical instruction. Only in the second half of the eighteenth century, with the founding of public midwifery schools and the formalization of surgical training within hospitals, did clinical obstetrical training for male surgeons develop.

Experiments with vaccination and artificial feeding emphasized the same kind of medical epistemology that transformed maternity wards into true clinics by the end of the eighteenth century. Foundlings, like illegitimate and desperately poor mothers, represented a particularly vulnerable group that could be exploited to promote the interests of an expanding public health apparatus. Moreover, easy recourse to autopsy, without the interference of resistant parents or concerned family members, facilitated the production of medical knowledge that advanced both obstetrics and the emerging field of pediatrics. Thus, even the deaths of mothers, newborns, or foundlings provided opportunities for surgeons to hone their skills, instruct students, develop their physiological understanding of the body, and conduct medical research.

Notes

1 Paolo Bernardo Calvo, *Lettera Istorica di Paolo Bernardo Calvo Chirurgo Collegiato in Torino* (Turin: G.B. Valetta, 1714); for more on Calvo, see Sandra Cavallo, *Artisans of the Body in Early Modern Italy: Identities, Families, and Masculinities* (Cambridge: Cambridge University Press, 2007), 16–30.
2 Cavallo, *Artisans of the Body*, 18.
3 These included the French Royal Academy of Surgery (Bertrandi, Moscati, Nannoni), the Etruscan Academy of Cortona (Tanaron, Nannoni), and the Academy of Sciences in Turin (Malacarne).
4 Valentina Cani and Paolo Mazzarello, "La difficile docenza pavese di Vincenzo Malacarne," *Bulletin d'Histoire et d'Epistémologie des Sciences de la Vie* 24, no. 2 (2017): 153–162.
5 On the professionalization of surgery in Italy between the seventeenth and eighteenth centuries, see T. M. Caffaratto, *L'Ospedale Maggiore di San Giovanni Battista e della Città di Torino. Sette Secoli di Assistenza Socio-Sanitaria* (Turin: U.S.L., 1984), esp. Ch. 11; Giorgio Cosmacini, *La vita nelle mani. Storia della chirurgia* (Bari: Laterza, 2003), Ch. 4; Cavallo, *Artisans of the Body*; Mario Nono and Domenico Bertero, *Storia della Chirurgia in Piemonte e varie vicende*

che l'accompagnano (Turin: Edizioni Minerva Medica, 2018); Renzo Dionigi, *Bernardino Moscati: Maestro di Chirurgia e Riformatore della Sanità Milanese nel Settecento* (Milan: EDRA, 2017).

6 Cavallo, *Artisans of the Body*, Ch. 10.

7 Ibid., Ch. 5.

8 The Vernas (Alberto, his nephew Andrea, and Andrea's cousin, Giovan Battista) in Turin's Ospedale Maggiore are a good example of this. The family held a near monopoly on surgical practice in the hospital from the late seventeenth through the eighteenth centuries, despite the state's efforts to place more control of surgery at the hospital in the hands of university professors. See Nano and Bertero, *Storia della Chirurgia*, 55–56.

9 See Cavallo, *Artisans of the Body*, 22–25, 27–29.

10 Paolo Savoia, "Skills, Knowledge and Status: The Career of an Early Modern Italian Surgeon," *Bulletin of the History of Medicine* 93, no. 1 (2019): 29.

11 Savoia, "Skills, Knowledge and Status," 29.

12 Calvo, *Lettera Istorica*, 8.

13 Filippo Masiero, *Opere Chirurgiche di Filippo Masiero* (Padua, 1724), part 2, 403–406.

14 Ibid., part 3, 631–633.

15 Cavallo, *Artisans of the Body*, 33.

16 T. M. Caffaratto, *L'Ostetricia, la ginecologia e la chirugia in Piemonte dalle origini ai giorni nostri* (Saluzzo: Edizioni Vitalità, 1973), 307–310.

17 Ibid., 308. Joannis Baptistae Bianchi, *De naturali in humano corpore, vitiosa morbosaque generatione historia* (Augustae Taurinorum, 1741), 193–221.

18 In fact, Bianchi was also present during Morano's labor as well as when Calvo autopsied her body. See Calvo, *Lettera Istorica*, 7, 11.

19 Ibid., 10–11, 13–14.

20 Sebastiano Rizzo, *Della Origine e dei Progressi dell'Arte Ostetricia, Prolusione Recitata il giorno 17 Settembre 1776* (Venezia: Carlo Palese, 1776).

21 During the planning for the midwifery school in Milan, Bernardino Moscati noted that several cities had sent surgeons and midwives to Paris to be trained in the absence of existing resources locally. ASMi, *Sanità, Parte Antica*, c. 268, "Riflessioni di Bernardino Moscati intorno allo stabilimento della nuova Scuola pe' Parti," 1767.

22 Dionigi, *Bernardino Moscati*, 50–52.

23 Ibid., 53–55.

24 André Levret, *L'Art des Accouchemens Démonté par des Principes de Physique et de Méchanique*, 1st ed. (Paris: Delaguette, 1753), 76.

25 Dino Carpanetto, *Scienza e Arte del Guarire: Cultura, Formazione Universitaria, e Professioni Mediche a Torino tra Sei e Settecento* (Torino: Deputazione Subalpina di Storia Patria, 1998), 98–102.

26 Carlo Vidoni, *Delle vicende dell'Ostetricia*. (Pavia: Bizzoni, 1838), 43.

27 Carpanetto, *Scienza e Arte del Guarire*, 301–302.

28 Benedetto Maja, *Lettera responsiva . . . all'illustrissimo signor dottor Luigi Calza* (Venice: Milocco, 1766).

29 ASV, *Sanità*, b. 171, Petition of Benedetto Maja, 9 May 1776.

30 Ibid.

31 Lorenzo Nannoni, *Trattato d'Ostetricia di Lorenzo Nannoni* (Siena: Luigi e Benedetto Bindi, 1788), Bk. 2, 106–108.

32 Ibid., Bk. 2, 203–205.

33 Vincenzo Malacarne, *Osservazione dello squarciamento dell'utero in una paralitica partoriente* (Verona: Mainardi, 1814).

34 Ibid., 11.

35 Ibid., 12.
36 Susan C. Lawrence, "Educating the Senses: Students, Teachers and Medical Rhetoric in Eighteenth-Century London," in *Medicine and the Five Senses*, ed. W. F. Bynum and Roy Porter (Cambridge: Cambridge University Press, 1993), 154.
37 Eve Keller, "The Subject of Touch: Authority in Early Modern Midwifery," in *Sensible Flesh: On Touch in Early Modern Culture*, ed. Elizabeth D. Harvey (Philadelphia: University of Pennsylvania Press, 2003), 64–65.
38 Elizabeth D. Harvey, "The 'Sense of All Senses'," in *Sensible Flesh: On Touch in Early Modern Culture*, ed. Elizabeth D. Harvey (Philadelphia: University of Pennsylvania Press, 2003), 1–21, 8. Harvey is following Norbert Elias here.
39 Michel Foucault, *The Birth of the Clinic: An Archaeology of Medical Perception* (Abingdon: Routledge, 1989), 202–204.
40 ASMi, *Sanità, Parte Antica*, c. 268, "Riflessioni di Bernardino Moscati intorno allo stabilimento della nuova Scuola pe' Parti," 1767.
41 G. B. Monteggia, trans., "Osservazioni Preliminari," in *Arte Ostetricia di G.G. Stein*, vol. 1 (Venice, 1800), 5–6.
42 ASMi, *Sanità, Parte Antica*, c. 268; "Riflessioni di Bernardino Moscati intorno allo stabilimento della nuova Scuola pe' Parti," 1767.
43 Monteggia, "Osservazioni Preliminari," 6.
44 Malacarne was following the Dutch obstetrician Hendrik van Deventer whose 1701 work, *A New Light for Midwives*, was the first to fully and accurately describe the relation of pelvic size and shape to childbirth. On Deventer, see Adrian Wilson, *The Making of Man-Midwifery: Childbirth in England, 1660–1770* (Cambridge, MA: Harvard University Press, 1995), 79–87.
45 Malacarne, *L'Esplorazione*, 49.
46 Ibid., 49.
47 Monteggia, "Osservazioni Preliminari," 29–30.
48 See Chapter 4, n. 68.
49 ASMi, *Sanità, Parte Antica*, c. 273. Letter from Vincenzo Malacarne, 9 November 1792.
50 Galletti, *Elementi di Ostetricia*, xiii.
51 ASMi, *Sanità, Parte Antica*, c. 273. Letter from Vincenzo Malacarne, 9 November 1792.
52 Galletti, *Elementi di Ostetricia*, xiv.
53 Ibid., xiii.
54 Ibid., xiv–xv.
55 For instance, Bonnie Blackwell, "*Tristram Shandy* and the Theater of the Mechanical Mother," *English Literary History* (2001): 81–133.
56 Jessica Riskin, "The Defecating Duck, or, the Ambiguous Origins of Artificial Life," *Cultural Inquiry* 29, no. 4 (2003): 601.
57 Darren N. Wagner, "Body, Mind and Spirits: The Physiology of Sexuality in the Culture of Sensibility," *Journal for Eighteenth-Century Studies* 39, no. 3 (2016): 335–358.
58 Wagner, "Body, Mind, and Spirits," 336.
59 Corinna Wagner suggests that eighteenth-century anatomical wax models, particularly the so-called anatomical Venuses, and obstetrical machines influenced literary constructions of female automata in the nineteenth century, at a time when there was a growing distaste for the spectacle of the dissected, fleshy, opened body. See Corinna Wagner, "Replicating Venus: Art, Anatomy, Wax Models, and Automata," *19: Interdisciplinary Studies in the Long Nineteenth Century*, 24. http://doi.org/10.16995/ntn.783
60 ASMi, *Sanità, Parte Antica*, c. 273. Letter from Vincenzo Malacarne, 9 November 1792.

61 Darren Neil Wagner, "Sex, Spirits, and Sensibility: Human Generation in British Medicine, Anatomy, and Literature, 1660–1780," unpublished PhD dissertation, University of York, 2013, 116–122.

62 See, for instance, Giovanni Fantoni, *Anatomia corporis humani ad usum theatri accomodata. Pars prima, in qua infimi, et medii ventris historia eaponitur* (Augustae Taurinorum, 1711); Pietro Simone Rouhault, *Osservazioni Anatomico-Fisiche di Pietro Simone Rouhault* (Torino: Gio. Francesco Mairesse, 1724), 91–105; Pietro Sografi, *Corso Elementare dell'Arte di Raccogliere i Parti* (Padua, 1788), 275–293.

63 See, for instance, *Lettere sopra la forza dell'imaginazione delle donne incinte* (Venice: Gio. Battista Pasquali, 1794); Rouhault, *Osservazioni Anatomico-Fisiche*, 24–41, 48–56.

64 Pam Lieske, "Configuring Women: William Smellie's Use of Obstetrical Machines and the Poor," *Studies in Eighteenth-Century Culture* 29 (2000): 65–86; Blackwell, "*Tristram Shandy* and the Theater of the Mechanical Mother."

65 On the so-called anatomical Venuses, see Ludmilla Jordanova, *Sexual Visions: Images of Gender in Science and Medicine Between the Eighteenth and Twentieth Centuries* (Madison: University of Wisconsin Press, 1993), 43–65; Lucia Dacome, "Women, Wax and Anatomy in the 'Century of Things'," *Renaissance Studies* 21 (2007): 522–550; Dacome, "Waxworks and the Performance of Anatomy in mid-18th-Century Italy," *Endeavor* 30 (2006): 29–35; Martin Kemp and Marina Wallace, *Spectacular Bodies: The Art and Science of the Human Body from Leonardo to Now*, exh. cat. (London: Hayward Gallery, 2000), 32–68; Rebecca Messbarger, "Waxing Poetic: Anna Morandi Manzolini's Anatomical Sculptures," *Configurations* 9 (2001): 65–97; Messbarger, "The Re-Birth of Venus in Florence's Royal Museum of Natural History and Physics," *Journal of the History of Collections* 25 (2013): 195–215; Roberta Panzanelli, ed., *Ephemeral Bodies: Wax Sculpture and the Human Figure* (Los Angeles: Getty Publications, 2008); Joan Landes, "Wax Fibers, Wax Bodies, and Moving Figures: Artifice and Nature in Eighteenth-Century Anatomy," in *Ephemeral Bodies, Wax Sculpture and the Human Figure*, ed. Roberta Panzanelli (Los Angeles: Getty Publications, 2008), 41–66; Joanna Ebenstein, *The Anatomical Venus: Wax, God, Death, and the Ecstatic* (New York: D.A.P., 2016).

66 On traveling wax exhibits, see Richard D. Atlick, *The Shows of London* (Cambridge, MA: Harvard University Press, 1978), esp. Chs. 4, 24; Pamela Pilbeam, *Madam Tussaud and History of Waxworks* (London and New York: Hambledon and London, 2003); Maritha R. Burmeister, "Popular Anatomical Museums in Nineteenth-Century England," PhD dissertation, Rutgers University, 2000.

67 Anna Maerker, *Model Experts: Wax Anatomies and Enlightenment in Florence and Vienna, 1775–1815* (Manchester: Manchester University Press, 2011), 120.

68 Anna Maerker has shown that anatomical models' association with middle-class public consumption was a major factor in their rejection by both surgeons and physicians in Vienna after Joseph II ordered an extensive collection from the Florentine workshop in the early 1780s. Maerker, "Florentine Anatomical Models and the Challenge of Medical Authority in Late-Eighteenth-Century Vienna," *Studies in History and Philosophy of Biological and Biomedical Sciences* 43 (2012): 730–740; Maerker, *Model Experts*, Ch. 5.

69 Johann Peter Frank, *Sistema Completo di Polizia Medica di G.P. Frank traduzione dal Tedesco del Dottor Gio. Pozzi*, vol. 15 (Milan: Giovanni Perotta, 1827), 293–294.

70 Frank was nonetheless acutely aware of the detriments and moral dubiety of subjecting pregnant women, poor and/or unmarried, in public hospitals to the

endless ministrations of unskilled surgeons and students. According to Frank, five, ten, or fifteen students practicing the 'exploration' of a pregnant woman would cause the poor woman not only shame and fear, but also negative physical effects, such as inflammation. In fact, he warned against turning pregnant patients into veritable 'rope dancers' (*ballerina da corda*), particularly in cases in which a professor was paid per student instructed. Frank, *Sistema Completo*, vol. 15, 271–272.

71   Frank, *Sistema Completo*, vol. 15, 292.
72   Giambattista Fabbri, "Antico Museo Ostetrico di Giovanni Antonio Galli, restauro fatto alle sue preparazioni in plastica e nuova conferma della suprema importanza dell'ostetricia sperimentale," in *Memorie dell'Accademia delle Scienze dell'Istituto di Bologna, serie III, tomo II* (Bologna: Gamberini e Parmeggiani, 1872), 143; Giovanni Calderini, "Come si deve imparare a fare le diagnosi e le operazioni ostetriche," *La Clinica Moderna: Repertorio delle Cliniche Italiane* 7 (1895): 185–187.
73   Frank, *Sistema Completo*, vol. 15, 292.
74   Ibid., 267–268.
75   Ibid., 274–275.
76   G.B. Monteggia, "Osservazioni Preliminari," 7–9.
77   Augusto Ferro, "Sulle Presenti Condizioni dell'Insegnamento Teorico Pratico di Ostetricia in tutte le Università e Ginnasi Comunali del Nostro Stato," speech read at the Accademia Medico-Chirurgico di Ferrara, 15 October and 19 November 1852.
78   Catherine Packham, *Eighteenth-Century Vitalism: Bodies, Culture, Politics* (New York: Palgrave Macmillan, 2012), 1. See also Peter Hanns Reill, *Vitalizing Nature in the Enlightenment* (Berkeley: University of California Press, 2005).
79   On the debates between preformationists and epigenesists, see Shirley A. Roe, *Matter, Life, and Generation: 18th-Century Embryology and the Haller-Wolff Debate* (Cambridge: Cambridge University Press, 1981).
80   Felice De Billi, *Sulla I.R. Scuola di Ostetricia ed Annesso Ospizio* (Milano, 1844), 12.
81   Paola Zocchi, "L'assistenza agli esposti e alle partorienti nell'Ospedale Maggiore di Milano e nell'Ospizio di S. Caterina alla Ruota tra sette e ottocento," *S.I.DE.S. Bolletino di Demografia Storica* 30, no. 31 (1999): 171.
82   Ibid., 171.
83   De Billi, *Sulla I.R. Scuola di Ostetricia ed Annesso Ospizio*, 6–10.
84   Zocchi, "L'assistenza agli esposti e alle partorienti," 172–173.
85   Paolo Assalini, *Nuovi Stromenti di Ostetricia e Loro Uso* (Milano: Stamperia Reale, 1811), vii–viii; Zocchi, "L'assistenza agli esposti e alle partorienti," 172.
86   Giuseppe Ferrario, *Della Vita del Professore Giovanni Battista Paletta* (Milan, 1833), 80–83.
87   Ibid., 81.
88   Luigi Sacco, *Trattato di Vaccinazione* (Milan: Mussi, 1809), 14. Quoted in N. Nicoli Aldini, L. Pontoni, P. Scarani, A. Ruggeri, "Documenti ed immagini sull' innesto del vaiuolo vaccino in Bologna al principio del xix secolo," *Medicina nei Secoli Arte e Scienza* 19, no. 1 (2007): 199.
89   Sacco, *Trattato di Vaccinazione*, 122.
90   Nicoli Aldini et al., "Document ed immagini," 202–204.
91   ASV, *Sanità*, b. 181, Report of Pietro Sografi, 30 April 1795.
92   ASP, *Sanità*, b. 400, 2 May 1794.

93 John Chircop, "'*Giusta la benefica intenzione del Re*': The Bourbon Cowpox Vaccination Campaign in Sicily," *Hygiea Internationalis* 9, no. 1 (2010): 170.
94 Reggiani, "Il 'materiale umano'," 570–571.
95 Similar methods were used in Turin, where in 1800 the *Ospizio delle partorienti* kept twelve goats on hand to feed foundlings when an insufficient number of wetnurses were available. T. M. Caffaratto, *L'Ospedale Maggiore di San Giovanni Battista e della città di Torino. Sette secoli di assistenza socio-sanitaria* (Torino: U.S.L., 1984), 52.
96 Reggiani, "Il 'materiale umano'," 570–571.
97 Ibid., 573f.

6   Contested deliveries

Even in light of increased regulation by state and medical authorities, midwives' most important source of legitimation continued to derive from community approval. Parish priests represented an outward face of this recognition; they could attest to a midwife's good morals and ability to perform an emergency baptism, and they often publicized the names of approved midwives in their churches. Yet, it was the reputation a midwife had among clients and neighbors that counted most. Precisely for this reason, midwives tended to be respected and integrated, if not necessarily the most economically solvent, members of the community. The presence or absence of an official license remained a distant consideration for much of the period being examined, though the establishment of midwifery schools and more aggressive licensing practices did begin to alter traditional interactions by the end of the eighteenth century.

This chapter considers moments of conflict between midwives and other community members both before and after the introduction of midwifery schools in the second half of the eighteenth century. An examination of the relationship among midwives and their clients, surgeons, and other midwives reveals periodic discord, but also surprising examples of support and collaboration. Although historians have often assumed constant tension between midwives and surgeons, for instance, the evidence from Italy reveals that the two groups could interact in mutually beneficial ways. On the other hand, the relationship between midwives and the women they served should not be romanticized. Although a number of midwives registered their understanding of midwifery as a female occupation, perhaps even a responsibility, by virtue of women's shared sex and experience of childbirth, individual births were not always moments of female solidarity.[1] Midwives' own concerns over payment, time investment, or personal safety might take precedence over any perceived obligation to protect another woman's welfare. In some cases, midwives assisted clients who desired secrecy and discretion to hide disagreeable situations, but they were generally not so loyal as to overlook a missing payment. In other cases, midwives policed illegitimacy and upheld patriarchal authority both informally and formally, in birth rooms, courtrooms, and early modern streets. And in the event of an infant or mother who died during childbirth, nothing shielded a midwife from the anger that rippled out of a family's loss and grief. In other words, gender was not the defining element shaping the majority of interactions discussed later in this chapter. Although midwives' status as women indeed shaped the contours of their practice and necessarily framed decisions about how to navigate a world dominated by men, midwives also interacted with their communities in ways that privileged religious, class, or professional commitments as much as gendered ones.

Clients, communities, and conflict

Most commonly, tensions arose between midwives and their clients when the former were not compensated adequately or in a timely manner for their services. In such cases, the midwife might make a complaint to the local health board or *protomedicato* for redress. In 1782, for instance, the Venetian midwife Angela Rizzardini wrote that, after delivering the wife of Sgualdo Campolin Murer, her payment was repeatedly delayed, until which time she felt compelled to solicit outside assistance.[2] Similarly, Anna Miotta, originally from Padua but living at the time in the S. Angelo neighborhood in Venice, petitioned the health board after she helped treat and eventually deliver the wife (*consorte*) of Marco Correr over the course of several weeks. During late June and July of 1791, Miotta reported that she was called "more and more times . . . to appear at the bed [of the pregnant woman] in the late hours of the night to assist her while [she was] bothered by excessive pains," ultimately resulting in a miscarriage.[3] Miotta claimed that during her long hours she was compensated only with chocolate and coffee, even though she seems to have, at her own expense, paid for and retrieved medicines prescribed by a doctor for the ailing mother-to-be. In consideration of the extended time spent at the pregnant woman's side and the expenses she supplied for the medicine, the midwife requested that she be reimbursed thirty *lire*.[4]

In some cases, a midwife might go beyond the legal bounds of her profession to help a client who was pregnant out of wedlock – only to be rebuffed in the end by the woman's suitor. The Venetian midwife Regina Servasoni was called by a certain Paolo (whose last name she never learned) in Calle de' Fabri to treat in utmost secrecy and at the most "inconvenient" times the man's pregnant consort.[5] Despite numerous entreaties, Regina never received compensation and was forced to take her case before the Venetian health board. Similarly, in 1796, the midwife Antonia Pasquetti petitioned the Venetian health board after Cristoforo Sasso failed to compensate her for services rendered nearly a year earlier. In this case, grief was no excuse – Pasquetti delivered Sasso's lover safely. In fact, Pasquetti delivered the anonymous young woman [*giovane*] in her own home and then kept her there for an undisclosed amount of time, suggesting the couple was unmarried and delivering an illegitimate child.[6] Statutes strictly prohibiting the secret care of pregnant women in a midwife's own residence meant that Pasquetti assisted Sasso at great risk.

The frequency of cases brought by midwives such as Angela Rizzardini, Anna Miotta, and Regina Servasoni suggest that fair and timely compensation for a midwife's services could be difficult to obtain, for a variety of reasons. First, as a group with no guild or professional organization to provide support, midwives could be particularly vulnerable to such abuses. Despite greater regulation and oversight by medical authorities during the eighteenth century, midwives, as women, were themselves never allowed to form a distinct college or professional organization.[7] Second, the strained emotions involved when a birth resulted in the infant's or mother's death likely resulted in some families' greater reluctance to pay their midwife, as may have been the case with Anna Miotta. In such cases, failure to pay a midwife may also have reflected the kind of power dynamics between patients and healers that existed historically in Italy and which have been described persuasively by Gianna Pomata. As opposed to a modern expectation of payment proffered for services rendered, the early modern cure system operated with a considerably different set of obligations and expectations. In particular, clients expected to negotiate payments with their practitioners and might expect to pay only when treatment was successful.[8]

Although many communities praised midwives who tended the poor for little or no compensation, often midwives were themselves of exceedingly modest means. In such cases, lack of payment or inability to practice for one reason or another could represent real hardship for a midwife and her family. In the city of Venice, we can get a sense of the social status of urban midwives from the professions of their husbands, many of whom were laborers or small merchants, including cooks, helmsmen (*nocchiero di nave*), tailors, servants, coffee makers (*caffattier*), bricklayers, lieutenants, printers, barbers, and shopkeepers.[9] In rural areas outside of large cities, however, midwives' backgrounds tended to be much more humble. Petitions to medical officials often cite the desperate economic conditions of many rural midwives. In the village of Carate outside of Milan, for instance, the licensed midwife Clara Madalena Galimberti, a widow, wrote that she was barely able to provide for her "poor, numerous family," particularly in the face of two unlicensed midwives with whom she was forced to compete.[10] In Venice in 1787, a midwife named Alessandra Longo Spinarol petitioned the health board to be approved and licensed despite the fact she had not attended the anatomical demonstrations and two years of schooling required for official recognition. Spinarol argued that she had practiced successfully for eleven years, two of which were in the company of her aunt, also Alessandra, and nine of which were under the guidance of her mother, Cristina Longo. Now, finding herself in a "miserable state because of having to tend to a numerous family, comprised of seven children in tender age. . . . and a husband without work,"

Alessandra was desperately seeking approval from the health board so that she could continue to practice as a midwife legally.[11]

In a similar case, 37-year old Anna Maria Niccoli petitioned the Venetian health board for permission to practice independently as a midwife after her mother was called away unexpectedly to care for her son abroad. Anna Maria had long assisted her mother, Catterina, a trained midwife, but was not herself licensed.[12] In addition to Anna Maria's petition to the health board, in which she proclaimed her abilities as a midwife, her parish priest sent an additional letter on her behalf. According the priest, Niccoli cared for four young children by herself, and besides her role as an assistant to her mother had no other source of income. The priest was confident in Niccoli's capacity as a midwife and even confided that the woman had in fact continued to assist women in her mother's absence, despite her lack of official approvals.[13]

It is clear that these women had no other recourse to income besides their midwifery skills. The death, injury, or abandonment of a spouse could quickly turn a meager supplementary income into a family's entire source of support. Rural midwives, in particular, seem often to have fallen into these categories, even as neighbors and priests frequently praised them for their acts of Christian charity toward other women. For Anna Maria Niccoli's priest, her upstanding character and practical experience clearly meant as much in his mind as an official license might. Other community members also tended to cite aspects of a midwife's character as well as her practical skills when describing local practitioners.[14] Negative appraisals often mentioned a midwife's tendency to drink too much, or gamble, or otherwise act conspicuously in some way.

Indeed, it was often a lack, or perceived lack, of Christian charity that caused tensions to erupt between midwives and the families in their communities. In 1723 in the Lecce region of southern Italy, for instance, a midwife named Antonella Seppi was accused of causing the death of a newborn after she refused to attend the mother during her labor. The records of Seppi's court case do not indicate exactly why she refused to treat the infant's mother, Maria Monte, but her lack of goodwill was perceived by both the family and other neighbors as an affront to the principles of mutual assistance and charity that were central to small, remote towns like Torre Santa Susanna where Monte and Seppi resided.[15]

The case of Antonella Seppi also reveals the potential for midwives' knowledge of healing rituals and remedies to cast suspicion back upon them when illness struck or death could not be prevented. Especially because pregnancy and infancy were periods seen as particularly vulnerable to outside forces, including magic, midwives came under natural scrutiny because of their intimate involvement at such times. Thus, while midwives in Italy were rarely accused of diabolical witchcraft, they were not infrequently associated with the practices of magical healing, which could be used either to heal or to harm. This was especially the case in remote areas where magical beliefs remained strong well into the eighteenth century.[16] Seppi, for instance, was known to her community not only as a midwife but also a healer. When Maria Monte's infant had trouble nursing, the mother accused Seppi of causing the child's decline. Sickness and harm without an available natural explanation could easily lead to accusations of magic and witchcraft.

Across Italy, ever present fears of a nursing woman's milk drying up resulted in widely held beliefs that envious women might magically "steal" another woman's milk. Given that there were no good feeding alternatives at this time,[17] and that malnutrition must have put a number of women at risk of a reduced or complete inability to nurse their infants, concern over milk was desperately real to early modern mothers. In 1722, another midwife and general healer, Camilla Rubino, was thus similarly accused of causing a mother to be unable to nurse. The episode began with the mother, Cecilia D'Adorante, requesting from Rubino some of her 'childbirth potion.' It is unclear what D'Adorante wanted the remedy for – perhaps because her child was already experiencing nursing issues. In any case, it was Rubino's refusal to provide the mother with the potion that sparked the accusation.

In general, a midwife's healing skills were eagerly sought out by community members, even if they incorporated magic or folk rituals officially frowned upon by the Church. In fact, in the case of Antonella Seppi, before Maria Monte accused her of harming her child, the mother made recourse to the healer for a *breve*, "a slip of paper on which was written the names of the Trinity of words from the gospel and worn on the person as a means of protection."[18] In other words, it was the same skillset that made a healer potentially harmful that also made her particularly useful, especially in the context of remote communities whose access to doctors, surgeons, or other kinds of practitioners might be extremely limited. Repeatedly, it was the refusal of assistance or charity, or the refusal of proper gratitude, that seems to have framed the distinctions community members made between helpful and harmful assistance, rather than the nature of the remedy or ritual itself.[19]

A dramatic example of the tensions that might arise if a midwife refused to provide aid occurred in Milan in the winter of 1798. Late one night that winter, the midwife, Gaetana Chiappuzzi, received a call from an unknown man requesting she come to assist his pregnant wife in the Chiossetto neighborhood of Milan. Chiappuzzi, who lived on Corso di Porta Tosa (today Porta Vittoria), was hesitant to leave with the man, whom she did not know and who had not offered his name. Rebuffed, the man, accompanied by a friend of his, went to the nearest authorities to plead his case. Rashly, a Captain Villa, in charge of the local national guardsmen that evening, ordered his sergeant, Gaetano Silvestri, and eight other troops to return with the man (who finally revealed his name to be Magni) to the midwife's house. Not only was Villa ready to force the midwife to assist the anonymous pregnant woman in Chiossetto, but also even to have her arrested if she refused. The by now large group of Magni, his friend, Sergeant Silvestri, and eight guardsmen returned to Corso di Porta Tosa where Magni's friend immediately began publicly insulting the midwife in "abusive and threatening language," even warning that he would seek to prevent her from continuing to serve as midwife. Despite the harangue, Chiappuzzi, who knew Silvestri well, was willing to return to Magni's home as soon as it became clear that the sergeant would be accompanying them. In stark contrast to the drama preceding her arrival, the midwife, upon entering Magni's home, found his pregnant wife seated calmly with another woman, not experiencing labor pains and, in her estimation, with no signs of impending birth.

In the wake of these events, Chiappuzzi wrote a formal complaint to the Milanese authorities requesting compensation for her trouble. Although Villa protested that he never intended to arrest the midwife, or even forcibly transport her to the pregnant woman, the episode suggests the heightened emotions and various considerations that might accompany a midwife's decision to assist – or not – a potential client. In an urban setting, a midwife was less likely to know potential clients, and therefore concerns for personal safety merged with those of professional responsibility. However, Villa's position that the midwife was obligated to help a woman in labor, regardless of the circumstances, was one increasingly supported by state authorities, who saw midwifery as essential to an ordered public health system.[20]

At the same time, the vicious response to Chiappuzzi's denial of assistance echoed the fear and anger that colored accusations against Camilla Rubino when she refused to provide her childbirth potion. Although the particular circumstances of each case were vastly different – one involving recourse to police in an urban setting, the other suspicion of witchcraft in an intimate village – the underlying assumption of a midwife's charitable duty to assist another woman in need suggests the still ambiguous nature of a midwife's work in eighteenth-century Italy. On the one hand, midwifery was a semi-professional paid occupation operating in the orbit of official medicine. On the other hand, midwifery was still clearly subject to older traditions of mutual assistance and Christian charity, particularly, but not only, in the context of small towns and villages where community members were likely to be intimately familiar with one another.[21]

Familiarity was indeed often key to midwives' success in small communities, which were notoriously suspicious of outsiders. Local officials caused a minor scandal in the small town of Canneto, not far from Mantua, when, in 1787, they dismissed the midwife Margarita Maltini in favor of the newly licensed Antonia Volpi.[22] Maltini had served for seven years in Canneto as a *levatrice condotto*, or salaried midwife, who served both rich and poor in exchange for an annual income from the community itself. While both she and Volpi were licensed midwives, Volpi had only very recently (eight days prior) received an official patent. Yet, Volpi was a native of Canneto and apparently appealing because of this, both to the town officials who approved Maltini's dismissal and members of the community, who were in favor of the exchange of midwives.[23]

The examples of Niccoli and Spinarol, Regina Servasoni and Anna Miotta therefore demonstrate the multifaceted nature of a midwife's work, which was at once economic, charitable, and communal. On the one hand, midwives such as Miotta and Servasoni were ready to take financial disputes with clients to a higher authority in order to receive the compensation they thought rightly owed to them. On the other hand, even midwives in miserable conditions were often esteemed for charitably helping others in need, though they might be more likely to do so when those requiring assistance were familiar members of the community. These examples may also suggest an urban/rural divide. While Servasoni, Miotta, and Angela Rizzardini were urban midwives in Venice, Niccoli and Spinarol operated in a much more intimate rural setting. The former seem to have had no problem bringing clients, even those in apparently delicate positions, to the health authorities when their work was not adequately compensated. The latter, by contrast, relied more on the goodwill of their neighbors and curates to shield them from outside intervention, as they provided an important and sometimes charitable service to the community.

Midwives and surgeons

Although male obstetrical writers were quick to accuse midwives of hesitating too long or failing entirely to call in the assistance of a surgeon in emergency cases, there is evidence that midwives often did request outside aid when deliveries became obstructed or dangerously protracted. The husband of Livia Catterina Valsecchi noted, for instance, that his wife's midwife, Elena Salvi Bosello, had recognized immediately that the baby was in a poor position, wedged against the mother's pelvic bone, and so requested the assistance of a surgeon, at which point Giovanni Menini was called. Unfortunately, Menini's attempt to dislodge the baby's head, push the fetus back into the womb, and then attempt an extraction by the feet proved ineffective, causing the death of the child and long laceration on its mother's vagina.[24]

In a case with a happier outcome, the delivery of Madalena Mande suggests that midwives and surgeons might even work systematically with one another, recognizing the professional competencies of each without, apparently, much animosity or rivalry. When Mande's midwife, Elena Zavattera, recognized the fetus's malpresentation and the increasing inflammation of the uterus, she recommended that the woman call in the surgeon Benedetto Maja. In fact, Maja was known as one of the only surgeons in the Venetian Republic to use specialized obstetrical tools in his practice. He called this instrument, which was of his own design, *tenaglie*, or 'pincers', but it was actually a revised version of the Levret forceps. According to Maja, the instrument could be used to help guide a fetus's head during delivery without damage to either the fetus or mother. According to patients' testimony, Maja's instrument proved successful in a number of cases and did not leave marks or lacerations on the baby.[25] In Mande's case, a healthy daughter was delivered with Maja's help.[26] Zavattera, for her part, having seen that Maja's use of the forceps could be helpful during obstructed deliveries, did not hesitate to recommend to her patient to call in his assistance.

Midwives' assistance did not necessarily end upon the arrival of a surgeon, either. A patient with a uterine rupture described by Vincenzo Malacarne illustrates both the continued involvement of the midwife in the case even after it became 'surgical', as well as the intimate negotiations that might take place in an emergency situation among practitioners, the laboring mother, and her relatives. When Malacarne was called to the bedside of a 35-year-old woman with paralysis in April 1778, she had already had a protracted labor of three days and was beset with convulsions and fever.[27] The baby was hopelessly lodged with an arm protruding from the woman's womb. After assessing the situation, the first thing Malacarne did was to ask the midwife, Maria Bagotta, for a complete rundown of the case up to that point, which Malacarne transcribed in full in his report. Bagotta, who had desperately tried to reposition the fetus, recorded that in the midst of these maneuvers, the mother began screaming that she felt she was ripping at the core, at which time she began to experience convulsions and her belly became distended and hard as a rock. Both Bagotta and Malacarne noted the lack of much blood or fluid escaping from the woman, though neither knew the reason was a uterine rupture, a complication rare enough that a practitioner might see such a case only a handful of times in a decades-long career.

Malacarne's ministrations, even given the general consensus that the child was already dead – the hand outside the woman's womb was dark and cold, no movement was felt – were cautious, restricted to an anodyne tincture in an almond emulsion, a small bleeding from the woman's arm, and manual attempts to reposition the fetus, much as the midwife had done in the hours before his arrival. In fact, with little luck after several hours, Malacarne asked Bagotta to try again herself to reposition the fetus, considering that she perhaps had smaller and more dexterous hands.[28] In his case report, Malacarne also noted in several places the extreme distress he felt at the agony the mother was experiencing – her screams were "heartbreaking", they "penetrated the heavens, and our hearts."[29] When Malacarne did finally suggest the use of embryotomy to remove the fetus in pieces, neither the mother nor her relatives consented to the operation, a decision the surgeon respected. Thus, while Malacarne presents himself as the protagonist in the story he tells, he is clearly sensitive to those around him, including the midwife, and, in particular, the mother, whose responses guided his own actions.

Of course, not all cases ended with surgeons and midwives on good terms. In a 1785 case in which the Florentine surgeon Lorenzo Nannoni was called in to assist a difficult labor, the midwife publically condemned the surgeon's actions for resulting in a poor outcome. The mother, who was near 40 years old and incredibly weak when Nannoni arrived, was in a labor that had failed to progress for more than ten hours as the baby's head was lodged awkwardly against her pelvic bone. Judging from the nature of the dystocia, the diminished state of the mother, and the case's similarity to another that had registered a fatal outcome, Nannoni told the woman's relatives that he thought surgical intervention with forceps was necessary – immediately. After a number of unsuccessful attempts with the forceps, Nannoni tried to push the fetus's head back in so that he might find the feet and deliver the child that way, a maneuver that also proved impossible given the contracted state of the uterus and the extent to which the head had already descended. At this point, believing the fetus to be dead, Nannoni resorted to craniotomy, ultimately removing what he noted was a large fetus. Hours later, the mother, too, succumbed, possibly from a hemorrhage or infection resulting from the "uterus having been wounded," both before and during the operation.[30]

Significantly, in the aftermath of the horrendous situation, the mother's family's anger was directed at the midwife, whom they charged hesitated too long to call in the surgeon, rather than at the latter's inability to remedy the situation even with surgical equipment. Clearly, some of the polemic obstetrical writers had directed at midwives' supposed ignorance must have filtered through by the second half of the eighteenth century. Nannoni recorded, paternalistically, that he himself had defended the midwife, despite her oversight in recognizing how difficult the labor was, because it was always "prudent to see what could be achieved by the mother's forces."[31] The midwife, however, along with another unnamed surgeon, countered by attacking the violence of Nannoni's interventions. Nannoni, from whose perspective the case was recounted, notes that he was surprised at the midwife's disloyalty, particularly given that the two had worked a birth together in the past in which she had apparently recognized the necessity of surgical intervention and supported his use of forceps.[32] Though it is impossible to know if the midwife's accusations were simply defensive, or even perhaps borne out of guilt, it is clear that the death of the mother and/or fetus could easily sow discord among all parties involved.

Perhaps because of the circulation of stories about cases like the one just recounted, it could sometimes be difficult to find a surgeon willing to take on a difficult delivery at all, even when a midwife did seek help. In some instances, a particularly remote area could mean the nearest surgeon was simply too far away to offer timely assistance. In others, the surgeon might refuse the case for a variety of reasons. A 30-year-old pregnant woman who experienced a violent hemorrhage as she neared full term called in a surgeon whose only advice was to rest, given that, as he explained, he was not knowledgeable in obstetrics. He recommended calling in another practitioner.[33]

Even when their training was sufficient, it seems some surgeons hoped to avoid desperate obstetrical cases altogether, given the frequently poor outcomes. A letter from a Venetian priest in 1793 described a harrowing case of a labor gone badly and the difficulty of finding a receptive surgeon to assist. When the wife of Stuttio Tachinetto found herself in an increasingly desperate condition during her labor, her attending midwife conscientiously requested the assistance of a surgeon. Tachinetto and his godfather immediately took to the streets to track down help. However, it took the men four hours and two failed attempts before they were able to find an amenable surgeon, at which point the pregnant woman was nearly dead:

> In company of his godfather, Girolamo Palladin, he [Tachinetto] went in search of a Professor, in order to call him in to help, to save his poor wife; and at the sixth hour in the night he went to the surgeon Sig. Zuanne Carminati at the Tolentini, begging him as an act of charity to come with them to assist a pregnant woman, who was in danger of death, he [Carminati] responded that he was sick at home, when in reality he wasn't; neither pleas nor displays were enough to remove him, and, seeing such resistance, they took themselves to another surgeon at San. Tomei, Sig. Carlo Gramarcola, who claimed the same misfortune as Carminati, who responded that he didn't want to come; finally they went to S. Giacomo dall'Orio, and appealed to the assistance of the surgeon Sig. Sento Novello, who promptly came with them, to find the poor woman nearly dead for having had to wait four hours for help.[34]

Perhaps because at the time recourse to a surgeon still commonly indicated a delivery that was beyond even surgical aid, it seems some male practitioners were hesitant to assist at emergencies at all.

As we saw in the previous chapter, the extensive theoretical knowledge a surgeon or physician might have obtained at university could be wholly inadequate when faced in person with a difficult labor. Neither bloodletting nor fumigations served much purpose for the complications of pregnancy, and a last-chance appeal to surgical operations in this period typically signaled that either the mother's or fetus's life had already been lost. Thus, regardless of official mandates to call in surgeons or physicians in emergency situations, midwives might find little aid available, either because of male professionals' own disinclination to involving themselves in such situations, or more simply because of the remoteness of the delivery. Rather than the oft-described situation in which male practitioners were chomping at the bit to usurp women's position as birth attendants, Tachinetto's case suggests that male practitioners might want to avoid entirely the risks of assisting at a delivery.

Despite the fact that the number of male surgeons trained in obstetrics remained limited in Italy throughout the eighteenth century, medical authorities in some areas nonetheless attempted to expand the range of activities of such practitioners at the expense of female midwives. In Venice, for instance, statutes issued in the last years of the century prohibited midwives from engaging even in manual operations, such as the internal or external version of a fetus in an unfavorable position. Although midwives across Italy were commonly excluded from the use of surgical instruments, the extension of the surgeon's competencies to include manual obstetrical maneuvers represented a significant encroachment on the midwife's traditional sphere of activity. Indeed, manual operations had in part defined the special expertise that distinguished midwives from the friends, neighbors, or other assistants that might attend a birth. By redefining certain procedures as *surgical*, however, medical authorities could legally keep them out of the hands of midwives, whose work was increasingly circumscribed vis-à-vis that of surgeons. Unsurprisingly, more than one midwife rejected this encroachment, both for its professional implications and for more practical concerns.

On 28 November 1800, Benedetta Fedeli Trevisan, a recently approved midwife, sent a petition to the Supreme Royal Health Tribunal (*Regio Supremo Tribunale di Sanità*) in Venice[35] requesting an examination to be granted the privilege of performing certain manual surgical operations.[36] As Trevisan argued in her petition, time was the key to successfully managing a troublesome delivery. The time it took to call and wait for the arrival of a surgeon in the case of a difficult birth could literally mean the difference between life and death. Moreover, as seen in the case of Stuttio Tachinetto's wife, surgeons with practical obstetrical training could be few and far between, if they were even willing to assist in a desperate situation. It was therefore sensible that, according to Trevisan, midwives be allowed to perform certain kinds of surgical procedures, with instruments if necessary, in cases of dire urgency. Trevisan, who had been officially licensed as a midwife in 1799, had already demonstrated excellent abilities during her training at the Venetian midwifery school. Not only had she obtained a prize for the highest performance in her class, but she had also designed a new kind of obstetrical chair that had received much praise from her instructor, Sebastiano Rizzo.[37] Despite her own obvious competency, and the undeniable practicality of her concerns, Trevisan's petition caused much debate among the officials of both the Venetian health tribunal and the College of Surgeons. In fact, the Venetian authorities would take nearly two years finally to issue a decision on the case.

Although Trevisan was eventually permitted to sit for an exam and was ultimately granted a license to use instruments, her case was atypical. For one, the Venetian college of surgeons was notably aggressive in its circumscription of midwives' activities, despite the fact that male surgical students in Venice had only been regularly instructed in obstetrical operations of this kind since 1780. The fact that Trevisan even petitioned for an official recognition of her capacity also distinguished her from other midwives, who tended to ignore rather than actively resist restrictions with which they disagreed. As we have seen, particularly in rural areas, where official oversight was much more limited, many midwives passively resisted state efforts to formally instruct, examine, and license them. In remote areas, where the timely assistance of a surgeon or physician was unlikely, midwives likely engaged in a range of activities that were officially prohibited to them, but which they nonetheless felt were appropriate and required under the circumstances. Indeed, health officials across Italy indignantly reported midwives who used instruments, prescribed internal medicines, and drew blood. Though in some cases likely exaggerated, the ubiquity of such reports suggests nonetheless that these activities were not uncommon.

In Venice in 1797, the death in childbirth of a 27-year-old woman named Domenica Lucchetta was investigated for just this kind of professional overreach by a midwife.[38] Lucchetta, a widow, had been staying with Antonio Vendramin and his wife, Giaccomina, in the San Trovaso neighborhood of the city during her pregnancy. According to Antonio, his wife had offered Domenica their home out of compassion for the woman's miserable state – pregnant, widowed, and without a stable residence. When, at the end of July 1797, Domenica experienced a prolonged uterine hemorrhage, Antonio called the midwife Lucia Satellico, fearful that Domenica was in immediate danger of miscarriage. After examining the woman, Lucia ordered a powdered remedy to be administered dissolved in a tonic and called for Domenica to be bled. The latter was performed by a surgeon, after which the pregnant woman seemed to rally slightly, though her bleeding never fully ceased.

Fifteen days later, Domenica's hemorrhage increased fearfully, such that Antonio and Giaccomina called again for the midwife, who, recognizing the direness of the situation, immediately requested the assistance of a surgeon. The surgeon, a Sig. Titella, recommended that the fetus be extracted surgically as soon as Domenica could regain some strength. Titella made plans to return the next afternoon, though when he did, he found Domenica experiencing consistent labor pains, causing him to reconsider the operation and instead suggest that they let nature take its course and Domenica deliver naturally with the midwife's assistance. As Domenica's labor progressed slowly into the evening, the midwife Lucia stepped out briefly so that she could attend a baptism, assuming nothing imminent would occur. Soon after her departure, however, Domenica again experienced heavy bleeding and her contractions increased in frequency, leading shortly to the delivery of a deceased fetus.[39] Giaccomina tried to strengthen the exhausted woman with some restoratives, but acknowledging the severity of the situation, called in a priest to perform the last rites.[40] Domenica was able to deliver the placenta, but she ultimately had lost too much blood during her travail and died before either the midwife or surgeon could be recalled to the house.

Domenica's case reveals the complex nature of the interactions that might occur across the childbed of a laboring mother. Although the midwife, Satellico, was ready to defer to the surgeon's expertise in the event of the surgical extraction of the fetus, she was clearly familiar with internal remedies to assist childbirth and unconcerned that her administration of such was overstepping her occupational bounds. The surgeon, for his part, was not overly aggressive in pushing a surgical remedy to the situation when Domenica went into labor, willing to let the midwife conclude what had nonetheless been a difficult and risky labor.

Even the medical authorities were forced to admit that sometimes midwives might have to perform procedures that would ideally be handled by surgeons but could not because of opposition borne out of women's modesty. After 1790, midwives who graduated from the midwifery school in Milan were therefore supplied with a dozen pessaries, to correct uterine prolapse, and a syringe, with which to administer enemas. The latter therapy would typically be performed by a surgeon, but since "pregnant women very often abstain from this treatment even when they have the need" because they do not want to be treated by a surgeon, midwives had to be prepared to step in.[41]

Interprofessional rivalries

As we have seen, one of the most dramatic results of the introduction of midwifery schools and more aggressive licensing procedures was the creation of two classes of midwives, one semi-professional whose training had been institutionalized, the other traditionally trained through apprenticeship and personal experience. Whereas the authority of the latter derived from community approval and trust, that of the former was more ambiguous. Officially examined and approved, licensed midwives were recognized by the state but not always accepted by the clients upon whose business they were ultimately dependent. As Claudia Pancino has observed, it was not only suspicion of the kind of training formally licensed midwives had received, or the setting in which that knowledge had been transmitted – though these were important elements. It was also that licensed midwives embodied a disruption in a pre-existing culture surrounding childbirth, obvious in "their younger age [and] their not always being mothers themselves."[42] In other words, if midwifery had traditionally been understood in some ways as an extension of women's own reproductive experience, midwives who were young and unmarried challenged the notion that managing childbirth was somehow intrinsically related to women's experience of their own bodies.

In the case of Madalena Oliva, rumor and community resistance functioned effectively to neutralize any legitimacy an official license theoretically offered. Although the aforementioned Maja apparently found some success with his forceps in Venice, he seems to have been one of a few Italian practitioners known for using such tools because of women's strong resistance to this kind of intervention. In Oliva's village of Binasco, outside of Milan, the competition between her and another midwife centered on accusations that Oliva used iron instruments in her practice. When Madalena Oliva left Binasco to study at the midwifery school in Milan, Catterina Mazzolletti, an unlicensed midwife, continued to practice in Oliva's absence. Mazzolletti apparently so thoroughly ingratiated herself with the community that upon Oliva's return from Milan the latter was unable to find any clients. Mazzolletti's trust had been earned not only through her practice, however, but also by spreading rumors among her clients that at the *Ospedale Maggiore* Oliva had been instructed to treat patients with surgical instruments. Though false, this accusation apparently turned even Binasco's parish priest against Oliva.[43] Just the mention of surgical instruments therefore registered fear and distrust in the eyes of female clients.

At the same time, the foregoing story clearly demonstrates that mothers saw professionally trained midwives as outsiders, bearing novel attitudes toward the management of birth that devalued women's own embodied experiences of labor. Be it fears that educated midwives would employ surgical instruments, or disgust that they had attended dissections,[44] or simply wariness that such midwives were often much younger and less familiar with their communities than traditional midwives, prospective clients overwhelmingly shunned the services of midwives returning from new midwifery schools during the last quarter of the eighteenth century. As the long-standing arbiters of local midwifery practice, parish priests might be sensitive to the state's increasing regulatory efforts, and even sympathetic to their overall aims, but they also tended to support traditional midwives with close community ties. Certainly, the priest in Binasco was uncomfortable with the idea of a midwife wielding surgical instruments at births.

In the unusual case of Angela Antonia Buzzi from Viggiù, near the southern tip of Lake Lugano, it was not an unlicensed midwife who threatened the trained woman's reputation but rather a local physician named Bassi. For reasons that are not entirely clear, Bassi, a salaried community physician, advised female patients not to call Buzzi, the only licensed midwife in the area. Instead, he recommended the services of the handful of traditional midwives who had remained active in the area while Buzzi attended school in Milan. Perhaps Bassi feared that his own medical authority in the community would be threatened by the arrival of a woman recently trained in the most up-to-date theoretical knowledge and practice of childbirth.[45]

Buzzi, who wrote to the medical authorities in Milan that she had "left her town, her home, her domestic responsibilities, and [had] incurred considerable expenses" in order to be educated at the midwifery school in Milan, was naturally outraged at the unexpected impediments to her ability to practice as a midwife.[46] The director of medical education in Lombardy, Giuseppe Cicognini, wrote personally that Bassi should be severely admonished, and the unlicensed midwives warned – again – to abstain from practice immediately.[47] At the same time, Claudia Pancino has argued that the petitions of licensed midwives forced to compete with unlicensed counterparts are distinct precisely because they do not share the same kinds of invective male practitioners used against traditional midwives. In other words, licensed midwives might request authorities' assistance in suspending abusive practitioners, but they rarely railed against such women's ignorance or lack of educational or anatomical training. That is, even given their own specialized training, professional midwives were, at least initially, respectful of the expertise and competencies of their unlicensed counterparts.[48]

On the other hand, what emerges from the countless petitions to health boards and medical officials from unlicensed midwives who sought to continue practicing without formal training is a picture of a competing system of training and authority. These women wrote of long periods of apprenticeship with respected midwives, often mothers, aunts, or other female relatives; experience with a wide variety of births, both uncomplicated and difficult; and the general approval of a number of clients. Practical experience, but not theoretical or anatomical training, was key. Annunziata Nava of Vimercate, a community situated between Milan and Bergamo, therefore considered the injunction that all practicing midwives had to attend lessons at the new midwifery school in order to be licensed "strange." After all, she was not in need of training in the company of novices – she had thirty years' experience as a midwife under her belt.[49] What more could theoretical lessons teach her?

Despite repeated warnings to desist practice, we know that unlicensed midwives such as Nava just mentioned, Maria Lucia Giudice from Viggiu, and many others continued to do exactly that. For the most part, such women seem to have faced little resistance from clients, who, as mentioned, tended to prefer older, traditionally trained, and familiar midwives. In the village of Mariano, near Como, for instance, the "old midwife," Barbara Ponti, despite being proclaimed insufficiently trained by the head of the Milanese midwifery school, Bernardino Moscati, was nonetheless the midwife of choice for local women. Francesca Maria Secca, who had spent two years training in Milan and touted an official license, lamented that not only was she almost never called upon to serve as midwife, but also that she had "been reduced to the joke of the community."[50] While many unlicensed midwives apparently practiced without ever facing significant repercussions, despite threats of fines or incarceration, in a least some cases abusive midwives might in fact be taken into custody. Nava, for instance, was briefly incarcerated in Vimercate, though her advanced age (she was 60) and long service to the community provoked sympathy for her plight. The priest in charge of prisoners in Vimercate even wrote on behalf of the "miserable detainee."[51]

As a result of widespread resistance to midwifery school graduates, officials in Milan and Vienna responded with measures aimed at raising the professional and social profile of the trained midwife. To counteract the anticipated suspicion of a figure who fit uneasily back into her local community, Johann Peter Frank stressed the important role such women had for the well-being of the entire state. The authorities in Milan and Vienna thus put themselves behind efforts to shore up acceptance for professional midwives in individual communities. Such communities, they believed, should demonstrate "all the possible regard" for such a useful practice, "upon which depends both the fate of Posterity, as well as that of all the Mothers of the Country." Eventually, it was expected that the trained midwife would

> Enjoy all the esteem and distinction that is owed a public figure, who the entire community can trust with issues of much importance. Each approved midwife will therefore enjoy the status of honored citizen within the community, and no one will dare offend her in any manner under a penalty much graver than those which would be merited for persons of lesser distinction.[52]

This respect would extend even to midwives' husbands, who should be "immune from obligations of public labor so that they can attend to their families and to domestic affairs when their wives are occupied at the service of the Community."[53]

Likewise, Frank and others highlighted the necessity of reducing inter-professional rivalries among midwives. It was deemed of great importance that midwives "live in good harmony with the colleague[s] of their profession" and not seek to arrogate another's position or sabotage the public's trust in her. In the same vein, a midwife should always be willing to assist a colleague when necessary and to fill in if one were sick or otherwise unavailable. Clearly, Frank and the other reformers were loathe to see repeated the confrontations among midwives which had been so prevalent in the years immediately after the opening of the midwifery school in Milan. By ensuring approved midwives' salaries from the outset and by stressing professional camaraderie as opposed to competition, the authorities aimed to avoid the tense atmosphere which had erupted in previous years as a result of divides among midwives newly trained in the Milanese school and illegally practicing ones whose traditional experience made them more familiar and often more appealing to prospective clients.

Between church and state: the case of Marianna Boi

The last case we consider is that of the midwife Marianna Boi, whom we met briefly in the introduction to this book.[54] In the fall of 1793, Boi assisted at the delivery of Antonia Volpi. In what was a tragic case, Volpi died after a prolonged illness, leaving the twins she was carrying in desperate risk of perishing along with their mother. Although such misfortunes were of course not unknown in early modern childbirth, what distinguishes Boi's case is the manner in which it entangled the interests of the Catholic Church, the Milanese state, and a professionalizing medical profession. An investigation into the case hinged around the actions Boi had performed to save the souls of the two imperiled infants, and the fact that she may have lied about the course of events to authorities. According to a priest present at the birth and a surgeon who arrived soon after, Marianna Boi had performed a postmortem cesarean section to extract the two fetuses once she had determined that the mother had died.[55] The responses of those involved, including the director of public health in Milan, a leading professor at the University of Pavia, and Church officials reveal the competing and sometimes contradictory interests in midwifery in late eighteenth-century Italy. Whereas the medical authorities in both Milan and Pavia were deeply condemnatory of Boi's actions, the priest present at the birth was impressed with the poise and composure Marianna Boi demonstrated in a moment of extreme duress.[56] The remainder of this chapter focuses on sorting out the responses of the various parties to Boi's actions and what those responses can tell us about the practice of midwifery at the end of the eighteenth century.

* * * *

One of the key reports in Marianna Boi's case came from Alessandro Vespa, a salaried town doctor (*medico condotto*) from nearby Melzo who was directed to go to Trucazzano and make inquiry into the events of Antonia Volpi's delivery from those who had been present. At the behest of the Milanese health director, Johann Peter Frank, Vespa questioned the local parish priest, who had been on the scene for the entire episode, and a town surgeon (*chirurgo condotto*) named Vailati who was called in to assist when the birth became difficult.[57] According to Vespa's report, Antonia Volpi had had a difficult pregnancy from the start. During nearly the entire period she had been in a "poor state of health," suffering from dropsy (indicating some kind of swelling or water retention) and fainting spells (*forte sincope*).[58] Despite her health problems, however, Volpi had apparently continued to undertake normal activity nearly every day until just before labor. On the afternoon of October 20, around four o'clock, Antonia found herself in such a state of distress that she summoned her parish priest to her house. The priest immediately sent for a surgeon, as well as the midwife, Marianna Boi, who, being closer, arrived first. It was not until early the next morning that the surgeon Vailati got word about the pregnant woman in difficulty and took off toward Trucazzano on horseback. When the surgeon arrived in the town square around four in the morning he was stopped immediately by the priest, who bore the news that he had arrived too late – the midwife had already performed an operation to remove two living infants, both of whom unfortunately died shortly thereafter.[59]

At this point, the surgeon Vailati thought it best to continue to the house of Antonia Volpi to observe the scene for himself. Once inside, he found Antonia still in bed with a large wound: there was an incision stretching from her sternum to pubis, as well as one extending transversally across the upper abdomen about ten fingers in width. On a nearby chest lay the two infants, who seemed to the surgeon to be full-term. Both Vailati and the investigating physician seem to have been shocked by the bloody scene and the witnesses' description of the midwife's actions. According to those present, very little time had passed between the apparent death of the pregnant Volpi and the cesarean extraction of the twins. In fact, it seemed to Vailati that Boi had done little to confirm adequately that the pregnant woman was indeed dead. Boi had only felt below the woman's nostrils and in front of her mouth, and then placed a lit candle in front of the woman's face to see if the flame flickered or moved, a test that Vespa noted was very equivocal and the least accurate of all those that could be done in such cases, particularly when conducted by only one person.[60] Nevertheless, with death seemingly confirmed, Boi proceeded to perform the cesarean operation, in Vespa's words, "without mercy" and with a poor (*cattivo*) instrument.[61] Medical director Scarpa's unhesitating conclusion in his report was thus that Marianna Boi had not conducted the cesarean operation "according to the rules of the art [of surgery]," and that she had not adequately conducted "the experiments that are required to assure that the mother is really dead."[62]

An additional statement came from the parish priest himself, who presented the entire episode in a quite different light than had the medical authorities. According to Ambrogio Amigone, Marianna Boi had acted bravely, without hesitation, and had performed the cesarean operation "skillfully" in the absence of a surgeon, who, though called, was too far away to provide timely aid. As soon as Boi had determined that the mother was dead, she borrowed the priest's penknife, which he stated was "fortunately very sharp," and made a straight cut, the length of a palm on the right side of the abdomen, cutting only the skin. Boi then "deepened the cut in the abdomen at the upper edge in order to insert a guiding finger and, slowly, widened the cut so that two fingers together could divide away all the parts overlying the uterus, without damaging it or the . . . intestines, which only with great care was she able to hold out of the way." Next, Boi felt carefully until she could stabilize the womb and, slowly and gingerly, made a cut about the length of a finger which she widened to permit the extraction of the fetuses, still in the amniotic sac, the membranes of which she then broke. The midwife brought out first one live and moving (*vegeto*) infant, and then a second, handing each in turn to the priest who immediately baptized them. Although the outcome for both mother and infants was ultimately a tragic one, the priest could nevertheless rejoice that the infants' eternal souls had been saved by the heroic actions of a skilled and unflinching midwife. Indeed, Amigone wrote that he had witnessed the events of the night "with surprise" but also "with joy."[63] With only the priest to offer direction and two other women to provide assistance, the "fearless and intelligent" Boi had successfully conducted a difficult surgical operation to achieve the most humane and charitable end: that of ensuring two innocent souls Christian salvation.[64]

Although surprisingly none of the documents relating to Boi's case mention whether she was an approved midwife or not, a Milanese survey conducted in 1790 states that for Trucazzano there was only one practicing midwife and that she was unlicensed. If this woman was Boi, it might further explain the harsh judgments of Frank, Scarpa, and the *medico-condotto* Alessandro Vespa in their review of her actions. Particularly for Frank and Scarpa, who had been intimately involved in Austrian Lombardy's efforts to expand midwifery education and better regulate practice, a midwife acting so audaciously while also impudently refusing to follow licensing procedures would likely have provoked a particularly strong response in these men. Regardless of her official status, the differing responses to Boi's actions underline the competing interests surrounding midwifery and childbirth in the late eighteenth century.

* * * *

As discussed in Chapter 2, there was much discussion by priests, lawmakers, and medical practitioners in the late eighteenth century about when and how to perform a postmortem cesarean section to save or at least baptize a fetus.[65] Although the procedure had been mentioned by theologians since the medieval period, the postmortem cesarean operation received increased attention amidst new scientific controversies in the eighteenth century.[66] Debates between rigorists and probabilists over the fate of unbaptized infants who died in the womb or shortly thereafter became entangled in this period with competing scientific theories about fetal development, resulting in a frenetic campaign on the part of some members of the Catholic Church to baptize at all costs. Religious authors such as the Sicilian friar and inquisitor Francesco Emmanuele Cangiamila, the Ferrrarese priest Girolamo Baruffaldi, and the Piedmontese friar P. Diodato da Cuneo all wrote lengthy treatises for audiences of priests, doctors, midwives, lawmakers, and officials on how best to ensure the salvation of the fetus's soul in every possible situation.[67] Fra Diodato argued, for instance, that a fetus should be baptized as soon as its delivery became difficult, even recommending the insertion of a syringe of holy water into the birth canal to accomplish the rite.[68] Both Cangiamila and Diodato were strong proponents of performing cesarean sections whenever the mother had died without delivering, even in early pregnancy.[69] In their treatises, such theologians made clear, moreover, that the cesarean operation was not just an obligation for doctors and surgeons; midwives and even priests were also expected to undertake the procedure if they found themselves in a situation that required such intervention.[70]

The proponents of what has been called 'theological embryology' propelled the Catholic Church to enter heatedly into discussions over medical and surgical thought and praxis in the eighteenth century.[71] Particularly in Italy, but also in other strongly Catholic countries such as Spain and its colonies, Catholic clerics renewed their efforts to oversee midwives and influence reproductive practices. At the same time, medical writers demonstrated deep interest in the cesarean operation, not only as a result of their shared religious sensibilities, but also because the operation represented a point of separation between the sphere of action open to male practitioners and that to midwives.[72] Public health officials such as Johann Peter Frank tended to advocate for a more restrained application of the cesarean operation, limited to qualified surgeons or physicians. Thus, while the medical profession in Italy was generally receptive to the Church's prescriptions regarding baptism, divisions did arise with respect to the cesarean operation between those, like Cangiamila, who argued that the procedure was of such great spiritual importance that priests, midwives, and even other laymen might be called upon to perform it, and those like Frank, who were not willing to put a surgical procedure in the hands of women or others not specifically trained in such matters.

In Boi's case there was clearly a significant divide between the interests of the parish priest, who likely directed and encouraged the midwife's actions, on the one hand, and the medical authorities who reviewed the case, on the other. For his part, the priest Amigone's response to the events in Trucazzano was informed not only by his religious worldview, but also by his own personal experience with the cesarean operation. In fact, Amigone had recently been instructed in how to perform the cesarean section by the surgeon Giacinto Beretta of Inzago, who also served Trucazzano as a *chirurgo condotto*. Amigone, and possibly other parish priests from the region, had been present when Beretta had demonstrated for the public (and clergymen in particular) the cesarean operation on a number of cadavers, courtesy of Trucazzano's last large epidemic.[73] Amigone was well aware, having also studied Cangiamila's *Embriologia Sacra*, that in the absence of another trained practitioner, it fell upon the parish priest or midwife to carry out such an operation.[74] Some writers had argued specifically that if parish priests were provided with a degree of medical instruction in the area of childbirth, they might be able to intervene in the absence of trained midwives, surgeons, or physicians in particularly remote areas, potentially saving many lives, or, at the very least, offering them eternal salvation.[75] In the case of Antonia Volpi, the priest worked in conjunction with the midwife Boi to achieve the desired goal of saving innocent souls from the prospect of eternal damnation. Both

Amigone and Boi were familiar with the cesarean procedure, its religious significance, and were prepared, unhesitatingly, to carry out the operation.

By contrast, the medical authorities who judged Boi's actions, the surgeon Antonio Scarpa and Alessandro Vespa, the town doctor sent to investigate the case, were deeply condemnatory. In their opinion, Boi had overstepped the boundaries of her profession while also failing to uphold the standards of medicine required in such a situation (in particular, by neglecting to ensure absolutely that Volpi was really dead). Perhaps unsurprisingly then, Vespa presented a report that clearly favored the surgeon Vailati's version of events, rather than that of the priest. Whereas the priest had praised Boi for her quick thinking and skillful handling under pressure, Vespa and Vailati instead noted that the procedure had been performed poorly and without proper tools. Neither Vespa nor Vailati made any note of what was likely the ultimate goal of Boi's act – the ability to baptize the two unborn infants still trapped within their mother's womb. Their focus was instead on Boi's actions with regard to the professional ambit of midwifery, a boundary that, at least in the medical men's eyes, Boi had transgressed by daring to use surgical instruments. Furthermore, the medical practitioners may have been wary of what they viewed as the Church's encroachment on their own jealously guarded territory. At a time when surgery was gaining in status, and male practitioners increasingly interested in the emergent field of obstetrics, Catholic writers' claims that any parish priest or midwife could perform a complicated surgical procedure was likely vexing.

As for Johann Peter Frank, who ultimately represented a moderating voice in the case – hardly condoning Boi's actions, he nonetheless argued that no criminal charges should be levied against her apart from a strong verbal reprimand – a considerable amount is known about his position on maternal assistance and the cesarean operation. Frank's role as a physician and government advisor grew immensely upon the 1779 publication of his treatise *A Complete System of Medical Police* which was intended to guide states in their management of the health and welfare of their populations. In German and Austrian territories, and also in Austrian Lombardy, Frank's influence was profound.[76]

In addition to sections on maternal welfare more generally, Frank discussed the cesarean operation directly in a chapter entitled, "On the operation of pregnant women who die before giving birth and of the preservation of the fetus." Frank supported performing the cesarean in cases in which the mother had died, arguing that both human law and good sense commanded that there at least be an attempt to save the fetus's life in the event its mother died prematurely. Those who impeded a surgeon from performing the operation could even be considered guilty of homicide.[77] At the same time, however, Frank criticized the zeal of those like Cangiamila, cautioning that too much ardor might lead to many instances in which the mother was cut into without ensuring she was truly dead. To prevent such a mishap, Frank outlined several tests that could be performed to be entirely sure of the woman's death. Ultimately, Frank advised caution, reasoning that the slight possibility of saving the baby's life was not worth ensuring the mother's death in cases in which there was any chance she was alive. Unlike Cangiamila, Frank's main motivation for performing a postmortem cesarean section was to save the infant's life, even though he acknowledged that successful outcomes in such instances were rare. Despite his overall approval of the postmortem cesarean operation, Frank was wary of the notion of a midwife or parish priest performing the procedure, preferring these to call in a physician or surgeon instead to undertake the actual operation. In the case of Marianna Boi, Frank's main concerns in regard to the cesarean operation were realized – a less-experienced practitioner had undertaken the operation without definitively ensuring the mother was dead.

What is absent from Scarpa's and Vespa's reports, and what may have been recognized by Frank, however, is that Boi and the priest Amigone did, in fact, call a surgeon immediately. However, because Trucazzano seems to have lacked a town surgeon or doctor of its own (and so shared these practitioners with nearby communities), Boi's assistance was the only kind immediately available for Antonia Volpi. As Lombardy's medical director, Frank was well aware of the necessity of locally salaried medical practitioners to aid rural communities; in fact, he had discussed this topic thoroughly in *A Complete System of Medical Police*. He was also aware that, however much he might desire otherwise, there were many instances in which midwives were compelled to act without the supervision of a surgeon or a physician, not because they refused to call in assistance, but because such trained individuals were not present in many remote areas. Frank was also acutely aware of the significance of the parish priest as a kind of gatekeeper through which state directives would have to pass to reach local communities. As Claudia Pancino notes, the priest's authority was always as much "temporal as it was spiritual," and thus alienating the priest for doing largely what Frank himself had advocated in the *Complete System* – counseling families to undertake measures that could potentially save a fetus's life – could hardly be in the authorities' best interests.[78] Future efforts to reform and rationalize public health in Lombardy would necessarily rely on the cooperation of local priests Amigone.

Conclusion

The case of Marianna Boi illustrates that conflicts surrounding who had authority over childbirth in eighteenth-century Italy were not limited to gendered contests between midwives and ambitious male medical practitioners. The Catholic Church's influence weighed heavily on both state and medical policy, and shaped the way practitioners navigated the care of and relationship between mother and fetus. The popularization of the cesarean operation began with the Church's campaign for fetal baptism, even though today the procedure has become synonymous with the medicalization and hospitalization of childbirth. Frank and other administrators' concerns with the preservation of citizens-subjects, and the Church's with souls, combined in the eighteenth century to surveil and access women's bodies in particularly invasive ways. Midwives were not, however, necessarily protectors of other women's bodies. Midwives like Boi were deeply persuaded by the Church's recommendations on fetal baptism, even at the expense of the mother's bodily integrity.

Looking beyond expectations of either gendered conflict or solidarity further reveals the nuanced landscape in which early modern midwives practiced. Midwives might police illegitimacy, for instance, or they might conceal it, though it was often a concern for timely compensation that ultimately drove such decisions. Similarly, midwives and surgeons might work together agreeably, respecting the professional bounds of the other, though more often than not midwives operated independently anyway, owing to the lack of surgeons trained in obstetrics. In fact, the most contentious relationships that developed out of state and medical attempts to regulate and professionalize midwifery were those among midwives themselves. Formally trained and licensed midwives found themselves back in communities that largely did not accept them, shunning the knowledge and instruction they embodied. Indeed, the resistance of local forms of authorization and knowledge transmission to outside intervention represented the single largest impediment to the success of formal midwifery education in eighteenth-century Italy.

Notes

1 On the myth of female solidarity in the context of early modern childbirth, see Linda A. Pollock, "Childbearing and Female Bonding in Early Modern England," *Social History*, 22, n. 3 (1997): 286–306; Laura Gowing, *Common Bodies: Women, Touch and Power in Seventeenth-Century England* (New Haven: Yale University Press, 2003), 50–51.
2 ASV, *Sanità*, b. 174, Supplica of Angela Rizzardini, 24 January 1782.
3 This term was used to refer to a number of situations that today we would distinguish, including a miscarriage early in pregnancy and a full-term stillbirth. ASV, *Sanità*, b. 178, Supplica of Anna Miotta, 7 September 1791.
4 Ibid.
5 ASV, *Sanità*, b. 181, Supplica of Regina Servasoni, 9 December 1795.
6 ASV, *Sanità*, b. 182, Supplica of Antonia Pasquetti, 12 December 1796.
7 Gianna Pomata, *Contracting a Cure: Patients, Healers, and the Law in Early Modern Bologna* (Baltimore: The Johns Hopkins University Press, 1998), 77.
8 Ibid., Ch. 2.
9 ASV, *Sanità*, b. 584, Register of Midwives, 1790.
10 ASMi, *Sanità*, c. 270, Supplica of Clara Madalena Galimberti, n.d.
11 ASV, *Sanità*, b. 589, Supplica of Alessandra Longo Spinarol, 26 April 1787.

12 ASV, *Sanità*, b. 181, Supplica of Anna Maria Niccoli, 2 December 1795.
13 Ibid., attached letter dated 23 November 1795.
14 For example, ASV, *Sanità*, b. 172, Supplica 5 February 1778.
15 David Gentilcore, *From Bishop to Witch: The System of the Sacred in Early Modern Terra d'Otranto* (Manchester and New York: Manchester University Press, 1992), 145.
16 Ibid., 144–148.
17 Foundling homes experimented with goat's milk and other substitutes, but the lack of effective bottles meant that such attempts were largely unsuccessful. On the practice of artificial nursing, see Chapter 5 in this book; A. Pasi, "L'allattamento artificiale presso il brefotrofio di Milano," in *Senza Famiglia: Modelli demografici e sociali dell'infanzia abbandonata e dell'assistenza in Italia (sec. XV–XX)*, ed. G. Da Molin (Bari: Cacucci Editore, 1983), 143–175.
18 Gentilcore, *From Bishop to Witch*, 101, 145.
19 Ibid., 144.
20 See, for instance, ASMi, *Sanità, Parte Antica*, c. 269, "Piano di Regolamento per le Levatrici e pe' Chirurghi Ostetricanti della Lombardia Austriaca," 1791.
21 On the lingering importance of conceptions of charity in medical practice well into the early modern period, see Pomata, *Contracting a Cure*, 36–37, 105–107. In this way, the power dynamics between patient and healer were such that the 'weak' party gained a certain degree of strength from their position as the rightful recipient of Christian charity.
22 ASMi, *Sanità*, c. 270, "Canneto," Report of the Regia Intendenza Provinciale Politica di Bozzolo, 5 September 1787.
23 ASMi, *Sanità*, c. 270.
24 ASV, *Sanità*, b. 171, Statement of Daniele Fabritius, 24 July 1776.
25 ASV, *Sanità*, b. 171, Statements of Madalena Mande and Giovanni Celossi, 20 July 1776; statement of Giovanni Battista Zanfardini, July 30, 1776.
26 ASV, *Sanità*, b. 171, Statement of Madalena Mande, 20 July 1776.
27 Vincenzo Malacarne, *Osservazione dello squarciamento dell'utero in una paralitica partoriente* (Verona: Mainardi, 1814).
28 Ibid., 10–11.
29 Ibid.
30 Lorenzo Nannoni, *Trattato d'Ostetricia di Lorenzo Nannoni* (Siena: Luigi e Benedetto Bindi, 1788), Bk. 2, 203–205.
31 Ibid., Bk. 2, 205.
32 Ibid.
33 Ibid., Bk. 3, 159.
34 ASV, *Sanità*, b. 179, 18 June 1793.
35 After the fall of the Republic, the Venetian health board (*Provveditori alla Sanità*) was reorganized and officially renamed the Royal-Imperial Supreme Tribunal of Health (*Imperial Regio Supremo Tribunale di Sanità*).
36 ASV, *Imperial Regio Supremo Tribunale di Sanità, Terminazioni,* 1802, b. 11, Petition of Benedetta Fedeli Trevisan, 28 November 1800. The case of Benedetta Trevisan is also discussed in Camillo Corner, *La scuola di ostetricia del collegio medicochirurgo di Venezia tratta degli atti priori dello stesso dissertazione di Camillo Corner* (Padova: Tipografia Tenada, 1841), 24–25; Nadia Maria Filippini, "Levatrici e ostetricanti a Venezia tra Sette e Ottocento," *Quaderni Storici* 58 (1985): 149–180; Nelli-Elena Vanzan Marchini, *I mali e i remedi della Serenissima* (Vicenza: Neri Pozza, 1995), 154.
37 Corner, *La scuola di ostetricia*, 24–25.
38 ASV, *Sanità*, b. 791, 28 August 1797, report of Ignazio Lotti, Protomedico, on the death of Domenica Lucchetta.

39 Ibid., testimony of Antonio Vendramin.

40 Ibid., testimony of Giaccomina Vendramin.

41 ASMi, *Sanità, Parte Antica*, c. 269, "Piano di Regolamento per le Levatrici e pe' Chirurghi Ostetricanti della Lombardia Austriaca," 1791.

42 Claudia Pancino, *Il Bambino e l'acqua sporca*, 127.

43 Archivio di Stato di Pavia (hereafter ASPa), *Università, Medicina*, 608. Supplica of Madalena Oliva, Giacomo Canaleri, n.d.

44 ASMi, *Sanità, Parte Antica*, c. 269, Letter from the community of Abbiate Guazzone, 15 August 1768.

45 ASMi, *Sanità*, c. 272, Viggiù, Letter of Paolo Baroffi, 9 June 1769.

46 Ibid., Supplica of Angela Antonio Buzzi, 1769.

47 Ibid., Letter of Giuseppe Cicognini, 7 July 1769.

48 Pancino, *Il Bambino e l'acqua sporca*, 132–133.

49 ASMi, *Sanità*, c. 272, Vimercate, Supplica of Emanuele Milani (Canonico, Protettore de' Carcerati) on behalf of Annunziata Nava, 1775.

50 ASMi, *Sanità*, c. 271, Mariano, Supplica of Francesca Maria Secca, 1769.

51 ASMi, *Sanità*, c. 272, Vimercate, Supplica of Emanuele Milani (Canonico, Protettore de' Carcerati) on behalf of Annunziata Nava, 1775.

52 ASMi, *Sanità, Parte Antica*, c. 269, "Piano di Regolamento per le Levatrici e pe' Chirurghi Ostetricanti della Lombardia Austriaca," 1791.

53 Ibid.

54 ASMi, *Sanità*, c. 272, "Trucazzano." Marianna Boi's case is also discussed in Claudia Pancino, *Il bambino e l'acqua sporca: Storia dell'assistenza al parto dalle mammane alle ostetriche (secoli XVI–XIX)* (Milan: Franco Angel, 1984), 140–69.

55 On the history of the cesarean operation, see Chapter 2 of this volume; Renate Blumenfeld-Kosinski, *Not of Woman Born: Representations of Caesarean Birth in Medieval and Renaissance Culture* (Ithaca: Cornell University Press, 1990); Nadia Maria Filippini, *La Nascita Straordinaria: Tra Madre e Figlio la Rivoluzione del Taglio Cesareo* (Milano: Franco Angeli, 1995); Carmen Trimarchi, "Politica, cultura, religione e corpo delle donne: la pratica del parto cesareo (sec. XVII–XVIII)," in *Donne, politica e istituzioni: percorsi, esperienze e idee*, ed. M. Antonella Cocchiara (Rome: Arcane, 2009), 164–174. More broadly, scholars have explored the cultural, medical, and religious implications of the dissection of the female body in Renaissance and early modern culture. See, for instance, Katharine Park, *Secrets of Women: Gender, Generation, and the Origins of Human Dissection* (New York: Zone Books, 2006); Jonathan Sawday, *The Body Emblazoned: Dissection and the Human Body in Renaissance Culture* (New York and London: Routledge, 1995).

56 ASMi, *Sanità*, c. 272, "Trucazzano," Report of Antonio Scarpa, 6 May 1794.

57 Like the original *supplica* from Marianna Boi, any direct testimony from the surgeon, Vailati, who appeared on the scene shortly after the cesarean section was performed, is now absent from the folder (if it was ever recorded).

58 ASMi, *Sanità*, c. 272, "Trucazzano," Report of Alessandro Vespa, 24 April 1794.

59 Ibid.

60 The question of how to definitively determine if someone was really dead was not an insignificant one in an era of pre-modern medicine. In fact, several eighteenth-century authors wrote treatises on the subject or discussed it in longer works. In his report, Vespa references Jacques-Jean Bruhier d'Ablaincourt's 1742 work, *The Uncertainty of the Signs of Death and the Danger of Precipitate Dissections and Burials*, which was itself a translation and expansion of a dissertation by the Franco-Danish anatomist Jacques Bénigne Winslow which was published in Latin in 1740. Within two decades, the Bruhier d'Ablaincourt

expansion had been translated from French into English, Italian, German, and Swedish and was well known throughout Europe. Martin S. Pernick writes that from about 1740–1850 "the scientific, social, and ethical effects of the Enlightenment combined to render the boundary between life and death frighteningly indistinct," resulting in a kind of epistemological crisis for physicians, theologians, lawmakers, and others who were plagued with newfound uncertainty about their ability to accurately diagnose death. Scientific experiments with artificial respiration, to, for example, revive a drowning victim resulted in even greater confusion. Such anxieties contributed to widespread fears and panic over the possibility of premature burial. As physicians and others attempted to wrangle with the problem, no fewer than fifty medical treatises were published on the subject of the signs of death (many saw putrefaction as the only reliable and sure sign of death). See Martin S. Pernick, "Back from the Grave: Recurring Controversies Over Defining and Diagnosing Death in History," in *Death: Beyond Whole-Brain Criteria*, ed. Richard M. Zaner (Dordrecht: D. Reidel, 1988), 7–74, esp. 20–29; Jan Bondeson, *Buried Alive: The Terrifying History of Our Most Primal Fear* (New York: W.W. Norton, 2001), especially Chs. 3–4.

61 ASMi, *Sanità*, c. 272, "Trucazzano," Report of Alessandro Vespa, 24 April 1794.
62 Ibid., Report of Antonio Scarpa, 6 May 1794.
63 Ibid., Report of Ambrogio Amigone, 30 April 1794.
64 Ibid.
65 Even before the eighteenth-century debates over the cesarean discussed in this article, the operation had been mandated in various synodal and conciliar legislation from at least the thirteenth century. See Kathryn Taglia, "Delivering a Christian Identity: Midwives in Northern French Synodal Legislation, c. 1200–1500," in *Religion and Medicine in the Middle Ages*, ed. Peter Biller and Joseph Ziegler (York: Boydell and Brewer, 2001), 77–90, esp. 86–87.
66 From the twelfth century, priests were prohibited from engaging in activities which involved spilling blood, meaning that they were not implicated in the Church's recommendations to perform the postmortem cesarean. The eighteenth-century religious proponents of the cesarean, by contrast, identified parish priests as responsible to undertake the operation when another trained practitioner was not present. Evidence suggests that postmortem cesareans were not performed on a large scale, despite the religious exhortations to perform them, during much of the medieval period. See Blumenfeld-Kosinski, *Not of Woman Born*, 24–27. Katharine Park argues that, at least by the sixteenth century, the postmortem cesarean section had become a fairly common procedure, particularly in the context of legal concerns over inheritance. This thesis remains, however, largely conjectural. See Katharine Park, "The Death of Isabella Della Volpe: Four Eyewitness Accounts of a Postmorem Cesarean Section in 1545," *Bulletin of the History of Medicine* 82, no. 1 (2008): 169–187.
67 F. E. Cangiamila, *Embriologia Sacra, ovvero dell'Uffizio de' Sacerdoti, Medici, e Superiori, circa l'Eterna Salute de' Bambini racchiusi nell'Utero* (Milano: Giuseppe Cairoli, 1751); P. Diodato, *Notizie Fisico-Storico-Morali Conducenti alla Salvezza de' Bambini Nonnati, Abortivi, e Projetti* (Venezia: Niccolò Pezzana, 1760). Girolamo Baruffaldi, *La Mammana Istruita per Validamente Amministrare il Santo Sacramento del Battesimo in caso di Necessità alle Creature Nascenti* (Venezia: Giambattista Recurti, 1746).
68 Eventually, in-utero baptism fell out of favor over questions as to its validity. The cesarean operation thus became the favored option for baptizing unborn infants. See Adriano Prosperi, *Dare l'anima: storia di un infanticidio* (Turin: Einaudi, 2005), 215.

69 On debates surrounding the practice of cesarean section in the eighteenth cen-
    tury and the broader ideological and religious shifts which began to favor saving
    the soul of the infant over the life of the mother in this period, see Filippini,
    La Nascita Straordinaria; Elena Brambilla, "La medicina del Settecento: dal
    monopolio dogmatico alla professione scientifica," in *Storia d'Italia. Annali 7.
    Malattia e medicina*, ed. Franco Della Peruta (Torino: Einaudi, 1984), 5–147;
    José G. Rigau-Pérez, "Surgery at the Service of Theology: Postmortem Cesarean
    Sections in Puerto Rico and the Royal Cedula of 1804," *The Hispanic American
    Historical Review* 75, no. 3 (1995): 377–404; Adam Warren, "An Operation
    for Evangelization: Friar Francisco González Laguna, the Cesarean Section, and
    Fetal Baptism in Late Colonial Peru," *Bulletin of the History of Medicine* 83,
    no. 4 (2009): 647–675.
70 Claudia Pancino, "La Comare Levatrice: crisi di un mestiere nel XVIII secolo,"
    Società e Storia 3 (1981): 619.
71 Ibid., 619–620. Theological embryology was based on contemporary under-
    standings of when the soul entered the embryo. In the early modern period,
    such thinking was employed in the service of legal and ecclesiastical rulings on
    abortion, the baptism of unborn embryos, the baptism of 'monsters,' etc. See
    Joseph Needham, *A History of Embryology* (Cambridge: Cambridge Univer-
    sity Press, 1959); David Albert Jones, *Soul of the Embryo: Christianity and the
    Human Embryo* (London and New York: Continuum, 2004); Shirley A. Roe,
    *Matter, Life, and Generation: Eighteenth-Century Embryology and the Haller-
    Wolff Debate* (Cambridge: Cambridge University Press, 2003).
72 A handful of male practitioners, including the midwifery manual author Orazio
    Valota, left open the possibility of midwives performing the postmortem cesar-
    ean. See Chapter 2.
73 ASMi, *Sanità*, c. 272, "Trucazzano," Report of Ambrogio Amigone, 30 April 1794.
74 Ibid.
75 On the intervention of parish priests in local medical practice in an English con-
    text, see Karen D. Scheib, "Christian Commitment to Public Well-Being: John
    Wesley's 'Sensible Regimen' and *Primitive Physick*," in *Religion as a Social
    Determinant of Public Health*, ed. Ellen L. Idler (Oxford: Oxford University
    Press, 2014), 113–132.
76 Johann Peter Frank, *System einer vollstandigen medicinischen Polizey*, 6 vols.
    (Mannheim: C. F. Schwann, 1779–1819). The massive work was published in
    several volumes between 1779 and 1817; it was translated into Italian as *Sistema
    Completo di Polizia Medica* beginning in 1807. For an English translation, see
    Erna Lesky, ed., *A Complete System of Medical Police: Selections from Johann
    Peter Frank* (Baltimore: The Johns Hopkins University Press, 1976). For more
    on Frank and the concept of medical police, see George Rosen, "Cameralism
    and the Concept of Medical Police" and "The Fate of the Concept of Medi-
    cal Police," in *From Medical Police to Social Medicine: Essays on the History
    of Health Care* (New York: Science History Publications, 1974); Ludmilla Jor-
    danova, "Medical Police and Public Health: Problems of Practice and Ideology,"
    Society of the Social History of Medicine Bulletin 27 (1980): 15–19; Guenter
    Risse, "Medicine in the Age of Enlightenment," in *Medicine in Society: Histori-
    cal Essays*, ed. Andrew Wear (Cambridge: Cambridge University Press, 1992),
    173–187.
77 Pancino, *Il Bambino e l'Acqua Sporca*, 147–150.
78 Ibid., 158–159.

Conclusion

During the eighteenth century, the development of the field of obstetrics and the emergence of the state as both moral guardian and motor of public health prompted significant changes to the management of reproduction in Italy. The creation of specialized maternity wards and formal schools for midwives perhaps best represents these shifts. At the same time, these two institutional responses to changing social, political, and professional landscapes derived from differing concerns about how to manage childbirth. On the one hand, maternity wards reflected a new response to long-standing social concerns about honor, shame, and illegitimacy. These sites aimed to provide unwed women with a safe and secretive place to give birth, but, for a time, they rarely emphasized improved birth outcomes or access to more specialized care. On the other hand, midwifery schools, although often located in close proximity to maternity wards, *were* shaped from the outset by the efforts of medical men and state officials interested in transforming the management of childbirth along more scientific and rational lines. Amidst these developments, the Catholic Church intensified rather than retreated from its traditional concerns related to childbirth, particularly in light of debates about embryology and fetal development.

Although orphanages and foundling homes had long been focal points of Catholic charity in Italy, the provision of maternal welfare on a broad scale only materialized in the context of the growth and centralization of state administrations in the eighteenth century. Migration patterns and changing legal and gender norms in this period tended to weaken the community bonds that had once regulated sexual relations on a local level. Public maternity wards therefore served women who might previously have been able to rely on local networks for support and to hold the father of an illegitimate child accountable. Instead, by the eighteenth century, a Catholic Church intent on preserving family integrity, and secular legal structures that increasingly privileged male autonomy and exculpated fathers of illegitimate children combined to leave single mothers dependent on new public institutions where they could give birth anonymously and abandon the newborn. In this way, maternity wards represented a new kind of institutional solution to what were otherwise long-held concerns about shame, honor, and wayward sexuality. Indeed, there were strong continuities between these eighteenth-century public spaces for childbirth and the many asylums for fallen women established in Italy in the era of the Counter-Reformation. Both kinds of institutions aimed to morally and spiritually rehabilitate women through strict confinement, manual labor, and religious tutelage.

In conjunction with these societal transformations, the medical profession itself demonstrated a newfound confidence and interest in intervening in the traditionally female realm of childbirth. Supported by rulers intent on preserving and growing their populations through the protection of maternal and infant welfare, medical men made strident claims to authority in this area based on their university training and superior understanding of anatomy. Whereas traditional midwives located their expertise in hands-on training and their own personal experience of childbirth, male practitioners countered this type of knowledge with a conviction in the masculine epistemology of objective, rational, theoretical science.

Across Europe, male practitioners essentially wrote the field of obstetrics into existence through a massive print campaign. Midwifery manuals and other emerging forms of scientific writing, such as the medical journal and the case study, allowed male practitioners to validate their own claims to expertise. In print, men could counter accusations of inexperience by highlighting their role in cases in which surgical intervention heroically saved the life of a mother or child. Even when cases registered poor outcomes, surgeons wrote in detail about their anatomical investigations of deceased patients. Surgeons' reputations could thus be built on the production of obstetrical knowledge through autopsy, even when they were unable to actually save the lives of mothers and babies. Indeed, surgeon-obstetricians greatly benefited from broader changes in medical epistemology during this period that made clinical instruction and pathological anatomy central to medical learning. By the end of the eighteenth century, clinical obstetrical training in hospitals and maternity wards was increasingly seen as necessary. In this transformed environment, maternity wards began to lose their primary identity as charitable sites and to emerge as spaces of specialized care and innovative medical research.

At the midwifery schools opened during the second half of the eighteenth century, male professors employed obstetrical models, anatomical drawings and demonstrations, and rote memorization in a manner that instilled in students a theorized and mechanized understanding of childbirth. As midwives came under stricter control by medical authorities, their professional activity was, in theory, circumscribed. Medical authorities increasingly warned midwives against intervening in difficult cases or employing techniques or tools that encroached upon the surgeon's domain. Midwives also saw a gradual erosion of the public authority they had traditionally held in the legal sphere. By the end of the century, midwives' expert testimony, once highly valued in cases of rape, infanticide, incest, and other kinds of sexual offenses, was neglected in favor of male experts.

At the same time, midwives and mothers in Turin, Milan, Venice, and their peripheries often found ways to challenge the initiatives of state reformers and medical practitioners. Despite legal requirements to do so, many midwives eschewed the process of licensing and formal instruction completely, sometimes with the sanction of a parish priest and often with the approval of past and prospective clients. This widespread preference of community members for traditional over formally trained midwives represents another kind of resistance to the intervention of outside forces in an intimate process long regulated and managed locally. Some midwives willingly enrolled in courses of formal instruction but then petitioned for an expansion of the sanctioned activities allowed to female practitioners (to include, for instance, the use of surgical tools). Furthermore, the elite surgeons who taught the first Italian midwifery courses, men who interspersed Latin into their medical treatises to emphasize their university training, typically had to adapt their courses to accommodate the needs of their female students. Some instructors were compelled to use their students' own colloquialisms and dialects in discussions of anatomy and physiology, and many had to revise text-based lessons for illiterate students. Long-standing modes of training, such as apprenticeship with a senior midwife, remained essential to midwifery education, even after formal courses were technically required for licensing.

Ultimately, the impact of formal midwifery schools and efforts to enforce licensing regulations fell well short of the ambitious goals set out by the reformers and medical men who had devised them. Although broad-minded reformers wished to extend midwifery education and the new scientific knowledge of childbirth far into the provinces, the enforcement capabilities of early modern states were limited. Moreover, reformers faced conflicting goals: even if they could have identified all unlicensed midwives and compelled them to enroll in courses or desist from practicing, it would have been impossible and reckless simply to ban large numbers of midwives. From the start, then, authorities made concessions to many long-practicing midwives, allowing them to continue their work with or without formal training. At the same time, the passive resistance of many midwives who simply refrained from enrolling in midwifery schools or from appearing for licensing inspections was sustained by the widespread preference of local women for traditional midwives. For many mothers, a license or course certificate meant less than a midwife's years of experience and intimate knowledge of the community. Partly because the midwifery schools were especially intent on recruiting younger women, regardless of their own experience of childbirth, many potential clients were wary of the new kind of 'scientific' midwife who contrasted radically with the figure of the mature midwife who had long been a familiar and intimate community figure.

Urban areas surely felt the greatest impact of increased midwifery regulations. Here, a relatively high percentage of active midwives were licensed and formally trained by the end of the eighteenth century. In provincial areas, however, very little changed because of the presence of one or a handful of midwifery schools in the state. Local contexts also shaped specific experiences and dictated how much of an impact new regulations and educational opportunities might have. A parish priest who advocated on behalf of a long-practicing midwife could shield his community from outside intervention, while one who reported the abuses of unlicensed practitioners might instead reinforce the new expectations about training and education of midwives.

Finally, any study of childbirth and its management in early modern Italy must contend with the powerful role of the Catholic Church. In regard to childbirth, the Church had a well-established tradition of intervention and regulation. As early as the 1200s, for instance, synodal decrees mandated that parish priests instruct midwives in the baptismal rite so that they could administer the sacrament in cases of emergency. The midwife's important spiritual duty in this regard remained one of the justifications for a close tie between midwives and parish priests throughout the early modern period. In the era of the Counter-Reformation, the Church directed local priests to work with midwives to help regulate the sexual and moral practices of community members. At least in theory, midwives might help to enforce the Church's official position on abortion, pre-marital sexuality, and magical or superstitious practices. In practice, midwives often did promote religious orthodoxy, though they might also protect clients from outside scrutiny given the right incentives.

Particularly in the eighteenth century, new discoveries in the field of embryology gave way to stringent debates over conception, animation, and fetal development in which the Catholic Church was a vocal participant. Because some of these discoveries were seen to suggest that life began at conception (as opposed to the long-accepted belief that there was a period of several weeks between fertilization and animation), they held profound meaning for the Church's outlook on and involvement in the emerging field of obstetrics. Indeed, the Church sanctioned an aggressive attitude toward the cesarean operation and began to advocate in favor of the life of the fetus at all costs, even if that meant compromising the life of the mother. By mid-century, several Catholic moralists, such as Francesco Cangiamila, were writing treatises that stressed the importance of baptizing any fetus who was potentially alive – whether in utero or not – and detailed the procedures for baptism in a variety of different childbirth outcomes. Although such authors generally acknowledged that the cesarean operation was properly the work of the surgeon, they argued that in his absence a midwife (or a parish priest for that matter) should be instructed in and ready to perform the procedure as well. As Cangiamila had begun to write of the fetus as a potential child even at the moment of conception, some secular reformers, like Johann Peter Frank, for the first time articulated a vision of the fetus as a future citizen endowed with rights. Thus, even as local priests often resisted the intrusion of state authorities in local affairs, the Church hierarchy saw the advanced training of midwives as key to the salvation of infant souls, and a greater oversight of midwives as the critical means to reduce sinful acts such as abortion and infanticide. The Catholic Church in Italy was therefore an advocate of maintaining women rather than men as birth attendants at the same time that it actively encouraged greater control over midwives' practice and the medicalization of women's bodies as a way of achieving spiritual ends.

Despite diverse local contexts, Savoy, Lombardy, and the Venetian Republic all developed policies toward maternal welfare and the practice of midwifery that aligned closely by the second half of the eighteenth century. Secular reformers in all three regions advanced pronatalist initiatives with the intent of growing populations and strengthening their states. To varying degrees, government officials in Turin, Milan, and Venice also began to see the tutelage of female honor and the management of reproduction as a prerogative of the state. At the same time, religion and medicine combined to medicalize women's bodies in new ways, particularly with respect to childbirth. The interests of Enlightened bureaucrats, medical practitioners, and moralist clergymen in Italy thus converged in ways that both protected women as rightful birth attendants and subjected female bodies to a greater degree of medical supervision and intervention.

Bibliography

Printed primary sources

Anonymous. *The English Midwife Enlarged*. London: Thomas Sawbridge, 1682.

Assalini, Paolo. *Nuovi Stromenti di Ostetricia e Loro Uso*. Milano: Stamperia Reale, 1811.

Bartholin, Thomas. *Bartholinus Anatomy*. London, 1668.

Baruffaldi, Girolamo. *La Mammana Istruita per Validamente Amministrare il Santo Sacramento del Battesimo in caso di Necessità alle Creature Nascenti*. Venezia: Pietro Savioni, 1774.

Bellet, Isaac. *Lettere sopra la Forza dell'Immaginazione delle Donne Incinte*. Venezia: Giambatista Pasquali, 1751.

Bernati, Natale. *Breve Istruzioni dell'Arte Ostetricia ad uso delle Comare Levatrici*. Treviso: Giannantonio Pianta, 1778.

Bertolotti, David. *Descrizione di Torino*. Torino: G. Pomba, 1840.

Bianchi, Joannis Baptistae. *De naturali in humano corpore, vitiosa morbosaque generatione historia*. Augustae Taurinorum, 1741.

"Bolletino di Notizie Statistiche ed Ecconomiche Italiane," *Annali Universali di Statistica; Economia Pubblica, Storia Viaggi* 45 (1855): 237–239.

Buckley, Theodore Alois. *The Canons and Decrees of the Council of Trent: Literally Translated into English*. Cambridge, MA: Harvard University Press, 1851.

Calderini, Giovanni. "Come si deve imparare a fare le diagnosi e le operazioni ostetriche," *La Clinica Moderna: Repertorio delle Cliniche Italiane* 7 (1895): 185–187.

Calvo, Paolo Bernardo. *Lettera Istorica di Paolo Bernardo Calvo Chirurgo Collegiato in Torino*. Turin: G.B. Valetta, 1714.

The Catechism of the Council of Trent; Published by the Command of Pope Pius the Fifth. New York: F. Lucas Jr., 1850.

Chamberlen, Hugh. *The Compleat Midwife's Practice Enlarged*. London, 1680.

Chamberlen, Peter. *Dr. Chamberlain's Midwifes Practice: Or, a Guide for Women in That High Concern of Conception, Breeding, and Nursing Children*. London: Thomas Rooks, 1665.

Corner, Camillo. *La Scuola di Ostetricia del Collegio Medicochirurgo di Venezia tratta degli Atti Priori dello stesso Dissertazione di Camillo Corner*. Padova: Tipografia Tenada, 1841.

Corradi, Alfonso. *Dell'Ostetricia in Italia dalla metà dello scorso secolo fino al presente*. Bologna: Gamberini e Parmeggiani, 1872.

De Billi, Felice. *Sulla I.R. Scuola di Ostetricia ed Annesso Ospizio delle Partorienti.* Milano: Società degli Editori degli Annali Universali delle Scienze e dell'Industria, 1844.

Decio, Carlo. *Notizie storiche sulla ospitalita e didattica ostetrica Milanese raccolte da carlo decio.* Pavia, 1906.

Desclee, Lefebvre. *Rituale Romanum Pauli V, Pontificis Maximi, jussu editum et a Benedicto XIV.* Tornaci Nerviorum, 1896.

Duboin, F. A. *Raccolta per ordine di materia delle leggi. editti. manifesti. emanate dai sovrani della real Casa di Savoia sino all'8–12–1798,* 23 toms. Turin, 1818–69.

Fabbri, Giambattista. "Antico Museo Ostetrico di Giovanni Antonio Galli, restauro fatto alle sue preparazioni in plastica e nuova conferma della suprema importanza dell'ostetricia sperimentale," in *Memorie dell'Accademia delle Scienze dell'Istituto di Bologna, serie III,* tomo II, 129–166. Bologna: Gamberini e Parmeggiani, 1872.

Fantoni, Giovanni. *Anatomia corporis humani ad usum theatri accomodata: Pars prima, in qua infimi, et medii ventris historia eaponitur.* Augustae Taurinorum, 1711.

Ferrario, Giuseppe. *Della Vita del Professore Giovanni Battista Paletta.* Milan, 1833.

Frank, Giovanni Pietro. *Sistema Completo di Polizia Medica,* vol. 1. Milan: Pirotta and Maspero, 1807.

Frizzi, Benedetto. *Dissertazione di Polizia Medica sul Pentateucho in riguardo alle legge spettanti alla Gravidanza, al Parto, Puerperio, all'Educazione della Fanciulezza, ed ai Patemi di animo, etc.* Pavia, 1788.

Galeotti, Pio Urbano. *Ostetricia Practica, Ove si Dimostra il Metodo più Semplice, e più Facile per Assistere i Parti Divenuti Difficli per la Cattiva Situazione del Feto, con un Breve Discorso sopra la Generazione, ed Avanzamenti della Gravidanza, e Parto Naturale.* Napoli: Donato Campo, 1787.

Galletti, Giuseppe, trans. *Elementi di Ostetricia, del Dottore Gio. Giorgio Roederer, Tradotti e Corredati di Figure in Rame da Giuseppe Galletti.* Florence: Albizziniana, 1791.

Guevarre, A. *La Mendicita Sbandita Col Sovvenimento Dei Poveri.* Turin, 1717.

Joubert, Laurent. *The Second Part of the Popular Errors,* trans. Gregorgy David de Rocher. Tuscaloosa: University of Alabama Press, 1995.

Le Fort, Léon. *Des maternités: Étude sur les maternités et les institutions charitables d'accouchement à domicile, dans lesprincipaux états de l'Europe.* Paris, 1866.

Levret, André. *L'Art des Accouchemens Démonté par des Principes de Physique et de Méchanique,* 1st ed. Paris: Delaguette, 1753.

Maja, Benedetto. *Lettera responsiva . . . all'illustrissimo signor dottor Luigi Calza.* Venice: Milocco, 1766.

Malacarne, Vincenzo. *L'Esplorazione Proposta come Fondamento dell'Arte Ostetricia.* Milano: Giacomo Barelle, 1791.

———. *Oggetti più interessanti di Ostetricia e di Storia Naturale esistenti nel Museo Ostetrico della Reale Università diPadova.* Padova, 1807.

———. *Osservazione dello squarciamento dell'utero in una paralitica partoriente.* Verona: Mainardi, 1814.

Masiero, Filippo. *Opere Chirurgiche di Filippo Masiero.* Padua, 1724.

Mauriceau, Francois. *The Diseases of Women with Child, and in Child-Bed,* trans. Hugh Chamberlen. London, 1672.

Melli, Sebastiano. *La comare levatrice; istruita nel suo ufizio; secondo le regole più certe, e gli ammaestramenti più moderni.* Venice: Gio Battista Recurti, 1721.

Mercurio, Girolamo Scipione. *La Commare o Raccoglitrice*. Venice: Giovanni Battista Ciotti, 1596.

———. *De gli errori popolari d'Italia. Libri Sette*. Venice: Giovanni Battista Ciotti, 1603.

Monteggia, G. B., trans. *Arte Ostetricia di G.G. Stein*, vol. 1. Venice, 1800.

Muratori, Ludovico Antonio. *Della pubblica felicità: oggetto de' buoni principi*. Lucca, 1749.

Nannoni, Lorenzo. *Trattato di Ostetricia e di lei Respettive Operatzioni*. Siena: Luigi e Benedetto Bindi, 1788.

Nardo, Luigi. "Dell'Anatomia in Venezia," *L'Ateneo Veneto* 20/1 (March–April 1897): 141–192.

Nessi, Giuseppe. *Arte Ostetricia Teorico Pratica*. Venezia, 1797.

O'Kane, James. *Notes on the Rubric of the Roman Ritual Regarding the Sacraments in General, Baptism, the Eucharist, and Extreme Unction*. New York: P. O'Shea, 1883.

Paré, Ambroise. *The Workes of That Famous Chirurgion Ambrose Paréy Translated Out of Latine and Comparéd with the French*, trans. Th. Johnson. London, 1634.

Patuna, Niccolò. *Relazione scritta all'Illustriss: Pierantonio Bruni Avvocato, intorno al Cadavere d'un Feto*. Venice, 1727.

Pechey, John. *The Compleat Midwife's Practice Enlarg'd*. London, 1698.

Plenk, Gioseffo Jacopo. *Elementi dell'arte Ostetricia*. Venezia: Francesco di Nicolò Pezzana, 1798.

Ployant, Teresa. *Breve Compendio dell'Arte Ostetricia*, 3rd ed. Bologna, 1803.

Rizzo, Sebastiano. *Della Origine e dei Progressi dell'Arte Ostetricia, Prolusione Recitata il giorno 17 Settembre 1776*. Venezia: Carlo Palese, 1776.

Rouhault, Pietro Simone. *Osservazioni Anatomico-Fisiche di Pietro Simone Rouhault*. Torino: Gio. Francesco Mairesse, 1724.

Sacco, Luigi. *Trattato di Vaccinazione*. Milan: Mussi, 1809.

Sharp, Jane. *The Midwives Book, or, the Whole Art of Midwifry Discovered*. London: S. Miller, 1671.

Siegemund, Justine. *Die Chur-Brandenburgische Hoff-Wehe-Mutter*. Cologne: A. D. Spree, 1690.

Sografi, Pietro. *Corso Elementare dell'Arte di Raccogliere i Parti, Diviso in Lezioni*. Padova: 1788.

Tanaron, Pietro Paolo. *Il Chirurgo-Raccoglitore Moderno*. Bassano, 1774.

Tranquillini, Giacomo. *Dottrina della Comare, o sia Breve Compendio d'Arte Ostetricia*. Verona, 1770.

Valota, Orazio. *La Levtrice Moderna, Opera Necessaria all Comari, ed Utile ai Principanti d'Ostetricia, ed ai Reverandi Parrochi*. Bergamo: Locatelli, 1791.

Vespa, Giuseppe. *Dell'Arte Ostetricia Trattato di Giuseppe Vespa Professore di Chirurgia, diviso in tre parti procedute da vari ragioanmenti*. Firenze: Appresso Andrea Bonducci, 1761.

Vidoni, Carlo. *Delle vicende dell'Ostetricia*. Pavia: Bizzoni, 1838.

Secondary sources

Accati, Luisa. "The Spirit of Fornication: Virtue of the Soul and Virtue of the Body in Friuli, 1600–1800." In *Sex and Gender in Historical Perspective: Selections from Quaderni Storici*, edited by Edward Muir and Guido Ruggiero, 110–140. Baltimore: The Johns Hopkins University Press, 1990.

Adams, Annmarie. *Architecture in the Family Way: Doctors, Houses, and Women.* Quebec: McGill, Queen's University Press, 2001.

Adams, Christine. *Poverty, Charity, and Motherhood: Maternal Societies in Nineteenth-Century France.* Urbana, Chicago and Springfield: University of Illinois Press, 2010.

Aikema, B. and D. Meyers, editors. *Nel regno dei poveri: Arte e storia dei grandi ospedali veneziani in età moderna, 1474–1797.* Venice: Arsenale, 1989.

Alessi, Giorgia. "Il Gioco degli Scambi: Seduzione e Risarcimento nella Casistica Catolica del XVI e XVII Secolo," *Quaderni Storici* 75 (1990): 805–831.

———. "Discipline: I Nuovi Orizzonti del Disciplinamento Sociale," *Storica* 2, no. 4 (1996): 7–37.

Allegra, Luciano. "Il parroco: un mediatore fra alta e bassa cultura." In *Storia d'Italia. Annali, vol. 4, Intellettuali e potere,* edited by C. Vivanti, 895–947. Torino: Einaudi, 1981.

Allerston, Patricia. "'Contrary to the Truth and also to the Semblance of Reality?' Entering a Venetian 'Lying-In' Chamber (1605)," *Renaissance Studies* 20, no. 5 (2006): 629–639.

Andrea, David D. "Charities and Confraternities." In *A Companion to Venetian History, 1400–1797,* editedy by Eric R. Dursteler, 421–449. Leiden: Brill, 2013.

Armanini, Carlo. "L'Ostetricia in Milano dagli albori dello Xenodochio di Dateo al Tramonto della Maternità di Santa Caterina alla Ruota," *L'Ospedale Maggiore* 4 (1956): 189–198.

Arrivo, Giorgia. *Seduzioni, Promessi, Matrimoni: Il Processo per Stupro nella Toscana del Settecento.* Roma: Edizioni di Storia e Letteratura, 2006.

Astarita, Tommaso. *Village Justice: Community, Family, and Popular Culture in Early Modern Italy.* Baltimore: The Johns Hopkins University Press, 1999.

Atlick, Richard D. *The Shows of London.* Cambridge, MA: Harvard University Press, 1978.

Bakos, Adriana E. "'A Knowledge Speculative and Practical': The Dilemma of Mid-wives' Education in EarlyModern Europe." In *Women's Education in Early Modern Europe: A History, 1500–1800,* edited by Barbara J. Whitehead, 225–250. New York: Routledge, 1999.

Balbo, Prospero. "Delle Diverse Proporzioni tra la mortalità de' fanciulli e quella delle età superiori,"*Memorie della Reale Accademia delle Scienze di Torino* XXXIV: 51–60.

Baldi, Silvana. "L'assistenza alla Maternita' a Torino nel XVIII Secolo," *Sanita' Scienza e Storia* 1, no. 2 (1992): 121–178.

Barchielli, Siliva. "L'istituto vaccinogeno all'ospedale di Santa Maria degli Innocenti di Firenze nel xviii secolo," *Nuncius* 13, no. 1 (1998): 247–264.

Barona, Josep L., editor. *Malaltia i Cultura.* Valencia: Seminari d'Estudis Sobre la Ciencia, 1995.

Barry, Jonathan and Colin Jones, editors. *Medicine and Charity Before the Welfare State.* London: Routledge, 1991.

Bashford, Alison and Claire Hooker. *Contagion: Historical and Cultural Studies.* London: Routledge, 2001.

Beales, Derek. *Enlightenment and Reform in Eighteenth-Century Europe.* London: I.B. Taurus, 2005.

———. *Joseph II: Volume 1, in the Shadow of Maria Teresa, 1741–1780.* Cambridge: Cambridge University Press, 2008.

Bell, Rudolph. *How to Do It: Guides to Good Living for Renaissance Italians*. Chicago: University of Chicago Press, 1999.

Bertoloni Meli, Domenico. *Mechanism, Experiment, Disease: Marcello Malphighi and Seventeenth-Century Anatomy*. Baltimore: The Johns Hopkins University Press, 2011.

Betri, Maria Luisa and Edoardo Bressan, editors. *Gli Ospedali in Area Padana fra Settecento e Novecento*. Milano: Franco Angeli, 1992.

Betri, Maria Luisa and Alessandro Pastore, editors. *L'arte di guarire. Aspetti della professione medica tra Medioevo ed Età contemporanea*. Bologna: CLUEB, 1993.

Bevilacqua, Fabio and Lucio Freggonese, editors. *Nuova Voltiana: Studies on Volta and His Times*, vol. 1. Pavia and Milan: Hoepli, 2000.

Biagi, Maria Luisa Altieri, et al., editors. *Medicina per le donne nel Cinquecento: Testi di Giovanni Marinello e Girolamo Mercurio*. Turin: UTET, 1992.

Bicks, Caroline. " 'Stones Like Women's Paps': Revising Gender in Jane Sharp's *Midwives Book*," *Journal of Early Modern Cultural Studies* 7, no. 2 (2007): 1–27.

Biller, Peter and Joseph Ziegler, editors. *Religion and Medicine in the Middle Ages*. Suffolk: York Medieval Press, 2001.

Black, Christopher F. *Italian Confraternities in the Sixteenth Century*. Cambridge: Cambridge University Press, 2003.

Blum, Carol. *Strength in Numbers: Population, Reproduction, and Power in Eighteenth-Century France*. Baltimore: John Hopkins University Press, 2002.

Blumenfeld-Kosinski, Renate. *Not of Woman Born: Representations of Caesarean Birth in Medieval and Renaissance Culture*. Ithaca: Cornell University Press, 1990.

Bonner, Thomas Neville. *Becoming a Physician: Medical Education in Britain, France, Germany, and the United States, 1750–1945*. Baltimore: The Johns Hopkins University Press, 2000.

Bossy, John. *Christianity in the West, 1400–1700*. Oxford: Oxford University Press, 1985.

Brambilla, Elena. "Il 'sistema letterario' di Milano: professioni nobili e professioni borghesi dall'età spagnola alle riforme teresiane." In *Economia, istituzioni, cultura in Lombardia nell'età di Maria Teresa*, edited by A. de Maddalena, E. Rotelli, and G. Barbarisi, vol. 3, 79–160. Bologna: Il Mulino, 1982.

———. "Tra teoria e pratica: studi scientifici e professioni mediche nella Lombardia settecentesca." In *Lazzaro Spallanzani e la biologia del Settecento. Teorie, esperimenti, istituzioni scientifiche*, edited by G. Montalenti and P. Rossi, 553–568. Firenze: Olschki, 1982.

———. *Alle Origini del Sant'Uffizzio: Penitenza, Confessione e Giustizia Spirituale dal Medioevo al XVI Secolo*. Bologna: Il Mulino, 2000.

———. "Scientific and Professional Education in Lombardy, 1760–1803: Physics Between Medicine and Engineering." In *Nuova Voltiana: Studies on Volta and His Times*, edited by Fabio Bevilacqua and Lucio Freggonese, vol. 1, 51–100. Pavia and Milan: Hoepli, 2000.

Brockliss, Laurence and Colin Jones. *The Medical World of Early Modern France*. Oxford: Oxford University Press, 1997.

Broman, Thomas H. *The Transformation of German Academic Medicine*. Cambridge: Cambridge University Press, 1996.

Broomhall, Susan. *Women's Medical Work in Early Modern France*. Manchester: Manchester University Press, 2004.

Brunton, Deborah. "The Emergence of a Modern Profession?" In *Medicine Transformed: Health, Disease and Society in Europe, 1800–1930*, edited by Deborah Brunton, 119–150. Manchester: Manchester University Press, 2004.

———. *Medicine Transformed: Health, Disease and Society in Europe, 1800–1930*. Manchester: Manchester University Press, 2004.

Burke, Peter, editor. *New Perspectives on Historical Writing*. University Park: Pennsylvania State University Press, 2001.

Burmeister, Maritha R. "Popular Anatomical Museums in Nineteenth-Century England," PhD disseration, Rutgers University, 2000.

Bynum, W. F. and Roy Porter, editors. *William Hunter and the Eighteenth-Century Medical World*. Cambridge: Cambridge University Press, 1985.

———. *Medicine and the Five Senses*. Cambridge: Cambridge University Press, 1993.

Byrne, Joseph P. *Health and Wellness in the Renaissance and Enlightenment*. Santa Barbara: ABC-CLIO, 2013.

Cady, Diane. "Linguistic Disease: Foreign Language as Sexual Disease in Early Modern England." In *Sins of the Flesh: Responding to Sexual Disease in Early Modern Europe*, edited by Kevin Siena, 159–186. Toronto: Centre for Reformation and Renaissance Studies, 2005.

Caffaratto, T. M. "Storia dell'Assistenza agli Esposti a Torino," *Minerva Medica* 54 (1963): 1752–1761.

———. "L'assistenza ostetrica in Piemonte dalle origini ai nostri tempi," *Giornale di Batteriologia, Virologia ed Immunologia* 6 (1970): 176–209.

———. *L'ostetricia, la ginecologia e la chirurgia in Piemonte, dalle origini ai nostri giorni*. Saluzzo: Edizioni Vitalità, 1973.

———. *L'Ospedale Maggiore di San Giovanni Battista e della Città di Torino: Sette Secoli di Assistenza Socio-Sanitaria*. Turin: Unità Sanitaria Locale, 1984.

Camporesi, Piero. *Il Sugo della Vita: Simbolismo e Magia del Sangue*. Milan: Edizioni di Comunità, 1984.

Camporesi, Piero, et al., editors. *Cultura popolare nell'Emilia Romagna: Medicina, erbe e magia*. Milan: Silvana Editoriale, 1981.

Canepari, Eleonora. "Svelare o Occultare? L'Eco delle Nascite Illegittime (Roma, XVIII Secolo)," *Quaderni Storici* 41, no. 1 (2006): 101–132.

Cani, Valentina and Paolo Mazzarello. "La difficile docenza pavese di Vincenzo Malacarne," *Bulletin d'Histoire et d'Epistémologie des Sciences de la Vie* 24, no. 2 (2017): 153–162.

Cannella, Maria, Luisa Dodi, and Flores Reggiani, editors. '*Si Consegna questo Figlio': L'Assistenza all'Infanzia e alla Maternità dalla Ca' Granda alla Provincia di Milano, 1456–1920*. Milano: Università degli Studi di Milano, Skira, 2008.

Cappelletto, Giovanna. "Infanzia Abbandonata e Ruoli di Mediazione Sociale nel Verona del Settecento," *Quaderni Storici* 53 (1983): 433.

Capra, Carlo. "Il Settecento." In *Il Ducato di Milano dal 1535 al 1796, vol. 11 of Storia d'Italia*, edited by Carlo Capra and Domenico Sella, 151–617. Turin: UTET, 1984.

Capra, Carlo and Domenico Sella, editors. *Il Ducato di Milano dal 1535 al 1796, vol. 11 of Storia d'Italia*. Turin: UTET, 1984.

Carbone, Angela. *Scritti in onore di Giovanna Da Molin. Popolazione, famiglia e società in età moderna*. Bari: Cacucci Editore, 2017.

Carbone, Salvatore. *Provveditori e Sopraprovveditori alla Sanità della Repubblica di Venezia*. Roma: Quaderni della Rassegna degli Archivi di Stato, 1962.

Carlino, Andrea. *Books of the Body: Anatomical Ritual and Renaissance Learning*, trans. John Tedeschi and Anne C. Tedeschi. Chicago: University of Chicago Press, 1999.

Carlyle, Margaret. "Phantoms in the Classroom: Midwifery Training in Enlightenment Europe," *KNOW: A Journal on the Formation of Knowledge* 2 (2018): 111–136.

Carpanetto, Dino. *Scienza e Arte del Guarire: Cultura, Formazione Universitaria, e Professioni Mediche a Torino tra Sei e Settecento*. Torino: Deputazione Subalpina di Storia Patria, 1998.

Carrier, Henriette. *Origines de la maternité de Paris. Les maîtresses sages-femmes et l'office des accouchées de l'ancien Hôtel-Dieu 1738–1796*. Paris: G. Steinheil, 1888.

Carroll, Berenice A., editor. *Liberating Women's History*. Urbana: University of Illinois Press, 1976.

Casarini, Maria Pia. "Maternita' e Infanticidio a Bologna: Fonti e Linee di Ricerca," *Quaderni Storici* 17, no. 1 (1982): 275–284.

Castellarin, Benvenutio, editor. *I Processi dell'Inquisizione nella Bassa Friulana (1568–1781)*. La Bassa: Associazione per lo Studio della Friulanita, 1997.

Cavallo, Sandra. "Assistenza Femminile e Tutela dell'Onore nella Torino del XVIII Secolo," *Annali della Fondazione L.Einaudi* 14 (1980): 127–155.

———. "Conceptions of Poverty and Poor Relief in Turin in the Second Half of the Eighteenth Century." In *Domestic Strategies: Work and Family in France and Italy, 1600–1800*, edited by Stuart Woolf, 148–200. Cambridge: Cambridge University Press, 1991.

———. *Charity and Power in Early Modern Italy: Benefactors and Their Motives in Turin, 1541–1789*. Cambridge: Cambridge University Press, 1995.

———. *Artisans of the Body in Early Modern Italy: Identities, Families, and Masculinities*. Manchester: Manchester University Press, 2007.

Cavallo, Sandra and Simona Cerutti. "Female Honor and the Social Control of Reproduction in Piedmont Between 1600 and 1800." In *Sex and Gender in Historical Perspective: Selections from Quarderni Storici*, edited by Edward Muir and Guido Ruggiero, 73–109. Baltimore: The Johns Hopkins University Press, 1990.

Cavazza, Silvano. "La Doppia Morte: Resurrezione e Battesimo in un Rito del Seicento," *Quaderni Storici* 50 (1982): 551–582.

Cerutti, Simona and Sandra Cavallo. "Onore femminile e controllo sociale delle riproduzione in Piemonte tra Sei e Settecento," *Quaderni Storici* 44 (1980): 346–383.

Chase, Vanessa Scharven. "The Casa delle Zitelle: Gender and Architecture in Renaissance Venice," PhD dissertation, Columbia University, 2002.

Chiappa, Paola Vismara. "Le soppressioni di monasteri benedettini. Un episodio dei rapporti Stato- Chiesa nella Lombardia teresio-giuseppina e napoleonica," *Ricerche storiche sulla Chiesa ambrosiana* 9 (1980): 138–201.

———. "La soppressione dei conventi e dei monasteri in Lombardia nell'età teresiana." In *Economia, istituzioni, cultura in Lombardia nell'età di Maria Teresa*, edited by A. De Maddalena, E. Rotelli, and G. Barbarisi, 3 vols., 481–500. Bologna: Il Mulino,1982.

Chinosi, Lia, editor. *Nascere a Venezia: Dala Serenissima alla Prima Guerra Mondiale*. Torino: Gruppo Editoriale Forma, 1985.

Chircop, John. " 'Giusta la benefica intenzione del Re': The Bourbon Cowpox Vaccination Campaign in Sicily," *Hygiea Internationalis* 9, no. 1 (2010): 155–181.

Chojnacka, Monica. "Women, Charity and Community in Early Modern Venice: The Casa delle Zitelle," *Renaissance Quarterly* 51, no. 1 (1998): 48–91.

Cipolla, Carlo. *Public Health and the Medical Profession in the Renaissance*. Cambridge: Cambridge University Press, 1976.

Cody, Lisa Forman. *Birthing the Nation: Sex, Science, and the Conception of Eighteenth Century Britons*. Oxford: Oxford University Press, 2005.

———. "Living and Dying in Georgian London's Lying-In Hospitals," *Bulletin of the History of Medicine* 78, no. 2 (2004): 309–348.

Cohen, Sherrill. *The Evolution of Women's Asylums Since 1500: From Refuges for Ex-Prostitutes to Shelters for Battered Women*. Oxford: Oxford University Press, 1992.

Cohn, Jr. Samuel K. *Cultures of Plague: Medical Thinking at the End of the Renaissance*. Oxford: Oxford University Press, 2009.

Cosmacini, Giorgio. *Storia della medicina e della sanità in Italia: Dalla peste europea alla guerra mondiale (1348–1914)*. Roma-Bari: Laterza, 1987.

———. *La Ca' Granda dei Milanesi: Storia del Ospedale Maggiore*. Rome: Laterza, 1999.

———. *Biografia della Ca'Granda: Uomini e idee dell'Ospedale Maggiore di Milano*. Rome: Laterza, 2001.

Cranshaw, Jane L. Stevens. *Plague Hospitals: Public Health for the City in Early Modern Venice*. Burlington, VT: Ashgate, 2012.

Crawford, Patricia. "The Construction and Experience of Maternity in Seventeenth-Century England." In *Women as Mothers in Pre-Industrial England*, edited by Valerie Fildes, 3–38. London: Routledge, 1990.

Cruciani, Gianfranco. *Cerusici e Fisici: Preciani e Nursini dal XIV al XVIII Secolo*. Arrone: Thyrus, 1999.

Cunningham, Andrew. "Fabricius and the 'Aristotle Project' in Anatomical Teaching and Research at Padua." In *The Medical Renaissance of the Sixteenth Century*, edited by Andrew Wear, R. K. French, and I. M. Lonie, 195–222. Cambridge: Cambridge University Press, 1985.

———. *The Anatomical Renaissance: The Resurrection of the Anatomical Projects of the Ancients*. Aldershot: Scolar Press, 1997.

———. *The Anatomist Anatomis'd: An Experimental Discipline in Enlightenment Europe*. Surrey and Burlington, VT: Ashgate, 2010.

Dacome, Lucia. "Women, Wax and Anatomy in the 'Century of Things'," *Renaissance Studies* 21, no. 4 (2007): 522–550.

———. "The Anatomy of the Pope." In *Conflicting Duties: Science, Medicine, and Religion in Rome, 1550–1750*, edited by Maria Pia Donato and Jill Kraye, 355–376. London: Warburg Institute, 2009.

———. *Malleable Anatomies: Models, Makers, and Material Culture in Eighteenth-Century Italy*. Oxford: Oxford University Press, 2017.

Daston, Lorraine and Elizabeth Lunbeck, editors. *Histories of Scientific Observation*. Chicago: University of Chicago Press, 2011.

De Bernardin, Sandro. "I Riformatori dello Studio di Padova: Indirizzi di Politica Cultural nell'Università di Padova." In *Storia della Cultura Veneta, vol. 4: Il Seicento*, part 2, 61–91. Vicenza: Neri Pozza, 1984.

De Boer, Witse. *The Conquest of the Soul: Confession, Discipline, and Public Order in Counter-Reformation Milan*. Leiden: Brill, 2001.

Del Negro, Piero. "Venetian Policy Toward the University of Padua and Scientific Progress During the 18th Century." In *Universities and Science in the Early Modern*

Period, edited by Mordechai Feingold and Victor Navarro-Brotons, 169–181. Dordrect: Springer, 2006.

De Maddalena, Aldo. *Prezzi e mercedi a Milano dal 1701 al 1860*, vol. 1. Milano: Banca Commerciale Italiana, 1974.

De Maddalena, Aldo, E. Rotelli, and G. Barbarisi, editors. *Economia, istituzioni, cultura in Lombardia nell'età di Maria Teresa*, 3 vols. Bologna: Il Mulino, 1982.

De Marchi, Elena. *Dai Campi alle Filande: Famiglia, matrimonio e lavoro nella "pianura dell'Olona" (1750–1850)*. Milan: Franco Angeli, 2009.

D'Errico, Gian Luca. "I Sortilegi." In *Sortilegi amorosi, materassi a nolo e pignattini. Processi inquisitoriali del XVII secolo fra Bologna e il Salento*, edited by Umberto Mazzone and Claudia Pancino, 119–170. Rome: Carocci, 2008.

Dionigi, Renzo. *Bernardino Moscati: Maestro di Chirurgia e Riformatore della Sanità Milanese nel Settecento*. Milan: EDRA, 2017.

Di Simplicio, Oscar. *Peccato, penitenza, perdono: Siena, 1575–1800; La formazione della coscienza nell'Italia moderna*. Milan: Franco Angeli, 1994.

Donato, Maria Pia. *Sudden Death: Medicine and Religion in Eighteenth-Century Rome*. Burlington, VT: Ashgate, 2014.

Donato, Maria Pia and Jill Kraye, editors. *Conflicting Duties: Science, Medicine, and Religion in Rome, 1550–1750*. London: Warburg Institute, 2009.

Donegan, Jane B. *Women and Men Midwives: Medicine, Morality, and Misogyny in Early America*. Westport, CT: The Greenwood Press, 1978.

Donnison, Jean. *Midwives and Medical Men: A History of Inter-Professional Rivalries and Women's Rights*. London: Heinemann Educational Books, 1977.

Dooley, Brendan M. "Giornalismo, Accademie, e Organizzazione della Scienza: Tentativi di Formare un'Accademia Scientifica Veneta all'Inizio del Settecento," *Archivio Veneto 5*, no. 120 (1983): 5–39.

———. *Science and the Marketplace*. Boston: Lexington Books, 2001.

Doriguzzi, Franca. "I Messagi del'Abbandono: Bambini Esposti a Torino nel' 700," *Quaderni Storii 53*, no. 2 (1983): 445–468.

Duden, Barbara. *Disembodying Women: Perspectives on Pregnancy and the Unborn*. Cambridge, MA: Harvard University Press, 1993.

———. *The Woman Beneath the Skin: A Doctor's Patients in Eighteenth-Century Germany*. Cambridge, MA: Harvard University Press, 1998.

Dursteler, Eric R., editor. *A Companion to Venetian History, 1400–1797*. Leiden: Brill, 2013.

Eamon, William. *Science and the Secrets of Nature: Books of Secrets in Medieval and Early Modern Culture*. Princeton: Princeton University Press, 1994.

Ebenstein, Joanna. *The Anatomical Venus: Wax, God, Death, and the Ecstatic*. New York: D.A.P., 2016.

Ehrenreich, Barbara and Deirdre English. *Witches, Midwives and Nurses: A History of Women Healers*. Old Westbury, NY: The Feminist Press, 1973.

Evenden, Doreen. *The Midwives of Seventeenth-Century London*. Cambridge: Cambridge University Press, 2000.

Feingold, Moredechai and Victor Navarro-Brotons, editors. *Universities and Science in the Early Modern Period*. Dordrect: Springer, 2006.

Ferraro, Joanne M. *Nefarious Crimes, Contested Justice: Illicit Sex and Infanticide in the Republic of Venice, 1557–1789*. Baltimore: The Johns Hopkins University Press, 2008.

Fildes, Valerie, editor. *Women as Mothers in Pre-Industrial England*. London: Routledge, 1990.

Filippini, Nadia Maria. "Il Bambino Prezioso: Maternità ed Infanzia negli Interventi Istituzionali del Primo Ottocento." In *Nascere a Venezia: Dala Serenissima alla Prima Guerra Mondiale*, edited by Lia Chinosi, 28–40. Torino: Gruppo Editoriale Forma, 1985.

———. "Levatrici e ostetricanti a Venezia tra sette e ottocento," *Quaderni Storici* 58 (1985): 149–180.

———. "Ospizi per Partorienti e Cliniche Ostetriche tra Sette e Ottocento." In *Gli Ospedali in Area Padana fra Settecento e Novecento*, edited by Maria Luisa Betri and Edoardo Bressan, 395–411. Milano: Franco Angeli, 1992.

———. *La Nascita Straordinaria: Tra Madre e Figlio: La Rivoluzione del Taglio Cesareo (Sec. XVIII–XIX)*. Milano: Franco Angeli, 1995.

———. *Generare, partorire, nascere: Una storia dall'antichità alla provetta*. Rome: Viella, 2018.

Filippini, Nadia Maria and Tiziano Cappelletto. "L'Arte Ostetrica a Venezia: Sull'Origine della Scuola Ostetrica," *Giornale Veneto di Scienze Mediche* 34, no. 1 (1982): 37–43.

Findlen, Paula, Wendy Wassyng Roworth, and Catherine M. Sama. *Italy's Eighteenth Century: Gender and Culture in the Age of the Grand Tour*. Stanford, CA: Stanford University Press, 2009.

Finucci, Valeria. *The Manly Masquerade: Masculinity, Paternity, and Castration in the Italian Renaissance*. Durham, NC: Duke University Press, 2003.

———. *The Prince's Body: Vincenzo Gonzaga and Renaissance Medicine*. Cambridge: Harvard University Press, 2015.

Finzsch, Norbert and Robert Jutte. *Institutions of Confinement: Hospitals, Asylums, and Prisons in Western Europe and North America, 1500–1950*. Cambridge: Cambridge University Press, 1996.

Fissell, Mary. *Vernacular Bodies: The Politics of Reproduction in Early Modern England*. Oxford: Oxford University Press, 2004.

Focaccia, Miriam. *Anna Morandi Manzolini: Una donna fra arte e scienza*. Florence: Leo S. Olschki, 2008.

Forbes, Thomas. *The Midwife and the Witch*. New Haven: Yale University Press, 1966.

Forth, Christorpher E. "Moral Contagion and the Will: The Crisis of Masculinity in Fin-de-siècle France." In *Contagion: Historical and Cultural Studies*, edited by Alison Bashford and Claire Hooker, 61–75. London: Routledge, 2001.

Foucualt, Michel. *The Birth of the Clinic: An Archaeology of Medical Perception*. London: Tavistock, 1973.

———. *Discipline and Punish: The Birth of the Prison*, trans. Alan Sheridan. London: Penguin, 1991.

French, R., et al., editors. *Medicine from the Black Death to the French Disease*. Aldershot: Ashgate, 1998.

Fuchs, Rachel G. *Poor and Pregnant in Paris: Strategies for Survival in the Nineteenth Century*. New Brunswick: Rutgers University Press, 1992.

Gambaccini, Piero. *I Mercanti della Salute: Le Segrete Virtù dell'Imbroglio in Medicina*. Florence: Le Lettere, 2000.

Gambacorta, Gorgias. *Antonio Scarpa: Anatomico Chirurgo e Occulista*. Milan: Asclepio Editrice, 2000.

Garofolo, Fausto, editor. *Quattro Secoli di Vita del Protomedicato e del Collegio dei Medici di Roma; Regesto dei Documenti dal 1471–1870*. Rome: Pubblicazioni dell'Istituto di Storia della Medicina dell'Universitá di Roma, 1950.

Gelbart, Nina Rattner. *The King's Midwife: A History and Mystery of Madame Du Coudray*. Berkeley: University of California Press, 1999.

Gelfand, Toby. *Professionalizing Modern Medicine: Paris Surgeons and Medical Science and Institutions in the Eighteenth Century*. Westport, CT and London: Greenwood Press, 1980.

Gelis, Jacques. "Sages-Femmes et Accoucheurs: l'obstetrique populaire aux XVIIe et XVIIe Siecles," *Annates: Economies, Sociétés, Civilisations* 32, no. 5 (1977): 927–957.

———. *La sage-femme ou le medecin: Une nouvelle conception de la vie*. Paris: Fayard, 1988.

———. *History of Childbirth: Fertility, Pregnancy and Birth in Early Modern Europe*. Cambridge: Cambridge University Press, 1991.

Gentilcore, David. *From Bishop to Witch: The System of the Sacred in Early Modern Terra d'Otranto*. Manchester: Manchester University Press, 1992.

———. "'All That Pertains to Medicine': *Protomedici* and *Protomedicati* in Early Modern Italy," *Medical History* 38 (1994): 121–142.

———. *Healers and Healing in Early Modern Italy*. Manchester: Manchester University Press, 1998.

———. "The Church, the Devil, and the Healing Activities of Living Saints in the Kingdom of Naples After the Council of Trent." In *New Perspectives on Witchcraft, Magic, and Demonology: Witchcraft, Healing, and Popular Diseases*, edited by Brian P. Levack, 200–221. New York and London: Routledge, 2001.

———. "The Protomedicato Tribunals and Health in Italian Cities, 1600–1800: A Comparison." In *Living in the City*, edited by E. Sonnino, 407–430. Rome: Casa Editrice Università La Sapienza, 2004.

———. "The 'Golden Age of Quackery' or 'Medical Enlightenment'? Licensed Charlatanism in Eighteenth-Century Italy," *Cultural and Social History* 3 (2006): 250–263.

———. *Medical Charlatanism in Early Modern Italy*. Oxford: Oxford University Press, 2006.

Gowing, Laura. *Common Bodies: Women, Touch, and Bodies in Seventeenth-Century London*. New Haven: Yale University Press, 2003.

Green, Monica. *Making Women's Medicine Masculine: The Rise of Male Authority in Pre-Modern Gynaecology*. Oxford: Oxford University Press, 2008.

Grendler, Paul F. *Books and Schools in the Italian Renaissance*. Aldershot, Hampshire: Variorum, 1980.

———. *Schooling in Renaissance Italy: Literacy and Learning, 1300–1600*. Baltimore: The Johns Hopkins University Press, 1991.

Guerci, Luciano. *La Sposa Obbediente: Donna e Matrimonio nella Discussione dell'Italia del Settecento*. Torino: Tirrenia, 1988.

Hacke, Daniela. *Women, Sex, and Marriage in Early Modern Venice*. Burlington, VT: Ashgate, 2004.

Hanlon, Gregory. "L'infanticidio di Coppie Sposate in Toscana nella Prima Eta' Moderna," *Quaderni Storici* 113 (2003): 453–498.

Haraway, Donna Jeanne. *Simians, Cyborgs, and Women: The Reinvention of Nature*. New York: Routledge, 1991.

Harding, Sandra G. *The Science Question in Feminism*. Ithaca, NY: Cornell University Press, 1986.

Harley, David. "Historians as Demonologists: The Myth of the Midwife-Witch," *Society for the Social History of Medicine* 3 (1990): 1–27.

Harvey, Elizabeth D. *Sensible Flesh: On Touch in Early Modern Culture*. Philadelphia: University of Pennsylvania Press, 2003.

Henderson, John, Peregrine Horden, and Alessandro Pastore, editors. *The Impact of Hospitals: 300–2000*. Oxford: Peter Lang, 2007.

Herrle-Fanning, Jeanette. "Of Forceps and Folios: Eighteenth-Century British Midwifery Publications and the Construction of Professional Identiy," PhD dissertation, City University of New York, 2004.

Hillman, David and Carla Mazzio, editors. *The Body in Parts: Fantasies of Corporeality in Early Modern Europe*. New York: Routledge, 1997.

Hsia, R. Po-chia. *Social Discipline in the Reformation*. London and New York: Routledge, 1989.

Huet, Marie-Hélène. *Monstrous Imagination*. Cambridge, MA: Harvard University Press, 1993.

Hull, Isabel V. *Sexuality, State and Civil Society in Germany, 1700–1815*. Ithaca: Cornell University Press, 1996.

Hunecke, Volker. *I Trovatelli di Milano: Bambini esposti e famiglie espositrici dal XVII al XIX secolo*. Bologna: Il Mulino, 1989.

Ingrao, Charles W. *The Habsburg Monarchy, 1618–1815*. Cambridge: Cambridge University Press, 2000.

Jacobus, Mary, Evelyn Fox Keller, and Sally Shuttleworth, editors. *Body Politics: Women and the Discourses of Science*. London and New York: Routledge, 1990.

Jordanova, Ludmilla. *Sexual Visions: Images of Gender in Science and Medicine Between the Eighteenth and Twentieth Centuries*. Madison: University of Wisconsin Press, 1989.

Jorland, Gérard, George Weisz, and Annick Opinel, editors. *Body Counts: Medical Quantification in Historical and Sociological Perspective*. Montreal: McGill-Queen's University Press, 2005.

Kapsalis, Terri. *Public Privates: Performing Gynecology from Both Ends of the Speculum*. Durham, NC: Duke University Press, 1997.

Katz, Barbara Rothman. *In Labor: Women and Power in the Birthplace*. New York: W.W. Norton, 1982.

Keel, Othmar. "The Politics of Health and the Institutionalization of Clinical Practices in Europe in the Second Half of the Eighteenth Century." In *William Hunter and the Eighteenth-Century Medical World*, edited by F. W. Bynum and Roy Porter, 207–258. Cambridge: Cambridge University Press, 1985.

Keller, Eve. "The Subject of Touch: Authority in Early Modern Midwifery." In *Sensible Flesh: On Touch in Early Modern Culture*, edited by Elizabeth D. Harvey, 62–80. Philadelphia: University of Pennsylvania Press, 2003.

Keller, Evelyn Fox. *Reflections on Gender and Science*. New Haven: Yale University Press, 1985.

Keller, Evelyn Fox and Helen E. Longino, editors. *Feminism and Science: Oxford Readings in Feminism*. New York: Oxford University Press, 1996.

Kemp, Martin and Marina Wallace. *Spectacular Bodies: The Art and Science of the Human Body from Leonardo to Now*, exh. cat. London: Hayward Gallery, 2000.

Kertzer, David I. "Gender Ideology and Infant Abandonment in Nineteenth-Century Italy," *Journal of Interdisciplinary History* 22 (1991): 1–25.

Kertzer, David I. and Marzio Barbagli, editors. *Family Life in Early Modern Times, 1500–1789*. New Haven: Yale University Press, 2001.

King, Helen. "As If None Understood the Art That Cannot Understand Greek': The Education of Midwives in Seventeenth-Century England." In *The History of*

Medical Education in Britain, edited by Vivian Nutton and Roy Porter, 184–198. Amsterdam: Rodopi, 1995.

Klestinec, Cynthia. "Practical Experience in Anatomy." In *The Body as Object and Instrument of Knowledge: Embodied Empiricism in Early Modern Science*, edited by C. T. Wolfe and O. Gal Dordrecht, 33–57. New York: Springer, 2010.

———. *Students, Teachers and Traditions of Dissection in Renaissance Venice*. Baltimore: The Johns Hopkins University Press, 2011.

Kostylo, Joanna. "From Gunpowder to Print: The Common Origins of Copyright and Patent." In *Privilege and Property: Essays on the History of Copyright*, edited by Ronan Deazley, Martin Kretschmer, and Lionel Bently, 21–50. Cambridge: Open Book Publishers, 2010.

Kuehn, Thomas. *Illegitimacy in Renaissance Florence*. Ann Arbor: University of Michigan Press, 2002.

Laget, Mireille. *Naissances: l'accouchement avant l'âge de la Clinique*. Paris: Seuil, 1982.

Landes, Joan. "Wax Fibers, Wax Bodies, and Moving Figures: Artifice and Nature in Eighteenth-Century Anatomy." In *Ephemeral Bodies, Wax Sculpture and the Human Figure*, edited by Roberta Panzanelli, 41–66. Los Angeles: Getty Publications, 2008.

Laqueur, Thomas. *Making Sex: Body and Gender from the Greeks to Freud*. Cambridge, MA: Harvard University Press, 1990.

Laughran, Michelle Anne. "The Body, Public Health and Social Control in Sixteenth-Century Venice," PhD dissertation, University of Connecticut, 1998.

Lawrence, Susan C. "Educating the Senses: Students, Teachers and Medical Rhetoric in Eighteenth-Century London." In *Medicine and the Five Senses*, edited by W. F. Bynum and Roy Porters. Cambridge: Cambridge University Press, 1993.

———. *Charitable Knowledge: Hospital Pupils and Practitioners in Eighteenth-Century London*. Cambridge: Cambridge University Press, 2002.

Levack, Brian P. *New Perspectives on Witchcraft, Magic, and Demonology: Witchcraft, Healing, and Popular Diseases*. New York and London: Routledge, 2001.

Lieske, Pam. "Configuring Women: William Smellie's Obstetrical Machines and the Poor," *Studies in Eighteenth-Century Culture* 29 (2000): 65–86.

———. " 'Made in Imitation of Real Women and Children': Obstetrical Machines in Eighteenth-Century Briton." In *The Female Body in Medicine and Literature*, edited by Andrew Mangham and Greta Depledge, 69–88. Liverpool: Liverpool University Press, 2011.

Long, Kathleen P., editor. *Gender and Scientific Discourse in Early Modern Culture*. Burlington, VT: Ashgate, 2010.

Longhurst, Robyn. *Maternities: Gender, Bodies, and Space*. London and New York: Routledge, 2008.

Longino, Helen E. *Science as Social Knowledge: Values and Objectivity in Scientific Inquiry*. Princeton: Princeton University Press, 1990.

Loudon, Irvine. *The Tragedy of Childbed Fever*. Oxford: Oxford University Press, 2000.

Maerker, Anna. "Florentine Anatomical Models and the Challenge of Medical Authority in Late-Eighteenth-Century Vienna," *Studies in History and Philosophy of Biological and Biomedical Sciences* 43 (2012): 730–740.

———. *Model Experts: Wax Anatomies and Enlightenment in Florence and Vienna, 1775–1815*. Manchester: Manchester University Press, 2015.

Magnello, Eileen and Anne Hardy, editors. *The Road to Medical Statistics*. Amsterdam: Rodopi, 2002.

Malamani, Anita. "L'Organizzazione sanitaria nella Lombardia Austriaca." In *Economia, istituzioni, cultura in Lombardia nell'età di Maria Teresa*, edited by A. De Maddalena, E. Rotelli, and G. Barbarisi, 3 vols., 991–1010. Bologna: Il Mulino, 1982.

Malanima, Paolo. *L'Economia Italiana: Dalla Crescita Medievale alla Crescita Contemporanea*. Bologna: Il Mulino, 2002.

Mangham, Andrew and Greta Depledge, editors. *The Female Body in Medicine and Literature*. Liverpool: Liverpool University Press, 2011.

Marcolini, Giuliana and Giulio Marcon. "Prostituzione e assistenza a Venezia nel secolo XVIII: il pio loco delle povere peccatrici penitenti di S.Iob," *Studi Veneziani* 10 (1985): 99–136.

Marland, Hilary, editor. *The Art of Midwifery: Early Modern Midwives in Europe*. New York and London: Routledge, 1993.

Martin, Emily. *The Woman in the Body: A Cultural Analysis of Reproduction*. Boston: Beacon Press, 1987.

Martin, John. "Out of the Shadow: Heretical and Catholic Women in Renaissance Venice," *Journal of Family History* 10, no. 21 (1985): 21–33.

Martin, Ruth. *Witchcraft and the Inquisition in Venice, 1550–1650*. Oxford: Blackwell, 1989.

Mazza, Barbara Boccazzi. "Governare i 'Luoghi Pii': La Casa delle Zitelle," *Studi Veneziani* 50 (2005): 293–299.

Mazzone, Umberto and Claudia Pancino, editors. *Sortilegi amorosi, materassi a nolo e pignattini. Processi inquisitoriali del XVII secolo fra Bologna e il Salento*. Rome: Carocci, 2008.

Mazzoni, Cristina. *Maternal Impressions: Pregnancy and Childbirth in Literature and Theory*. Ithaca: Cornell University Press, 2002.

McClive, Cathy. "The Hidden Truths of the Belly: The Uncertainties of Pregnancy in Early Modern Europe," *Social History of Medicine* 15, no. 2 (2002): 209–227.

———. "Blood and Expertise: The Trials of the Female Medical Expert in the Ancien-Régime Courtroom," *Bulletin of the History of Medicine* 82 (2008): 86–108.

———. *Menstruation and Procreation in Early Modern France*. New York: Routledge, 2015.

McGough, Laura J. " 'Raised from the Devil's Jaws': A Convent for Repentant Prostitutes in Venice, 1530–1670," PhD dissertation, Northwestern University, 1997.

———. *Gender, Sexuality, and Syphilis in Early Modern Venice: The Disease That Came to Stay*. Basingstoke and New York: Palgrave Macmillan, 2011.

McLaren, Angus. *Reproductive Rituals: The Perception of Fertility in England from the Sixteenth to the Nineteenth Century*. London: Methuen, 1984.

———. *Impotence: A Cultural History*. Chicago: Chicago University Press, 1997.

McTavish, Lianne. *Childbirth and the Display of Authority in Early Modern France*. Burlington, VT: Ashgate, 2005.

Messbarger, Rebecca. "Waxing Poetic: Anna Morandi Manzolini's Anatomical Sculptures," *Configurations* 9 (2001): 65–97.

———. "As Who Dare Gaze the Sun: Anna Morandi Manzolini's Wax Anatomies of the Male Reproductive System and Genitalia." In *Italy's Eighteenth Century: Gender and Culture in the Age of the Grand Tour*, edited by Paula Findlen, Wendy Wassyng Roworth, and Catherine M. Sama, 251–274. Stanford, CA: Stanford University Press, 2009.

———. *The Lady Anatomist: The Life and Work of Anna Morandi Manzolini*. Chicago: University of Chicago Press, 2010.

Messbarger, Rebecca, Christopher M. S. Johns, and Philip Gavitt, editors. *Benedict XIV and the Enlightenment: Art, Science, and Spirituality.* Toronto: University of Toronto Press, 2016.

Montalenti, G. and P. Rossi, editors. *Lazzaro Spallanzani e la biologia del Settecento. Teorie, esperimenti, istituzioni scientifiche.* Firenze: Olschki, 1982.

Muir, Edward and Guido Ruggiero, editors. *Sex and Gender in Historical Perspective: Selections from Quaderni Storici.* Baltimore: The Johns Hopkins University Press, 1990.

Murphy-Lawless, Jo. *Reading Birth and Death: A History of Obstetric Thinking.* Bloomington: Indiana University Press, 1998.

Musacchio, Jacqueline Marie. *The Art and Ritual of Childbirth in Early Modern Italy.* New Haven: Yale University Press, 1999.

Nicoli Aldini, N., L. Pontoni, P. Scarani, and A. Ruggeri. "Documenti ed immagini sull' innesto del vaiuolo vaccino in Bologna al principio del xix secolo," *Medicina nei Secoli Arte e Scienza* 19, no. 1 (2007): 195–208.

Nono, Mario and Domenico Bertero. *Storia della Chirurgia in Piemonte e varie vicende che l'accompagnano.* Turin: Edizioni Minerva Medica, 2018.

Nutton, Vivian. "Humanist Surgery." In *The Medical Renaissance of the Sixteenth Century*, edited by Andrew Wear, Roger Kenneth French, and Iain M. Lonie, 75–99. Cambridge: University of Cambridge Press, 1985.

Nutton, Vivian and Roy Porter, editors. *The History of Medical Education in Britain.* Amsterdam: Rodopi, 1995.

Oakley, Ann. *Women Confined: Towards a Sociology of Childbirth.* New York: Schocken Books, 1980.

———. *The Captured Womb: A History of the Medical Care of Pregnant Women.* New York: Basil Blackwell Publisher Ltd., 1984.

O'Neil, Mary. "Magical Healing, Love Magic, and the Inquisition in Late Sixteenth-Century Modena." In *New Perspectives on Witchcraft, Magic, and Demonology: Witchcraft, Healing, and Popular Diseases*, edited by Brian P. Levack, 172–199. New York and London: Routledge, 2001.

Onger, Sergio. "The Formation of the Hospital Network in the Brescian Region Between the Eighteenth and Twentieth Centuries." In *The Impact of Hospitals, 300–2000*, edited by John Henderson, Pergrine Horden, and Alessandro Pastore, 257–274. Bern: Peter Lang AG, 2007.

Owen, Harry. *Simulation in Healthcare Education: An Extensive History.* New York: Springer, 2016.

Packham, Catherine. *Eighteenth-Century Vitalism: Bodies, Culture, Politics.* New York: Palgrave Macmillan, 2012.

Palmer, Richard. "Physicians and Surgeons in Sixteenth-Century Venice," *Medical History* 23 (1979): 451–460.

Pancino, Claudia. "La Comare Levatrice: Crisi di un Mestiere nel XVIII Secolo," *Storia e Società* 15 (1981): 593–638.

———. *Il Bambino e l'acqua sporca: storia dell' assistenza al parto dale mammane alle ostetriche (secoli XVI–XIX).* Milan: Franco Angeli, 1984.

———. *Politica e salute: dalla polizia medica all'igiene.* Bologna: CLUEB, 2003.

Pancino, Claudia and Jean d'Yvoire. *Formato nel segreto. Nascituri e feti fra immagini e immaginario dal XVI al XXI secolo.* Rome: Carocci, 2006.

Panzanelli, Roberta, editor. *Ephemeral Bodies: Wax Sculpture and the Human Figure.* Los Angeles: Getty Publications, 2008.

Park, Katherine. *Doctors and Medicine in Early Renaissance Florence*. Princeton: Princeton University Press, 1985.

———. "The Rediscovery of the Clitoris." In *The Body in Parts: Fantasies of Corporeality in Early Modern Europe*, edited by David Hillman and Carla Mazzio, 171–193. New York: Routledge, 1997.

———. "Stones, Bones, and Hernias: Specialists in Fourteenth- and Fifteenth-Century Italy." In *Medicine from the Black Death to the French Disease*, edited by R. French et al., 110–130. Aldershot: Ashgate, 1998.

———. *Secrets of Women: Gender, Generation, and the Origins of Human Dissection*. New York: Zone Books, 2006.

Parma, Anna. "Didattica e Pratica Ostetrica in Lombardia (1765–1791)," *Sanità, Scienza e Storia* 2 (1984): 101–155.

———. "Johann Peter Frank e l'Introduzione della polizia medica nella Lombardia Austriaca." In *Sanità e Società: Veneto, Lombardia, Piemonte, Liguria, Secoli XVII–XX*, edited by Franco della Peruta, 95–107. Udine: Casamassima, 1989.

Pasi, Antonia. "Mortalita infantile e cultura medica in Italia nel XIX secolo." In *Malaltia i Cultura*, edited by Josep L. Barona, 117–152. Valencia: Seminari d'Estudis Sobre la Ciencia, 1995.

Pastore, Alessandro. *Il Medico in Tribunale: La Perizia Medica nella Procedura Penale d'Antico Regime (secoli XVI–XVIII)*. Bellinzona: Edizioni Casagrande, 1998.

Patriarca, Silvana. *Numbers and Nationhood: Writing Statistics in Nineteenth-Century Italy*. Cambridge: Cambridge University Press, 2003.

Pecchiai, Pio. *L'Ospedale Maggiore di Milano nella Storia e nell'Arte*. Milan: Pizzi e Pizio, 1927.

Pelling, Margaret. "Medical Practice in Early Modern England: Trade or Profession?" In *The Professions in Early Modern England*, edited by Wilfred Prest, 90–128. London: Croom Helm, 1987.

———. *The Common Lot: Sickness, Medical Occupations, and the Urban Poor in Early Modern England*. London: Longman, 1998.

———. *Medical Conflicts in Early Modern London: Patronage, Physicians, and Irregular Practitioners 1550–1640*. Oxford: Oxford University Press, 2003.

Peruta, Franco Della, editor. *Storia d'Italia, Annali, vol. 7, Malattia e medicina*. Turin: Einaudi, 1984.

Pilbeam, Pamela. *Madam Tussaud and History of Waxworks*. London and New York: Hambledon and London, 2003.

Pillon, Daniela. "La Comare Istruita nel Suo Ufficio. Alcune Notizie sulle Levatrici fra il '600 e il '700," *Atti dell'Istituto Veneto di Scienze, Lettere ed Arti* 140 (1981): 67.

Pomata, Gianna. "Madri Illegittime tra Ottocento e Novecento," *Quaderni Storici* 15, no. 44 (1980): 497–542.

———. "Barbieri e comari." In *Cultura popolare nell'Emilia Romagna: Medicina, erbe e magia*, edited by Piero Camporesi et al., 161–183. Milan: Silvana Editoriale, 1981.

———. *Contracting a Cure: Patients, Healers, and the Law in Early Modern Bologna*. Baltimore: The Johns Hopkins University Press, 1998.

———. "Observation Rising: Birth of an Epistemic Genre, 1500–1650." In *Histories of Scientific Observation*, edited by Lorraine Daston and Elizabeth Lunbeck, 45–80. Chicago: University of Chicago Press, 2011.

Porter, Roy. "William Hunter: A Surgeon and a Gentleman." In *William Hunter and the Eighteenth-Century Medical World*, edited by W. F. Bynum and Roy Porter, 7–34. Cambridge: Cambridge University Press, 1988.

———. "History of the Body Reconsidered." In *New Perspectives on Historical Writing*, edited by Peter Burke, 233–260. University Park: Pennsylvania State University Press, 2001.

Poska, Allyson M. *Regulating the People: The Catholic-Reformation in Seventeenth-Century Spain*. Leiden: Brill, 1998.

Premuda, Loris. *Personaggi e vicende dell'ostetricia e della ginecologia nello studio di Padova*. Padova: Attualità di Ostetricia e Ginecologia, 1958.

Prest, Wilfred, editor. *The Professions in Early Modern England*. London: Croom Helm, 1987.

Prodi, Paolo and Carla Penuti, editors. *Disciplina dell'Anima, Disciplina del Corpo, e Disciplina della Società tra Medioevo e Età Moderna*. Bologna: Il Mulino, 1994.

Prosperi, Adriano. *Dare l'Anima: Storia di un Infanticidio*. Torino: Einaudi, 2005.

Pullan, Brian. *Rich and Poor in Renaissance Venice: The Social Institutions of a Catholic State, to 1620*. Cambridge, MA: Harvard University Press, 1971.

———. *Tolerance, Regulation and Rescue: Dishonoured Women and Abandoned Children in Italy, 1300–1800*. Manchester: Manchester University Press, 2016.

Quazza, Guido. *Le Riforme in Piemonte nella Prima meta' del'700*. Modena: Società Tipografica Editrice Modenese, 1957.

Ramsey, Matthew. *Professional and Popular Medicine in France, 1770–1830*. Cambridge: Cambridge University Press, 1988.

Ray, Meredith K. *Daughters of Alechmy: Women and Scientific Culture in Early Modern Italy*. Cambridge, MA: Harvard University Press, 2015.

Read, Sara. *Menstruation and the Female Body in Early Modern England*. Basingstoke: Palgrave Macmillan, 2013.

Reggiani, Flores. "Responsibilità Paterna fra Povertà e Beneficienza: 'I Figli dell'Ospedale' di Milano fra Seicento e Settecento," *Ricerche storiche* 2 (1997): 287–314.

———. " 'Si Consegna questo Figlio': Segnali, Messaggi, Scritture." In *'Si Consegna questo Figlio': L'Assistenza all'Infanzia e alla Maternità dalla Ca' Granda alla Provincia di Milano, 1456–1920*, edited by Maria Cannella, Luisa Dodi, and Flores Reggiani, 135–158. Milano: Università degli Studi di Milano, Skira, 2008.

———. "Il 'materiale umano'. Note su didattica ostetrica, pratiche vaccinali e sperimentazioni alimentari nel brefotrofio di Milano dal XVIII al XIX secolo." In *Scritti in onore di Giovanna Da Molin. Popolazione, famiglia e società in età moderna*, edited by Angela Carbone, 559–578. Bari: Cacucci Editore, 2017.

Reill, Peter Hanns. *Vitalizing Nature in the Enlightenment*. Berkeley: University of California Press, 2005.

Rich, Adrienne. *Of Woman Born: Motherhood as Experience and Institution*. New York: W.W. Norton, 1976.

Richter, Simon. *Missing the Breast: Gender, Fantasy, and the Body in the German Enlightenment*. Seattle: University of Washington Press, 2006.

Riskin, Jessica. "The Defecating Duck, or, the Ambiguous Origins of Artificial Life," *Cultural Inquiry* 29 (2003): 599–633.

Risse, Guenter B. "Before the Clinic Was 'Born': Methodological Perspectives in Hospital History." In *Institutions of Confinement: Hospitals, Asylums, and Prisons in Western Europe and North America, 1500–1950*, edited by Norbert Finzsch and Robert Jutte, 75–96. Cambridge: Cambridge University Press, 1996.

Roberts, Helen, editor. *Women, Health and Reproduction.* London: Routledge & Kegan Paul, 1981.

Roe, Shirley A. *Matter, Life, and Generation: Eighteenth-Century Embryology and the Haller-Wolff Debate.* Cambridge: University of Cambridge Press, 1981.

Romeo, Giovanni. *Esorcisti, confessori e sessualità femminile nell'Italia della Controriforma. A proposito di due casi modenesi del primo Seicento.* Florence: Casa Editrice le Lettere, 1998.

Rosen, George. *From Medical Police to Social Medicine: Essays on the History of Health Care.* New York: Science History Publications, 1974.

Rublack, Ulinka. "Childbirth and the Female Body in Early Modern Germany," *Past and Present* 150 (1996): 84–110.

Rusnock, Andrea. "Quantifying Infant Mortality in England and France, 1750–1800." In *Body Counts: Medical Quantification in Historical and Sociological Perspective,* edited by Gérard Jorland, George Weisz, and Annick Opinel, 65–88. Montreal: McGill-Queen's University Press, 2005.

———. *Vital Accounts: Quantifying Health and Population in Eighteenth-Century England and France.* Cambridge: Cambridge University Press, 2009.

Savoia, Paolo. "Skills, Knowledge and Status: The Career of an Early Modern Italian Surgeon," *Bulletin of the History of Medicine* 93, no. 1 (2019): 27–54.

Sawday, Jonathan. *The Body Emblazoned: Dissection and the Human Body in Renaissance Culture.* London and New York: Routledge, 1995.

Schiavoni, Claudio. "L'attività delle levatrici o 'mammane' a Roma tra XVI e XVIII secolo: storia sociale di una professione," *Sociologia* 2 (2001): 41–61.

Schiebinger, Londa. *The Mind Has No Sex? Women in the Origins of Modern Science.* Cambridge, MA: Harvard University Press, 1989.

Schleiner, Winfried. "Modern Controversies About the One-Sex Model," *Renaissance Quarterly* 53, no. 1 (2000): 180–191.

Schnalke, Thomas. *Diseases in Wax: History of the Medical Moulage,* trans. Kathy Spatschek. Carol Stream, IL: Quintessence Publishing, 1995.

Scotti, Aurora. "Malati e strutture ospedaliere dall'età dei Lumi all'Unità." In *Storia d'Italia, Annali, vol. 7, Malattia e medicina,* edited by Franco della Peruta, 235–297. Turin: Einaudi, 1984.

Seitz, Jonathan. *Witchcraft and Inquisition in Early Modern Venice.* Cambridge: Cambridge University Press, 2011.

Semi, Franca. *Gli "Ospizi" di Venezia.* Venice: Helvetia, 1983.

Sheridan, Bridgette. "Whither Childbearing: Gender, Status, and the Professionalization of Medicine in Early Modern France." In *Gender and Scientific Discourse in Early Modern Culture,* edited by Kathleen P. Long, 239–258. Burlington, VT: Ashgate, 2010.

Siena, Kevin, editor. *Sins of the Flesh: Responding to Sexual Disease in Early Modern Europe.* Toronto: Centre for Reformation and Renaissance Studies, 2005.

Sirasi, Nancy G. *Medieval and Early Renaissance Medicine: An Introduction to Knowledge and Practice.* Chicago: University of Chicago Press, 1990.

Smith, Hilda. "Gynecology and Ideology in Seventeenth-Century England." In *Liberating Women's History,* edited by Berenice A. Carroll, 97–114. Urbana: University of Illinois Press, 1976.

Smith, Mark M. *Sensing the Past: Seeing, Hearing, Smelling, Tasting, and Touching in History.* Berkeley: University of California Press, 2007.

Sonnino, E., editor. *Living in the City.* Rome: Casa Editrice Università La Sapienza, 2004.

Speert, Harold. *Obstetrics and Gynecology: A History and Iconography*. New York: Parthenon Publishing, 2004.

Sperling, Jutta Gisela. *Convents and the Body Politic in Late Renaissance Venice*. Chicago: University of Chicago Press, 1999.

Spiller, Elizabeth. *Science, Reading, and Renaissance Literature*. Cambridge: Cambridge University Press, 2004.

Storrs, Christopher. *War, Diplomacy and the Rise of Savoy, 1690–1720*. Cambridge: Cambridge University Press, 1999.

Symcox, Geoffrey. *Victor Amadeus II: Absolutism in the Savoyard State, 1675–1730*. Berkeley and Los Angeles: University of California Press, 1983.

Szabo, Frank A. J. *Kaunitz and Enlightened Absolutism, 1753–1780*. Cambridge: Cambridge University Press, 1994.

Taglia, Kathryn. "Delivering a Christian Identity: Midwives in Northern French Synodal Legislation, c. 1200–1500." In *Religion and Medicine in the Middle Ages*, edited by Peter Biller and Joseph Ziegler, 77–90. Suffolk: York Medieval Press, 2001.

Tatlock, Lynne. "Speculum Feminarum: Gendered Perspectives on Obstetrics and Gynecology in Early Modern Germany," *Signs* 17, no. 4 (1992): 725–760.

Terrall, Mary. "Maternal Impressions: Conception, Sensibility, and Inheritance." In *Vital Matters: Eighteenth-Century Views of Conception, Life, and Death*, edited by Mary Terrall and Helen Deutsch, 109–129. Toronto: University of Toronto Press, 2012.

Terrall, Mary and Helen Deutsch, editors. *Vital Matters: Eighteenth-Century Views of Conception, Life, and Death*. Toronto: University of Toronto Press, 2012.

Tisci, Caterina. "La vaccinazione antivaiolosa nel Regno di Napoli (1801–1809): il ruolo del clero," *Medicina & Storia* 3 (2003): 89–117.

Tittarelli, L. "Gli Esposti all'Ospedale di S. Maria della Misericordia in Perugia nei Secoli XVIII–XIX," *Bollettino della Deputazione di Storia Patria per l'Umbria* (1985): 23–130.

Traub, Valerie. "Gendering Mortality in Early Modern Anatomies." In *Feminist Readings of Early Modern Culture: Emerging Subjects*, edited by Valerie Traub, M. Lindsay Kaplan, and Dympna Callaghan, 44–92. Cambridge: Cambridge University Press, 1996.

———. *The Renaissance of Lesbianism in Early Modern England*. Cambridge: Cambridge University Press, 2002.

Traub, Valerie, M. Lindsay Kaplan, and Dympna Callaghan, editors. *Feminist Readings of Early Modern Culture: Emerging Subjects*. Cambridge: Cambridge University Press, 1996.

Trombetta, Simona. "Le Strategie dell'Abbandono: Luoghi, Esposti, Espositori nei Fascicoli Processuali del Tribunale Criminale Comasco (1815–1860)," *Il Risorgimento* 1 (1994): 89–138.

Tucci, Ugo. "Una statistica sanitaria bresciana di fine Settecento." In *L'arte di guarire. Aspetti della professione medica tra Medioevo ed Età contemporanea*, edited by Maria Luisa Betri and Alessandro Pastore, 105–118. Bologna: CLUEB, 1993.

Tuttle, Leslie. *Conceiving the Old Regime: Pronatalism and the Politics of Reproduction in Early Modern France*. Oxford and New York: Oxford University Press, 2010.

Vannozzi, Francesca. "Fantocci, marchingegni e modelli nella didattica ostetrica senese." In *Nascere a Siena. Il parto e l'assistenza alla nascita dal Medioevo all'età moderna*, edited by Francesca Vannozzi. Siena: Nuova Immagine, 2005.

———. *Nascere a Siena. Il parto e l'assistenza alla nascita dal Medioevo all'età moderna*. Siena: Nuova Immagine, 2005.

Van Teijlingen, Edwin, George Lowis, Peter McCaffery, and Maureen Porter, editors. *Midwifery and the Medicalization of Childbirth: Comparative Perspectives*. New York: Nova Publishers, 2004.

Vanzan Marchini, Nelli Elena, editor. *Le Leggi di Sanita della Repubblica di Venezia, vol. 1*. Veneto: Neri Pozza, 1995.

———. *I Mali e I Remedi della Serenissima*. Vicenza: Neri Pozza, 1995.

Venturi, Franco. *Settecento Riformatore: Da Muratori a Beccaria*. Turin: Giulio Einaudi, 1969.

Verga, Andrea. *Intorno all'ospitale maggiore di Milano nel secolo diciotto. e specialmente intorno alle sue scuole d'anatomia e chirurgia: cenni storici*. Milano: Fratelli Richiedei, 1871.

Versluysen, Margaret Connor. "Midwives, Medical Men and 'Poor Women Labouring of Child': Lying-in Hospitals in Eighteenth-Century London." In *Women, Health and Reproduction*, edited by Helen Roberts. London: Routledge & Kegan Paul, 1981.

Vicker, Nancy J. "Members Only." In *The Body in Parts: Fantasies of Corporeality in Early Modern Europe*, edited by David Hillman and Carla Mazzio, 3–23. New York and London: Routledge, 1997.

Viora, Mario. *Le Costituzioni Piemontesi, 1723, 1729, 1772. Storia Esterna della Compilazione*. Turin: Fratelli Bocca, 1928.

Virdis, Raffaelle. "The Beginning of Smallpox Vaccination in the Duchy of Parma," *Acta Biomed* 90, no. 2 (2019): 321–326.

Vivanti, C., editor. *Storia d'Italia. Annali, vol. 4, Intellettuali e potere*. Torino: Einaudi, 1981.

Von Greyerz, Kasper. *Religion and Culture in Early Modern Europe*. Oxford: Oxford University Press, 2007.

Wagner, Corinna. "Replicating Venus: Art, Anatomy, Wax Models, and Automata," *19: Interdisciplinary Studies in the Long Nineteenth Century* (2017). http://doi.org/10.16995/ntn.783

Wagner, Darren Neil. "Sex, Spirits, and Sensibility: Human Generation in British Medicine, Anatomy, and Literature, 1660–1780," PhD dissertation, University of York, 2013.

———. "Body, Mind and Spirits: The Physiology of Sexuality in the Culture of Sensibility," *Journal for Eighteenth-Century Studies* 39, no. 3 (2016): 335–358.

Warren, Adam. "An Operation for Evangelization: Friar Francisco González Laguna, the Cesarean Section, and Fetal Baptism in Late Colonial Peru," *Bulletin of the History of Medicine* 83, no. 4 (2009): 647–675.

Watt, Jeffrey R. "The Impact of the Reformation and Counter-Reformation." In *Family Life in Early Modern Times, 1500–1789*, edited by David I. Kertzer and Marzio Barbagli, 125–156. New Haven: Yale University Press, 2001.

Wear, Andrew, Roger Kenneth French, and Iain M. Lonie, editors. *The Medical Renaissance of the Sixteenth Century*. Cambridge: University of Cambridge Press, 1985.

Wertz, Richard W. and Dorothy C. Wertz. *Lying-In: A History of Childbirth in America*. New Haven: Yale University Press, 1989.

Whitehead, Barbara J., editor. *Women's Education in Early Modern Europe: A History, 1500–1800*. New York: Routledge, 1999.

Wiesner, Merry E. "The Midwives of South Germany and the Public/Private Dichotomy." In *The Art of Midwifery: Early Modern Midwives in Europe*, edited by Hilary Marland, 77–94. New York and London: Routledge, 1993.

———. *Christianity and Sexuality in the Early Modern World: Regulating Desire, Reforming Practice*. London: Routledge, 2000.

———. *Women and Gender in Early Modern Europe*. Cambridge: Cambridge University Press, 2000.

———. "Early Modern Midwifery: A Case Study." In *Midwifery and the Medicalization of Childbirth: Comparative Perspectives*, edited by Edwin Van Teijlingen, George Lowis, Peter McCaffery, and Maureen Porter, 63–74. New York: Nova Publishers, 2004.

Wilson, Adrian. *The Making of Man Midwifery: Childbirth in England, 1660–1770*. Cambridge, MA: Harvard University Press, 1995.

———. *Ritual and Conflict: The Social Relations of Childbirth in Early Modern England*. Farnham: Ashgate, 2013.

Woolf, Stuart J. "Sviluppo Economico e Struttura Sociale in Piemonte da Emanuele Filiberto a Carlo Emanuele III," *Nuova Rivista Storica* 46, no. 1 (1962): 1–57.

Zocchi, Paola. "L'assistenza agli esposti e alle partorienti nell'Ospedale Maggiore di Milano e nell'Ospizio di S. Caterina alla ruota tra Sette e Ottocento," *S.I.De.S. – Bollettino di Demografia storica* 30–31 (1999): 165–184.

Index

Note: Numbers in *italics* indicate a figure.

Abbiate Guazzone 128–129
abortion 15; baptisms performed
  following 70; Church's position
  on 21, 194–195; as crime 23,
  69, 93–94; involuntary 69, 79;
  maternity wards in response to 86;
  and midwives, instruction in causes
  of 116; and midwives, prohibition
  against inducing 37n30; midwives'
  testimony regarding 23, 27–28;
  obstetrical manuals, discussion of
  58, 141; sinfulness of 20–21, 54,
  195; and the state 108–109; women
  suspected of 72–73; *see also* Amico,
  Anna de; infanticide; miscarriage
Accati, Luisa 25
accoucheur see man-midwife
Amico, Anna de 21
Amigone, Ambrogio 181–185
Amoretti, Maria Pellegrina 113
anatomical venus 149, 161n59
animation (of the fetus) 2, 6, 68–69,
  194; *see also* ensoulment
Appiana, Cristina 128, 135n114
Aranzio, Giulio Cesare 79n131
Arezzo 89, 91
Aristotle 44–47, 55, 68, 140
artificial feeding 84, 157–158,
  187n17
Asdrubaldi, Francesco 142
Assalini, Paolo 154–155
automata 121, 148–149, 161; *see also*
  obstetrical machine
autopsy 7, 83, 142, 144–145, 158
Avicenna 140

Bagotta, Maria 171
Baldi, Silvana 98, 103n65

baptism 1–2, 4, 9, 182; and abortion
  70; emergency 15–16, 28, 33, 68,
  164; fetal 186; infant 1, 17–18, 20,
  26, 69; in-utero 69, 182, 190n68; and
  maternity wards 88; and the medical
  profession 183; and the soul 17–22;
  of the unborn 1–2, 69–70, 184,
  189n68; *see also* baptism performed
  by midwives; unbaptized; unborn
baptismal registration and ceremonies
  35, 36n3
baptism performed by midwives 15–20,
  26, 33, 109, 122, 175; bishop's
  intervention in 131n15; and Boi,
  Marianna 184, 186; ignorance of
  28; in midwifery texts 68; and parish
  priests 16, 30, 35, 109, 127, 134,
  194; *see also répit* miracle
barbers 7, 29, 139, 166; college of 30,
  109, 131n18
Baruffaldi, Girolamo 68, 182
Bassi, Laura 113
Bassi (physician) 177–178
Bell, Rudolph 44
Benedict XIV (Pope) *see* Lambertini,
  Prospero Lorenzo
Berengario da Carpi, Jacopo 51, *54*
Beretta, Giacinto 183
Bernati, Natale 60–63
Bertapaia, Vienna 27
Bertrandi, Ambrogio 117, 139
Bianchi, Giovanni Battista 137, 141
biopower 107, 109, 129; *see also*
  Foucault, Michel
birth *see* childbirth
birth attendants 3, 5–6, 35, 90, 98,
  106; men as 44, 173, 195; midwives
  as 95, 107, 111–112

birthing room 2, 15–16, 31, 34–35; and male obstetrical writers 43, 59, 73; midwives in 164
bloodletting 34, 140, 173
Boi, Marianna 1–3, 11, 180–185, 188n57
Bologna 7, 21, 29–31, 33, 48; midwife training programs in 108, 113; obstetrical instruction in 77n56; *see also* Galli, Giovanni Antonio
Bonnet, Charles 139
Bossa, Elena 87
Bourgeois, Louise 43, 76n38
Bramano, Catterina 116
Brambilla, Orsola 106
breastfeeding 87, 101n28, 154, 168; *see also* artificial feeding; wetnurse
breast milk 87–88, 97, 98, 168
breast size 47, 121
breve, brevi 26, 168
Bruhier d'Ablaincourt, Jacques-Jean 189n60
Bulgarelli, Matilde 35, 42n117
Buzzi, Angela Antonia 177–178

cadaver 116–118, 146, 153; female 111, 151, 183; fetal 111, 150–151
Caima, Angela Maria 128
Calegari, Virginia 31
Calvo, Paolo Bernardo 137–138, 140–142, 144
Calza, Luigi 60, 124–125, 143, 156; obstetrical models, collection of 8–9, 119, 146
Cangiamila, Francesco Emanuele 69–71, 182–185, 194
Caomino, Giovanni 81
Carminiati, Zuanne 173
Casa del Santo Bambino (Catania, Sicily) 89
Castelnuova, Isabella 135n114
Catherina (midwife) 27–28
Catholic Church 2–4, 6, 9, 16–19; and Boi, Marianna 180, 185; and the Counter-Reformation 22–24, 91–94; re-Catholicization 25; *Embriologia sacra*, influence of 69; newborn souls, salvation of 68–69, 191, 194; reform 35; *see also* baptism; embryology
caul 26
Cavallo, Sandra 7, 93, 100n23, 140
Celsus 140
Ceriana, Camila 106
Cerutti, Simona 93

cesarean operation: Catholic Church's stance on 4, 6; history of 11n4; "internal" 141; on live women 70–72, 80n134, 141; postmortem 1, 10, 69–71, 180–186, 188n57, 189n65–66; surgical instruction in 138, 141; and theological embryology 68–73; *see also* cadaver
Chamberlen, Peter 46
Chapman, Edmund 67
Charles III (King of Sicily) 70, 143
charity 3, 82–87, 89; Christian 85, 128, 152, 167, 169, 182, 191; foundlings as focus of 153; hospital as institutional expression of 83, 154; maternity wards as sites of 9, 81, 192; in medical practice, conceptions of 187n21; midwives' duty to perform 169–170, public 86; refusal of 168; religious 89; as a virtue 55, 87
Chiappuzzi, Gaetana 168–169
childbirth 1–11, 15–20, 22–28, 30–36, 191–195; and cesarean intervention 68–73, 141, 182–186; infants dying during 20; and maternity hospitals/wards 84–85, 87–92, 94–99, 153–157; male involvement in 6; mechanical principles driving 148–149; and medical men 43–44, 57, 73, 130, 135n109; and midwives, conflicts with clients over 164–166, 168–169, 172–178, 180, 182–186; in midwifery education 106–109, 111–113, 115–119, 121–122, 127–128; in midwifery manuals 44–45, 48, 50–51, *52–53*, 73; mother's death due to 1–2, 15–17, 20; in obstetrical texts 55–68, 73; surgeons' knowledge of 138, 141–151; Virgin Mary, role in 16, 25, 27–28
Chojnacka, Monica 88, 104n96
Cicognini, Giuseppe 110, 127, 178
Cody, Lisa Forman 5, 100n15
Cohen, Sherrill 82, 89
conception (pregnancy) 25, 44, 47, 66; and animation 71; and ensoulment 68–70; false 58, 61; life beginning at 194; midwife manuals, discussed in 73; midwife's knowledge of 117; obstetrical treatises, discussed in 55, 141
contraception 15

Corpus juris cononici 23
Correr, Marco 165
Council of Canterbury 17
Council of Trent 18, 23, 39n53, 91–92
Council of Trèves 17
Counter-Reformation 3, 9–10, 16–17, 20, 22, 91; era of 82, 88–89, 98, 192, 194
Cromeri, Guglielmo 27–28
Culpeper, Nicholas 46–47

Dacome, Lucia 119–120
D'Adorante, Cecilia 168
Decio, Carlo 105n106
Decree Tametsi 23, 39n53, 91; *see also* Council of Trent
defloration 23–24, 122; *see also* virginity
Deventer, Hendrik van 58, 73, 79n134, 141, 160n44
Diodato da Cuneo, P. (friar) 1, 182
Di Simplicio, Oscar 19, 22
dowry 83, 91–92

embryology 4, 6, 151, 191, 194; theological 68–73, 183, 190n71; and vitalism 151; *see also* Cangiamila, Francesco Emanuele
end of life 2
ensoulment 4, 21, 38n34; Aristotelian and Thomist doctrine concerning 68–69; Cangiamila's position on 70
epigenesis 38n34, 68, 151, 162n79
esplorazione, l' (internal examination of the genitals) *see* exploration, manual (of a woman's genitals)
exorcism 2, 25
exploration, manual (of a woman's genitals) 59, 65, 137, 154, 162n70; instruction of 145–146; *see also* Malacarne, Vicenzo

Fabricius 140
Falloppio, Gabriele 140
Feltivato, Domenica 114
female honor 3–4, 82, 84–94, 98, 107, 112, 152, 195
Ferrara 68, 77n56, 151
Ferrari, Domenica 114
Ferrari, Domenico 142
Ferrari, Giovanni Battista 23–24
Ferro, Augusto 151
fertility and fertilization 25, 27, 108, 194

fetal development 38n34, 138, 182, 191, 194; *see also* epigenesis; preformationism
fetus 22, 111, 184–186; abnormal presentation of 62–63, 66–67; baptism of 17, 69, 182, 194; as child and citizen 194; deceased 34, 51, 55, 60–61, 131, 137, 141, 151, 173, 175; and forceps 143–144, 155, 170–172; malpresenting 61, 141, 170–172; and maternal death 70–71, 172, 184; midwifery manuals, discussion of 45; "monstrous" 118–119; and obstetrical machines and models 146–151; obstetric manuals, discussion of 58; obstructed 80n135; positions of 45, 48, 56, 64, 145, 174; repositioning of 154; soul of 1, 6, 37n33, 47; and the state 71; surgical extraction of 176–177, 180–182; vs tumor 50; turning of 63, 67, 97, 146–147; womb, development outside 137, 141–142; *see also* animation; ensoulment; mother, life of; uterus; womb
Filippini, Nadia Maria 6, 71, 83–84
Florence 57, 77n56, 89, 108; midwifery schools in 113, 134n96
forceps 2, 4, 7; Assalini's design experiments of 15; fetus, extraction using 143–144, 155, 170–172; Levret's development of 58, 142–143, 170; Maja's use of 170–171, 177; and touch, learning to use via 150
Forbes, Thomas 40n75
Foucault, Michel 83–84, 109, 146
foundling assistance 152
foundling homes and hospitals 20, 22, 39n48, 81–83, 92–93, 95, 152; abuses at 97–98; Catholic charity 191; midwives working at 97; and milk, chronic lack of 88, 111, 163n95, 187n17; and pregnant women 89; *Quarto delle Balie* 125; San Celso 90–91; wetnurses in 87
foundlings 10, 105n107, 111, 153, 155; experimentation on 156–158
Frank, Johann Peter 8, 70–71, 93, 103n68, 112, 114, 122, 149–150, 152, 162n70, 179–180, 182–186; on the fetus, rights of 194
fumigation 10, 141, 173

Galen 44, 55, 140
Galeotti, Pio Urbano 64, 66–67
Galletti, Giuseppe 121, 147–148, 152
Galli, Giovanni Antonio 60, 119–121, *119–120*, 148, 150
Gentilcore, David 7, 21
Giudetti, Giuseppe 144
Giudice, Maria Lucia 178
Graaf, Regnier de 38n34
gravide occulte 87, 91
gravid uterus *see* uterus
Guillemeau, Jacques 55, 141

Hacke, Daniela 23
Harvey, William 38n34
Herrle-Fanning, Jeanette 64–65
Hippocrates 44, 55, 140
honor *see* female honor
Hunter, William 117
hymen 46, 48, 75

illegitimacy 3, 5, 21–23, 107–108; and poverty 95, 103n69; social attitudes towards 93
illegitimate birth and offspring 10, 23, 81, 86–88; fathers of 90, 94, 99, 191; *see also* paternity
illegitimate pregnancy 21, 55, 67, 82, 85, 91–92; midwives' policing of 109, 112, 164–165, 186; and mothers, marginalization of 158
Immaculate Conception 68
incest 192
infant baptism *see* baptism
infanticide 15, 20–21, 23, 72, 86; criminalization and decriminalization of 93–94, 103n65; foundling homes as response to 87; maternity wards as preventative of 88; and midwives, oversight of 192, 195; and the state 108; women suspected of 73, 102n62
infertility 15, 23, 141; *see also* fertility
Ingenhousz, Jan 155
inoculation 155–156; *see also* vaccination
Inquisition 18, 20, 24–28, 37n16, 69, 182

Jordanova, Ludmilla 5

Keller, Eve 65, 67
Kertzer, David 11

Lambertini, Prospero Lorenzo 14n24
Landi, Lucia 122

Lawrence, Susan 145
Levret, André 57–58, 117, 158
Levret forceps 142–143, 170
Lombardy 8, 71, 106, 112, 195; Austrian 106, 150, 182, 184–185; medical education in 178
Lombriasco 81
Longo, Cristina 166; *see also* Spinarol, Alessandra Longo
Louis, Antoine 143
Lucchetta, Domenica 175–176

Madonna 28
Madonna of Terlago 20
Maerker, Anna 161n68
Magni (resident of Corso di Porta Tosa) 168–169; *see also* Chiappuzzi, Gaetana
Maja, Benedetto 143, 170–171, 177
Malacarne, Vincenzo 117, 139, 144–150, 152; obstetrical machine 121; treatise on childbirth 57; and midwives 171
Malthus, Thomas 107
Maltini, Margarita 169–170
Mande, Madalena 170–171
Manfredini, Giovanni Battista 160n48
man-midwife 3, 5, 50, 56, 84, 65, 76n38, 145, 149; *see also* Levret, André; Smellie, William; Willughby, Percival
Mantua 169
Manzolini, Anna Morandi 120
Manzolini, Giovanni 120
Marchesini, Bortola 33
Maria Teresa (Empress) 127, 142
marriage 15; and the courts 22–24; fertility determined prior to 55; and illegitimate children 99; and premarital sex 91, 93; promise of 23, 92, 98; as sacrament 39n53; and sexuality 22–24; *verba de futuro* 23; *see also* Decree *Tametsi*; sex and sexuality
Mary, Mother of Christ *see* Madonna; Virgin Mary
Masiero, Filippo 141
maternity care: public 81–99; in Turin 85–88, 91; in Milan 90–91, 95–98, 152–155
maternity hospital 3–4, 7; as institution 82–85; public 8
maternity wards 8, 57, 85–99; 'clinicalization' of 84, 137, 152–157; specialized 191–192

Mauriceau, Francois 55, 141
Mazzoletti, Catterina 129, 177
Mazzuchelli, Francesca 106, 128
McClive, Cathy 21
McKeown, Thomas 85
McTavish, Lianne 5, 56, 65–66
Melli, Sebastiano 43, 55–56, 58
menstruation 15, 20–21, 40n65;
    'blockages' 47
Mercurio, Girolamo Scipione 20, 24,
    32; caesarean operation, description
    of 71; *La commare o riccoglitrice* 43,
    48–55
Mioli, Appolonia 81–82
Mioli, Giovanni 81
midwife: female 2; clients 165–170;
    compensation of 1, 11, 22, 28, 125,
    165; disputes and conflicts over
    164–186; interprofessional rivalries
    of 176–180; licensed/unlicensed
    3–4, 7–8, 10–11, 28–36, 48,
    106, 109–110, 113, 193; secretive
    behavior of 22–23, 26; *see also*
    baptism performed by midwives;
    birth attendants; man-midwife
midwifery: Catholic Church's interest in
    16–17; regulation and legislation of
    9, 11, 30–36, 107, 186; scientific 139
midwifery education 106–130; *see also*
    midwifery schools
midwifery, professionalization of
    2–6, 9–11, 32, 107, 169, 191; and
    medical professionals 28; midwives'
    opposition to 186
midwifery schools 3–4, 7–11, 106,
    110–130, 138, 152, 158, 191–192;
    in Milan 152, 159n21, 176–180; in
    Venice 108, 113, 118, 123, 129, 156;
    see also Ospedale Maggiore (Milan)
midwifery texts, manuals, and treatises
    55, 60, 65, 71, 73, 191–192;
    female-authored 74n2; *La commare
    o riccoglitrice* (Mercurio) 20–21,
    48–55; and male professional
    authority 74n12; physicians,
    authored by 59–60
midwifery training 82, 85, 150, 154,
    178; in foundling hospitals 90; in
    France 12n12, 85–86, 111, 143
Milan 8, 86, 166, 168–169, 193;
    maternity care, institutionalized 89;
    maternity hospital 87; maternity
    wards 97; midwifery instruction in
    108–114, 117–118, 123, 126–129,
    135n107; midwifery, oversight of 29,

34, 92; midwifery schools in 152,
    159n21, 176–180; obstetrics, courses
    for surgeons in 77n56; postmortem
    cesarean, endorsement of 70;
    protomedicato 30, 33, 109; *Quarto
    delle Balie* 91, 94–95, 111, 125,
    129, 152–153; San Celso hospital
    90–91, 97, 157; *see also* Monteggia,
    Giovanni Battista; Moscati, Pietro;
    Ospedale Maggiore (Milan)
milk 88, 111; alternative sources
    157; breast milk 87, 168; *see also*
    wetnurse
Miotta, Anna 165–166
miracle *see répit* miracle
miscarriage 25, 31, 144–145, 165, 175;
    as "involuntary abortion" 69, 79
modesty 112, 121, 142, 149, 176
Molin, Andrea 22
Monteggia, Giovanni Battista 146–147,
    150–151, 154
Monte, Maria 168
Morano, Angela Francesca 137,
    141–142, 159n18
Moscati, Bernardino 117, 139,
    142–143
Moscati, Pietro 153, 155
mother, life of 6, 72, 144, 173,
    184–185; fetus, priority over 194
Muratori, Ludovico Antonio 3,
    108–109
Murer, Sgualdo Campolin 165

Nannini, Angela 30–31, 35
Nannoni, Lorenzo 67, 139, 142, 144,
    171–172; case studies 64, 66
Nava, Annunciata 178–179
Nessi, Giuseppe 57, 64, 114, 124
Niccoli, Anna Maria 167, 170
Nihell, Elizabeth 76n38

obstetrical machines 7, 64, 75,
    116–118, 120–122, 130; and touch,
    instruction on 75n17, 120, 124, 138,
    145–150
obstetrical models 7, 61, 64, 116,
    118–122, 153, 192; collections of
    152; terracotta 133n68, 160n48;
    wax 9, 118, 120, 124, 149, 151,
    156, 161n59; wood 151; *see also*
    obstetrical instruments
obstetrical treatises and texts 5, 9,
    43–73
obstetrical instruments 7, 66, 170,
    177, 184; midwives prohibited from

using 30, 131n11, 192–193; *see also* forceps

obstetricians 3, 10, 84, 139, 148; *see also* Calza, Luigi; Galli, Giovanni Antonio; Levret, André; Moscati, Bernardino; Nannoni, Lorenzo; Smellie, William; van Deventer, Hendrik

obstetrics 56–60, 62–65, 73, 108, 184, 191, 194; and childbirth, views regarding 117; and the clinic 84; courses in 107 77n56, 110, 116; and infant care 157; male professors and practitioners of 10, 34, 57, 142–144, 150–151, 154, 157, 191–192; training of surgeons in 130, 138–142, 158, 186

Olivia, Maria Maddalena 129

Orbatello, Florence 89

Ospedale Maggiore (Milan) 83, 91, 95–98; and foundlings and *Quarto delle Balie* 91, 94–95, 111, 125, 129, 152–153; midwives and midwifery school at 106, 110–112, 118, 125, 129, 135n105, 177; *see also* Milan; Moscati, Bernardino; Verna family

Padua 57, 59–60, 115; midwifery education in 114, 118–119, 124, 126–127, 152, 156; obstetrics in 9, 77n56, 135n109, 152; *see also* Calza, Luigi; Masiero Filippo; Sografi, Pietro

Pagiola, Francesco 143–144

Pancino, Claudia 2, 176, 178, 185

Paré, Ambroise 46, 55, 140

parish priests 2–4, 6, 10, 16, 19, 22; and childbirth culture 20; and the Council of Trent 18; and maternity hospitals 95–96; and midwives, recruitment of 112, 114–116, 127–129; and the Marianna Boi case 180–185; and midwives, sanctioning and support of 30, 32, 34–35, 107, 164, 167, 177, 193; postmortem cesareans performed by 70, 72, 189n66

paternity 46, 98

patriarchy, structures and authority 5, 73, 164; birth as destabilizing 28; female sexuality as threat to 91

pelvimetry 2, 58

pelvis: abnormal 119; and difficult birth 144, 154; and labor 51, 58–59; of

an obstetrical machine 120, 122, 150–151

pessaries 118, 141, 176

Pietro Leopoldo (Grand Duke) 122

Pillon, Daniela 32

placenta 35, 118, 176; artificial 151; detached 173; extraction of 127, 138, 145

Ployant, Teresa 74n2

Pomata, Gianna 7, 31, 33, 166

Ponti, Barbara 178

populationism 10, 71, 103, 107–110

preformationism 38n34, 68–69, 79n108, 151

pregnancy: ambiguity of 38n41, 46–47; Church's views of 69; death of woman during 17, 30–31, 35, 70; extrauterine 137, 141–142; folk practices regarding 24–25; hospital care for 83–85; male writing on 43–44; and religion 27; unwanted 20; *see also* abortion; childbirth; illegitimate pregnancy; quickening; uterus; womb

procreation and procreativity 107–108

pronatalism 10, 93, 103, 107–110, 195

Prosperi, Adriano 19, 22, 70, 72; on foundling hospitals 92; on infanticide 102n62; on in-utero baptism 189n68

Protestant Reformation 17, 19

protomedicati 9, 28–29; in Bologna 30–31; in Milan 30, 33, 109; in Naples 7; in Rome 33–34; in Turin 29; in Venice 32, 122, 165

Provveditori alla Sanità see Venice

puerperal fever 83, 85, 105n106

Quarto delle Balie see Milan

quickening 21, 37n33, 38n41, 47

rape 15, 23, 192; *see also* sexual assault

Regazzi, Lucia 116

Reggiani, Flores 91, 157

répit miracle 19–20, 25

Riskin, Jessica 148

Risse, Guenter 83

Rizzardini, Angela 165–166, 170

Rizzi, Teresa 114–115

Rizzo, Sebastiano 60, 118, 123–124, 142, 174

Robbles, Maria Teresa 97

Roccati, Cristina 113

Roederer, Johann Georg 117

Romeo, Maria 21, 27
Rouhault, Pietro Simone 86, 100n20, 143Rubino, Camilla 168–169
Rueff, Jacob 46

Sacco, Luigi 155
sacred, the 20, 24–26, 112
San Celso hospital, Milan 90–91, 97, 157
San Cristoforo, Arezzo 89, 91
San Giovanni hospital, Turin 8, 83, 85–86, 88, 94, 98
Santa Catarina maternity home, Milan 104n86, 129, 150, 152–156
Santa Maria Maddalena hospital, Bologna 31
Santa Maria Nuova hospital, Florence 57
Satellico, Lucia 175–176
Savoy 8, 82–83, 85–86, 88, 195; criminal code 93; surgeons unlicensed in 139; *see also* Turin
Sburlato, Girolamo 145
Scarpa, Antonio 1, 181–182, 184–185
Secca, Francesca Maria 178
secrets: of birth 26; books of 44, 74n10; of female body 2, 9, 45, 57; of generation 43; language of 45; *see also gravide occulte*; "women's secrets"
secretive behavior *see* midwives
Seppi, Antonella 168
Servasoni, Regina 165–166, 170
sex and sexuality 22–24, 44, 82, 108, 112; deviant 99; disciplining 10, 84, 88–94; illicit 3, 21, 24, 81; marital 17; of obstetrical machines 121, 149; and pleasure 148; premarital 5, 91–93, 98; regulation of 9, 191–192; as sin 94
sexual assault 23
sexual functioning 15
sexual morality 4, 94, 194
sexual problems 45
sexual shame 85, 99, 192
shame 3, 191; maternity care in response to 88, 99, 107, 112; and pregnancy 81–83, 86–88, 94, 162n70; and religious education 97; and sexual relations 22, 85, 93
Sharp, Jane 43
Siegemund, Justine 43
Siena 29, 77n56, 122

Silvestri, Gaetano 168–169
Medical simulation 148; critiques of 149–152
Smellie, William 58, 73, 117, 149, 158
Sografi, Pietro 57–59, 118–119, 127, 156
sorcery *see* witchcraft
spina bifida 118
Spinarol, Alessandra Longo 166, 170
Stephanson, Raymond 79n108
sterility 58
stillbirth 186n3
suppositories 141
surgeons 1–3; and difficult births 43, 57, 60–66, 70–73; and maternity hospitals 82–83; and midwives 11, 30–31, 34, 51, 55, 61–64, 129–130, 170–176; obstetrical models, use in training of 119, 122; obstetrical training 10, 64–65, 73, 96–97, 110, 138–152; social milieu of 7; and surgery, heightened status of 139, 192; touch, importance of 59, 75n17; *see also* Calvo, Paolo Bernardo; Louis, Antoine; Malacarne, Vincenzo; Masiero, Filippo; Mioli, Giovanni; Moscati, Bernardino; Nannoni, Lorenzo; obstetricians; Paré, Ambroise; Rouhault, Pietro Simone

Tachinetto, Stuttio 173
Tametsi *see* Decree Tametsi
Tanaron, Pietro Paolo 57–59, 72, 139, 142, 158n3
Thomism 68
"*toccamento, il*" *see* exploration, manual (of a woman's genitals)
Toretta, Maria 19
Torre Santa Susanna 167
touch: gendering of 77n71; of the midwife 50, 77n71, 118, 121; and obstetrical machines 120, 124, 138, 145–150; of the surgeon 50, 75n17, 137; vocabulary related to 119; *see also* exploration, manual (of a woman's genitals); Tranquillini, Giacomo 60–63
Trevisan, Benedtta Fedeli 174–175
Treviso 60
Trucazzano, Italy 180–183, 185
Turin 8, 19; foundling hospitals in 36n10; maternity care in 85–88; obstetric courses in 77n56; *protomedico* in 29

unbaptized 37n24, 69, 93, 189n68; *see also* baptism
unborn 1–2, 69, 71, 184, 189n68; *see also* cesarean operation
uterus 33, 51, 58, 147; diseased or defective 137, 141–142, 154, 170, 172; dissection 145; extracted *54;* fetus, position in 62–64, 73, 117; glass 120; gravid 117–118, 146; hemorrhage 141, 172–173, 175; holy water inserted into 69; mechanistic understanding of 148; of an obstetrical machine 120–121, 150–151; prolapsed 118, 151, 176

vaccination 84, 139, 155–156, 158
Vailati (surgeon) 180–181, 184, 188n57
Valota, Orazio 62–64, 72, 190n72
Vannozzi, Francesca 122
Vendramin, Antonio 175–176
Vendramin, Giaccomina 175–176
Venetian Health Board (*Provveditori alla Sanità*) *see* Venice
Venice 8, 22–23, 25, 27; caul, use of 26; cesareans in 70–72; health boards 29–30, 165; maternity wards 152; midwife training and schools 108, 113, 118, 123, 129, 156; midwifery in 32, 34, 48, 57, 112, 166, 170, 193, 195; obstetrics in 174–175, 177; *Provveditori alla Sanit*à 28, 30–31, 115, 122, 126
verba de futuro (promise of marriage) *see* marriage

Verna family (surgeons: Alberto, Andrea, and Giovan Battista) 159n8
Versluysen, Margaret Connor 84, 131n11
Vespa, Alessandro 182, 180–182, 184–185, 189n60
Vespa, Giuseppe 57, 142
Victor Amadeus II (Duke) 82, 85
virginity (female) 23, 46, 48, 55, 75n21
Virgin Mary 16, 25, 27–28, 36n2; *see also* Immaculate Conception
vitalism 138, 151
Volpi, Antonia 1, 169, 180–181, 183–185

Wagner, Darren Neil 148
Walcher's position 51
Watt, Jeffrey 92
wetnurse 44, 87, 90–91, 97–98, 107; in the *Quarto delle Balie* 125, 152
Willughby, Percival 50, 67
Wilson, Adrian 5, 160n44
wise woman 27
witchcraft 25–27, 167–169
womb 32; death of fetus/child in 72, 131n11, 170, 182, 184; diseased 31; dissection of 48; fetus in 58, 61, 69–73, 97, 122, 146, 171, 181; glass 120, 148; magical power of 26; mandrake to protect 25; mechanistic understanding of 120–121, 149; midwife's access to 47; models of 160n48; power of 46–47; pregnant 50–51, 55–56; touching 59
"women's secrets" 2, 32

Zavattera, Elena 170–171